THE
OLAVO DE CARVALHO
READER

THE
OLAVO DE CARVALHO READER

A selection of Olavo de Carvalho's writings compiled, translated, and edited by his students in the Online Philosophy Course coordinated by Mariana Dean.

Academica Press
Washington~London

Library of Congress Cataloging-in-Publication Data

Names: de Carvalho, Olavo (author)

Title: The olavo de carvalho reader | Olavo de Carvalho

Description: Washington : Academica Press, 2025. | Includes references.

Identifiers: LCCN 2024945493 | ISBN 9781680534283 (hardcover) | 9781680534306 (paperback) | 9781680534290 (e-book)

Contents

Acknowledgements

This publication has been made possible thanks to the generosity of Roxane Carvalho, who supported the endeavor from the beginning with a view to promote her late husband's philosophical legacy in the United States, the country they called home for sixteen years.

Special thanks to Vide Editorial, the Brazilian imprint that has published Olavo de Carvalho's work since 2010. Vide Editorial authorized the use of all of their editions, thirty of which appear in this volume.

This work has also benefited from the support of Seminário Online de Filosofia ("Online Philosophy Seminar"), which has live-streamed and hosted Olavo de Carvalho's courses and digital supplements since 2008, when online courses were yet to become popular.

Appreciation is extended to all former students who, in spite of demanding family and professional obligations, generously contributed to this edition, offering crucial insights, and helpful suggestions.

All their contributions have been invaluable.

Who Is Olavo de Carvalho?

A brief introduction

This *Reader* brings to the American public, for the first time, a selection of the writings of Brazilian philosopher, professor, and journalist Olavo de Carvalho, from the early 1990s to some of his last articles, published before he passed away on January 24, 2022, in Hopewell, Virginia.

Anyone sincerely interested in making sense of the world will profit from a first encounter with Carvalho's writings—and will likely ask for more. His clear-eyed, tell-it-like-it-is assessment of the ailments of our culture makes for urgent reading. In the many thousands of pages he left behind, a large part of which remains unpublished, and in the hundreds of hours of recorded lectures of his "Online Philosophy Course," started in 2009, he is always at work rendering intelligible the ongoing cultural chaos, tracing its origins, debunking its myths, revealing what's at stake. He does so not only as a cultural or literary critic, but as a seeker of truth, as a philosopher in the fullest sense.

The uniqueness and power of Carvalho's works rest in a simple fact: he is a true philosopher, in the Socratic tradition, as the reader will realize as he proceeds through this selection of some of his best writings. He never preaches how to build a better world but strives to depict, in minute detail, the world as it is, and how it turned out to be that way. Averse to fads and herd mentality, endowed with an innate disposition for investigation and debate, Carvalho goes back to the foundations of the Western philosophical tradition, to Socrates, Plato and Aristotle, bringing them to life and listening to what they have to say to us. The more ingrained in that great tradition, as his work matured, the more innovative, original, and insightful he became, writing pieces of permanence against the backdrop of the ephemeral and trivial contemporary culture of self-imposed Western decadence.

From his very original and fruitful insight into the philosophy of Aristotle, to his critique of some of the main tenets of modern philosophy and his dissection of the "revolutionary mind" (a concept he himself created) and its consequences, to his essays on political power, the new global order, the corruption of science, to his more pedagogical essays, Carvalho's breadth and depth of interests cover a vast mosaic of the cultural landscape of the West, especially in its last bastion, America. He does so with a unique voice and style, more concerned with concrete, real-life questions than with academic abstractions or the ever-sillier demands of fashionable nonsense. This is what gives his writings and teachings their freshness and renders them so relevant to us.

He was a staunch champion of freedom who fought against right and left-wing obscurantism in his native Brazil and beyond. As he was also a political conservative, the reader may find possible parallels and connections in some of Carvalho's works and ideas with the likes of Russell Kirk, Leo Strauss, Thomas Sowell, or Roger Kimball in the U.S., or still with Sir Roger Scruton, Leszek Kołakowski, or Eric Voegelin. But as will became abundantly clear in this volume, Carvalho was his own man: largely self-taught, vastly erudite, he addressed some of the perennial questions of human existence, dedicating his life to study, teaching, writing, and analyzing, as a sort of cultural pathologist, the spiritual diseases of our time.

A thorough biography of Olavo de Carvalho remains to be written.[1] A brief look at his life itinerary, as unconventional and adventurous as it was, sheds light not only on the sources of his thought in life, but also on the form of his mind and work. In his late sixties, asked why he would not take time to write an autobiography, he usually replied, only half-jokingly: "It cannot be contained in a single volume, I lived many lives."

Without intending to summarize in a few pages all those "many lives," this introduction highlights, in a chronological commentary, some aspects of Carvalho's biography, especially those which may provide useful context and clues to understanding his thought and work.

Olavo Luiz Pimentel de Carvalho was born in the city of Campinas, in the State of São Paulo, Brazil, on April 27, 1947, to a middle-class Catholic family, which soon moved to the city of São Paulo. His father, a modest lawyer, and his mother, a worker in the printing industry, separated when he was eight. According to his own writings, he spent most of his early childhood sick and bedridden, afflicted with fevers and recurrent ailments that prevented him from regularly

---

[1] Preliminary biographical sketches published in Brazil provided useful information for this introduction: *O Mínimo sobre Olavo de Carvalho*, by Ronald Robson; and *Olavo de Carvalho: o filósofo e sua circunstância. Fotografias entre 2015 e 2021*, by Josias Teófilo, both from Vide Editorial (2023). Robson is also the author of the most successful attempt at a first synthesis of Carvalho's Philosophy, in his *Conhecimento por Presença: em torno da filosofia de Olavo de Carvalho* [Knowledge through presence: on the philosophy of Olavo de Carvalho] (Campinas, BR: Vide Editorial, 2020).

attending school. Reflecting on this period fifty years later, he would attribute his first philosophical insight to the time when he could not leave his bed:

> I became accustomed to a vertical perspective of the world, which began on the ground (imaginarily extending below to the center of the Earth) and rose to the limitless depths of the sky, which I could divine beyond the ceiling. From time to time, the fever would leave me, and I would discover, to my astonishment, that I had to learn to walk again. But the rotation of my person from the horizontal to the vertical position was accompanied by a concomitant reverse rotation of the picture of the world. Thus, a scheme of proportions was naturally formed, which once and for all structured, for me, the relational framework of things: above-below, ahead-behind, near-far. These lines, which crossed with my humble little person as their center, did not only designate directions of space, but different senses of the experience of living. The horizontal was health, life, action: playing and running, meeting my friends, participating in the dramas and joys of the tribe. The vertical was solitude, the presence of death, but also the opening to the infinite sky, to a superhuman peace. [2]

When he recovered, he attended elementary school in the Catholic parish of Our Lady of Peace, in São Paulo. From a young age he was a voracious reader. When he was twelve, the *História da Literatura Ocidental* (History of Western Literature) by Otto Maria Carpeaux, an Austrian *émigré,* was published in Brazil, one of the greatest critical panoramas of its subject ever written by a single author anywhere. Not long after, Carvalho discovered it and made a personal commitment to read as many (if not all) of the works listed for each of the authors reviewed in the 2,300 pages of the book, beginning with the literature of Classical Antiquity all the way to the 1950s. By sixteen, the young Carvalho had read all of Dostoevsky, and much of Shakespeare, Goethe, and Dante, and the classics of Brazilian and Portuguese literature. He would never stop devouring books. That would be the backbone of his education, since, at about that time, he decided to drop out of school. He was disappointed with his classes and wished to pursue studies in literature and the humanities on his own, dreaming about becoming a writer. He immediately began working, first as an office boy, and then as copydesk editor and reporter for newspapers in São Paulo. By this time, he also read some of his first philosophical works, by Heidegger and Ortega y Gasset.

---

[2] "O filósofo-mirim" [The child philosopher], February 26, 2004.

In 1966, two years after military commanders led a bloodless coup and took power in Brazil, thwarting the brewing movement towards communist revolution, Carvalho decided to join the Brazilian Communist Party (PCB). He was nineteen and avidly studying Marxism. At that time, by an interesting coincidence, he would share the same student lodgings[3] with some of the most die-hard Brazilian communists, such as José Dirceu,[4] and militant journalist Rui Falcão. Less than twenty years later, the two of them would lead a successful rebranding operation of the communist movement, founding the Workers' Party, which ruled Brazil from 2003–2015 and returned to power in 2023.

Carvalho was soon disappointed in the unethical behavior of his comrades in the Communist Party and left it in 1968, distancing himself from political activity. But he continued reading not only Marx and Engels, and Lenin and Stalin, but also the authors of "cultural" Marxism, György Lukács, Antonio Gramsci, and the members of the Frankfurt School who had emigrated to the United States—Max Horkheimer, Theodor Adorno, and Herbert Marcuse—and Walter Benjamin, who didn't make it to the U.S. He would remain a serious student of Marxism and the Communist movement throughout his life and would pen some of his most effective criticism against totalitarian ideology and practice.[5] He amassed a vast and thorough Marxist bibliography of several thousand volumes, part of which, in a demonstration of his regard for Communism, adorned the walls of the bathroom in his library in Virginia.

In August 1968, he married his first wife, with whom he would have four children, in a civil ceremony. In September 1972, his father passed away at fifty-six.

By that time, in the aftermath of the Second Vatican Council, Carvalho, now in his mid-twenties, became disenchanted with Catholic Church practice and embarked on a long spiritual quest that would take him to the study of "comparative religions and spiritual traditions," with stops at New Age spirituality, alchemy, astrology, Buddhism and Hinduism, perennialism and Sufi Islam. Describing the situation of the Church in São Paulo at that time, he would note:

---

[3] *Casa do Estudante* at Av. S. João provided lodging for low-income students in downtown São Paulo.
[4] Dirceu, arrested by the military regime, was released in exchange for the American Ambassador in Brazil, Charles Burke Elbrick, who was kidnapped by communist guerrillas in 1970. Dirceu ended up in Cuba, where he received military training. Years later, after plastic surgery, he returned to Brazil under a false identity.
[5] See Chapter 6, "Marxism, Intellectuals and Cultural Revolution."

The content of the sermons that were heard in churches became increasingly thinner: they only talked about social justice and morality (specifically sexual morality), and nothing else. Catholic circles began to seem just like a club, a social movement or something similar; they gradually left Catholic doctrine aside . . . I, like many other people, without breaking with the Church, began to investigate what was around me, looking for possible alternatives, in order to find something that I called (and many still call) "spirituality." Obviously, what was closest at hand were Eastern doctrines, especially Buddhist and Hindu—Islam only entered the orbit of my interests later. I was also interested in indigenous and African religions and the entire New Age movement . . . I spent almost twenty years exploring this area of study. Not only did I read Mircea Eliade, Carl Jung, Daisetsu Suzuki and many related authors, I also translated "Taboo," by Alan Watts, the New Age guru in the United States. At the same time, thanks to Watts—because he drew many parallels between Buddhism and the teachings of the Anglo-American analytical school, especially Ludwig Wittgenstein—I immersed myself in the *Tractatus Logico-Philosophicus*, which impressed me greatly.[6]

A narrative of the whole odyssey could fill an entire volume, in a riveting and sometimes paradoxical story that brought together, in Carvalho's experience, influential Islamic writers and intellectuals, such as René Guénon, Frithjof Schuon, Titus Burckhardt, Martin Lings, and Seyyed Hossein Nasr, as well as Catholic converts like Rama Coomaraswamy, along with some colorful and farcical characters. Carvalho didn't settle for the superficial elements of what was then a fashionable cultural trend among some intellectuals in the West, but delved deeply into these doctrines. He collaborated in perennialist studies with French painter and martial arts instructor Michel Veber, then living in São Paulo, who also initiated him in the practice of *tai-chi*. He developed a particularly influential friendship with Juan Alfredo César Muller (1927–90), an Argentinian psychologist residing in São Paulo, who had studied at the C.G. Jung Institute in Zurich, and who opened the whole field of symbolic studies and post-Freudian psychoanalysis to Carvalho, introducing him to the works of Maurice Pradines, Leopold Szondi, Igor Caruso, Paul Diel, René Le Senne, Viktor Frankl, Julian Jaynes, and others.

---

[6] "De volta à Igreja: um depoimento" [Back to the Church: a testimony], published posthumously in *O saber e o enigma* [Knowledge and the enigma] (Vide, 2022), 176–7.

It was around this time, in the early 1980s, that Carvalho's first marriage was dissolved. Sometime later, he began a common law union with his second wife, with whom he had two children. They broke up in 1985. The following year, Carvalho married Roxane de Andrade, who would remain his spouse until the end of his life. They had two children.

During that period, Carvalho wrote many articles, pamphlets, and opuscules with modest circulation, on many symbolic and perennialist topics. He later considered this his "pre-philosophical" work, though some of them contain valuable indications of the development of his mature thought, for example on medieval symbolism, and the critique of modernity. His intellectual respect for Guénon's and Schuon's work would be reflected in many of his later writings on the topic of the "Islamization of the West,"[7] of which the two were certainly pioneers, though he did not fail to expose what he considered the shortcomings and inconsistencies of their doctrines, including the mistaken claims of Guénon about a purported "esoteric Catholicism."

Carvalho's interest in the perennialist movement and Sufi Islam would culminate in 1986 with him joining *Maryamiyya,* the tariqa led by Schuon in Bloomington, Indiana. He confesses to being deceived by the environment of moral laxity he encountered there and, after some quarrels and court litigation, he was eventually expelled, about a year after having entered. In a series of lectures on the subject of "Esoterism in history and today," he summarized his experience:

Being expelled from the Schuon tariqa was the best thing that ever happened to me. From that day on, I realized that I no longer needed a sheik or a guru. I had to seek what I needed by relying solely on my own resources. When I put the esoteric field aside, I realized that what I had been searching for so long was simply what is called God, eternity, and life after death. I had studied Kant, from whom I had learned that everything related to God and eternity is beyond the possibilities of our experience. In fact, we can only know what God Himself shows us. But how does He show us? I found the answer in the verses of the Gospel of Matthew in which John the Baptist, while imprisoned, tells his disciples to ask Jesus: "Are thou he that art to come, or look we for another?" to which Jesus responds: "Go and tell John what you have heard and seen: the blind see, the lame walk, the lepers are cleansed, the deaf hear, the

[7] See in Chapter 8, "In the Claws of the Sphinx: Réne Guénon and the Islamization of the West."

dead rise again, the poor have the gospel preached to them" (Mt 11:2–5).[8]

After a long search, Carvalho was finally ready to begin tracing his way "back to the Church," to rediscover the religion of his childhood, a process that would still take a few years. He would also gradually turn his attention to philosophy and the foundations of Western culture. In 1987, the same year he left Schuon's tariqa, he began teaching the course "Introduction to Intellectual Life," at the "Instituto de Artes Liberais," in São Paulo, which a decade later would evolve into "The Philosophy Seminar," which he taught in Rio de Janeiro, where he moved with his family in 1989.

It was there, in 1990, that Carvalho finally met someone he considered a true philosopher, who would—for the first (and only) time in his life—teach him philosophy, in a graduate course, albeit a rather unique one, at an independent department of the Pontifical Catholic University of Rio de Janeiro (PUC). This is how he described the encounter:

> Until then, although I had accumulated more philosophical knowledge than any professor I knew, and although I occasionally gave lectures here and there, I did not feel confident in publishing anything on philosophical subjects, because I still lacked the essential: personal experience, direct learning from an authentic philosopher in the fullness of his creative powers. This did not exist in any Brazilian university.[9]

The "authentic philosopher" was the Latvian Jesuit priest and professor Stanislavs Ladusãns, who had emigrated to Brazil in 1947, after a period in Poland, where he befriended Karol Wojtyła, future Pope John Paul II, who later had, according to Carvalho, "entrusted Ladusãns with the impossible task of reintroducing some Catholicism into a Catholic university in Brazil." The encounter would seal Carvalho's fate as a philosopher. It is worth recalling his own account of that fruitful eureka moment:

> In the very first class I was shocked. The man presented the fundamental problems of the theory of knowledge, divided them into a few questions and announced: "We are going to examine each of these questions from the point of view of the main philosophical schools, comparing them

---

[8] Published posthumously in *O saber e o enigma* [Knowledge and the enigma] (Vide, 2022), 175–188.

[9] "Miséria sem Grandeza: a filosofia universitária no Brasil" [Misery without Greatness: university philosophy in Brazil], in *A filosofia e o seu inverso* [Philosophy and the inverse thereof] (Vide, 2012), 145.

with each other, and then we are going to outline a personal solution that seems most appropriate to each of them." He then went on to analyze 'knowledge through the senses' as seen by Plato, Aristotle, the Stoics, and continued on to Husserl and Merleau-Ponty. But it was not just a historical account. Each new chapter was a laborious and problematic stage in a dialectical process that was unfolding in the speaker's mind at that very moment, with twists and turns that, reflecting the intensity of an inner search, did not forego any difficulties. There was nothing of a school exposition there. It was our professor's own philosophical quest, which, adopting the language of History, saw in the advances and retreats of intelligence in the struggle with a problem over time the expanded image of a present, living cognitive effort before us. It was not ready-made knowledge, nor an analysis of texts, it was a philosophy, the struggle of intelligence to pierce the opacity of thought and reach the reality of things.

"That's it, my God in heaven!" I exclaimed to myself. That was what I was missing, that was what was missing in all the supposed teaching of philosophy that I had known up until then in Brazil: not historical erudition, not analysis of texts, not mere exposition of ready-made doctrines, but the living experience of philosophizing, the example of how to do it. It was as if a deaf person, having read sheet music and known only the mathematical structure of music, suddenly had his ears unstopped and his soul flooded by the chords of a Bach cantata.[10]

Fr. Ladusãns passed away in 1993, and Carvalho saw no point in further pursuing his studies without his mentor. He continued his work as journalist, writing for several newspapers in São Paulo and Rio, and in 1992–93 administered a course on the introduction of Edmund Husserl's *Logical Investigations.* He was now ready to embark in the philosophical phase of his work, living the experience of philosophizing, as he had learned from his late professor.

* * *

To grasp the impact that the publication of Carvalho's first philosophical works had in Brazil in the mid-1990s—and since—one must bear in mind the extent to which one political current, namely the left, had come to dominate the country's cultural landscape and political life. It may seem paradoxical that the same political movement that had been removed from power by right-wing

---

[10] Id. Ibid., 147–8.

military in the 1964 coup, and then again utterly defeated in the "armed fight" of the late 1960s early 1970s, in both cities and rural areas, would make such an impressive comeback barely two decades later. The historical explanation for this strange phenomenon is actually quite simple, and rests almost entirely on the adoption of the strategy of one man: the founder of the Italian Communist Party, Antonio Gramsci.

Gramsci's strategy was cultural, not armed, revolution. Its basic tenet was replacing the violent seizure of political power by the communist movement with the infiltration and domination of cultural institutions, which, according to him, would inevitably lead the communists to power. It sounded very attractive to recently-defeated Brazilian guerrillas—mostly a few thousand middle-class intellectuals in a country of ninety million. The old Leninist approach to revolution was gradually put aside, and militants of the Communist movement, which of course included many "fellow travelers" or useful idiots outside the Party (then outlawed by the military regime), began the "long march into the state apparatus" devised by Gramsci. It entailed a three-pronged approach: a) control of educational institutions, especially the universities, through professors and administrators, entrusted with disseminating the ideology by indoctrination; b) control of the flow of information by infiltrating the media, publishing, and the entertainment industry; and c) infiltration of the Catholic Church so as to change it from the inside.

By now the reader will have realized that such a strategy, *mutatis mutandis*, has also been widely employed in the United States and other Western countries, with varying degrees of success. But Brazil was very likely the first country, before any other, where Gramscian hegemony came to reign supreme, after two decades of gradual and continuous institutional subversion, practically unmitigated by any other political force. In the early 1990s, the country having just adopted a new and very liberal 1988 Constitution, humanities and education departments were run by outright Communists or close sympathizers, major newsrooms and television studios were massively overtaken by leftist militants, and the hierarchy of the Catholic Church had been infiltrated by "liberation theology," with priests openly preaching communist revolution from the pulpit.[11] It was no surprise, therefore, that beginning in the mid-1990s the left would be in power for over twenty years, first with the social democrats, then with the Communist hard-left, under the brand of the Workers' Party. It became an increasingly illiberal and intolerant environment, with the leftist government attempting to establish formal, widespread censorship and actively curtail

---

[11] See "Corpse in Power," in Chapter 7.

freedom of expression in university departments, newsrooms, and entertainment. A country of 150 million in 1990, formally a democracy, did not have one single truly conservative political party. The left ruled alone, in all domains of life.

As if to seal the leftist hegemony, an initiative led by Cuban life-long dictator Fidel Castro and future Brazilian president Luiz Inácio Lula da Silva resulted in a fateful meeting in São Paulo in July 1990 of some fifty radical leftist parties from Latin America and the Caribbean. It included all the openly communist parties and terrorist (e.g. the *Movimiento Izquierda Revolucionaria* from Chile, *Sendero Luminoso,* from Peru, etc.) and drug trafficking (the Colombian FARC and ELN) organizations. The São Paulo Forum became the most important organization for coordinating the communist movement in the region, having held annual meetings ever since. For fifteen years it operated discreetly, covered by an invisibility mantle provided by the mainstream media, in Brazil and elsewhere, including in the United States. Many historians, journalists, and politicians peremptorily denied its existence. It is still going strong today: the 2023 meeting took place in Brasilia and was attended by president Lula, who in his speech proclaimed he was "proud to be called a communist."

* * *

It is against this backdrop of quasi-totalitarian control of cultural life in Brazil that Olavo de Carvalho, then a little-known journalist, published, within a relatively short period, a trilogy of interconnected books. In February 1994, the first of them came out, *A Nova Era e a Revolução Cultural: Fritjof Capra and Antonio Gramsci* (New Age and Cultural Revolution: Fritjof Capra and Antonio Gramsci). A short book connecting the dots of the two major strains of the revolutionary movement in the country, it would, in his words, "sound the alarm" about the seriousness of the cultural crisis in Brazil. It would be shortly followed, in July 1995, by what he considered his best written book, *O Jardim das Aflições* (The Garden of Afflictions—from Epicurus to the resurrection of Caesar: An essay on materialism and civil religion), which traced the roots and historical evolution of the ideas that contributed to the Brazilian tragedy. Considering its historical breadth, covering over two millennia of Western history, and scope, reviewing some of the most influential philosophers since Epicurus in a single chain of argument, it was a rather unique work, for which the Brazilian intelligentsia was not prepared. And in 1996 he published *O Imbecil Coletivo* (The Collective Imbecile), almost 500 pages of examples of the cultural disease he had diagnosed in the preceding work. It would become an instant best-seller (by Brazilian standards), with successive editions selling out monthly. The title, of course, mocked the "collective intellectual" preached by Gramsci and gleefully adopted by his followers in Brazil.

One of the fundamental issues denounced in the book was "the denial of objective knowledge and the consequent reduction of intellectual activity to propaganda and manipulation of consciousness," a denial jointly embraced by both Gramscian Marxists and Pragmatists such as Richard Rorty, then much revered by Brazilian intellectuals. From there, things would only get worse, with either the "academic collective," according to Rorty, or "the collective intellectual," according to Gramsci, unmercifully imposing their politically correct dogmas on everybody else.

The unifying aspect of the essays gathered in *The Collective Imbecile* is the corruption of higher education, the consequent degradation of cultural life, and the role played by the leftist intellectuals in this process, both those in cushy jobs in universities (whom he dubbed "intellocrats") and the "beautiful people" in show business. No controversial issue was left out: the attempt to impose racial quotas and "compensation" for descendants of slaves in a country where the majority of the population is of mixed race; the ideological demolition of higher education; the beatification of criminals while condemning their victims and demonizing policemen; the campaign to legalize drugs; the association of leftist militants and common criminals, which led to the creation of some of the largest criminal organizations in the country (e.g. "Red Command"); radical feminism and queer ideology. These are just some of the issues covered in mostly unanswerable essays and articles.

The Brazilian establishment did not receive Carvalho's ideas well. He had unrelentingly poured salt on the wounds created by the leftist intelligentsia, exposing its contradictions and absurdities—and outright lies and ugliness— while documenting its destructive effects on all aspects of cultural life. The left would not forgive him for that brutal exposé. Over many years, and even to this day, he has been the target of smear campaigns and character assassination attempts written by militants disguised as journalists. At one point, a politician of a radical party, frustrated with the incapacity of leftists to win the debate of ideas with Carvalho, gave marching orders to fellow militants: "Olavo de Carvalho is not to be talked about." The idea was to censor the publication of his articles in the major newspapers and condemn him to silence. The orders were obediently followed by the "collective intellectuals," but they didn't have the desired effect: Carvalho would use technology to circumvent the tacit censorship and outright persecution. First, he created his own website in the late 1990s, on which he posted practically everything he wrote, granting open and free access, a novelty at the time. The website aptly adopted old biblical wisdom as its motto: *Sapientiam autem non vincit malitia* ("*No evil can overcome wisdom*," Wis 7:30). Later he launched an online version of his Philosophy Seminar on the internet.

In 1996, Carvalho also published a revised version of his work on Aristotle, which had appeared in a limited edition two years before, *Aristóteles em Nova Perspectiva* (*Aristotle in a New Perspective: The Theory of the Four Discourses*). It presents a simple but brilliant idea, which unifies different and previously unconnected works of the Stagirite. As the author put it: "it can be summarized in one sentence: human discourse is a single power, which actualizes itself in four different ways: the poetic, the rhetorical, the dialectical, and the analytic (logical)." As he observes, "phrased in this way, the idea doesn't seem particularly remarkable. However, if we consider that the names of these four modes of discourse are also the names of four sciences, we see that from this perspective, Poetics, Rhetoric, Dialectic, and Logic, studying the modalities of a single potency, also constitute variations of a single science." The long essay goes on to show that the difference between each of the four modes of discourse is their increasing degree of credibility, beginning with the realm of the *possible* (Poetics), moving to the *plausible* (Rhetoric), and then to the *probable* (Dialectics), and finally to the *provable* (Logic or Analytics, what came to be known as scientific discourse). It also demonstrates that their sequence is not without reason, and that historically they appeared in a succession, following a certain order, so that scientific knowledge was necessarily preceded by dialectical, rhetorical, and poetic discourse.

In the following years, Carvalho proceeded with intense intellectual activity, giving a series of lectures on the history of philosophy, an introduction to the thought of Aristotle, and writing articles, essays, and books. A notable conference was his intervention in the UNESCO symposium "Forms and Dynamics of Exclusion," in Paris in June 1997, where he presented a paper on "The most excluded of the excluded," which, according to him, are not this or that aggrieved minority, but a "group made up of the vast majority of the human species ... who never protest and who express themselves with silence which we, too easily, often take as a signal of indifference or approbation."[12] He was referring to the *dead*, to those who preceded us, and denouncing the *chronocentrism* of our epoch, which makes dialogue with the past impossible, thus rendering us incapable of learning from those who came before us, or of seeing our present situation in the light of their ideas. The criticism of what he called "the absolutization of time," which

---

[12] *O futuro do pensamento brasileiro* [The future of Brazilian thought] (Rio de Janeiro: Faculdade da Cidade Editora, 1997; Vide, 2016).

locks us up in a solipsistic present moment or enslaves us to history, would remain a constant in his thought. In the same year he published a detailed commentary on Arthur Schopenhauer's classic *The Art of Winning an Argument*[13] and the second volume of *The Collective Imbecile.*[14]

It was in 1999 that the political rage against Carvalho reached a boiling point: he received a tip that radical leftist militants were studying his daily movements in Rio and very probably plotting his assassination. Not to put his family at risk, he decided to leave Brazil for a while, visit friends in France, and then spend some time in Romania, at the invitation of the Brazilian ambassador in Bucharest. There, he gave lectures and acquainted himself with some of the philosophers who fought and survived the Ceausescu dictatorship. He also famously took a picture sitting on the head of a gigantic fallen statue of Lenin.

Carvalho returned to Brazil at the end of that year and launched the "Library of Philosophy," putting in circulation philosophers not widely known in Brazil, such as Eugen Rosenstock-Huessy and Constantin Noica, or simply forgotten, like the great Aristotelian Émile Boutroux. More importantly, he would bring back, from the memory hole to which decades of Gramscian "occupation of spaces" in Brazilian universities had relegated him a philosopher whom he considered the greatest in Brazil: Mario Ferreira dos Santos, the creator of "Concrete Philosophy," proposing a synthesis of all dialectics, from the ancient Greeks all the way to Nietzsche. The task of introducing or reclaiming unknown or censored authors in Brazil culminated in the work of the publisher CEDET, under the intellectual guidance of Carvalho, which has published some 2,000 titles, under several imprints, since its creation in 2011.

In another pioneering initiative, in 2002 he launched a series of thirty-six lectures on the *História Essencial da Filosofia* (Essential History of Philosophy), which were filmed and released on DVD and in booklets. Beginning with the Socratic project, it covered the core of the history of Western philosophy. The series showed Carvalho entirely at ease with bringing the most dissimilar philosophical doctrines alive, in their own context and in dialogue with the present, not trying to subject them to his own view, but illuminating what was unique about each of them.

At this point, in his early fifties, Carvalho's writings and lectures had reached a degree of intellectual and philosophical maturity that he was able to produce

---

[13] Arthur Schopenhauer, ed. Olavo de Carvalho, *Como vencer um debate sem precisar ter razão, em 38 estratagemas*. Dialética Erística (São Paulo: Topbooks, 1997; Auster, 2019).
[14] *A longa marcha da vaca para o brejo* [The cow's long march to the swamp] (Rio de Janeiro: Topbooks, 1998; Vide, 2020).

some of his most long-lasting contributions. He would also single-handedly denounce the São Paulo Forum in the press as the organization responsible for the strategic coordination of the communist movement in Latin America.

In 2005, Carvalho took a decisive step: fed up with the unrelenting persecution and (failed) attempts to ostracize him, as well as with the depressing cultural environment in Brazil, he decided to move to America; not to any trendy urban center, but to rural Virginia. He didn't want to be too far away from the action in Washington, however, and ended up in Carson (pop. 1,400), in Southeastern Virginia. When he left Brazil, he still wrote weekly columns for some of the major Brazilian newspapers and magazines. Just a few months later, he was fired from all of them, except *Diário do Comércio*, for which he continued to write the column "Real World," as the paper's U.S. correspondent. His work spanned a whole decade and resulted in about ten volumes of collected articles, a treasure trove of concrete applications of many of the concepts and ideas he was working on in his philosophy courses.

Beginning in December 2006, Carvalho launched the weekly internet radio program "True Outspeak," broadcast from his home in Carson, in which he reviewed cultural and political developments, in both the U.S. and Brazil. The program reached an increasingly large audience and consistently ranked in the top five of the platform Blog Talk Radio. Once more, he proved that he would not be easily silenced. He soon published another collection of essays, *A dialética simbólica* (Symbolic Dialectics), a compilation of twenty years of writings, which he considered a "long preface" to his philosophical work proper.

After some difficulties with technology, as there was no fast internet connection available in Carson at the time, in 2009 Carvalho launched what he considered his greatest achievement in teaching philosophy: the *Curso Online de Filosofia*, the "Online Philosophy Course." It started with an audience of a few dozen, mostly in Brazil, and over time some eighty thousand students joined from around the world, including thousands in America and Europe. It was a pioneering effort in distance education, to say the least, and remains to this day one of the most successful initiatives for the online teaching of philosophy ever undertaken by an individual.

The Online Philosophy Course was unique, not because it lacked a fixed syllabus and provided no diploma, but because of the method employed by Carvalho. He would not teach "philosophical culture," as he called it— the contents of this or that influential philosopher's doctrines, or an outline of the history of philosophy. He would teach what it is to *philosophize* by doing it in front of his students. His very rich and apparently chaotic intellectual and spiritual trajectory in life, the many influences he received from the most disparate quarters, the fateful years studying with Fr. Ladusañs, the libraries he had read—in short, the life he had lived up to then—all seemed to converge and contribute to something unique: a real philosopher doing real philosophy in real time. It proved very attractive for young and not-so-young students who were searching for understanding and truth in a world dominated by the tyranny of relativism, and who believed their lives have meaning—one they earnestly wanted to know themselves. Carvalho provided the tools and a living example.

From the first class—interrupted several times by failing internet connections—to the last one on New Year's Day 2022 (barely three weeks before he passed away), Carvalho taught 585 classes, always on Saturday evenings. They would last anywhere from one to three hours, depending on the topic and on the questions raised by students. In small towns around Brazil, groups of students would spontaneously form to watch the classes together, and read and discuss the dozens of books mentioned or recommended. Other groups would work diligently to transcribe the lectures and then edit the texts. In a conservative estimate, Carvalho left over twenty-five thousand pages of transcriptions of his courses, mostly unpublished, some published for the first time in this volume.

The issues Carvalho dealt with varied wildly: from a close reading and critique of classics of philosophy, always with a view to discussing *real* problems, to a philosophical critique of intellectual trends (such as political correctness, climate hysteria, pseudo-science and scientific fraud, racialism, globalism, the Islamization of the West, queer theory, gender ideology, wokeism, etc.), to the workings and history of the revolutionary movement, and the development of many aspects of his own philosophy in metaphysics, epistemology, political science, psychology, and so on. He also introduced several original concepts and analyses, which would later be printed in essays and books. They are well documented in this volume: e.g. *cognitive parallax* and the structure of the *revolutionary mind, metacapitalism, knowledge through presence, radical intuitionism, circle of latency*, and *the rotatory perspective* method, among many others. Several of his lectures were prescient. For instance, he would frequently revisit the issue of scientific ideology posing as "science" and expose its fraudulent character. A piece he wrote in 2013 would prove rather prophetic:

> Almost imperceptibly, the circular reasoning that considers all issues resolved before the mere possibility of discussion, and consecrates pressure, intimidation, and fraud as the only valid judgment criteria for solving all problems, has spread beyond the university milieu, now dominating virtually all Western governments, big media, and

international organizations. Imposing scientific theories through massive propaganda campaigns and the criminalization of objections, blocking discussions via slander and moral assassination, prohibiting, through psychological blackmail, the investigation of facts adverse to the interests of pressure groups, have all become universally accepted and even obligatory procedures in the media, public discussions, and government decisions. The "thirst for power" has replaced reason and expelled it from decent society. We already live in the world of the Queen of Hearts in Alice in Wonderland, where the verdict precedes the trial, and, moreover, it's always the same: "Off with their heads."[15]

Carvalho believed that the purpose of a philosopher is not only to transmit the content of the philosophic tradition, but "to make philosophers." Therefore, he hoped that his Online Course would contribute to the creation of a new intellectual class in Brazil, to replace the "collective imbeciles" who dominate the establishment in universities and the media.

In 2011, Carvalho received an unusual invitation, which he accepted as another opportunity to fulfill his mission: to debate with the Russian philosopher Aleksandr Dugin, then professor at the Moscow State University. Dugin is a proponent of so-called "National Bolshevism" and "neo-Eurasianism" and said to be influential with Russian president Vladimir Putin. The topic of the debate was "the role of the U.S. in the New World Order."[16] Carvalho readily denounced Dugin's proposals for a "Eurasian Union" under Russian leadership. He also claimed that there are three projects for "global domination:" the Sino-Russian alliance, the Islamic Caliphate, and Western globalism. He argued that only part of the U.S. elite is involved in the latter, while most Americans are still patriots, who live according to traditional Christian values, under the framework of the U.S. Constitution. He added: "The USA is not the command center of the globalist project but, on the contrary, its primary victim, marked for destruction." A close look into this debate (an excerpt appears in Chapter 8) shows that, in 2011, Carvalho deftly anticipated some of the core elements of the platform of national populism that would be the basis for Donald Trump's election as president in 2016.

---

[15] "O mundo da Rainha de Copas" [The world of the Queen of Hearts], November 26, 2013, unpublished handout of the Online Philosophy Course.
[16] Os EUA e a Nova Ordem Mundial: um debate entre Olavo de Carvalho e Aleksandr Dugin (The USA and the New World Order: a debate between Olavo de Carvalho and Aleksandr Dugin) (Vide, 2012).

After a hiatus of almost five years without publishing, Carvalho broke his literary silence in 2011 with *Maquiavel ou A confusão demoníaca* (*Machiavelli or the Demonic Confusion*), a chapter of a longer work he was planning, dedicated to "The Revolutionary Mind." In the form of a long essay, this work reconstitutes Machiavelli's thought in his own time and circumstances, putting aside the images and fictions posterity attributed to him. The figure that emerges in the end is not the cunning and unscrupulous counselor to the prince, which over the centuries has become a bad description of politicians and self-interested rulers, but the pathetic figure of a diabolical liar (in his writings) and loser (in his political ambitions).

Shortly after, in 2013, Carvalho dedicated another book to the founder of modern philosophy: *Visões de Descartes* (Visions of Descartes: Between the Evil Genius and the Spirit of Truth). Carvalho applied to the work of the French philosopher the method he had learned from Paul Friedländer in his classic studies of Plato, and from the works of Eric Voegelin,[17] according to whom "understanding philosophical ideas cannot be achieved by analyzing texts alone or by reconstructing the cultural atmosphere from which the texts emerged. It requires the meditative tracking of the real experiences from which ideas were born."[18]

Carvalho does exactly that to Descartes' works, especially his *Meditations on First Philosophy*, painstakingly reconstituting the whole argument that leads to the famous *cogito*. After demonstrating the impossibility of radical questioning as proposed by the philosopher, Carvalho shows that Descartes, who began his exposition talking about his *real* self, halfway through switches his object, and begins talking about an *abstract* self, without realizing it. Carvalho explores some of the consequences of this basic mistake of Cartesian philosophy, which exerted an enormous influence in Western tradition.

The year of 2013 also marked the beginning of a shift in Brazilian politics that would bring Carvalho's name to the public square. Protests initially launched by the left would be overtaken by conservatives, who, for the first time in decades, rose up against the ruling Workers' Party's blatant and widespread corruption and increasing tyranny. It was at that time that a 700-page anthology of his writings, organized by a young journalist who was his student, topped the best-seller

---

[17] Paul Friedländer, *Plato, An Introduction,* 3 vols. (Pantheon Books, 1958); Eric Voegelin, *Complete Works* (Louisiana University Press, 1995–2006).
[18] "Descartes and The Psychology of Doubt," in Chapter 4 of this *Reader.*

charts.[19] Along with a new edition of *The Collective Imbecile*, over 300,000 of Carvalho's books were sold in a relatively short period. Olavo de Carvalho became a household name in Brazil.

At that time and in the following years, Carvalho also successively published the ten volumes of the yearly collection of his articles for *Diário do Comércio*,[20] selections of essays in *A filosofia e o seu inverso* (Philosophy and the inverse thereof & Other studies), a guide to the study of the philosophy of Mário Ferreira dos Santos, and other books. He also taught courses on specific authors and issues, usually in five or six lectures, including "Knowledge and morality," "Principles and methods of self-education," "Introduction to the philosophy of Louis Lavelle," "Sociology of philosophy," "How to become an intelligent reader," "The crisis of intelligence according to Roger Scruton," "Personality formation," and "Esotericism in History and today."

The spontaneous emergence of a mass conservative movement, which peacefully took to the streets, would lend decisive support to the impeachment and removal from power of President Dilma Roussef. In the late 1960s, Roussef had participated in terrorist organizations that fought to impose a Cuban-style dictatorship in Brazil. She was impeached in 2016, on corruption charges related to the federal budget. Two years later, the movement would usher in the election of the first conservative president in many decades. In street demonstrations throughout Brazil, from well-off neighborhoods to bus stops and slum quarters, homemade placards would read *Olavo tem razão* ("Olavo is right"). On October 28, 2018, in his first public address after winning 55% of the popular vote, in a live streamed video, President Jair Bolsonaro had in front of him four books: the Bible, the Brazilian Constitution, Winston Churchill's memoirs, and Carvalho's *The Minimum You Need To Know Not To Be An Idiot* (in Portuguese).

In the following year, Brazilian filmmaker Josias Teófilo would release his documentary *O Jardim das Aflições* (The Garden of Afflictions), about Carvalho's philosophy. The American premiere took place at a special session at the Trump Hotel, in Washington, on the eve of President Bolsonaro's first official visit to the United States, in March 2019.

The left's reaction against Carvalho reached new paroxysms of rage. Soon major news outlets forbad anyone from calling him a philosopher and would label

---

[19] Olavo de Carvalho, *O mínimo que você precisa saber para não ser um idiota* [The minimum you need to know not to be an idiot], ed. Felipe Moura Brasil (Rio de Janeiro: Record, 2013).

[20] Series *Cartas de um Terráqueo ao Planeta Brasil* [Letters from an Earthling to Planet Brazil].

him as the "guru of the president," in an attempt to portray him as a trivial political ideologue. It's worth quoting his reaction to this caricature:

> A fundamental distinction, which clearly escapes all the pundits who opine about me in the media and in almost the entire academic world, is that which exists between a "conservative thinker," who is essentially dedicated to the exposition and defense of conservative ideals, and a philosopher in the strict sense, whose sphere of interests and achievements infinitely transcends that of conservatism, who enters it as a mere part, and not as a living center articulating the whole. Such is, for example, the difference between Russell Kirk and Eric Voegelin, or between Edmund Burke and Samuel Taylor Coleridge. I do not see, for example, how one could call my analyses of Aristotle and Descartes "conservative doctrines" (or anti-conservative doctrines), and even less so my long studies on "knowledge through presence," so skillfully summarized in Ronald Robson's book … Since the ideological struggle is the supreme or only interest of those media and academic pundits, they map my thinking according to the format of their own, placing at the center and top of mine what is only their own, and thus reducing me to their own meager stature.[21]

In 2021, he would release his last three books: *A consciência de imortalidade* (The conscience of immortality], *Inteligência e verdade* (Intelligence and truth), and the first volume of his massive philosophical diary, which includes a selection of his daily posts on social media.[22]

For a few years, and increasingly more seriously since 2018, Carvalho had suffered from debilitating pulmonary and heart disease, aggravated by sepsis. He went to Brazil for treatment in June 2021 and returned to Virginia in November. On New Year's Day 2022, he gave what would be his last lecture on the Online Philosophy Course. On January 24, at the age of 74, he passed away in a hospital in Hopewell, Virginia. He was survived by his wife, Roxane, eight children, and eighteen grandchildren.

As goes the famous verse by Mallarmé, which Carvalho often quoted:

Tel qu'en Lui-même enfin l'éternité le change.

---

[21] "Corção, palavrões e a miséria cultural," *Mídia Sem Máscara*, September 17, 2020.
[22] *Diário filosófico*, Vol. 1, 2013–2015. A second volume of the *Philosophical Diary* would appear posthumously in 2022.

"Such as into Himself at last eternity changes him."

Carvalho liked to begin many of his courses by inviting students to meditate on a passage from French metaphysician Louis Lavelle, one of his favorite contemporary philosophers, who wrote:

> There are privileged moments in life when it seems that the universe lights up, that our life reveals its meaning to us, that we desire the very destiny that has been ours, as if we had chosen it ourselves. Then the universe closes in on itself again: we become lonely and miserable once more, and we can only walk along a dark path where everything becomes an obstacle to our steps. Wisdom consists in preserving the memory of these fleeting moments, in knowing how to revive them, in making them the fabric of our daily existence and, so to speak, the habitual abode of our spirit.[23]

Olavo de Carvalho dedicated his life to preserving, reviving, and teaching those moments, so that each of his many thousands of students could perhaps one day make them the habitual abode of their spirit. It is an invitation here renewed to the reader.

* * *

---

[23] Louis Lavelle, "Témoignage," *De l'Intimité spirituelle* (Paris: Aubier, 1955).

A Note About This *Reader*

Faced with the daunting task of selecting, from a universe of forty books, over twenty-five thousand pages of lecture transcriptions, and countless articles, essays, and unpublished class handouts, a sample that would be representative of the extraordinarily broad territory covered by the philosophical work of Olavo de Carvalho, the editors chose to cast their net broadly and deeply. Aside from many "obvious" picks—for their originality, repercussions, or interest to the English-speaking audience—*The Olavo de Carvalho Reader* contains writings from about thirty of his works, covering a period of three decades, as well as many unpublished texts prepared especially for the Online Philosophy Course. Inevitably, much was left out, including important works, which will have to wait for a complete collection of Carvalho's works in English.

Most of the texts chosen are presented in their entirety, but a few had to be edited for reasons of length. Carvalho's texts speak for themselves. Still, the editors added a few notes, either on sources or to clarify specific points and context.

Following the express wishes of the author for the publication of his works, inclusive language is used throughout this *Reader,* in keeping with the tradition of Western languages, beginning with Latin and Classical Greek. Therefore, consistent with that tradition, the third person masculine pronoun is used to include both genders in the subjective case or as a possessive: e.g. *the philosopher, if he knows his sources*. The ungrammatical current fad suggested in "*the philosopher, if they know their sources*" is avoided.

To provide some guidance for a first encounter with Carvalho's vast opus, the *Reader* is divided into nine chapters organized around Carvalho's definition of philosophy: "the search for the unity of knowledge in the unity of consciousness and vice versa," and then dealing with some of the main topics of his writings, more or less in the order in which he developed them, but with occasional recapitulation and fast-forwards.

As suggested by Carvalho's definition, the first two chapters, closely intertwined, present the centrality of individual consciousness as the fulcrum of all knowledge: "The Unity of Consciousness" deals with personal experience, self-awareness, and consciousness of consciousness as indispensable steps for any philosophical activity. "The Unity of Knowledge" opens with an introduction to his theory of the unity of the four discourses in Aristotle, one of his indelible contributions to the philosophy of culture and theory of knowledge. It then goes on to address the problem of truth and the importance of the experience of the most beautiful things for anyone interested in fulfilling the highest human spiritual qualities.

The next chapter introduces some of the elements that led to "The Crisis of Consciousness," the dominant cultural and spiritual pathology of our time. It traces the emergence of individual consciousness to the roots of our civilization, and its retraction since the sixteenth century. It goes on to describe the role played by the "new elite," including intellectuals, in spreading the disease, highlighting some of its features, as the "cult of the East," or the cultural relativism that strives to abolish any sense of the good and the beautiful and forbids judging the value of different cultures.

The next stage down the road was the advent of what Carvalho called *cognitive parallax*. Aside from explaining the concept he created to describe a phenomenon typical of modern philosophy, the texts gathered in this chapter present Carvalho's critique of specific aspects of the philosophy of Machiavelli, Descartes, and Kant. The dissolution of consciousness that led to cognitive parallax will contribute to the formation of the *revolutionary mind*, which, according to Carvalho, "is not essentially a political phenomenon but a spiritual and psychological one, although its most visible field of expression and its fundamental instrument is political action."

A whole chapter is dedicated to "Marxism, Intellectuals, and Cultural Revolution," with original insights into Marxism as a culture and a scathing critique of the corruption of intellectuals and the *collective imbecile*. The essay "The New World Order Guru" presents an apparently unlikely candidate for that prestigious position: Immanuel Kant.

The chapter "Revolutionary Minds in Action" documents the extension of the devastation wrought by over two centuries of the revolutionary movement. Of particular interest is the depiction of two major Brazilian contributions to revolution: communist infiltration in the Catholic Church in Latin America, via so-called "liberation theology," whose effects are still being felt today in America and the Vatican; and the São Paulo Forum, the strategic coordination of the communist movement in the Western hemisphere.

"On Power and the New Global Order" brings an excerpt of Carvalho's debate with Aleksandr Dugin in 2011, still immensely relevant to understand what is at stake in geopolitical confrontations in Eastern Europe and across the globe. Other essays in this chapter go on to debunk myths about the Cold War and lay bare the shortcomings and ultimate failure of doctrines that guided American foreign policy in the twentieth century. They also describe the roots of the Islamization of the West that began over seventy years ago. An in-depth interview with Carvalho provides a unique insight on why he changed some of his views on the United States and its role in the world after he moved to Virginia in 2005.

The final chapter, "Return to Consciousness" serves as a coda, recapitulating the difference between ideology and philosophy according to Carvalho, and the misery brought about in Brazil by erasing that distinction. It ends with an overview of the role of truth in civilization and the current challenges posed by the "reign of consensus."

When reading Carvalho's works, one should heed the advice he gave to his students on "the only possible learning of philosophy," which is: "To read the expositions of philosophers by imaginatively reconstructing the inner activity that generated them. This is like reading a musical score and gradually learning to perform it with all the implied emotional nuances and emphases that the score hints at but doesn't show."[24]

The Editors

---

[24] "Notes for an Introduction to Philosophy," in Chapter 1.

Chapter 1

The Unity of Consciousness

Who Am I?

A filosofia e seu inverso & Outros estudos (2012)

One of the most significant moments in the history of philosophy arrived when Socrates, about to meet with Gorgias, is consulted by Chaerephon regarding the question he wishes to ask the renowned sophist:

"Ask him who he is (Ὅστις ἐστίν)," responds Socrates.

Commenting on this passage, Eric Voegelin observes: "That is for all times the decisive question, cutting through the network of opinions, social ideas, and ideologies. It is the question that appeals to the nobility of the soul; and it is the question that the ignoble intellectual cannot face."

For greater clarity, the author of *Order and History* emphasizes: "The substance of man is at stake, not a philosophical problem in the modern sense."[25]

Carefully avoiding "philosophical problems in the modern sense" appears to be, therefore, a *sine qua non* condition for the practice of philosophy in the Socratic-Platonic sense. To avoid them, or at least not engage with them without a clear awareness of the difference between philosophy proper and a discussion with the anti-philosopher. The first is the education of the soul in the pursuit of the eternal Good. The second is the removal of obstacles that do not arise from the pursuit itself but from the culture around it, from the political society entirely focused on the immediate goals of earthly life, where men do not speak with the voice of their hearts but with the voices of the social roles that suit them at the moment. The anti-philosopher can, of course, be another person or an aspect of the philosopher's own soul. In this case, the discussion with him becomes a stage of philosophical learning. The main occupation of the anti-philosopher, whether internal or external, is to place obstacles in the philosopher's path to make him give up the pursuit. Removing these obstacles requires some technique, the acquisition of which makes the philosopher more capable of surviving in a hostile environment and overcoming his own inner hesitations. The technique—rhetoric, dialectic, and logic—includes training in the art of anticipating obstacles in order to avoid surprises in the debate. The apprentice plays the role of the devil's advocate, arguing against his own fondest hopes with the tenacity and cunning of a true demon. The problem begins when the individual takes pleasure in this exercise, making it an end in itself, independent of the original goals of philosophy. This is how "philosophical problems in the modern sense" are born.

---

[25] Eric Voegelin, *Plato and Aristotle*, in *Order and History*, vol. 3, *The Collected Works of Eric Voegelin*, vol. 16 (Columbia and London: University of Missouri Press, 2000), 78.

They grow until they dominate the entire horizon of the apprentice's concerns and, over time, end up institutionalizing themselves as prestigious academic activities, highly professionalized and highly developed from a technical perspective. In the discussions that unfold in this environment, the most abstruse questions are examined in their tiniest details with admirable precision. There is only one question considered inconvenient there, so inconvenient that it doesn't need to be banned because no one dares to ask it out loud. That question is:

"Who are you?"

To answer it, the person being questioned would need to strip away their professional identity and speak from the living core of their flesh-and-blood self. However, this is not compatible with either standardized technical language or the decorum that should prevail in academic institutions. Therefore, Gorgias, or any other "ignoble intellectual," is safe from ever being put in an embarrassing situation by Socrates' inconvenient curiosity.

That's the reason why, keeping my distance from such sophisticated environments, in the etymological sense of the term as well, I feel comfortable moving freely between academic discourse and the voice of the heart. I don't disdain the former but subject it to the demands of the latter, and not the other way around.

In this book, readers will find, in a baroque blend that some may find a bit obscene, subtly elaborated technical analyses and direct outpourings of a human soul that has never learned to deal with anyone impersonally. I prefer to come across as coarse in the eyes of others rather than as insincere to myself.

It so happened that, since my adolescence, finding myself alone, without guidance in a confusing and unwelcoming world, I quickly understood that to avoid losing myself entirely, I had no other means than to come to terms with myself, to immediately find the center of my real person and settle there with the utmost humility and the absolute certainty that someone seated on the ground does not fall. Around me, there was so much confusion, so much deception, so much madness, so much falsehood, so much disorienting pretense that if I were not sincere with myself, no sense of direction in life would be possible for me. I chose inner sincerity not for some lofty moral reason, but for a simple matter of psychic survival.

I never managed or even attempted, in the theater of the world, to play any other role than that of myself. I appear before the human audience without any social or professional adornment, almost naked.

This has brought me many problems. The first is that anyone who talks to me for five minutes already feels like they're intimately acquainted with me and starts giving unsolicited advice about my life. I have no defense against it. I've grown accustomed to being treated with that affectionate disrespect that befalls those who are considered cousins by everyone.

Of course, there are those who, from a distance, are intimidated by a certain intellectual superiority they see in me, and they shield themselves with falsely ceremonious airs, poorly concealing that inevitable intrusiveness which, deep down, is shared by the rest of my acquaintances. I can't say that I detest these people, but if I could, I'd hide from them under the couch.

Even so, their presence is a small price to pay for the indescribable comfort of never having to police myself, evaluate my performance by the judgment of others, or shape my language to fit the expectations of the respectable public.

I often say that, excluding sexual and excretory activities, which would subject me to legal penalties if displayed in front of the public eye, there is nothing I do in private that I can't repeat in public. To the curious who wish to probe our domestic life, my wife always responds that I am just the same at home as what everyone sees in my classes and lectures.

Similarly, I would like my philosophy not to be the editorial and didactic crystallization of a professional identity but the direct and candid expression of what I see, feel, and think in everyday life. Especially of what, far from the world, I say and confess before God.

It is so, not due to any exhibitionist impulse on my part, which, if it existed, would prevent me from keeping my thoughts to myself as I did until the age of forty-eight, when I published my first book.

It is so, I say, because I am convinced that one can only see life realistically by first adjusting his inner focus, speaking from the center of himself and not from an external pseudo-personality adopted for professional purposes, neurotic self-compensation, or anything else. The philosopher, I believe, should speak not as a professor from his lectern, a preacher from his pulpit, a speaker from his platform, but as a sincere believer who examines his conscience and confesses what he knows about himself and the world. Without this, even the practice of the phenomenological method, which aims to describe things as they appear, becomes unworkable. After all, *to whom* do they appear? To an abstract and generic consciousness, morally and legally unaccountable? To a social identity of a professor and intellectual hastily glued onto a well-camouflaged and inaccessible self? This would divert the focus so much that even the most meticulous phenomenological description risks becoming what it least desires to be: a logical construct, a structure of hypotheses, a "theory" in the current sense of the term. Clearly, fidelity to the object should be articulated, with equal rigor, to the coincidence of the subject with himself, to the perfect honesty of the sinner before a God whom he knows he cannot deceive. This was the root of what I came to call the *confessional method*—the judgment of theoretical truth in the court of inner sincerity.

On the other hand, it was, of course, not autobiographical sincerity. Philosophy had to be confession, but not in its content, but in its form, in its cognitive strategy. The goal was not to talk about myself but to speak from within me, from the depths of my soul, about whatever I saw in it or around it.

Hence, the language to be employed should be the most strictly personal, yet, somewhat paradoxically perhaps, the occasional use of the technical and impersonal vocabulary of academic philosophy should not be in any way disregarded or dispensable. It becomes strictly necessary at certain moments, even to crystallize the most personal and intimate impressions with clarity.

As a result, the impossibility, at least occasionally and intermittently, of presenting my thoughts in a systematically academic or treatise-like format emerges.

Friends and foes, from time to time, demand from me a systematic exposition of a philosophy, a part of which I have scattered in oral and written fragments while the other part remains implicit, between the lines, trusting in the hermeneutic or divinatory ability of anyone who possesses it.

The former group makes this demand because they believe it would be good to explain more systematically a thought in which they glimpse something valuable without being able to fully grasp it. The latter group makes this demand to prove that I am incapable of meeting it.

Both are correct, but the latter more so.

I have no talent whatsoever for doing something that I firmly believe should not be done.

From the beginning of my scholarly adventure, I have been convinced that wisdom—an ideal both elusive and ultimate of philosophy—does not consist of general truths crystallized into repeatable doctrinal formulas, but in the apprehension of the universal meaning of the particular, unique, and concrete situations experienced by real human beings.

In the moral sphere, this is exemplarily obvious. A good person is not one who can recite the commandments by heart, but one who can transmute them into wise decisions and actions amid the confusing demands and conflicting pressures of immediate existence, where they often become unrecognizable or take on a scandalous and paradoxical appearance.

Similarly, in aesthetics, there are no general principles capable of accounting on their own for the bewildering variety of unpredictable forms that the experience of beauty can assume, sometimes even under the camouflage of the ugly, the misshapen, and the monstrous. Aesthetic sensibility lies in the ability to apprehend the unity of beauty behind these forms, even without being able to condense it into general principles.

Why wouldn't the same apply to the higher philosophical disciplines of purely theoretical nature: metaphysics and epistemology?

No metaphysical system, when examined closely, fails to reveal some internal contradiction or a mismatch with experience. None exists whose errors do not provide, in return, inspiring suggestions for addressing a thousand and one metaphysical problems that spring from real experience. Just as there can be no completely literal language without ambiguities, there always remains, in reading the great works of philosophy, the possibility of symbolically interpreting something that, in the literal sense, is manifestly wrong. In doing so, one can trace it back to the original perception of an obscure truth that the philosopher failed to convert into an explicit doctrinal conclusion.

There is a significant difference between reading philosophers to know their doctrines as such and reading them in pursuit of the truth. A doctrine crystalized in texts is only a historical truth, or more accurately, a philological truth, if not an editorial one. But no philosopher created his doctrines solely for us to know them; rather, he created them so that, through them, we could seek the truth. The truth, which, at best, his doctrines can only partially grasp or, in most cases, symbolically insinuate (not being, in this, any more exact or precise than a poem or a play). Yes, the text and doctrine must be historically acquired and possessed. But this is still not philosophy; it is merely philosophical culture.

At times, a theory that is in itself unacceptable remains valid as a critique to another theory. When Hume denies the existence of the "self," he is merely led to an absurd conclusion by the automatism of his own reasoning. Still, who can deny that, in doing so, he dismantled the deductive machinery of Cartesianism, showing that Descartes, while proving the existence of thought, erred in thinking that he had thereby also proven the existence of a "thinking substance?" Indeed, if the *cogito* is an instantaneous experience, without duration, it is impossible to deduce from it the persistence of the self between the instant when it has this experience and the moment when it narrates it.[26] By demonstrating the non-existence of the Cartesian "self," Hume may have wrongly denied the existence of any "self" at all—an unwarranted extension like that which he criticizes in Descartes. However, it is certain that by exposing the difficulty of finding proof of the "self's" existence, Hume created the eloquent symbol of a constitutive paradox of the human ego. It can only apprehend itself as a substance from a retrospective standpoint, where *"tel qu'en Lui-même enfin l'éternité le change"*?[27]

Those who attempt to declare universally valid literal truths almost always succeed only in sketching a symbol. Conversely, when we seek to move towards the universal truths we see outlined in concrete situations, the order is reversed. Instead of inadvertently arriving at a symbol, we intentionally start from one, knowing that, no matter how much we analyze it, we cannot transform it into a definitive literal truth but merely into another, clearer, more intelligible, and perhaps more satisfactory symbol. The limit we reach by this means is not determined by ultimate truth, but only by the degree of our demand for understanding. This demand, in turn, is determined by personal, cultural, and historical factors that define the scope and course of the investigation.

I have never had any other intellectual ambition.

Hence, my impatience with those generic philosophical problems—the "philosophical problems in the modern sense"—that professors and textbook authors seem to consider the purest and loftiest expressions of philosophical inquiry: materialism and idealism, determinism and free will, the foundations of morality, the logic of meaning, and so on.

I cannot, of course, entirely avoid these questions, which I stumble upon at every step in the attempt to explain myself to an audience preoccupied with them. However, I try to address them only superficially, as occasional complements to what I want to say about concrete realities of life.

All my writings are therefore strictly *of occasion*: reactions of a curious and sincere intellect to the experiences of a moment, recorded and analyzed in multiple keys, in shameless cognitive opportunism immune to any presumption of systematization and, even more so, subsequent textual organization. If they do not entirely dissolve into a dust pile of impressions, it is because, from the multiplicity of occasions that elicit them, the perspectives that shape them, and even the literary genres in which they are expressed, they always refer to a central

---

[26] See further "Descartes and the Psychology of Doubt," in Chapter Four—Eds.
[27] "Such as into Himself at last eternity changes him." Stéphane Mallarmé, *The Poems in Verse,* trans. Peter Manson (Miami University Press, 2012).—Eds.

core of concerns that unify around a constant, unique, almost obsessive goal: the pursuit of the Supreme Good, and therefore also the removal of obstacles that may arise along the way.

The texts collected in this book[28] reflect both the kaleidoscopic disorder of fragments and the unity of light that permeates them.

In this sense, the absence of any order, whether in the chronology of the writings or in the distribution of subjects, is intentional, harmless, and even opportune.

The reader of this collection will have, among the many shifts in perspective and tone throughout the pages, the opportunity to verify what I am saying. I only hope he does not become irritated by it but rather be encouraged and pleased to find that, amidst the baroque multiplicity I present, his own point of view is perhaps not entirely excluded.

Philosophy and the Inverse Thereof

A filosofia e seu inverso & Outros estudos (2012)

If there is a historical fact beyond doubt, it is that philosophy was born in Greece and acquired its classical form definitively with Plato and Aristotle (both under the original inspiration of Socrates). You can become a philosopher while ignoring Sartre, Husserl, Nietzsche, even Hegel, Leibniz, or Saint Thomas Aquinas. But those who have not immersed themselves in the teachings of the two founding fathers will remain forever estranged from the spirit of philosophy.

No one described this spirit better than Eric Voegelin when he stated that, as the old "cosmological" sense of life orientation, in which the order of existence appeared as an image of the cosmos, was lost, philosophy emerged as an attempt to find a new ordering principle, no longer in the contemplation of the physical universe, but in the interiority of the soul. In the general confusion of the world, the philosopher seeks to order his own soul to take it as a measure for assessing the external disorder.

Among the various styles of thought that universal philosophy offers us, students always end up, ultimately, attaching themselves to one. Whether formally

---

[28] The author is referring to the book where this introduction originally appeared, but it could well refer to this *Reader*.—Eds.

or informally, they become Kantian, Hegelian, Marxist, Nietzschean, structuralist, neo-empiricist, or something else. But none of these lines of orientation makes the slightest sense in and of itself if separated from the original ordering project inaugurated by Plato and Aristotle. Mainly because those various schools define each other within the limits of a "professional" philosophical debate, with problems and terms established by a long academic tradition, whereas the Greek classics provide us with a much broader sense of orientation, not within the framework of academic discussions, but in life in general. Descartes, Kant, Husserl, or Wittgenstein teach us "philosophy," meaning certain philosophical problems and sophisticated ways to approach them. But only in Plato and Aristotle will you learn what it means *to be* a philosopher. Being a philosopher is not the same as mastering only a set of intellectual techniques that make you a recognizable or even respectable member of a particular academic corporation (assuming that the university actually teaches them, rather than just giving you a title to cover up their absence). These techniques allow you to understand what philosophers are discussing and even formulate your speculations in academically acceptable language, but no one in their right mind would think of applying them to real life, to everyday life outside of the professional sphere. No one, when making decisions about marriage, employment, child rearing, household management, or even more so when dealing with the great crises of personal existence, will act based on Hegel or Wittgenstein. In fact, the mere idea of seeking philosophical guidance in real life sounds strange in academic circles today. Philosophy, they say, is serious intellectual activity, not self-help. In times of trouble, they forget seriousness and seek the help of a psychotherapist (or even a spiritualist, like many professors at the University of São Paulo). But it is precisely in the decisive moments of life, in times of crisis and perplexity, that Plato and Aristotle (and, hovering above them, the spirit of Socrates) come to our aid, infusing us with the sense of the inner order of the soul. This inner order will make each of us not a professional academic but a *spoudaíos*, a truly mature person, humanly developed to the utmost limit of their cognitive powers, capable of perceiving reality and making decisions from the center and the pinnacle of their consciousness, and not from the passing passions of the moment, from professional opportunism, from the fear of peer judgment, or from some fashionable prejudice.

   In terms of pedagogical power, in terms of the power to order the soul, the writings of Plato and Aristotle are second only to the Bible and the words of the Saints and Doctors of the Church—with one advantage in their favor: the Bible is written in symbolic language, sometimes difficult to interpret, and the writings of the Fathers and Doctors fill entire libraries, which you will not be able to read in a lifetime, assuming you emerge unscathed from the theological controversies that clutter the path. It is also true that many scholars see in Plato and Aristotle only what they find in Descartes, Kant, or Husserl: "philosophical questions" to fuel scholarly research and enliven academic debates. But they do this because they want to, because they love philosophy as a profession, not as a norm and meaning of life. Nothing obliges them to do so, except the decision they have freely taken to seek the security of a professional identity rather than the order of inner life. They reconcile, without any great crisis of conscience, the rigor of academic research with the fragmentation, disharmony, and deformity of their souls. That these individuals typify, in the eyes of the multitude, the image of "philosophers" par excellence is one of the greatest ironies of today's society. For the orientation they have adopted in life is the exact opposite of the philosophical life as understood by Socrates, Plato, and Aristotle. They are "professional philosophers" precisely to the extent that they ignore or despise the spirit of philosophy.

Philosophy and Self-Awareness

A handout from the Online Philosophy Course, 2012

With Socrates, philosophy was born as a critical analysis of collective knowledge in the light of the unity, integrity, and self-transparency of individual consciousness. Not just any individual consciousness, but one that has struggled to achieve this unity, integrity, and self-transparency, having dug and built them up amidst the tumultuous confusion of passions and self-deception, which partly arise from the passive, disordered, and uncritical absorption of collective beliefs.

It is this struggle that provides the philosopher with both the authority and cognitive tools to analyze, judge, and if necessary, condemn established beliefs. This struggle becomes possible and necessary because of the dual and self-conflicting constitution of individual consciousness. On the one hand, this consciousness is shaped by various genetic and environmental influences pulling it in different directions, awakening mutually contradictory demands. On the other hand, it tends towards unity due to the continuity of bodily existence and the need for decisions and choices that require the unity of an acting subject with self-remembrance, perseverance in actions, and the ability to respond to other agents.

A second layer of conflicting demands arises from the fact that the individual not only needs to develop as an acting subject but also to find or accept a place in society, often sacrificing a portion of his sense of internal unity to the demands of his social role and the sense of group identity that sustains and protects, but also limits and distorts, his individuality.

No human being could rise to the status of an independent critic of collective beliefs if the only forces at play in the process of self-discovery—or self-constitution—of his individual consciousness were his own individuating drive and the social environment's demands and pressures. On the one hand, this drive is not self-caused but depends on stimuli and cognitive means, including language, that come from the social environment itself. On the other hand, this environment is founded, in part, on needs inherent in the biological constitution of the individual being. Any evolutionary conflict that may arise between these two forces, therefore, takes place within the framework of an inseparable symbiotic relationship. In asserting their sovereignty, individuals rely on the social context and implicitly confess their dependence on it. This is most evident in cases of congenital or acquired maladaptation, where individuals, by rebelling against the human environment, are expelled to a lower social level where they have even less freedom of movement than their better-adapted peers.

Socrates, of course, does not fall into this category. His inner independence is real and, instead of restricting him, expands his freedom of movement, allowing him the space to perform a unique social role, which in many aspects is superior to that of other members of society, some of whom admire him to the point of veneration, while others envy and fear him to the extent of desiring his death.

The acquisition of this inner independence—and to some extent even outer independence—would not be possible in a framework exclusively delimited by the biological and social factors of the symbiotic competition between the individual and society, a competition that unfolds within the existing social patterns and ultimately reaffirms the primacy of society. The independence that Socrates achieves, exercises, and demonstrates is evidently based on the interference of a third element, superior and independent both of himself and the social environment, and irreducible, therefore, either to the natural constitution of individuality or to the available socio-cultural data.

It is this element that Socrates calls his *daimon*, the spirit that guides him amid the demands of life, imposing choices and behaviors that transcend both the impulses of his mere individuality and the rules and precepts of society.

What underlies and defines the philosopher's activity is not merely the critique of society, or, much less, the use of the natural and social faculty of "reason" as an instrument of that critique. Instead, it is the appeal to a higher instance, authorized to guide and judge both the individual and society.

By consciously and voluntarily submitting to the dictates of this higher instance, the philosopher becomes its emissary, but not the perfect and sole embodiment of its authority. He acknowledges that this authority is also distributed, albeit degraded and confused, within the existing social order. This apparent paradox is the reason why even the most independent of Athenian citizens obediently bows to the judgment of the court that condemns him, thus refusing to assert an independence in the empirical social realm equivalent to the one he demonstrated in the domains of thought and personal ethics.

Socrates is a spokesperson for the "unwritten laws" that transcend the existing social order, but not a prophet-legislator entrusted with modifying that order according to the standards set by those laws. His function is to remind people of the existence of the transcendent order rather than to establish it in the world through the force of authority.

This will continue to be the mission of philosophers throughout the centuries and the very definition of their way of being.

The Consciousness of Consciousness

Diário do Comércio, May 5, 2008
A Inversão Revolucionária em Ação (2015);
A consciência de imortalidade (2021)

The fact that, in the so-called human sciences, the subject and the object of knowledge are the same has often been lamented as a cause of subjective distortions incompatible with the claims of scientific rigor. In an effort to eliminate these distortions, many scholars have tried to constitute that object as an entity of the external world, like facts of nature, neutralizing the subjective bias of the observer. However, this coincidence of subject and object is the true and effective situation of knowledge in the human sciences, and I see no reason to avoid this situation through analogies with models borrowed from other sciences. It should be taken seriously from the outset as an inescapable given of reality.

Every attempt to constitute the object "man" as an external thing—and worse, to cut it out from its concrete background by selecting its mathematizable aspects, excluding the rest—can only result in producing an analogy, a figure of speech, a poetic simile. Studies oriented in this way may create interesting metaphors, but not true science. You can compare a human to ants, laboratory rats, computer programs, or, as Dr. Freud did, to a hydraulic pressure system. All of this is very suggestive, but as the number of similes is unlimited by definition, the whole endeavor is bound to be entirely inconclusive, just as the reading of the masterpieces of world literature is inconclusive.

On the contrary, the coincidence of subject and object is a privileged position that should be assumed from the beginning as a premise and guiding norm in the field of the human sciences. The technique for the study of an object defined in this way already exists and is one of the most refined cognitive instruments available to human beings. It is called "meditation" and should not be confused with any of the peculiar practices that pseudo-Eastern sects have circulated under that name. Hugh of St. Victor explained that thinking is moving from one idea to another (whether wandering through the forest of analogies or moving up and down the scale of propositions, from the general to the particular and vice versa). On the other hand, meditation is the systematic retreat from a thought to its foundation or root in the experience that made it possible. Classic models of meditation are the investigations into the nature of the "self" undertaken in St. Augustine's *Confessions*, in Vedanta, in René Descartes' *Meditations on First Philosophy*, in Husserl's phenomenology, in numerous passages of Louis Lavelle, or in Eric Voegelin's *Anamnesis*.

To go through these famous descriptions would already provide material for an entire course. Schematically, the central question is: "To whom do you properly refer when you use the word 'self' in everyday life?" The path to the answer leads from a mere idea or verbal convention to the experience of a reality that is both immediate and profound, which that word simultaneously conceals and reveals.

The self—not the philosophical, abstract self, a hypothetical subject of metaphysical demonstrations, but the concrete, real self—is not the body, not the sensations, not the emotions, not the thoughts. Nor is it pure memory, but it is the memory of memory, the memory that remembers having remembered and answers to others and to itself as the sole author and bearer of its own contents. Consciousness, as defined by Maurice Pradines, is a memory of the past prepared for the challenges of the present. The "self" is the one who answers for what it knows and, even more, for what it *knows that it knows*. The highest self-knowledge consists only in the admission of prior knowledge taken on responsibly.

But this self does not exist only in the heights of philosophical meditation. It is the one who answers for the demands of the world around it in everyday tasks and leisure. The self that answers—the responsible self—is the most direct, universal, and permanent human reality. Even cultures that did not have a clear concept of psychic individuality already knew this, as evidenced by the fact that in all of them, the one who is called to answer for their actions is the author of them, not a third party. There is no society, no matter how primitive, where the notions of authorship, guilt, and merit are not perfectly aligned with each other.

The self could not be created by the incorporation of social roles if it were not already prefigured, on the one hand, in physical individuality and, on the other, in the memory of memory—the recollection of inner states relived in the pure intimacy of the individual with himself.

The responsible self—the consciousness of consciousness—exists not as a thing or state but only as a permanent tension towards *more* consciousness, *more* responsibility, *more* comprehensiveness, and greater integration. Consciousness grows as it recognizes itself, and it can only recognize itself by permanently opening up to knowledge that transcends its previous repertoire. The opening to transcendence—to that which is beyond the current horizon of experience—is therefore a permanent datum of the structure of consciousness. Suppressing it falsifies the foundation of the knowledge situation.

The responsible consciousness is the true situation of the human being in the world. This is observed in the simplest interactions, in which the one who speaks always expects the other to understand him: not only to grasp the meaning of a sentence but to guess an intention and behind it to perceive the presence of a conscious self similar to his own. The opposite would be talking to walls.

The responsible self is one of the primary foundations of human society. This self is the origin of all ideas, creations, institutions, laws, habits, and structures. Everything in society that cannot be traced back to its origin in the conscious self takes on the appearance of an external thing that has come into the world by pure spontaneous magic. It's the coefficient of phantasmagoria that remains in every society as a result of alienation and loss of memory. That many social scholars prefer to concentrate their attention on this objectified residue, evading the inconvenience of demanding self-awareness, whose demands can continue to be met as common citizens outside of working hours, shows that what is called the honorable name of "science" is often nothing more than an elegant form of escape from reality.

Witnessless

O Globo, July 22, 2000
O leão e os ossos (2021)

"We have to unmask ourselves to achieve that inner authenticity of a culture in which we may one day recognize ourselves and feel fulfilled."—J. O. de Meira Penna.[29]

Albert Schweitzer, in *Memoirs of Childhood and Youth*, recalls the moment when he felt shame for the first time. He was about three years old and playing in the garden. A bee stung his finger, and in tears, the young boy was comforted by his parents and some neighbors. Suddenly, little Albert realized that the pain had subsided several minutes before, and he was still crying just to get the attention of the audience. When he recounted the incident, Schweitzer was in his seventies. He had a fulfilled life behind him, a great life as an artist, a doctor, a philosopher, a Christian soul dedicated to helping the poor and the sick. But he still felt the shame of that first deception. This feeling had crossed the years, hidden deep in his memory, giving him a twinge of conscience every time he faced a new temptation to self-deception.

Note that no one around had noticed anything. Only young Schweitzer knew of his shame, only he had to answer for his act to his conscience and his God. I am convinced that experiences of this kind—witnessless acts, as I often call them—are the only possible foundation upon which a person can develop an authentic, rigorous, and autonomous moral conscience. Only someone who, in solitude, can be strict and just with himself and against himself—can judge others fairly, instead of being swayed by the crowd's shouts, the propaganda stereotypes, or self-interest disguised in beautiful moral pretexts.

The reason for this is self-evident: a person must be free from all external surveillance to be sure he is looking at himself and not at a social role—and only then can he make a completely sincere judgment. Only those who are masters of themselves are truly free, and no one is their master if they cannot even look inside their own heart alone.

Even the most candid conversation, the most spontaneous confession, cannot replace this inner examination, because they are only valuable when they are its expressions, not fleeting outbursts induced by a casually stimulating atmosphere or vain sincerity.

---

[29] Brazilian diplomat and writer (1917–2017).—Eds.

Furthermore, it is not only the moral dimension of consciousness that develops in this confrontation: it is the whole consciousness—cognitive, aesthetic, practical. For it is both an approximation and a distancing: it is the solitary judgment that creates the true intimacy of a person with himself, and it is also the judgment that creates the distance, the inner space in which lived experiences and acquired knowledge are assimilated, deepened, and personalized. Without this space, without this personal "world" conquered in solitude, a person is merely a conduit through which information enters and exits—like food—transformed into waste.

Now, not all human beings have been blessed by Providence with a spontaneous insight and a precise judgment of their sins. Without these gifts, the desire for justice is perverted into projecting blame onto others and into "rationalization" (in the psychoanalytic sense of the term). Those who did not receive them from birth must acquire them through education. Moral education, therefore, consists less of memorizing lists of right and wrong than creating a moral environment conducive to self-examination, inner seriousness, and the responsibility of each person knowing what he did when no one was watching.

For two thousand years, such an environment was created and sustained by the Christian practice of "examination of conscience." There are equivalents of it in other religious and mystical traditions, but none in contemporary secular culture. There are psychoanalysis and psychotherapies, but they only work in this sense when they retain the religious reference to personal guilt and its redemption through confession before God. And, as society becomes less Christian (or, *mutatis mutandis*, less Islamic, less Jewish, etc.), this reference dissolves, and clinical techniques tend to produce the opposite effect: abolishing the sense of guilt, replacing it with self-serving selfishness disguised as "maturity," or with self-complacent adaptability, which is flabby and callous, disguised as "sanity."

The difference between religious technique and its modern substitutes is that it synthesized in a single dramatic experience both the pain of guilt and the joy of complete liberation—and this is what "secular ethics" cannot do, precisely because it lacks the dimension of the Last Judgment, the confrontation with an eternal destiny that, by giving this experience a metaphysical meaning, elevated the desire for personal responsibility to the heights of a noble soul with which the externals of "civil ethics" cannot even dream of.

For two centuries, modern culture has done what it can to weaken, suffocate, and extinguish in each person's soul the ability to have this supreme experience, in which self-awareness is demanded to the maximum, and where—only there—a person can gain a true understanding of the possibilities and responsibilities of the human condition. "Secular ethics," "citizenship education" is what remains on the outside when the inner consciousness is silent and when a person's actions mean nothing more than infringements upon or obedience to a code of conventions and casual interests.

"Ethics," in that context, is pure adaptation to the outside world, with no other inner resonance than what can be obtained through the forced internalization of slogans, clichés, and catchphrases. "Ethics," in that context, is the sacrifice of conscience on the altar of the official lies of the day.

How to Read Philosophy

Course delivered in Rio de Janeiro, 1992–1993
Edmund Husserl contra o psicologismo (2020)

Edmund Husserl's thoughts in written form can be read as if we were thinking what he thinks, exactly in the order in which he did. We hear the subject thinking, and this is good to dispel the notion of philosophy as a literary genre. Philosophy is not in the book. A literary work is materially in the work itself, but philosophy is in the philosopher, in the knowledge he has, and in those to whom he transmits it. For this reason, in philosophy, there is no eminent way of learning other than oral transmission. Writing presents additional difficulties, and its full apprehension presupposes a kind of connaturality between the reader's mind and the writer's mind, which is not always achieved. Only a philosopher who is also a poet, capable of creating the atmosphere in which his thoughts are understood, achieves a maximally efficient text. Almost nothing replaces the living presence of the subject, his intonation, his gestures. Only an immense confluence of mentalities can remedy the absence of this presence, as in the case of a St. Thomas, who read Aristotle in a Latin translation of an Arabic translation and was still the greatest interpreter of Aristotle.

The philosophical text is to philosophy what the score is to music: once read, it has to be played. This is different from what happens in a poem or novel, in which the aesthetic experience is exhausted in reading, regardless of the fact that it can later be remembered or analyzed—this, in the end, will be yet another act that does not merge with that experience. In the case of music, true understanding is only reached if we are able to perform it, which can even be done mentally. Similarly, the reproduction of an intellectual experience occurs in philosophy, and if you do not re-experience it, you cannot embrace an entire philosophy. An example of this would be someone who, after reading René Descartes, seeks out some technique that would allow him to imaginatively abstract the senses and suspend everything, in doubt. Only in this way will this individual know if he has understood Descartes or not, a task for which analytical reading is only accessory, as it provides clues for the better reconstitution of the reported experience. Reading is only the beginning; analysis serves only to break it down so that you can clarify for yourself the sequence of operations necessary for the reconstitution of the philosopher's thought. It is only at this point that philosophy proper begins.

Notes for an Introduction to Philosophy

A filosofia e seu inverso & Outros estudos (2012)

There's no elementary philosophy. Wherever you enter a philosophical question, no matter what it is, you'll end up right at the heart of the matter. Nothing can assist you except mastering philosophical technique. Philosophical technique is the ability to trace a theme, a problem, an idea, back to its roots in the very structure of reality. It's about thinking about the subject until thought finds its limits and reality itself begins to speak. "Thinking" here isn't talking to oneself, combining words, or arguing to prove something. It's not even constructing logical deductions, no matter how elegant they may seem (the constructive activity of the mind belongs to mathematics and not to philosophy). It is, first and foremost, delving into the inner experience to accurately remember how something came to your knowledge and where it emerged in the broader framework of reality. Gradually, you will distinguish what came from reality and what you added yourself, and why you added it. When you're sure you have the clean data without additions (but without discarding the additions, which are sometimes useful later), you can look around it and see the surrounding and preceding conditions that made its presence possible. You can't do this without deepening your own self-awareness in the very act of meditating on the object. This effort requires a level of mental concentration and sincerity that far exceeds the capacity of the ordinary person (including the "intellectuals," even the authentic ones; not to mention their imitators). It's a task as demanding and even more laden with psychological obstacles than the effort required to overcome neurotic resistances during psychoanalytic treatment (and psychoanalytic treatments can extend for years).

To gauge the distance that separates philosophical inquiry from any form of "argumentation" (valid or invalid), just note that in the early steps, the inner perception of the object, if it goes in the right direction, already transcends its immediate capacity for expression in words. It's about becoming aware, not "reasoning." Verbal thought serves only as initial support. It's about making present, through all available mental means, the entire framework of the real conditions that made it possible for you to know the object. From there to knowledge of the conditions that made its existence possible is only a step, but it's the decisive step. It is only at this moment that the verbal exposition of this experience becomes possible, for placing a real object in the framework of conditions that made it possible is to place it automatically at some point in a logical deduction.

All you can do is verbalize this deduction, not the inner path traveled. But it's the journey that gives logical deduction all its substantial meaning. Read or heard by someone who cannot reconstruct the corresponding inner experience, the deduction will be just a formal scheme that, like any other formal scheme, can fuel endless and fruitless discussions and refutations. These discussions and refutations may be an imitation of philosophy, but they are as different from genuine philosophy as a MIDI file of a Bach cantata is different from a Bach cantata. They can serve as logical training, but training for a constructive mental activity, useful as it may be for other purposes, is precisely the opposite of learning philosophical analysis: you cannot open yourself to reality by building something in its place.

The only possible learning of philosophy is to read the expositions of philosophers by imaginatively reconstructing the inner activity that generated them. This is like reading a musical score and gradually learning to perform it with all the implied emotional nuances and emphases that the score hints at but doesn't show.

Before becoming a composer, you have to learn to do this with many pieces by other composers. Before analyzing your first philosophical problem, you will have to play many pieces composed by philosophers of old. And, just as happens with the apprentice musician, you won't offer a public recital with the first pieces you've barely learned to play. Aristotle studied for twenty years with Plato before he began teaching. Learning to philosophize is learning to listen—and then to play—the secret melody behind mere verbal signs. If all goes well, after many years of practice, you'll eventually discover your own secret melodies—and when you write them down, you'll find that practically no one will know how to play them, but everyone will want to imitate them in the form of "arguments."

Philosophy professors—especially in Brazil—generally have no idea what philosophical inquiry is. Instead of philosophy, they teach argumentation, at best. Most of the time, they don't even do that: they teach ready-made arguments and call anyone who doesn't want to repeat them a fascist. It's a kind of drug trafficking.

Spirit and Personality

Diário do Comércio, January 31, 2013
O progresso da ignorância (2019)

The spirit is that which only reaches us through thought, but thought, by itself, cannot create or attain it. The spirit is the truth of the thought, which, by definition, is beyond thought, even in cases where thought creates its own object.

When, for example, we mentally create a triangle, it already carries within itself all its geometric properties that thought, at that moment, is completely unaware of. And when it discovers them one by one over time, it must confess that they were in the triangle simultaneously before it grasped them. Even when it apprehends just one, it grasps something that is in the triangle and not in itself.

In the realm of the mental, there is no difference between thinking the false and thinking the true. Thought only becomes truthful when it touches something beyond it, something that is in no way reducible to the act of thinking or the thought itself. This something is what we call "truth." As seen in the example of the triangle, truth is beyond thought even when the object of thought is created by thought itself: thought does not control or create the truth even of purely thought objects. Truth only appears beyond a boundary that thought sees but does not traverse. Truth is the realm of the spirit.

Truth is spirit, even when apprehended in a material object. Our senses can grasp the presence of an object, but they cannot, by themselves, decide if this presence is real or imaginary. Thought must intervene, asking questions that complete and correct mere impressions. It does so in pursuit of the truth of the object, but when it touches it, it knows that it is not only beyond the senses but beyond itself; otherwise, it would not be truth at all, but merely an impression modified by thought.

Truth is always transcendent to the realm of thought, sensations, emotions, and everything that constitutes the "mental." IQ tests do not measure the quantity of mental activity but its efficiency in transcending itself, in apprehending the truth of the object—the ability to glimpse beyond the realm of the thought, into the kingdom of the spirit.

This ability is not called "thought" but intelligence. It is entirely unrelated to the quantity, intensity, or formal elegance of thought. In Brazil, there is a saying that goes, "a donkey died from thinking." Thinking falsehoods is as laborious, sometimes even more so, than arriving at the truth. Good thought is not the one that delights in the richness of its own movements but the one that humbly withdraws to make way for intelligence, for the perception of truth.

Formal correctness of thought may be important at times, but thought, by itself, cannot even grasp the truth of its own formal correctness. Becoming aware of the formal correctness of a syllogism is not a thought; it is the instantaneous perception—intuitive, if you will—of a necessary connection between two thoughts. If it were otherwise, it would be just a third thought, whose connection with the other two would have to be proven syllogistically, and so on until the end of time. Even mere formal truthfulness is truthfulness and transcends thought.

People who think a lot are called "intellectuals," but that is wrong: the life of the intellect only begins at the border where thought fades away to give place to the glimpse of truth.

Both thought and impressions, memory or emotions, only accumulate reasons for truth to emerge later, in an instant perception. This accumulation can be long and laborious, but it is never an end in itself.

Every education of the intellect should take these obvious facts into account, but this has become almost impossible in an era that has turned its back on the very notion of truth—not to mention the spirit—replacing it with that of subjective projection, adequacy, utility, class interest, cultural creation, etc., as if all these notions did not implicitly assert their own truth and thus restore, somewhat blindly, what they would like to suppress.

In the course of his temporal evolution, the individual comes to have an "intellectual personality" when the submission of his thought to the spirit becomes an acquired habit and integrates into his soul as a usual and almost unconscious reaction.

Strictly speaking, leading the student to this ascent would be the goal of all higher education, but the reduction of universities to the status of professional schools or centers of ideological training for militants has made this goal entirely utopian, restricting it to an elite, instead of democratizing access to the higher assets of the spirit, as all the governments of the world promise to do.

Certainly, the path is not blocked for students who have personal initiative and some resources. The problem is that achieving an intellectual personality in an environment that is unaware of the mere existence of this human possibility—the case, undoubtedly, of the Brazilian university environment today—is a source of innumerable psychological difficulties for the student, starting with the almost impossibility of finding people of the same level of consciousness with whom he can have dialogue and friendship. The intellectual personality can only be understood by another intellectual personality: dialogue with individuals devoid of it is a transmission without a receiver, an occasion for misunderstandings and endless suffering.

The Retreat to Personal Experience

Introdução à filosofia de Louis Lavelle (2021)

It's important to note that, from the beginning, Louis Lavelle's philosophy demands from the reader a continual retreat into his deepest personal experience and the willingness to confess that he knows what he knows, he has seen what he's seen, felt what he's felt, and wants what he wants. Now, this is an activity that can only be performed by concrete, flesh-and-blood human beings, not by social roles. It's not as a philosophy professor, not as a holder of a master's or doctoral degree that you will do this; *it must be your real self.* The set of social roles that define professions serves precisely the opposite, to protect the individual against the display of his real person; that is, in a professional circle in which everyone speaks only as professionals. Your personal testimony has no validity and no place there. In this circle, the individual can only say what can be verified not by the real testimony of concrete people but by the codes that validate professional practice.

In this sense, philosophy can never be a profession, even though it can use a profession as an occasional instrument to make itself viable in a particular social context. My friend Antonio Donato says that the decline of modern philosophy began not in the Renaissance, as is often pointed out, but in the heart of the Middle Ages, when the statutes of the University of Paris were created, and the profession of philosophy professor was officially established. And perhaps he is right because, even within scholasticism, the richness of technical terminology, while allowing dialogue among professionals on the one hand, relegated the contribution of personal confession on the other. At the time, this was not a major problem because those involved were devout Catholics accustomed to the sacrament of confession and, therefore, to self-examination. But a division is already established: the lower level, consisting of real people who examine themselves, confess, and receive communion; and the upper level, the dialogue among professors, in which personal experience no longer matters.

When the university establishment broke with its roots in the Church, personal input threatened to disappear completely, unless the philosopher became aware of the situation and insisted on introducing personal confession into his philosophy. Obviously, it was not a confession of sins, sacramental confession, but a confession of his cognitive consciousness—as Descartes did when writing his spiritual biography in the *Meditations on First Philosophy*. However, by this point, the cultural perspective had already changed so much that Descartes himself became confused: he began his text as a narrative of personal experiences and, at a certain point, transformed it into an abstract deduction. Until he discovered the *cogito*, he was writing an autobiography, but from then on, it became a deduction based on the abstract concept of the thinking self—even so, Descartes continued to believe that he was giving personal testimony.

A true return to personal confession only occurred in the nineteenth century with a figure absolutely extravagant and alien to the European university milieu, the Danish philosopher Søren Kierkegaard. He realized that no deeper philosophical penetration was possible without the presence of personal consciousness. Later, when Louis Lavelle appeared, we saw that the alarm sounded by Kierkegaard was heard for the first time—although later, the philosophy called *existentialist* took different paths and, in many cases, paths which were terribly unfaithful to the spirit that originated them.

Consciousness and Form

A handout from the Online Philosophy Course, March 1, 2014
A consciência de imortalidade (2021)

"Matter" presents itself to me as a conscious *datum*, but consciousness never presents itself as material data. Assuming I could observe all the neuronal reactions in a conscious human brain in activity, they would tell me nothing about the contents of that consciousness at that moment. A greater activation of visual areas would not inform me, for example, whether the subject in observation is seeing a cat or a photo of a cat, a naked woman or a painting of a naked woman, a plate of food or the image of the food on the restaurant menu. However, a subject incapable of instantly apprehending these differences would be condemned to perish due to an absolute incapacity to deal with the physical environment around him. The intensity of reactions in the verbal area would not tell me whether they are mentally composing an advertisement for soap or *King Lear*. If obtaining such information were possible through brain examination, every neuroscientist would be a new Shakespeare.

These difficulties arise from another, more serious one. If, as Husserl claimed, there is no consciousness "in itself," empty consciousness, but all consciousness is consciousness of something, it is absurd to say that consciousness is "in" the cognizant subject: it is in a relationship established between the subject and the object, which cannot be entirely in this or that, but simultaneously in both. When the subject apprehends any quality of the object, be it its size, position, or color, it's because the object shows him, exhibits to him, that quality; it does not arise from within as a pure autonomous creation of the subject, but as a molding, so to speak, of the perceptive capacity of the subject to the form of something that is not him, that is not his consciousness, but offers itself as an object. Therefore, if consciousness is not in the subject, inside the subject, much less could it be in one of its parts, whether we call it "soul" or "brain."

If we name the psyche the set of internal, immanent, activities of the soul or brain, it is evident that consciousness only appears once the border is crossed, where the psyche transcends itself, overcomes itself, and reaches an object. Even supposing, *ad argumentandum*, that all activities of the psyche are determined by those of the brain, that they are ultimately material and governed by the laws of physicochemistry, and that, on the other hand, there are no objects in the world except material ones governed by these same laws, consciousness, that is, the relationship established between psyche and object in the act in which it becomes aware of it, remains perfectly immaterial and cannot be physically present in the subject or the object.

When I see a cat, there is a present subject, which we admit to be entirely material and governed by material laws, and an equally material object governed by these same laws. The psychic act by which I perceive the cat may also admittedly be determined by the material functioning of my brain and my sense organs. But the coincidence, the total or partial identity between the form of the thing perceived as it appears to my brain and the form of the object that presents itself to me as a cat cannot, in itself, be material because, for that, it would have to be an object itself and, like me and the cat, occupy a place in space. Now, it is only this identity that guarantees that I saw a real cat and did not just produce an imaginary cat within my psyche. Any and all objective knowledge depends on the formal identity between the perceived and the data.

More gravely still, of all possible relationships that can be established between the psyche and its object, none, absolutely none, can be said to be material because, for that, it would have to occupy a place in space and be perceived itself as an object; and its relationship with the knowing psyche would be a new spatial object, and so on indefinitely, making the perception of anything impossible.

When we discuss whether "consciousness" is material or immaterial, we usually confuse consciousness with the psyche. The latter may perhaps be entirely explained by the functioning of the brain, but when we leap from the realm of the psyche to that of consciousness, we are talking about a relationship with objects that transcend the sphere of the psyche (even when they are themselves psychic facts taken as objects), and there we could only speak of a cerebral cause of consciousness if we attributed to the brain the gift of creating by itself all spatial objects, and creating them spatially, not knowing how such a large number of things could fit into a cranial box.

The problem of consciousness, therefore, cannot be solved by the study of the psyche or the brain. It refers to a world of formal identities and differences that, in themselves, cannot be material or occupy a place in space. All discussions that claim to reduce consciousness to matter, matter to consciousness, or proclaim the existence of two distinct and separate spheres of reality, stem from the confusion between psyche and consciousness and do not go beyond it.

The universe around us, with our own being within it, is composed of material objects structured in forms, being therefore inseparably material and immaterial, bodily and spiritual. Consciousness is the relationship established between two forms, the form of an individual human psychophysical presence and the form of a bodily presence.

Revisiting the Philosophers

A filosofia e seu inverso & Outros estudos (2012);
O império mundial da burla (2016)

Expressing real experience in words is a daunting challenge even for great writers. So serious is this difficulty that to overcome it, an entire range of literary genres had to be invented, each suppressing parts of experience to highlight the remaining aspects. For instance, if you are Balzac or Dostoevsky, you string together facts in a narrative order, but to make the narrative readable, you must relinquish the poetic resources that would allow expressing the full richness and confusion of the involved feelings. On the other hand, if you are Arthur Rimbaud or Giuseppe Ungaretti, you can compress this richness into a few verses, but they won't have the immediate intelligibility of a narrative.

These observations suffice to show that ideas and beliefs emerging in public and private discussions rarely form from experience, at least not from direct personal experience. They come from ready-made verbal schemes received from the cultural environment, forming, on top of personal experience, a condensed set of clichés quite detached from life. If you carefully read the Socratic dialogues, you will see that the main occupation of the founder of the Western philosophical tradition was to dissolve these verbal conglomerates, forcing his interlocutors to reason from real experience, that is, to speak of what they knew instead of repeating what they had heard. The problem is that if you repeat once or twice what you've heard, not only do you come to consider it your own, but you identify and cling to that verbal fetish as if it were a treasure, a lifesaver, or the sacred symbol of a divine truth.

To make things worse, these ready-made phrases are well-crafted, in cultured and prestigious language, whereas personal experience, due to the difficulties mentioned earlier, can barely express itself in clumsy and childish words. There's a serious reason for people preferring to speak elegantly about what they don't know rather than exposing themselves to the embarrassment of expressing in naïve words what they do know. One result of this almost obligatory hypocrisy is that, by constantly feeding on insubstantial verbal symbols, intelligence ends up secretly disbelieving in itself or even openly proclaiming the impossibility of knowing the truth. Since this impossibility, in turn, is also a prestigious symbol these days, it serves as the ultimate and invincible pretext for escaping the only fruitful mental activity, which is the search for truth in real experience.

The very word "experience" often comes loaded with a deceptive nuance, as it generally refers to "scientific facts" cut out from conventional methods, which conceal and eventually replace direct personal experience. In these conditions, public or private discussion becomes an exchange of stereotypes in which, fundamentally, none of the participants believes. This is the essence of the popular expression "idle talk": 'the speaker buys attention, whether his own or others,' on credit and doesn't pay with substantive words for the time spent. (I've always found it unjust that laws punish pecuniary offenses but not the theft of time. Lost money can be earned again—time, never.)

From Socrates to today, philosophy has developed myriad techniques to burst the bubble of stereotyped conversation and bring the speakers back to reality. *Zu den Sachen selbst*—"to go to the things themselves"—the motto of the great Edmund Husserl, remains the most urgent message of philosophy after twenty-four centuries. No one but Husserl himself was aware of the linguistic and psychological obstacles opposing the realization of his call. The entire technical vocabulary of philosophy—and Husserl's is one of the heaviest—is aimed only at opening a way back from the illusions of the lettered class to actual experience. Mastering this vocabulary may itself be a formidable difficulty, but surely not as formidable as the risks of discussing empty words while the world collapses around us. By incorporating itself into the ambient culture as an academically respectable activity, philosophy itself tends to lose its original strength as an enlightening activity and becomes just another brick in the wall of artificialities that rises between thought and reality.

Chapter 2

The Unity of Knowledge

Aristotle in a New Perspective:
The Theory of the Four Discourses

Aristóteles em Nova Perspectiva:
Introdução à Teoria dos Quatro Discursos (1996, 2013)

Embedded in Aristotle's works is a core idea that has escaped the perception of almost all his readers and commentators, from antiquity to the present day. Even those who did perceive it—and there were only two, as far as I know, over the millennia—limited themselves to noting it in passing, without explicitly attributing decisive importance to it for the understanding of Aristotle's philosophy.[30] However, it is the very key to this understanding, if by understanding we mean the act of grasping the unity of a man's thought from his own intentions and values, rather than judging him from the outside; an act that implies carefully respecting the unexpressed and the implied, instead of suffocating it in the idolatry of the "text" as an objectified entity, the tomb of thought.

To this idea, I give the name *Theory of the Four Discourses*. It can be summarized in one sentence: human discourse is a single power, which actualizes itself in four different ways: the poetic, the rhetorical, the dialectical, and the analytic (logical).

---

[30] These two were Avicenna and St. Thomas Aquinas. Avicenna (ca. 980–1037 AD) categorically affirms, in his work *Kitāb al-najāt* (*Book of Salvation*), the unity of the four sciences under the general concept of "logic." According to Baron Carra de Vaux, this "shows how vast was his idea of this art," incorporating "the study of all various degrees of persuasion, from rigorous demonstration to poetic suggestion" [free translation] Baron Carra de Vaux, *Avicenne* (Paris: Alcan, 1900), 160–161. St. Thomas Aquinas also mentions, in his *Commentary on the Posterior Analytics*, I, lec I,1–6, the four degrees of logic, which he probably became aware of through Avicenna, but attributing to them the unilateral sense of a descending hierarchy from the most certain (*analytical*) to the most uncertain (*poetic*), implying that, from the *Topics* "downwards," we are dealing only with progressive forms of error or at least deficient knowledge. This does not exactly coincide with Avicenna's conception or with the one presented in this book, which seems to me to be that of Aristotle himself, according to which there is not properly a hierarchy of value among the four arguments, but rather a difference of articulated functions between them, all equally necessary for the perfection of knowledge. On the other hand, it is certain that St. Thomas Aquinas, like all medieval Westerners, did not have direct access to the text of the *Poetics*. If he had, it would be almost impossible for him to see in poetic work only the representation of something "as pleasant or repugnant" (loc. cit., 6), without reflecting more deeply on what Aristotle says about the philosophical value of poetry (*Poetics*, 1451a). In any case, it is an admirable feat of Aquinas to have perceived the unity of the four logical sciences, reasoning, as he did, from second-hand sources.

Phrased in this way, the idea doesn't seem particularly remarkable. However, if we consider that the names of these four modes of discourse are also the names of four sciences, we see that from this perspective, Poetics, Rhetoric, Dialectic, and Logic, studying the modalities of a single potency, *also constitute variations of a single science*. The very diversification into four subordinate sciences must be based on the unity of the object they focus on, lest they fail to adhere to Aristotle's rule of divisions. And this means that the principles of each of them presuppose the existence of common principles that subordinate them, that is, principles that apply equally to fields as different from each other as scientific demonstration and the construction of tragic plots in theatrical plays. Thus, the idea I have just attributed to Aristotle begins to seem strange, surprising, and extravagant to us. And the two questions it immediately suggests to us are: did Aristotle really think this way? And if he did, did he think correctly? The question is therefore twofold: a historical-philological investigation and a philosophical critique. Within the scope of the present communication, I cannot satisfactorily achieve either; I can only inquire into the reasons for the strangeness. The astonishment that the idea of the Four Discourses provokes at a first encounter arises from a deeply rooted habit in our culture of viewing poetic language and logical or scientific language as separate and distant universes, governed by sets of laws that are not commensurable among themselves. Since a decree of Louis XIV separated "Letters" and "Sciences" into different buildings, the gap between poetic imagination and mathematical reason has never ceased to widen, until it established itself as a kind of constitutive law of the human spirit. Evolving like parallel lines that sometimes attract each other and sometimes repel each other but never touch, the *two cultures*, as C. P. Snow called them, solidified into separate universes, each incomprehensible to the other. Gaston Bachelard, a poet who doubled as a mathematician, imagined being able to describe these two sets of laws as contents of radically separate spheres, each equally valid within its limits and in its own terms, between which man moves as from sleep to wakefulness, disengaging from one to enter the other, and vice versa:[31] the language of dreams does not challenge that of equations, nor does the latter penetrate the world of the

---

[31] Bachelard's work, reflecting the methodical dualism of his thought, is divided into two parallel series: on the one hand, the works of philosophy of science, such as *Le Nouvel Esprit Scientifique* [The New Scientific Spirit] and *Le Rationalisme Appliqué* [Applied Rationalism], etc. and on the other hand, the series dedicated to the "four elements," such as *La Psychanalyse du Feu* [The Psychoanalysis of Fire], *L'Air et les Songes* [Air and Dreams], etc. In this latter series, the vacationing rationalist freely exercises what he called "the right to dream." Bachelard seemed to possess a mental switch that allowed him to move from one of these worlds to the other, without the slightest temptation to build any other bridge between them other than the freedom to activate the switch.

former. So deep was the separation that some wished to find an anatomical foundation in the theory of the two cerebral hemispheres, one creative and poetic, the other rational and organizing, and believed they saw a correspondence between these divisions and the dual *yin-yang* of Chinese cosmology.[32] Moreover, they thought they had discovered in the exclusive predominance of one of these hemispheres the cause of the ills of Western man. A somewhat mystified view of Chinese ideography, propagated in pedantic circles by Ezra Pound,[33] gave this theory a literary backing more than sufficient to compensate for its lack of scientific foundations. The ideology of the "New Age" finally consecrated it as one of the pillars of wisdom.[34]

In this scenario, old Aristotle was depicted, alongside the nefarious Descartes, as the very prototype of the rationalistic warden who, with ruler in hand, kept our inner Chinese under strict repression. Readers imbued with such beliefs can only receive with indignant amazement the idea I attribute to Aristotle. It presents, as an apostle of unity, someone whom everyone used to view as a guardian of schizophrenia. It contests a stereotyped image that time and popular culture have enshrined as an acquired truth. It stirs up old wounds, healed by a long sedimentation of prejudices.

Resistance is thus a *fait accompli*. The task remains to confront it, proving, first, that the idea is indeed Aristotle's; second, that it is an excellent idea, worthy of being resumed, with humility, by a civilization that hastened to retire the

---

[32] Jerre Levy, *Right Brain, Left Brain: Fact and Fiction* (Psychology Today, May 1985), 43*ff.*

[33] Ezra Pound made a huge fuss about Ernest Fenollosa's essay, *The Chinese Characters as a Medium for Poetry* (London: Stanley Nott, 1936), giving the West the impression that the Chinese language constituted a closed world, governed by thought categories inaccessible to Western understanding except through a true twisting of the very concept of language. However, Chinese symbolism is much more similar to the Western one than enthusiasts of cultural abysses imagine. One glaring similarity that has escaped these individuals is that between the structure of the I Ching and Aristotle's syllogistics.

[34] The belief in the theory of the two hemispheres is common among all theorists and gurus of the "New Age," such as Marilyn Ferguson, Shirley MacLaine, and Fritjof Capra. Regarding the latter, see my book *A Nova Era e a Revolução Cultural: Fritjof Capra & Antonio Gramsci* [The New Age and the Cultural Revolution: Fritjof Capra & Antonio Gramsci]. The most curious aspect of this theory is that it aims to overcome the schizophrenia of Western man and begins by providing it with an anatomical foundation (fortunately, fictional).—It is evident, as we shall see, that I do not take too seriously the attempts, as commendable in intention as they are pitiful in results, to transcend dualism through the widespread methodological hodgepodge that accepts rhetorical persuasiveness and imaginative effusion as criteria for scientific validity—see for example, Paul Feyerabend, *Against Method* (1975).

teachings of its old master before examining them thoroughly. Here, I can only roughly indicate the directions where these two demonstrations must be sought.

Aristotle wrote a *Poetics*, a *Rhetoric*, a book on Dialectics (the *Topics*), and two treatises on Logic (*Analytics I and II*), as well as two introductory works on language and thought in general (*Categories* and *On Interpretation*). All these works practically disappeared, like Aristotle's other works, until the first century B.C., when a certain Andronicus of Rhodes organized a comprehensive edition, upon which our knowledge of Aristotle is based to this day.

Like any posthumous editor, Andronicus had to impose some order on the manuscripts. He decided to base this order on the criterion of dividing the sciences into *introductory* (or logical), *theoretical*, *practical*, and *technical* (or *poietic*, as some would say). This division had the merit of being Aristotle's own. But, as Octave Hamelin astutely observed, there is no reason to suppose that the division of a philosopher's works into volumes must correspond exactly to his conception of the divisions of knowledge.[35] Andronicus assumed this correspondence and therefore grouped the manuscripts into four divisions. However, lacking other works that could fit under the technical label, he had to include *Rhetoric* and *Poetics* there, disconnecting them from the other works on the theory of discourse, which formed the apparently closed unity of the *Organon*, the set of logical or introductory works.

Added to other circumstances, this editorial decision was fruitful in consequences, which multiply to this day. First of all, Rhetoric—the name of a science abhorred by philosophers, who saw in it the very emblem of their main adversaries, the sophists—did not arouse, from the first edition by Andronicus, the slightest philosophical interest. It was read only in rhetoric schools, which, to make matters worse, were then entering into rapid decline because the extinction of democracy, by eliminating the need for orators, deprived the art of rhetoric of its *raison d'être*, enclosing it in the cocoon of narcissistic formalism.[36] Soon after, *Poetics*, in turn, disappeared from circulation, only to reappear in the sixteenth century.[37] These two events seem fortuitous and unimportant. But, taken together,

---

[35] Octave Hamelin, *Le Système d'Aristote* (Paris: published by Léon Robin, 4e. éd., J. Vrin, 1985), 82.

[36] I am referring to the period of the so-called "school rhetoric." See Ernst Robert Curtius, *European Literature and the Latin Middle Ages*, trans. Willard R. Trask (Princeton University Press, 1953), ch. 4.

[37] This makes the plot of *The Name of the Rose* by Umberto Eco even funnier, a deliberately impossible plot that uninformed viewers take as plausible fiction: for how could there be a dispute over the missing Second Part of Aristotle's *Poetics* in a time that was unaware of even the First Part?

they result in nothing less than the following: all Western Aristotelianism, which, initially slowly but gaining in velocity from the eleventh century on, was forming in the period from the eve of the Christian Era to the Renaissance, completely ignored *Rhetoric* and *Poetics*. Since our image of Aristotle is still an inheritance from this period (since the rediscovery of *Poetics* in the Renaissance aroused interest only from poets and philologists, without touching the philosophical public), to this day what we call "Aristotle," either to praise him or to curse him, is not the man of flesh and blood, but a simplified scheme, assembled during the centuries that ignored two of his works. In particular, our view of Aristotle's theory of discursive thought is based exclusively on analytics and topics, that is, on logic and dialectics, amputated from the foundation Aristotle had built for them in poetics and rhetoric.[38]

But the mutilation didn't stop there. From the edifice of discourse theory, only the two upper floors remained—dialectics and logic—floating without foundations in the air. It didn't take long for the third floor also to be suppressed: dialectics, considered a lesser science since it dealt only with probable demonstration, was sidelined in favor of analytic logic, consecrated since the Middle Ages as the very key to Aristotle's thought. The image of an Aristotle constituted by "formal logic + cognitive sensationalism + theology of the Unmoved Mover" became a historical truth never contested.

Even the prodigious advancement of biographical and philological studies inaugurated by Werner Jaeger[39] did not change this. Jaeger only toppled the stereotype of a fixed and fully formed Aristotle, to replace it with the living image of a thinker who evolves over time towards the maturity of his ideas. But the final product of the evolution was not, in the aspect addressed here, very different from

---

[38] In the medieval context, the phenomenon I describe certainly has some relation to a social stratification that placed scholars and philosophers, the priestly class, above poets, who were servants of the court or street artists. The lower status of the poet in relation to the scholars is evident both in the social hierarchy (consider the decisive role played by the wandering clerics, or goliards, in medieval literary development, an entire "ecclesiastical proletariat" on the margins of universities) and in the hierarchy of the sciences themselves: literary studies were strictly outside the educational system of scholasticism, and the highest philosophical conceptions of the Middle Ages were written in a rather crude Latin, without this causing any strangeness at the time, let alone aesthetic scandal reactions as those that would erupt in the Renaissance. Cf., in this regard, Jacques Le Goff, *Les intellectuels au Moyen Age* (Paris: Éditions du Seuil, 1957), *Intellectuals in the Middle Ages*, trans. Teresa Lavender Fagan (Cambridge, MA: Blackwell, 1993).
[39] *Aristoteles: Grundlegung einer Geschichte seiner Entwicklung*, 1923; *Aristotle: Fundamentals of the History of His Development* (Oxford: Oxford University Press, 1962).—Eds.

the system consecrated by the Middle Ages: above all, dialectics would be a Platonic residue, absorbed in and surpassed by analytic logic.

But this view is contested by some facts. The first, highlighted by Éric Weil, is that the inventor of analytic logic never used it in his treatises, always preferring dialectical argumentation.[40] Secondly, Aristotle himself insists that logic does not bring knowledge but serves only to facilitate the verification of already acquired knowledge, confronting it with the principles that underlie it, to see if they do not contradict it. When we do not possess the principles, the only way to seek them is through dialectical investigation, which, by confronting contradictory hypotheses, leads to a kind of intuitive enlightenment that highlights these principles. Dialectics in Aristotle is therefore, according to Weil, a *logica inventionis*, or a logic of discovery: the true scientific method, of which formal logic is only a complement and a means of verification.[41]

But Weil's timely intervention, while dispelling the myth of a total hegemony of analytic logic in Aristotle's system, set aside the question of rhetoric. The academic world of the twentieth century still subscribes to the opinion of Sir David Ross, who in turn follows Andronicus: *Rhetoric* has "a purely practical purpose;" "it does not constitute theoretical work," but is "a manual for the orator."[42] However, Ross attributes effective theoretical value to *Poetics*, without noticing that, if Andronicus erred in this case, he may also have been mistaken regarding *Rhetoric*. After all, since its rediscovery, *Poetics* has also been seen mainly as "a practical manual" and interested the literati more than the philosophers.[43] On the other hand, the very book of the *Topics* could be seen as a "technical manual" or at least "practical"—for in the Academy, dialectics

---

[40] This observation in turn sparked the dispute between interpreters who consider Aristotle a systematic thinker (who always starts from the same general principles) and those who see him as an aporetic thinker (who tackles problems one by one and moves towards the general without being very sure where he is going to end up). The approach suggested in this work aims, among other things, to resolve this dispute.

[41] Éric Weil, "La Place de la Logique dans la Pensée Aristotélicienne," *Essais et Conférences* I, *Philosophie* (Paris: Vrin, 1991), 43–80.

[42] Sir David Ross, *Aristotle* (Methuen & Company, 1923).—Eds.

[43] Since its first annotated translation (Francesco Robortelli, 1548), the rediscovered *Poetics* would shape literary taste standards for two and a half centuries, while in the field of Natural Philosophy, Aristotelianism receded, ousted by the victorious advance of the new science of Galileo and Bacon, Newton and Descartes. This demonstrates, on the one hand, the complete separation between literary thought and philosophical and scientific evolution (a characteristic separation of the modern West, which will worsen over the centuries); on the other hand, the indifference of philosophers towards the rediscovered text. Regarding the Aristotelian roots of European classicism aesthetics, see René Wellek, *A History of Modern Criticism* (Yale University Press, 1955).

functioned exactly as such: it was the set of practical norms of academic debate. Finally, Andronico's classification, once followed to the letter, results in endless confusion, which can be resolved at once by admitting the following hypothesis, however disturbing it may be: as sciences of discourse, *Poetics* and *Rhetoric* are part of the *Organon*, the set of logical or introductory works, and are therefore neither theoretical nor practical nor technical. This is the core of the interpretation I defend. However, it implies a profound revision of the traditional and current ideas about Aristotle's science of discourse. This revision, in turn, risks having far-reaching consequences for our view of language and culture in general. Reclassifying the works of a great philosopher may seem like an innocent endeavor of scholars, but it is like moving the pillars of a building. It may require the demolition of many nearby constructions.

The reasons I allege to justify this change are as follows:

1. The four sciences of discourse deal with four ways in which man can, through words, influence the mind of another man (or his own). The four modalities of discourse are characterized by their respective levels of *credibility*:

(a) Poetic discourse deals with the *possible* (δυνατός, *dínatos*), addressing primarily the imagination, which captures what it presumes (εἰκαστικός, *eikástikos*, "presumable;" εἰκασία, *eikasia*, "image," "representation").

(b) Rhetorical discourse concerns the *plausible* (πιθανός, *pithános*) and aims to produce *firm belief* (πίστις, *pístis*), which presupposes, beyond mere imaginative presumption, the consent of the will; and man influences the will of another man through persuasion (πειθώ, *peitho*), which is a psychological action based on common beliefs. If poetry resulted in an *impression*, rhetorical discourse must produce a *decision*, showing that it is the most appropriate or convenient within a certain framework of accepted beliefs.

(c) Dialectical discourse no longer merely suggests or imposes a belief, but subjects beliefs to testing through trials and attempts to challenge them with objections. It is thought that goes back and forth, by transverse paths, seeking truth among errors and error among truths (διά, *diá* = "through" and also indicates duplicity, division). Hence dialectic is also termed *peirastic*, from the root *peirá* (πειρά = "proof," "experience," from which come πειρασμός, *peirasmos*, "temptation," and *empiric, empiricism, experience,* etc., but also, through πειρατής, *peirates*, "pirate": the very symbol of adventurous life, aimless travel). Dialectical discourse ultimately measures, through trials and errors, the greater or lesser *probability* of a belief or thesis, not according to its mere agreement with common beliefs, but according to the higher demands of rationality and accurate information.

(d) Logical or analytical discourse, finally, always starting from premises taken as indubitably certain, arrives, through syllogistic reasoning, at certain demonstration (ἀπόδειξις, *apodêixis*, "indestructible proof") of the truth of conclusions.

It is evident that there is a scale here of *increasing credibility*: from the possible we ascend to the plausible, from this to the probable, and finally to the certain or true. The very words used by Aristotle to characterize the objectives of each discourse demonstrate this gradation: therefore, among the four discourses, there is less of a difference in nature than in degree.

Possibility, *plausibility*, *reasonable probability*, and *apodictic certainty* are thus the key concepts on which the four respective sciences are built: Poetics studies the means by which poetic discourse opens the imagination to the realm of possibility; Rhetoric, the means by which rhetorical discourse induces the listener's will to accept a belief; Dialectics, the means by which dialectical discourse investigates the reasonableness of accepted beliefs, and finally, Logic, or Analytics, studies the means of apodictic demonstration, or scientific certainty. Now, the four basic concepts are relative to each other: one cannot conceive of the plausible outside the possible, nor this without confrontation with the reasonable, and so on. The consequence of this is so obvious that it is astonishing that almost no one has perceived it: the four sciences are inseparable; taken individually, they make no sense. What defines and differentiates them are not four isolable sets of formal characteristics, but four possible human attitudes towards discourse, four human motives for speaking and listening: man speaks to open the imagination to the immensity of possibility, to make some practical resolution, to critically examine the basis of the beliefs that underlie his resolutions, or to explore the consequences and extensions of judgments already admitted as absolutely true, constructing with them the edifice of scientific knowledge. *A discourse is logical or dialectical, poetic or rhetorical, not in itself and by its mere internal structure, but by the objective it tends to achieve as a whole*, by the human purpose it aims to accomplish. Hence, the four are distinguishable but not isolatable: each of them is only what it is when considered in the context of culture, as an expression of human intentions. The modern idea of delimiting a "poetic language in itself" or "logical language in itself" would seem to Aristotle like an absurd substantialization; worse still: an alienating objectification.[44] He was not yet tainted by the schizophrenia that has now become the normal state of culture.

2. But Aristotle goes further: he points out the different psychological dispositions corresponding to the listener of each of the four discourses, and the four dispositions also form, in the most obvious manner, a gradation:

(a) The listener of poetic discourse is tasked with loosening his demand for verisimilitude, admitting that "it is not probable that everything always happens in a probable manner," to grasp the universal truth that may be suggested even by a seemingly improbable narrative.[45] Aristotle, in short, anticipates the *suspension of disbelief* that Samuel Taylor Coleridge would later speak of. By admitting a more flexible criterion of verisimilitude, the reader (or viewer) acknowledges that the misfortunes of the tragic hero could have happened to himself or to any other person; in other words, they are permanent human possibilities.

(b) In ancient rhetoric, the listener is called a judge, because a decision, a vote, a sentence is expected from him. Aristotle, and in his wake the entire rhetorical tradition, admits three types of rhetorical discourses: forensic discourse, deliberative discourse, and epideictic discourse, or discourse of praise and blame (to a character, work, etc.).[46] In all three cases, the listener is called upon to decide: about the guilt or innocence of a defendant, about the usefulness or harmfulness of a law, a project, etc., about the merits or demerits of someone or something. Therefore, he is consulted as an authority:

---

[44] Four facts from the history of contemporary thought highlight the importance of these observations. 1) All attempts to isolate and define by their intrinsic characteristics a "poetic language," materially differentiating it from "logical language" and "everyday language," have utterly failed. See, Mary Louise Pratt, *Toward a Speech Act Theory of Literary Discourse* (Bloomington: Indiana University Press, 1977). 2) On the other hand, since Kurt Gödel, the impossibility of eradicating all intuitive residue from logical thought has generally been recognized. 3) The studies of Chaïm Perelman et Lucie Olbrechts-Tyteca, *Traité de l'argumentation. La Nouvelle Rhétorique* (Brussels: Université Libre, 1978); Thomas S. Kuhn, *The Structure of Scientific Revolutions* (1962), and Paul Feyerabend (cited) converge to show the impossibility of eradicating from scientific-analytical proof all dialectical and even rhetorical elements. 4) At the same time, the existence of more than a mere parallelism between aesthetic (that is to say, poetic, in a broad sense) and logical-dialectical principles in the medieval worldview is strongly emphasized by Erwin Panofsky, *Gothic Architecture and Scholasticism* (Meridian Books, 1957). These facts and many others in the same direction indicate not only the convenience but also the urgency of the integrated study of the four discourses.

[45] *Poetics*, 1451 a–b.

[46] About the three modalities in the rhetorical tradition, see Heinrich Lausberg, *Handbook of Literary Rhetoric: A Foundation for Literary Study* (Brill Academic Publishers, 1963).

he has the power to decide. If in the listener of poetic discourse it was important for the imagination to take the reins of the mind, to lead it to the world of possibility in a flight from which no immediate practical consequence was expected, here it is the will that listens and judges the discourse, to create, by deciding, a situation in the realm of facts.[47]

(c) The listener of dialectical discourse is, internally at least, a participant in the dialectical process. This does not aim at an immediate decision but at an approximation of truth, an approximation that can be slow, progressive, difficult, tortuous, and not always leads to satisfactory results. In this listener, the impulse to decide must be indefinitely postponed, even repressed: the dialectician does not wish to persuade, as the rhetorician does, but to arrive at a conclusion that ideally should be deemed reasonable by both contending parties. To do so, he must restrain the desire to win, humbly being willing to change his opinion if the opponent's arguments are more reasonable. The dialectician does not defend a party but investigates a hypothesis. Now, this investigation is only possible when both participants in the dialogue know and admit the basic principles on which the question will be judged, and when both agree to honestly adhere to the rules of dialectical demonstration. The attitude here is one of impartiality and, if necessary, self-critical resignation. Aristotle expressly warns disciples not to venture into dialectical arguments with those who are ignorant of the principles of that science: it would expose them to objections of mere rhetoric, thereby prostituting philosophy.[48]

(d) Finally, on the plane of analytic logic, there is no more discussion: there is only the linear demonstration of a conclusion which, starting from premises admitted as absolutely true and proceeding rigorously by syllogistic deduction, cannot fail to be certain. Analytical discourse is the monologue of the master: to the disciple, it is only left to receive and admit the truth. If the demonstration fails, the matter returns to dialectical discussion.[49]

From discourse to discourse, there is a progressive narrowing, a tightening of the admissible: from the unlimited openness of the world of possibilities, we move to the more restricted sphere of beliefs actually accepted in collective praxis; however, from the mass of beliefs subscribed to by common sense, only a few survive the rigors of dialectical screening; and, of these, even

---

[47] *Rhetoric,* 1358a–1360a.

[48] *Topics,* VIII, 164b.

[49] Between analytics and dialectics, "the difference, according to Aristotle, is that between the course of teaching given by a teacher and the discussion held in common, or, to put it another way, that between monologue and scientific dialogue" [Free translation—Ed] (Éric Weil, *op. cit.,* 64).

fewer can be admitted by science as absolutely certain and ultimately function as premises for scientifically valid reasoning. The proper sphere of each of the four sciences is therefore delimited by the contiguity of the antecedent and the subsequent. Arranged in concentric circles, they form the complete mapping of communications among civilized humans, the sphere of possible rational knowledge.[50]

3. Finally, both scales are demanded by Aristotle's theory of knowledge. For Aristotle, knowledge begins with sensory data. These are transferred to memory, imagination, or fantasy (φαντασία), which groups them into images (εἰκόνες, *eikones*; in Latin *species, speciei*), according to their similarities. It is upon these retained and organized images in the imagination, and not directly on the sensory data, that intelligence exercises the sorting and reorganization based on which it will create eidetic schemas, or abstract concepts of species, with which it can finally construct judgments and reasoning. From the senses to abstract reasoning, there is a double bridge to be crossed: fantasy and the so-called simple apprehension, which captures isolated notions. There is no leap: without the intermediation of fantasy and simple apprehension, one does not reach the higher stratum of scientific rationality. There is a perfect structural homology between this Aristotelian description of the cognitive process and the Theory of the Four Discourses. Indeed, it could not be otherwise: if the individual human does not arrive at rational knowledge without passing through fantasy and simple apprehension, how could the collectivity—whether the polis or the smaller circle of scholars—reach scientific certainty without the preliminary and successive collaboration of poetic imagination, the organizing will that is expressed in rhetoric, and the dialectical screening undertaken by philosophical discussion?

Once Rhetoric and Poetry are removed from the "technical" or "poietic" exile, in which Andronicus placed them, and restored to their condition as philosophical sciences, the unity of the discourses leads us to a surprising verification: embedded within it is an entire Aristotelian philosophy of culture as the integral expression of *logos*. In this philosophy, scientific reason emerges as the supreme fruit of a tree whose root is poetic imagination, planted in the soil of sensible nature. And since sensible nature is not for Aristotle merely an irrational

---

[50] It's almost impossible that Aristotle, a natural scientist with a mind full of analogies between the sphere of rational concepts and the facts of the physical order, did not notice the parallelism—direct and inverse—between the four discourses and the four elements, differentiated, too, by the scale from the densest to the subtlest, in concentric circles.

and hostile "externality," but the materialized expression of the divine *Logos*, culture, rising from the mythopoetic ground to the summits of scientific knowledge, appears as the humanized translation of that divine Reason, mirrored in miniature in the philosopher's self-consciousness. Indeed, Aristotle compares philosophical reflection to the self-cognitive activity of a God which consists, fundamentally, of self-awareness. The pinnacle of philosophical reflection, which crowns the edifice of culture, is, in fact, *gnosis gnoseos*, knowledge of knowledge. Now, this is achieved only at the moment when reflection comprehends retrospectively its complete trajectory, that is, when, having reached the sphere of scientific reason, it understands the unity of the four discourses through which it has progressively risen to this point. There it is prepared to move from science or philosophy to wisdom, to enter Metaphysics, which Aristotle, as Pierre Aubenque aptly emphasized, prepares but does not fully achieve, since its realm is not of this world.[51] The Theory of the Four Discourses is, in this sense, the beginning and end of Aristotle's philosophy. Beyond it, there is no more proper knowledge: there is only the "knowledge that is sought," the aspiration for supreme knowledge, of *sophia* whose possession would mark both the realization and the end of philosophy.

How to Become a Seeker of the Truth

A handout from the Online Philosophy Course, 2015

Introduction to Zetology

Even people who deny the existence of truth, or the possibility of knowing it, still believe that what they say is true. This alone is enough to demonstrate, or at least suggest, that complete skepticism is merely a mental exercise, not a serious attitude. Everyone considers himself possessor of some truth, and self-proclaimed skeptics are no exception. Even those who extol the universal power of deceit understand that it only serves a purpose when it carries a persuasive force of *truth*, not mere deception. It is also true that no one can lie without knowing the truth his lie distorts or conceals.

Everyone, whether more or less consciously, acknowledges that truth is a good, a highly desirable one at that. Many people even create or nurture specific

---

[51] Pierre Aubenque, *Le problème de l'être chez Aristote. Essai sur la problématique aristotélicienne* (Paris: P.U.F., 1962).

practices, which they believe are means of discovering truths: logic, the experimental method, historical criticism of documents, the art of police investigation, and so forth. All these methods presume in their students or practitioners the natural ability to know the truth. These methods merely adapt this inherent ability to the specific requirements of particular fields of knowledge, according to rules and norms generally accepted by the professionals in their respective domains. They are taught at universities, and those who learn them consider themselves, with some justification, more qualified than laypersons to uncover truths within their professional sphere, if not in all others as well.

However, when we speak of "natural ability," we conceive its possessor as man in general, man as member of an animal species, man as representative of humanity. A natural ability presupposes a nature, and we claim that all men possess this ability because they share the same human nature. The problem is that, when we are not discussing this generic man but real, concrete individuals, experience shows that they do not possess this ability in equal measure. The capacity to discover or accept the truth varies greatly from one individual to another.

From the start, differences in intelligence levels make some individuals more or less suitable for learning logic, the scientific method, or any other technique taught in universities to seek the truth. But there are even more significant differences. Some people can be blind to certain truths. Others may distort them according to their interests or passions. Certain individuals may obstinately deny the most obvious and patent truths if they perceive them as a threat to their psychological security or self-image. Some simply cease to seek certain truths because they believe they already know them. Some may not even imagine that these truths could or should be known.

Thus, if the natural ability to know the truth exists in all human beings, there is, by necessity, an individual difficulty in knowing it, some cognitive obstacle stemming from genetic heritage, cultural upbringing, acquired vices, fears, prejudices, and so on. In summary, all men have the ability to know the truth, but none is entirely, naturally, and spontaneously qualified to exercise this ability satisfactorily in all life situations or even within their preferred sphere of action. No one is a perfect, flawless truth-discovering machine, immune to defects, wear, and various impediments.

Correcting these defects, preventing these impairments, and removing these obstacles are absolutely essential precautions for anyone who does not want to be deluded by the illusion that everything natural in humans functions perfectly and infallibly. Just like all other animals, such as lion cubs learning to hunt with their mothers, fledgling birds learning to fly, or puppies being taught by adult dogs to track prey or herd a flock, human beings must learn *to harness* the skills their nature has bestowed upon them.

Now, if we ask whether any of the techniques taught in universities to seek the truth help humans acquire this possession, the answer is a resounding "No!" None of these techniques offer such assistance, for four fundamental reasons (though there are others I won't detail here). Firstly, all of these techniques presuppose that the student has already undergone the personal development necessary to acquire them. Clearly, no teaching can provide beginners with what it demands of them, from the outset, as a condition for acceptance. Secondly, they all focus on the *object* of knowledge, whether it is coherent speech, natural or historical facts, the authorship of a crime, and so on, rather than the person studying. Thirdly, these techniques are taught uniformly to everyone, largely ignoring the individual's unique needs or difficulties. Fourthly, each of them only pertains to the pursuit of specific types of truths, not all truths. For example, logic teaches you the truth of coherent discourse but not the truth of correct sensory perception. The science of history teaches you to evaluate documents and testimonies using specific criteria but does not make you a trustworthy witness in the court of your own conscience. The scientific method teaches you to collect, compare, and organize certain types of sensory data obtained through direct observation or equipment, but it never tells you if these data and the resulting conclusions make sense within the context of human existence or if they are mere unhealthy curiosities pursued for sheer pleasure or foul purposes.

In sum, these techniques and methods teach you how to perform a specific cognitive activity according to the standards accepted by a professional community but do not pertain to your *personal capacity* to know the truth. If this capacity is impaired, and you adorn it with one of these techniques, you will only learn to make technical mistakes and feel very confident in your errors, especially when they are shared by a significant portion of your professional community.

Although no one in universities is ignorant of what "prejudices," "ideological distortions," or "rationalizations" are, no university discipline teaches students how to overcome these inner obstacles that hinder their pursuit of truth.

The existing psychotherapeutic practices also do not address this issue. They aim to help patients achieve a state of harmony, well-being, and integration into society, rather than to empower them to seek the truth.

Similarly, religious practices focus on saving the soul, not on the sanity and efficiency of intellectual life.

In short, the health of cognitive consciousness, the foremost and most fundamental condition for the pursuit of truth in all intellectual disciplines—even in personal life situations—is entirely neglected in education, psychotherapy, and religious practices. All these domains assume that this condition will naturally and spontaneously fulfill itself without any special help, which only happens by sheer luck in a minuscule number of cases.

In principle, preserving the sanity of cognitive consciousness (or, to abbreviate it, intelligence) should be the task of philosophy, as understood in the Socratic-Platonic tradition. However, in the twentieth century, philosophy increasingly became a specialized profession, losing interest in the student's personal development. Some schools focus on addressing isolated obstacles, such as logical fallacies or ideological distortions, but they fixate on these points as if they were the sole issues, neglecting the student's personal growth. In some cases, it is about imposing a diminished concept of philosophy, reducing it to mere language analysis; in others, it is about combating ideologies other than the professor's own. The student is used as a tool to achieve these ends, rather than being the ultimate goal of the educational process.

The prevailing philosophy, as commonly understood in university settings today, also does not resolve our problem: how to train the student to seek the truth?

Given this state of affairs, I created, developed, and have applied a set of self-educational practices in my Online Philosophy Course with reasonable success. The goal is to (1) make students aware of cognitive obstacles, whether internal or external, that hinder them from seeking the truth and (2) gradually overcome these obstacles. I named these educational practices *zetology* (from the Greek ζητέω, *zeteo*, "to seek" or "search"), although without claiming they already constitute a science.

Circle of Latency

O saber e o enigma (2022)

The Starting Point of Symbolism

Susanne Langer asserted that a symbol is a "matrix of intellections." This isn't a complete definition, but it points to a property of the symbol.

When we become aware of a symbol, it somehow prompts various perceptions or intellections in us. In doing so, the symbol isn't teaching us anything, but it's offering us an opportunity to learn; it thus plays a hormonal role for intelligence (such that any study on symbolism should have a beneficial influence on intelligence, even if you're not interested in the topic of symbolism itself).

One characteristic of the symbol—emphasized in Langer's definition—is its openness to various "intentions." I use the word "intention" here in the sense given by Edmund Husserl. According to him, all consciousness is consciousness of something, and intention is this reference of our thought to something. When we think, we don't think in a vacuum or about nothing; there is always something to which we direct our thought. It can be an elephant, a cup of coffee, a stock in the stock market, or a presidential speech. That would be the intention.

Each term or word we use doesn't indicate just one thing (one intention), but possibly many. This happens because every word signifies the many other words that correspond to it in a dictionary. Human communication, therefore, is never based on a sign or an exclusive meaning. It implies not only a constellation of possible meanings but also a multitude of referents, which are the objects. "Elephant" signifies an animal with such and such characteristics given in the verbal meaning of the word; on the other hand, its referent is the actual elephant. It can be an elephant, all elephants, a portion of elephants, and so on.

So, we understand many things, but we have no idea how we understand them amid the immense range of intentions that can be actualized. All the time, we speak using words that we imagine mean specific things, but that, in reality, mean many things; and when we are speaking, we never have to bring all these possible meanings or referents to our consciousness.

Given this, how do we understand each other? If every word someone uses can mean a thousand things, and when I hear it, I can recall a thousand different things related to it, how do I understand what the person is saying? This phenomenon of the functionality of human language is the starting point for the study of symbolism.

The Three Functions of Language

Karl Bühler[52] used to say that language has three functions: a) the denominative function, which consists of naming things; b) the expressive function, which seeks

---

[52] *Theory of Language: The representational function of language* (Philadelphia: John Benjamins Publishing Company, 2011).—Eds.

to make a feeling or inner state visible; and c) the communicative function, which aims to act on the listener's mind. If the meanings we refer to correspond to countless referents that are merely latent, or that we sometimes don't even know, then language is being used in the expressive or communicative key, but not in the denominative key because we are not talking about a specific referent. We are just expressing a feeling or acting on the listener. For example, I come across a text in which Teilhard de Chardin talks about the "progress of the universe."[53] A company can have more or fewer employees, can have higher or lower revenue, and thus can have its progress measured. Cars can leave factories worse or better, and can therefore regress or progress. That is, progress is necessarily a comparative term. But what would be the "progress of the universe": would it be becoming larger, would it function better than it did up to a given moment (whatever "functioning" means), or would it become, perhaps, denser? It is impossible to know. The "progress of the universe," for which Teilhard de Chardin invites us to work for the good of a humanity on the verge of self-destruction in a nuclear conflagration, simply means nothing. This is a simple example, but it makes the predominance of the expressive and communicative functions in human language quite clear.

There will be those who react to this predominance. The essence of the analytic school, for example, lies in reducing philosophy to the analysis of language—all of Bertrand Russell's work is based on this. He realizes that there is something nebulous and tremendously imprecise in all language (including scientific language) and decides to analyze it to the last consequences, to make it perfectly objective, referentially specific. Thus, with the help of Whitehead, he intends, in the *Principia Mathematica,* to create a kind of general encyclopedia of the sciences, a universal philosophy in which all scientific terminologies are perfectly defined, without any ambiguity. Suppose they had finally managed to elaborate this system of concepts and judgments that puts order into language. There would be the various terms and concepts that define and justify them all the way, so that each concept is linked to the next concept with the utmost rigor, and so on. It would be a beautiful system, all neat, expressed in a work of almost two thousand pages. But here's what happens: I can't remember the whole system at once. When I refer to it, it is also a latent intention. I suppose that maybe I remember such and such a part, if asked about it. But I can't have an integral view of the entire system in a single instant. In the desire to eliminate the latency of language, a system was created that also exists in latency. The fundamental

---

[53] Pierre Teilhard de Chardin, *The Future of Man* (New York: Image Books, 2004).—Eds.

problem was not solved. I always have to continue visualizing only aspects. Imprecision is not a defect of our language—it is of its very nature.

The Rotatory Perspective

I called this possibility of rotating and capturing various intentions without ever exhausting them *rotatory perspective*.

Let's suppose I see a painting depicting a horse. The same word is used for the painted horse as for the real one, but at this moment, I am referring to the horse in the painting. Thus, one referent comes forward, to the forefront of consciousness, and the other goes to the background, as I am referring to the painted horse, not the zoo horse.

Each word we use has a stock of contents that can be actualized, which at a given moment do not come to the surface because we are not using them. But if we are pressed to seek in the word its correspondence with a specific thing, it is possible that these background contents will be actualized.

This is not just a phenomenon peculiar to language but common to any object of knowledge. The simplest example I can give refers to a cubic object. We can only see three sides of it at the same time, but it is not possible for a cube to have only three sides. If it does not have another three, it will not be a cube. We can only see all six sides of the cube at the same time if we disassemble it, as is done in descriptive geometry. In it, the various sides are placed on paper so that they form a cross to be assembled. But this is not a cube, it is a sheet of paper. Similarly, it is not possible to know a house entirely and instantly. If we are outside it, we will see at most three of its sides, while the others will remain hidden. Nor can we traverse all its rooms at the same time. It is only through memory that we perceive the unity of the house: when we go from one room to another, we still remember the previous one—if we forget, we will never form the image of the house and will keep only, perhaps, this and that isolated room.

Similarly, when you see a dog lying down and then see it walking, you know it's the same dog. There is unity or continuity in it. But it is only through memory that you know this. It is not possible to see the entire dog at once, in all its possible positions and moments, from its birth to its death. I have had my dog Big Mac for twelve years, an English Mastiff (a breed that lives an average of eight years, so you can imagine the elderly situation he is in); I remember when he was tiny, but it is a vague memory. It is impossible to imagine him when he was small as clearly as I see him now. I can only connect one thing to another through my memory and imagination.

The same applies to the logical system that would explain the unity and coherence of language. You cannot see it all at once: you only see a little piece of it and potentially remember the rest. Note that, in this sense, a philosophical system is like a dog, a painting, or anything else. You can only see a piece of it at a time, while the rest exists in your memory, as a latent possibility. Absolutely everything we know is like this. By reading *this* word, you know that I have already said others and that the exposition has coherence and continuity (I hope). You know this only because of your memory, remembering vaguely what I said before and articulating it with what I say now.

The Known Announces the Unknown

When you're hunting and come across a bear, what you see is not the complete bear but only its external surface because you cannot see its internal organs. However, if the bear were empty, if it had no stomach, lungs, and heart, it would be just a bear appearance, and that's not possible. Even though we don't see them, the bear's internal organs not only must be present but must be functioning. That's what makes the bear a bear: it is because of everything that we don't see. Similarly, I cannot see it at one month old and at two years old at the same time. I have to subdivide the bear and see only a little piece of it, be content with that, and guess all the rest that is behind what I see.

We often reason, forgetting that the world consists of little pieces whose totality does not immediately manifest to us. David Hume said that when we talk to someone, we perceive a sound, which may even make sense, but we don't see any conscious self behind it. What we see is just a speaking body, but how do we know if it has a conscious self?

Now, we know numerous things that do not present themselves to us. If we could not rely on everything we are not seeing (including the self that Hume is asking about), all human knowledge would be impossible, including the most elementary. We must be honest and confess that large portions of what we know depend on things whose direct knowledge generally escapes us.

Nevertheless, someone may conceive a "critical analysis" of knowledge and pretend not to know what they know. This creates an unsolvable logical problem because there is no way to prove that you—returning to the example—have a conscious self behind what you say. But everything we speak is based on the assumption that we have a conscious self, that each of us speaks his own words because he has thought them and wants to say them. With the abstraction of this, only the word remains popping in the void like a soap bubble.

On the Necessity of Proof or Not

We can only prove something because we have some knowledge about that something. Knowledge is the condition of proof, not the other way around. Proof is always secondary, as shown by the fact that the number of things we need to prove is always very small, as almost everything we know comes to us without the need for proof. It is indeed impossible to prove that you are yourself. It is also impossible to prove that I am giving this lecture now. You know that I am giving this lecture not because of some proof, but through your testimony. Socrates never endeavors, in Platonic dialogues, to prove what he says; what he does is invoke the testimony of his interlocutors, inviting them to pay attention to their real experience and sincerely testify. By doing so, they will notice possible inconsistencies in their own discourse or the interlocutor's discourse and thus move towards expressing the truth given in their experiences.

Not only is everything we know composed of fragments, behind which there is a whole universe guessed by us, but also our entire knowledge is based on this exchange of guesses. Worse: it works. Not only is everything like this, but our entire concept of honesty, sincerity, and love for others is also based on this. The commitment not to demand that the other prove what you also cannot prove is the number one condition for human coexistence. Our communication is based on trust. Of course, it can fail, to the extent that the other lies or tries to deceive me— the referents of lies cannot be actualized: lies do not point to anything—or erroneously testifies to his experience.

Aristotle said that one should not argue with someone who does not recognize or perceive the principles of proof. This is fine, provided it is recognized that the principles of proof depend on the reliability of the interlocutors. There is no way to eliminate human honesty as a fundamental element of knowledge and communication. Nothing can defend us from this fact. And wanting to defend oneself from it, desiring an absolutely apodictic knowledge that does not depend on anyone's testimony, only proves that you are a coward, that you are not qualified to live human life; you want to live in a completely protected world, in a kind of geometric world.

On the contrary, we live in the human community, and our destiny depends on finding people with whom we can dialogue honestly. A dishonest person does not recognize the need to accept any proof. At most, you can demoralize him, make his lack of sincerity manifest, but you cannot force him to accept the truth he insists on denying.

The Universe as a Total System of Latencies

All objects, even ideal ones, present themselves as latencies. The fact that objects of Euclidean geometry (a triangle, a rhombus, a right angle) are conceived by our minds does not mean that they can be known in the totality of their aspects. If that were possible, there would be no Euclidean geometry. Suppose I define a figure and you think you know it; then I deduce its internal properties, and you realize you did not know them. More concretely, suppose you know that a square is a flat figure with four equal sides and four right angles; however, you may not know that, by dividing it along the diagonal, we obtain two isosceles triangles, or that, by drawing a perpendicular from the middle to the other side, we get several right-angled triangles, and so on. More and more properties can be extracted that we had not perceived initially.

All of Euclid's geometry proves that even a purely ideal figure like a square cannot be known entirely and instantaneously. The very concept of a square only presents itself to me in the compact summary of a term, not in the complete unfolding of its properties. All we know are bundles of latencies: we know one aspect, and this aspect reveals to us a whole bundle, a whole constellation of latencies. By bringing an aspect from latency to patency, we realize that we somehow already knew it, even if we were not aware of it.

Furthermore, we not only guess the latency of all the properties that make up the objects we are talking about, but also their connections, what relations exist between them. What we know does not emerge as a tangle of elements but as a system of ordered latencies. There is nothing that exists on its own without any relation to anything else, for in that case, the detached thing would be the finished thing, the thing perfectly delimited and closed in on itself—and such a thing simply does not exist. We have never seen even one object in a state of absolute isolation. Objects always appear inserted in a system of latencies that links them to countless other objects. The universe is the total system of latencies.

However, there is an entire Kantian tradition according to which all we perceive are isolated and disconnected data, and we are the ones who articulate them. Thus, we would create in our mind, in our imagination, the idea of the world; in other words, the idea of a system or a totality would be a projection of our mind, while everything we receive from the world would actually come to us in a fragmented form.

This is a monstrous error committed by a great philosopher. He makes this mistake because he has inaccurately described his own experience by assuming that everything he perceives is, in some way, isolated fragments. But how, in the case of apprehending an isolated fragment, could you perceive that it is a fragment, since it would have no relation to anything else? How would you distinguish a fragment from a whole, element from element, and so on? It makes no sense. I see the external appearance of the bear, which is a fragment of it, and I know that there is a bear behind this appearance, a bear that completes it, without which I would not be able to perceive that I captured an appearance of a bear or even any appearance as appearance. I take the bear necessarily inserted in a system of latencies somewhere and at some time. I cannot see a bear outside of time or outside of space.

The unity of the world is presupposed in every act of perception. If my thought were responsible for the unity of the world, I would continuously have to reconstruct this unity because I would only have at my disposal the isolated, atomistic data that I would encounter at each moment. However, when I wake up every morning, I realize that I am in the same room as the day before. Did I mentally reconstruct this room, or did I simply recognize something I already knew? If I had reconstructed it, I could not know that it is the same room, because every time I reconstructed it, I would be doing something entirely new with no comparison to anything else—in short, it would be an entirely new room, not the old room always reconstructed.

The Given and the Constructed

Sometimes, philosophers propose that there are given elements that precede categorical thought. There would be pre-categorical elements, inherently chaotic and fragmentary, that you would arrange according to the categories of your thought and, thus, create an image of the world. But, as we have just seen, these pre-categorical elements, or fragments or parts that we perceive, are only fragments or parts because they contain latency within them. We only perceive a separate thing, distinct from another, because we articulate it with others. I am able to distinguish between a bear and a bear's paw. I cannot see a bear if it doesn't have a paw (it may have had its paws cut off, but it once had them). And I also cannot conceive of a bear's paw without the bear of which it is a part.

You don't get the data separately because they present themselves that way; or rather, the data never present themselves, all that presents itself is aspects of latencies. The data is something you abstract, something you isolate from the other powers and latencies that make up the object. You pretend that the data has no connections with the other elements and refer to it as if it were an isolated thing. But that, indeed, is a creation of your mind. What comes to you is the world itself, a world that you chop up, divide, and from which you obtain something you call "data."

In general, what philosophy professors call "data" is precisely the element constructed by their minds (abstraction, elements taken as atoms), and what they call construction is precisely what comes already given in reality (the unity of the world). But this is an inversion of the order of the real. Meaning, that is, the unity of the world, is what is eminently apprehensible, what is given even in the humblest of perceptions. Not that one properly arrives at meaning. Through speech, I recover the awareness I have of the presence of the ultimate meaning in each of my perceptions, I speak of it, and when I speak, other people recognize it. They know they have this experience, they know what I'm talking about because they have experienced it.

The idea of the unity of the world, as it appears in the mind of a philosopher when he is elaborating a doctrine, is not the same as the unity of the world as it appears in our real experience; it is a poorly made translation of the latter. In fact, the unity of real experience is indescribable. And when philosophers try to say it, they say it purely analogically.

No doctrine of the unity of the world corresponds to the unity of the world, only indicates it, because this unity of the world, for us, is infinite. It is only one because it is infinite. Given finitude, by definition, there would be another finitude beyond its limits, and so on, so that there would be a multiplicity of universes. (Note that I am not talking about spatial, material infinity, but about infinity from the point of view of latencies).

The Circle of Latency and the Unity of the World

In summary, if the only certain things were the fragmentary data of reality, while everything else was interpretation that we make, then all knowledge would be reduced to knowledge of fragments, without realizing that these fragments owe their fragmentary nature precisely to the *circle of latency* in which they are embedded.

To explain what I call the *circle of latency*—and notice that I have been alluding to various aspects of it—I usually give the following example. A person is walking down the street when he comes across a lying dog. He doesn't know if the dog will bite him, bark at him, run away, wag its tail, or just keep sleeping; but he knows that the dog can do any of these things, and above all, he knows that the dog will not recite Pindar's odes or fly away. If he didn't know any of this, he wouldn't know what a dog is. That is, if he saw no element of latency in the external figure of the dog, he would be unable to identify the dog. Perceiving an object is perceiving its circle of latency; and, even though it is impossible to perceive an entire circle of latency, you know that it is present. There is no physical object and, separate from it, the entirely arbitrary interpretation you make of it; the latencies you perceive are given in the circle of latency of which the physical appearance of the object is just one aspect.

Everything I perceive, I perceive at the same instant by operating a synthesis of its entire circle of latency and of all its links with the latencies of everything around it. I don't need to discursively think about the definition of a dog to eventually conclude that it doesn't fly. It is an immediate perception given in the apprehension of the dog, which is inseparable from its circle of latency. There is a kind of anticipation in the act of perception, but an anticipation that is not done by our thinking, but by the very perceptual structure; it is instantaneous. Edmund Husserl called this *protension*. If *retention* is the act by which the individual collects in memory what is no longer present, *protension* is the act by which he projects what is not yet present but may become present. But this waiting is not a thought: it is present, as I said, in the perception itself. It cannot be said to be an extra-sensory perception because it occurs through the senses. It is sensory, but at a level, so to speak, almost unconscious, provided it is understood that if there were no permanent transit from the unconscious to the conscious and from the conscious to the unconscious, we could not think and could not perceive anything, because we would have to be constantly conscious of everything. I don't know what word I will say next, but in a moment it moves from my unconscious to my conscious and I say it. (Conscious and unconscious are not things; they are not even states; they are almost like adverbs. Substantializing them leads to unsolvable problems, starting with the problem of how to characterize the relationship between one and the other).

Knowledge through Presence

What we merely anticipate, guess, arrives to us as *knowledge through presence*. It is something that the simple division between given [*datum*] and constructed is not capable of clarifying. It is not something intuited, nor is it something constructed rationally, discursively, but something that is the condition of possibility for any intuition and reasoning. The circle of latency that allows us to conceive the unity of the world is a precondition for any subsequent kind of knowledge (the way we come to perceive it, which I designated as *knowledge through presence*, had already been glimpsed, by the way, by a 12th-century Iranian philosopher, Suhrawardi).

I only know objects by the parts they show me of themselves and by what they insinuate to me about their system of latencies and connections. I also know myself in the same way. I cannot, at this exact moment, know myself in complete totality. I know that this totality is present, I know that at some point I was a baby, for example, but I cannot remember every moment of my infancy, also because if I started to remember, that memory would last as long as those moments lived in the past. If the passage of time in memory had the same duration as the passage of time in the physical world, memory would be impractical. Therefore, I must abstract certain moments from the past, separate them for the purpose of recollection, but knowing that they are articulated to each other in an unlimited series of moments, and that this is what gives them the density of a real thing.

Knowledge through presence starts from the understanding that there are things that are not in our mind, do not happen in our mind; on the contrary, it is our mind that is within a system, outside of which it would not function, and we could not know anything. Considering this fact carefully is all the more important because for three or four centuries the idealistic conception that everything is articulated by our minds has so predominated that the entire Western culture ended up addicted to clichés like "you are what you think," or beliefs like the "power of positive thinking," not to mention things like neurolinguistic programming. Implicit in all of this is the fundamental philosophical error of believing in the omnipotence of thought.

Loving Contemplation

It is even possible to expand the latency circle of the world. Beyond what you know, you know that there are things you ignore but would need to know to compose a more complete picture of reality. Being aware of this gives you a kind of heightened sensitivity, whereby you allow the object to be what it is, expecting it to spontaneously reveal itself. You are not interested in altering the object; you are interested in it remaining eternally as it manifests to you, as if it were speaking and you were listening. I call this *loving contemplation*.

The Objective of Philosophy

O saber e o enigma (2022)

Philosophy aims to encompass ever-wider circles of latency to which we only have access through presence. Most people may not be able to express them, but it is the philosopher's task to know the necessary technique for doing so. Viewed from the *theory of the four discourses*,[54] this would be the poetic phase of philosophical activity. It begins with the perception of the senses to then give it expression (an "expression of impressions," as put by Benedetto Croce).

The philosopher will then notice that in his expression, various elements are confused, which, once clarified, allow for the arrival at a generic concept of the object, which will no longer include its latency circle. This marks a progression in the levels of credibility of discourses, ascending to the dialectical or even apodictic level. At this point, the philosopher needs to strive to ensure that the concept does not lose its connection with the perception from which it originated, or else it will become a formalism that means nothing.

In such a case, you might go to war, as Franz Rosenzweig did, and there you will wonder about the value of all the philosophy you studied. Are you going to war to face the real issues of life, or are you going there to defend yourself from them? The early philosophers, like Heraclitus and Parmenides, were interested in fatally important issues, pregnant with references. Fundamental principles are all formulated in the face of life and death. Socrates showed that he took his philosophy deadly seriously by his willingness to die for it. But you won't want to die for analytical philosophy. (This is also the theme José Ortega y Gasset thought about when talking about the only ideas that matter, the "ideas of shipwrecked people," those to which you will cling in your final and decisive moment).

The need to analyze concepts without having the presence of the concrete object in front of you is a problem derived from the institutionalization of philosophy. In a college of philosophy, objects or things are not examined; only concepts and judgments are examined all the time, and this creates the habit of examinations that never appeal to the object itself. When you enter a college of philosophy, you receive an entire philosophical vocabulary, a set of concepts and judgments to examine, but you don't know where they were extracted from. The examination thus begins from concepts forward, in the illusion that these will be applied to things.

One should not study philosophy, but study other subjects and then philosophically analyze what was studied. Philosophy is not a discipline in the strict sense, but an activity on acquired knowledge. If there is no knowledge, there is no philosophy because philosophy is a reflection on that; and, in the absence of knowledge, there is only knowledge of reflection. Therefore, it is not possible to teach philosophy to children because they do not yet have something to

---

[54] See "Aristotle in a New Perspective: The Theory of the Four Discourses."—Eds.

philosophize about; at most, they will have heard words from the teacher's mouth, which they will get used to employing in certain contexts that will be directed to them, in a spirit of philosophical verbalism that mutilates intelligence. In short, to start philosophizing, it is necessary to have not only life experience but also accumulated knowledge (of history, life, art) to meditate on. Otherwise, you will try to digest what you have not eaten, which will cause an ulcer in one's intelligence. We can speak of institutionalized philosophy as masochistic self-mutilation.

In the time when Socrates met with his friends in the square or at one of their homes, they were very close to the real world, to nature, referring to events in their daily lives. But as philosophical debate solidified into institutions over the centuries, equipped with regulations and their own professional hierarchy, philosophy came to be more clearly constituted as an object of study and not as a certain way of addressing real problems.

This is how terrible perceptual errors arise, as we find in a book by Cláudio Costa, a Brazilian philosophy professor. He defines philosophy as "an investigation aimed at obtaining a set of true generalizations, which is carried out by members of a supposed critical community of ideas, the community of philosophers."[55] This cannot be philosophy at all. Philosophy only begins in the awareness of the isolated thinker, or he wouldn't even have anything to say to his friends, or if he did, they wouldn't recognize what he was talking about because they themselves had not solitarily observed their experience. Socrates's friends recognize what he is talking about because they had some similar experience before talking to Socrates. Philosophy cannot be seen as a social activity before being an activity of the concrete human individual. Philosophical meditation works when philosophical dialogue takes place with fully present individuals, that is, individuals invested with all their memory, all their feelings, all their real history. This is generally far from what happens at a philosophy congress, where the dialogue is not between real people but between social roles; there, professors can only discuss concepts and terms that are already, in some way, consolidated in the vocabulary of their profession. This is not philosophical dialogue but a second-degree imitation of what a true philosophical dialogue would be. The awareness of belonging to a professional philosophical community can be an impediment to true philosophical activity.

---

[55] [Free translation—Eds.] Cláudio Costa, *Uma introdução contemporânea à filosofia* (São Paulo: Martins Fontes, 2002).

Self-Awareness, Birthplace of Truth

Inteligência e verdade (2021)

It is important to learn to admit what you know to be true. Even if they are insignificant truths, meditating on the obvious is perhaps the best way to get accustomed to the truth and to lose the fear of it and the unjust suspicion regarding the power of intelligence. For example, even though almost all knowledge may be relative or doubtful, you know that you cannot seriously doubt that you are here at this moment; you can pretend that you are not, but you cannot doubt effectively. If there are so many obvious truths about insignificant things, imagine where we could go if we achieved such evidence for truly important matters! The sense of truth develops from the very sense of evidence, and the sense of evidence has its roots in what you already know and know that you know. When you truly know something, you automatically know that you know, and if you know that you know, you know that you know that you know. This means that any effective knowledge also implies awareness of this knowledge and the full admission of its truth. Intelligence, therefore, has a volitional aspect, inseparably linked to the cognitive aspect.

Where does the training of consciousness to admit the truth begin? The first step in learning the truth is for you to recognize those truths that only you know and that no one, other than you, can confirm or deny. For example, only you know your intentions, only you know the acts you have done in secret, only you know the feelings you have not confessed. In these cases, you are the only witness, and this is where you will know the radical and insurmountable difference between truth and falsehood. People who constantly deny the existence of truths do not know this experience; they have only borne false witness of themselves before the tribunal of conscience, lying to themselves and thus feeling that everything in the world is a lie. As Hegel said, self-awareness is the birthplace of truth. Also, Giambattista Vico observed that we only know perfectly well what we ourselves have done.[56] God alone knows nature perfectly well because He made it. But our own actions, only we ourselves can know, just as our thoughts and our inner states. There is no one there who can monitor us, no one who can defend us from ourselves.

---

[56] In Latin, *verum factum* principle.—Eds.

The Problem of Truth and the Truth of the Problem
A handout from the Philosophy Seminar, May 20, 1999

1. Radical Questioning

§ 1.1. On Frivolity Satisfied

Quid est veritas? This is the most serious and the most frivolous of questions. It depends, evidently, on the intention of the one who asks. Some admit that the meaning and value of human life depend on the existence of some eminently certain and reliable truth that can serve as a measure of the validity of our thoughts. Others think that life can perfectly well go on without any truth and without any foundation. Among these was surely old Pilate. When he exclaimed—"What is truth?"—he was not really asking a question, but expressing, with a shrug, his lack of inclination to take this question seriously. The prospect of there being no truth, which would lead to despair those who believe that life needs it to justify itself, was for Pilate a relief and a consolation— the guarantee of being able to continue living without worry. Some bet on the existence of truth and *cherchent en gémissant.*[57] Others turn their backs on it and wash their hands.[58] The verbal formula they use is the same: *Quid est veritas?* But in the difference of their nuances lies the whole range from the tragic to the comic.

The frivolous, or comic, school is widely dominant today, whether in universities or in culture in general. Even those who seek to believe in an effective truth surround it with all sorts of limits and obstacles, for example, reducing it to the type of partial and provisional truth given to us by some experimental sciences. Others cling to faith, saying that truth exists, but is beyond our understanding.

In any debate about the problem of truth, nowadays, the program almost invariably consists of challenging the observations that philosophers, from Pyrrho to Richard Rorty, have made about the limits of human knowledge again and again. These limits, taken together, form a formidable mountain of obstacles to any claim to know the truth. And this mountain is growing, with a peak that moves further and further away as we climb. For example, from the simplistic objections of the Pyrrhonian school against the validity of knowledge through the senses to the enormously complex constructions with which psychoanalysis denies the

---

[57] An expression coined by Pascal in his classic *Pensées* that means 'seek while groaning.'—Eds.
[58] There are also those who believe in the existence of truth and are confident in possessing it without any investigative effort. However, they are outside the philosophical debate and do not interest us.

priority of consciousness, or Gramsci reduces all truth to the expression of ideologies that succeed each other through History, the machine for injecting discouragement into the seeker of truth has evolved greatly. It is not surprising that many of the builders of this machine, instead of lamenting the increase of human impotence when they add a new piece to it, have a smile similar to Pilate's on their lips. The non-existence of truth, or the impossibility of knowing it, is for them a comfort. We will see later what the deepest reasons for this strange satisfaction are.

§ 1.2. Temporary Definition of the Truth

For now, let's set aside these creatures and focus, on our own terms, on the question of truth. Since we still don't know if truth exists or what it asserts, we must resort to a provisional formal definition, one that allows us to begin the investigation without prejudging its outcome. This provisional definition, to meet this requirement, must express the mere intentional meaning of the term, as it appears even on the lips of those who deny the existence of any truth, since to deny the existence of something one must understand the meaning of the term that designates it.

I say, therefore, that truth—that truth which we still do not know whether it exists or not, that truth whose existence and consistency will be the object of our investigation as they have been of so many investigations that preceded us—is *the permanent and universal cognitive foundation of the validity of judgments*. If we say, for example, that the only foundation of the validity of our judgments is their *utility*, we deny the existence of a *cognitive* foundation, that is, we deny the existence of truth by denying one of the elements that compose its definition. The same happens if we say that all valid judgments are based on faith. If we affirm, however, that there are no valid judgments of any kind, then we deny the existence of any foundation, cognitive or not. If we affirm that judgments are only valid for a certain time and place, we deny that the foundation is permanent. If we affirm that judgments are only valid subjectively for the one who pronounces them, we deny that the foundation is universal. If we say that the foundation of the validity of judgments is only logical-formal, without any reach on the real objects mentioned in the judgment, we deny that this foundation has cognitive significance. All these denials of truth presuppose the definition of truth as *the permanent and universal cognitive foundation of the validity of judgments*. Likewise, if we say that truth exists, that it is knowable, that based on it we can build a set of valid knowledge, we will have added or removed nothing from this definition, but we will have only affirmed that the object defined in it exists. Our provisional definition, therefore, being compatible with the two maximally opposite currents of opinion that dispute around the question, is a superior and neutral ground from which the investigation can be initiated without prejudices and with all honesty and rigor.

§ 1.3. Is Radical Questioning of the Truth Possible?

We start, therefore, from a consensus. The next step in the investigation consists of asking whether truth, thus defined, can or cannot be the object of radical questioning. By the term radical questioning, I mean the type of questioning that, admitting *ex hypothesi* the nonexistence of its object—as has often been done with the existence of God, innate ideas, or the external world—ultimately concludes, either in favor of this same nonexistence, or of existence.

The radical questioner of God, innate ideas, or the external world can question them because he places himself, from the outset, outside the divine, innate, or worldly realm, that is, he reasons as if God or innate ideas or the world did not exist. Depending on the progress of his investigation, he will either conclude that his premise is absurd, which will therefore lead him to admit the existence of that which he had postulated as nonexistent, or conversely, to the conclusion that the premise holds perfectly well and that what was supposed to be nonexistent really does not exist.

The most classic example of the use of this method is that of Descartes. He assumes the nonexistence of the external world, sensory data, his own body, etc. and continues reasoning along this line until he encounters a limit—*cogito ergo sum*—which forces him to retreat and admit the existence of everything he had initially denied.

Radical questioning is the toughest test to which philosophy can subject any idea or entity claiming existence.

What we must ask, therefore, immediately after obtaining the formal definition of truth, is whether truth thus defined can be the object of radical questioning. The answer, which may surprise many, is a categorical *no. Truth cannot be the object of radical questioning.*

No investigation into truth, however radical it may claim to be, can presuppose the nonexistence of any permanent and universal cognitive foundation for the validity of judgments and continue to reason consistently with this premise until it reaches some result, positive or negative. And it cannot for a very simple reason: the assertion of the absolute nonexistence of any permanent and universal cognitive foundation for the validity of judgments would itself constitute the permanent and universal cognitive foundation for the subsequent judgments made along the same line of investigation. The investigation would be paralyzed as soon as it was formulated.

Let us briefly examine some of the classic strategies of negation of truth that the questioner could resort to in order to escape from this *cul-de-sac*.

Let us try, for example, the pragmatist's strategy. It asserts that the validity of judgments rests on their practical usefulness, and therefore that the foundation of this validity is not cognitive. If we were to say that the nonexistence of a universal and permanent cognitive foundation for the validity of judgments is not itself a universal and permanent cognitive foundation, but only a practical foundation, either this practical foundation would have to be universal and permanent, or only partial and provisional.

In the first hypothesis, there would be two problems: on the one hand, we would fall into the paradox of a universal utility, that is, of something that could usefully serve all practical purposes, even the most contradictory ones. It would be the universal means to all ends, or more clearly still, the universal panacea. On the other hand, we would have to ask whether belief in this panacea itself had a cognitive foundation, or whether it was only a practical utility, and so on infinitely.

In the second hypothesis—that is, in the hypothesis that the questioner admits that the assertion of the nonexistence of truth is only a partial and provisional foundation for the validity of subsequent judgments—then, obviously, the possibility would always remain unshaken that outside the thus delimited realm, other permanent and universal cognitive foundations could validate a multitude of other judgments, and the investigation could continue indefinitely, leaping from provisional foundation to provisional foundation, without ever being able to ground itself in its own presupposition, that is, in the radical nonexistence of truth.

Let's attempt a second strategy, that of subjective relativism. This proclaims, with Protagoras, that "man is the measure of all things," which is commonly interpreted to mean that "each person has his own truth," in other words, that what is true is true only from the perspective of the thinker, and may be false from the perspective of all others. Can this assertion constitute the basis for a radical questioning of truth, in such a way that the denial of the existence of any universal and permanent cognitive foundation for the validity of judgments does not itself become the universal and permanent cognitive foundation on which the validity of subsequent judgments in the same line of investigation is based? Put another way, and more simply: can relativism deny the existence of valid judgments for all humans without that denial itself becoming a valid judgment for all humans? To do so, it would have to deny the universality of this denial, which would result in admitting the existence of some or several or an infinity of judgments valid for all humans. Thus, subjective relativism would itself be relativized and would ultimately amount to a platitude without any philosophical significance, that is, to the assertion that some judgments are not valid for all humans, which implies the possibility that other judgments perhaps are. No, subjective relativism cannot carry out a radical questioning of truth, just as pragmatism cannot.

Can historicism do it, then? It declares that all truth is merely the expression of a temporally located and limited worldview. Do humans think this or that not because this or that imposes itself as universally and permanently obligatory truth, but only because it imposes itself in a limited place and for a limited period. By proclaiming these limits, can historicism prevent the assertion of these limits from becoming itself the universal and permanent cognitive foundation of the validity of judgments? To do so, it would be necessary to admit that there may be some foundation that denies this assertion; but if this foundation exists, then there is some truth whose validity is unlimited in time and space, some truth whose validity escapes historical conditioning—and historicism would be reduced to the miserable observation that some foundations of validity are historically conditioned, others are not, without even being able to apply this distinction to concrete cases without affirming in the same act the invalidity of the historicist principle taken as a universal rule.

I will spare the reader the enumeration of all possible forms of subterfuge and their detailed refutation. He can perform them himself, as an exercise, if he wishes. I even suggest that he do so. And as many times as he does, he will always end up returning to the same point: it is not possible to deny the existence of a universal and permanent cognitive foundation for the validity of judgments, under any pretext whatsoever, without that denial, together with its respective pretext, having to affirm itself as the universal and permanent cognitive foundation of the validity of judgments, thus paralyzing the subsequent denial by which the investigation should continue, if it could. Truth as we have defined it cannot, in short, be the object of radical questioning. Nor can the possibility of knowing it. Denied that it is possible to know any universal and permanent cognitive foundation for the validity of judgments, or this impossibility itself would become such a foundation, affirming in the same act its own lack of any foundation, or else, not to assume this vexatious role, it would have to limit itself to affirming that some judgments have no foundation and others probably do, an assertion within the reach of any schoolboy.

Unable to reach the intended target, the enemy of truth is therefore condemned to gnaw at it around the edges, eternally, without ever reaching the vital center of what he would like to destroy. He will deny one truth, then another, now under one pretext, now under another, varying the strategies and directions of the attack, but he can never rid himself of his fate: each denial of a truth will be the affirmation of another, and both that denial and this affirmation will always result in the affirmation of truth itself, that is, the actual existence of some universal and permanent cognitive foundation for the validity of judgments.

This also explains the continuous, unlimited, and unstoppable proliferation of denials of truth, and their total incapacity to wipe off from the face of the Earth the belief in the existence of truth, the belief in the possibility of knowing the truth, the belief in the actual and full possession of some truth capable of providing a universal and permanent foundation to the validity of judgements.

For this reason, the number and variety of attacks on the truth, from Pyrrho to Richard Rorty, surpass by far the number and variety of defenses that formally present themselves as such: it is because the attacks themselves, even against the will of their authors, always end up constituting defenses and praises of truth, not only sparing the apologist effort but also invigorating what they would wish to bury and honoring what they would wish to humble.

This is also the reason why the beginner, impressed by the variety and continuous resurgence of attacks on truth observed in the history of philosophy—at a remarkably increasing speed in today's world—quickly adheres to skepticism in order not to feel he is a member of an isolated and weakened minority, but, continuing his studies and overcoming the first impression based only on apparent quantity, he cannot maintain this position and ends up realizing that strength lies not in the number of deniers, however impressive it may seem, but in the quality of the happy few who serenely affirm truth.

2. The Truth Doesn't Belong to Judgments

§ 2.1. Truth and Truthfulness

The impossibility of radical questioning, which we noted in the previous chapter, leads to the conclusion that truth can only be attacked in parts, but that each denial of a part reaffirms the validity of the whole. Put another way: what can be questioned are *truths*. "The" truth cannot be questioned and indeed never has been, except in words, that is, through a feigned denial that ultimately results in an affirmation.

But this takes us a step further in the investigation. A venerable tradition, initiated by Aristotle, asserts that truth lies in judgments, that it is a property of judgments. Some judgments "possess" truth, others do not. We call the former true judgments, the latter false judgments. The set of true judgments is therefore a subset of the set of possible judgments. Possible judgments, in turn, are a subset of the set of human cognitive acts, which are a subset of the set of mental acts, which are a subset of the set of human acts, and so on. The territory of truth is thus a small area carved out within the vast world of thoughts, acts, and beings.

Is this really possible? How could truth be both the foundation of the validity of all judgments and a property of some of them in particular? Is there not a glaring contradiction or, at least, a problem here?

To address and resolve it, it is necessary to make a distinction here between *truth* and *truthfulness*. Truth is the universal and permanent cognitive foundation of the validity of judgments. Truthfulness is a quality observed in some judgments, according to which their validity has a universal and permanent cognitive foundation.

Once this is understood, it becomes clear that truth is a foundational condition of truthfulness, and not vice versa. If there were no universal and permanent cognitive foundation of the validity of judgments, no judgment could have a universal and permanent cognitive foundation. However, if a particular judgment possesses this foundation, nothing in the world can determine that only it possesses it, that is, that the existence of the foundation depends on the existence of that particular judgment. Yet that particular judgment could not exist and be truthful if there were no truth at all. Truth is, therefore, logically prior to truthfulness and constitutes its foundation.

But, being the foundation of truthfulness, truth is also the foundation of falsity, because false judgments are only false insofar as they can be impugned veraciously, either by their simple negation—itself truthful—or by the assertion of the contrary true judgment.

Being the foundation not only of the truthfulness of true judgments but also of the falsity of false judgments, if truthfulness is only present in true judgments and cannot be present in false judgments, then truth, in turn, must be present in both, as the foundation of the truthfulness of the former and the falsity of the latter. The territory of truth, therefore, is not identical to the set of possible true judgments, but encompasses this and the set of possible false judgments.

§ 2.2 Is the Basis of All Judgments a Judgment?

Is truth, the foundation of all judgments, necessarily a judgment itself? Can only a judgment be the foundation of another judgment? The answer is both yes and no. Yes, if by foundation we mean, restrictively and conventionally, the premise upon which the proof of the judgment is based. But the premise asserts something about something, and this something, in turn, is not a judgment but an object of it. For instance, I say that turtles have shells. This judgment is grounded in the definitions of "turtle" and "shell," which are judgments, but these definitions are grounded in observation—which is not a judgment—of turtles and shells, which are also not judgments. Shouldn't this observation also be true, capturing truly present traits in truly existing objects? Or shall I resort to the subterfuge that observation must be merely *exact*, exempt from the concept of "true"? But what does "exact" mean in this case, if not that which informs me nothing beyond or below what was truly observed in what an object truly showed? And furthermore, is it genuine exactness or just a semblance of it? There is no escape: either there is truth in the observation itself, or it cannot be exact, correct, adequate, or possess any other quality except if that quality is, in turn, true.

Thus, the foundation of the truthfulness of a judgment lies not only in the truthfulness of the judgments serving as its premises but also—in the case of judgments concerning objects of experience—in the truthfulness of the data from which I extract these premises and in the truthfulness of what I know from them through experience.

Moreover, if the foundation of judgments had to always be a judgment itself, the first foundation of all judgments would itself be a judgment devoid of any foundation. Aristotle, faced with this dead-end, asserted that knowledge of first principles is immediate and intuitive. But by this, he meant only that these principles had no proof, not that they lacked foundations. The principle of identity, for example, as expressed in the judgment A = A, has no judgment behind it that could serve as a premise for its demonstration, but it has an objective foundation in the ontological identity of each being with itself, which is not a judgment. Now, what can be known intuitively is this ontological identity, not the judgment A = A which merely manifests it. The intuition of the first logical principle does not occur in the form of a judgment but from one immediate evidence that, in itself, is not a judgment. There cannot be judgment without signs that transform this immediate evidence into a *verbum mentis*, a conscious assent that, while not yet a proposition, a statement in words, is no longer pure and simple intuition but a mental reflection of it, and therefore a derived and secondary cognitive act, not a primary one.

Thus, if the territory of logical premises begins with judgments affirming the first principles, this territory by no means encompasses the entire field of cognitive foundations, which extends, on the contrary, into the domain of intuitive perception, whether of objects of experience or of first principles.

With this, the falsehood of the image in which truth is a small zone carved out in the vastness of the territory of possible judgments becomes evident. All judgments, true and false, are but a modest cut in the immense territory of truth.

3. Where Is the Truth?

§ 3.1. The Truth as a Domain

Thus, we are led to understand that truth, being the criterion of the validity of judgments, cannot be either an immanent property of the judgments themselves or something entirely external to the judgments that, from the outside, judges them; for this judgment would in turn be a judgment. If I say that *the hen laid an egg*, where can the truth of this judgment lie? In the judgment itself, independently of the hen, or in the hen, independently of the judgment? The absurdity of the first hypothesis led Spinoza to proclaim the futility of judgments of experience, which are never valid or invalid in themselves and always depend on something external: a true judgment, for him, would have to be true in itself, regardless of whatever it may be, such as $a = a$ independent of what a is and of any other external verification. But the identity of a with a is also not only in the judgment that asserts it, but in the consistency of a, whatever it may be. There is no purely logical judgment that can be true or false in itself and without reference to something that is what the judgment speaks of. Even a judgment that speaks only of itself unfolds into the judgment that affirms and the judgment of which something is affirmed, and this certainly is not that. Saying that a judgment is true in itself cannot mean complete detachment from the *world*, which is assumed in the very possibility of enunciating a judgment. The flight to the domain of formal identity does not absolutely resolve the problem. Shall we then say, with an old tradition, that truth lies in the relationship between judgment and thing? Well, this relationship is in turn affirmed in a judgment, which in turn must have a relationship with its object (the affirmed relationship), and so on infinitely.

The other hypothesis, that the truth of the judgment *the hen laid an egg* lies in the hen independently of the judgment, would lead us to equally insurmountable difficulties. It would result in saying that the truth of the judgment does not depend on the fact that this judgment is uttered, that is, once the hen has laid an egg, the judgment affirming it is true even though, as a judgment, it does not exist. Edmund Husserl would subscribe to this without hesitation: the truth of the judgment is a matter of pure logic, which has nothing to do with the merely empirical question of a particular judgment being affirmed one day by someone. The confusion between the sphere of the truth of judgments and the sphere of their psychological production has indeed done much harm to philosophy, and Husserl definitively cleared up this confusion. But if the hen laid an egg and no one said anything about it, the truth in this case is not in the judgment but in the fact. The judgment that has not been uttered cannot be true or false yet; it can only have the conditions to be so; if it is true that the hen laid an egg, the judgment affirming it will be true if formulated, whereas the truth of the fact is already given with the appearance of the egg.

But if the truth of the judgment *the hen laid an egg* is neither in the judgment independently of the hen, nor in the hen independently of the judgment, nor in the relation between hen and judgment, where on earth can it be?

Well, we have just seen that, regardless of the judgments that affirm them, the objects intended in the judgments can also be true or false, regardless of the judgments that may be uttered about them. *The hen laid an egg* is opposed to *the hen did not lay an egg*, regardless of whether someone says it or not. There is contradiction and identity in reality, independently and before any judgment affirms or denies anything about it. Or, what amounts to the same thing: truth exists in reality and not only in judgments, or else it could not exist in judgments at all. There is truth in the fact that the hen laid an egg, there is truth in the judgment that affirms it, and there is truth also in the relation between judgment and fact as well as in the judgment that affirms the relation between judgment and fact: truth cannot then be *in* the fact, nor *in* the judgment nor *in* the relation, but it must be in all three.

Furthermore, if it is in all three, it must also be in something more, unless we admit that a single fact, the judgment that affirms it, and the relation that binds them together can, together, be true in the hypothesis that everything else is false. But this "everything else," which is not contained in either the fact, the judgment, or the relation, necessarily includes the very existence of facts, as well as the logical principles implied in the judgment and the relation. If there are no facts or logical principles, chickens will lay eggs in vain in the domain of non-fact and the search for a relation between fact and judgment will be futile in the domain of illogic. Therefore, the truth of a single fact, a single judgment, and their relation presupposes the existence of truth as a domain that transcends and encompasses facts, judgments, and relations.

To seek truth in the fact, the judgment, or the relation is like seeking space in bodies, in their measurements, and in the distance from one to another; just as space is not in the bodies, nor in the measurements, nor in the distances, but bodies, measurements, and distances are in space, so too truth is not in the fact, nor in the judgment, nor in the relation, but all are in truth or are nowhere, and even this "not being," if it means anything and is not just a *flatus vocis*, must be in truth.

Truth is not a property of facts, judgments, or relations: it is the *domain* within which facts, judgments, and relations occur.

§ 3.2. Is Truth an "a priori" Form of Knowledge?

The Kantian temptation here is practically unavoidable. As a condition of possibility for facts, judgments, and relations, truth is indeed an *a priori* condition. But is it an *a priori* condition for the *existence* of these three things or only for their *knowledge*?

This problem is resolved in a simple and brutal manner: if we say that truth is an *a priori* form of knowledge and claim that this is *true*, then knowledge must be in truth and not truth in knowledge, because the *a priori* could not be inherent to what it itself determines. To be an *a priori* condition of knowledge, truth must necessarily be an *a priori* condition of something else, which in turn is not knowledge but its object. Knowledge, like facts, judgments, and relations, is within the domain of truth, regardless of whether we consider knowledge solely in its eidetic content or as a fact: the truth of the known, the truth of the knower, and the truth of knowing are aspects of truth, and truth is not an aspect of any of them. There is no Kantian escape route. Either knowledge is in truth or it is nowhere.

Message to the Survivors

Bravo! magazine, October 1997
A longa marcha da vaca para o brejo (1998, 2019)

As *higher education* is usually understood as mere training for better professions, one concludes, correctly, that every normal person is fit to receive it and that, in the selection of candidates, any elitism is unjust, even when it does not result from intentional discrimination, but merely from an unequal distribution of luck. However, if by *higher education* we mean the overcoming of intellectual limitations of one's environment, access to a universal view of things, the realization of the highest human spiritual qualities, then there exists within many aspirants a personal impediment that, sooner or later, will exclude them. Thus, higher education, in the strong and non-administrative sense of the term, continues to be, in fact and in law, a privilege for the few.

This impediment, thankfully, is not of an economic, social, ethnic, or biological nature. It is one of those human afflictions, like cancer and marital disputes, distributed more or less fairly among classes, races, and sexes. It is the only type of imperfection that could, with justice, be invoked as the basis for elitist selection but, in fact, does not need to be, as it operates that selection by itself, so naturally and spontaneously that the excluded are unaware of what they have lost and even feel quite satisfied with their condition, the most perfect harmony reigning between the few fortunate and the many unfortunate, safeguarded by the insurmountable distance that separates them.

What is this decisive impediment? What defect is it that forever distances a human being from the coveted privileges of a spiritual elite? Protein deficiency? Low IQ? Lack of a reading habit? Any of these explanations would return us to social, racial, and economic causes, which we have already excluded.

The factor I am referring to is neither material nor quantifiable, at least according to known methods. Sociology completely ignores it, and the Census Bureau does not recognize its existence. Nevertheless, it exists, has a name, and has been known for over two millennia. A trained mind immediately recognizes its presence, in an intuitive perception as simple as the difference between day and night.

The Greeks called it *apeirokalia* and considered that an individual affected by this formidable deficiency would be, in Plato's Academy, Aristotle's Lyceum, or Plotinus's auditorium, only an inconvenient and embarrassing presence, both for others and for himself.

Apeirokalia simply means "lack of experience of the most beautiful things." Under this term, it was understood that an individual who was deprived, during the decisive stages of his formation, of certain inner experiences that would awaken in him the craving for the beautiful, the good, and the true, could never understand the conversations of the wise, no matter how much knowledge he acquired and how well he was trained in literature and rhetoric. Plato would say that such a person is the eternal prisoner of the cave. Aristotle, in more technical language, said that the rites of mysteries are not intended to transmit a defined teaching to men but to leave a *deep impression* on their souls. Anyone familiar with the decisive importance that, in Aristotle's psychology, imaginative impressions have as a bridge between the senses and the higher activities of intelligence understands the extreme gravity of what he means: these deep impressions exert an illuminating and structuring impact on the soul. In their absence, intelligence flounders on the multitude of sensory data, failing to grasp the symbolic connection that, so to speak, gives flesh and blood to abstractions and prevents them from dispersing into an empty formalism, into a hallucinatory combination of empty syllogisms, into a pedantic verbosity that translates only the impotence of knowledge.

Of course, the inner experiences to which Aristotle refers are not provided only by the "rites of mysteries"—a category that naturally extends to the Catholic Mass, Jewish rites, Islamic canonical recitation, etc. Theater and poetry—when they have the spiritual support they had in Aeschylus and Sophocles—can eventually open the soul to an influx from above. To music—to certain kinds of music—one cannot deny the power to generate a similar effect. The mere contemplation of nature, a providential chance, or even, in sensitive souls, certain very special states of amorous ecstasy, when associated with an appeal to goodness and moral conversion (think of Raskolnikov before Sonia in *Crime and Punishment*), can place the soul in a kind of ecstasy that meets Aristotle's requirements and frees a man forever from the cave and *apeirokalia*.

However, more likely, the most intense experiences a man has had throughout his life will be of a nature to divert him from the kind of thing Aristotle has in mind, to throw him into a kind of an *Ersatz*, a surrogate soul quality required for access to the understanding of higher things. Because what characterizes the vivifying impression that the philosopher mentions, and whose opposite is designated by the term *apeirokalia*, is precisely the impossibility of separating, in its content, truth, goodness, and beauty. From Plato to Duns Scotus, there was not a single philosopher worthy of the name who did not emphatically proclaim the unity of these three aspects of Being. And here begins the problem: many men have never had any inner experience, no matter how wonderful and intense it may seem to them, in which the beautiful, the good, and the true did not appear separated by impassable chasms. These men are victims of *apeirokalia*, and many spiritual universes are forever closed to them.

Unfortunately, the number of these victims seems destined to grow. As early as 1918, Max Weber noted, as one of the prominent features of the emerging era, the loss of unity of ethical-religious, aesthetic, and cognitive values. Good, beauty, and truth were rapidly moving away from each other in a centrifugal movement, and as a result,

> precisely the ultimate and most sublime values have retreated from public life either into the transcendental realm of mystic life or into the brotherliness of direct and personal human relations. It is not accidental that our greatest art is intimate and not monumental, nor is it accidental that today only within the smallest and intimate circles, in personal human situations, in pianissimo, that something is pulsating that

corresponds to the prophetic pneuma, which in former times swept through the great communities like a firebrand, welding them together.[59]

The two fortresses of the sublime, which Weber mentions, did not take long to fall: mystical life, besieged by the tide of pseudo-esotericism that appropriated its language and prestige, ended up withdrawing to marginality and silence to avoid contamination from profane chatter and, at the moment it is spoken of the most, has become more inaccessible, perhaps, than at any other time in history.

Intimacy, scrutinized by TV and cinema, violated by state intrusion, turned into an object of hysterical exhibitionism and sadistic snooping, deprived of its language by the commercial and ideological exploitation of all its symbols, simply no longer exists. Day by day, the closest relationships, from father to son, from husband to wife, from friend to friend, and even from each to himself, tend to be governed by media stereotypes: with the language of feelings atrophied, each visualizes the other through the makeshift mirrors of fashion, without direct perception.

All the literature of the twentieth century reflects this state of affairs: first, the "incommunicability" of egos, then the suppression of the ego itself: the "dissolution of the character." But much has changed since Weber. As the end of the millennium approaches, what is understood by *mysticism* is a cerebralism of philologists; and by *intimacy*, at best, carnal contact between strangers, through a rubber film. The three supreme values are no longer just autonomous and strangers to each other, as Weber saw them in his time, but antagonistic. The beautiful is no longer unrelated to the good: it is decidedly evil; the good is decidedly hypocritical, pseudo-sentimental, and foolish; the truth is ugly, stupid, and depressing. Aesthetics celebrates vampires, the death of the soul, cruelty, the male who inserts his arm up to the elbow into another's anus. Ethics is reduced to an accusatory discourse of each against his enemies, allied with the most cynical self-indulgence; truth, to the arbitrary consensus of an academic community corrupt to the core.

Under these conditions, it is a true miracle that an individual can momentarily escape the leaden dome of *apeirokalia*, and another miracle that, upon returning to the nightmare he calls "real life," these moments do not seem to him merely a vain dream, worthy of being forgotten as soon as possible.

It is not surprising that, in most inhabitants of this world, especially in the upper classes, certain innate, intuitive capacities that for millennia were the

---

[59] *From Max Weber: Essays in Sociology* (New York: Oxford University Press, 1946)—Eds.

common possession of all human beings have atrophied to the point where their mere recollection seems an unattainable dream, surrounded by the mystical prestige of the unreal.

But nothing forbids a writer from addressing, in his works, the survivors of the spiritual shipwreck of the twentieth century, in the hope that they exist. Harassed by the joint siege of banality and brutality, these may still retain a vague suspicion that in their dreams and most hidden hopes there is a truth more certain than everything that today's world imposes on us with the label of "reality," guaranteed by the endorsement of the academic community and the Food and Drug Administration.

It is those that I address exclusively.

Chapter 3

The Crisis of Consciousness

Human Consciousness in Peril

A filosofia e seu inverso & Outros estudos (2012); *O mundo como jamais funcionou* (2014)

Once again, I invite readers to join me in a brief philosophical investigation. The subject—the foundations, or lack thereof, of human self-awareness—may seem distant from immediate political relevance, but those who read this article to the end will see that it is not so.

Never, as today, when an elite of enlightened bureaucrats whimsically disturbs the pillars of civilization like a troop of asylum escapees playing scientists in a nuclear laboratory, has it been so vital for every inhabitant of the planet to acquire a clear idea of the constants defining the human condition—before the very design of humanity fades from memory under the impact of globally imposed deforming experiments. However, one of these constants is precisely that every human constancy reveals itself, as if in a watermark, against the background of incessant historical change. Only the knowledge of the comparative history of civilizations and cultures shows, amid the almost hallucinatory variety of forms, the durability of the general structure of the human spirit. And, as what is at immediate risk of loss in the maelstrom of forced transformations is, above all, the unity of each individual's self-awareness—the fragmentation of culture resulting in the shattering of souls—it has never been more important to know the historical mutations of the "self" over the ages. This is necessary to distinguish in it what is accidental and transitory from what is essential, permanent, and indispensable for the ultimate defense of human dignity.

One of the richest deposits of materials for this study is autobiographies. The historical development of this literary genre clearly highlights the transformations of individual self-awareness over the ages, parallel to the changes in the respective experiences of time, memory, and the very act of narrating.

Among the many works on this subject, *Memory and Narrative: The Weave of Life-Writing* (The University of Chicago Press, 1998) by James Olsey, a professor of English at Louisiana State University, is one of the most useful. By focusing on the history of the autobiographical genre from Augustine's *Confessions* (397) to Samuel Beckett's scenic monologue *Company* (1979), Olsey delineates very clearly, in the journey between these two extremes, the progressive loss of the sense of unity of self-awareness. Without this unity, the very intention of narrating one's life becomes absurd.

The structural model of the narrative is the same in both cases. Augustine summarizes it with the example of prayer. When he recites a psalm, he already knows it by heart, entirely, beforehand. While reciting it, the words that follow aloud are updated in time against the static background of the complete text that remains in memory. Once the recitation is finished, the psalm has completed itself in time and is returned to memory, ready to be recited again and again. Almost all autobiographical writing has this structure. The life to be told is complete in memory, but it continues in the act of remembering it and continues after the narration is finished, returned to memory to be narrated again, read, or heard. What is the "substance" of this narrative? Time, but which time? The past, which no longer exists? The present, an infinitesimal atomistic moment that dissolves as soon as it appears? The future, which has only conjectural existence? The enigma appears more or less the same in the *Confessions* and in *Company*.

United in their common concern with time, memory, and the self, the two books could not be more antagonistic in their respective views.

Augustine's memories are the formal confession of a soul that, fully assuming authorship, responsibility, and the consequences of each of its acts, thoughts, and inner states, even the most obscure and remote in time, appears at its own judgment as if displaying an integral identity. Augustine achieves this because he composes his narrative before an all-knowing audience, God Himself. "Walking before God" means nothing other than acting and thinking in permanent confrontation with the symbol of "omniscience"—the unreachable and inescapable source of all consciousness, the only guarantee of the sincerity of thoughts, actions, and their recollection. Although the expression appears in the Bible, Augustine was the first to explicitly articulate the sense of the experience summarized there. The man who walks before God governs and conceives himself at every moment as if he were before the Final Judgment, in the complete form of his individual being consciously responsible for choosing his own eternal destiny. The complete life of the future is, therefore, the measure of the remembrance of the past, which the narrator undertakes in the present.

It is also from there that Augustine extracts the solution to the problem of the insubstantiality of time. God is not only omniscient but eternal. Boethius, later, will define eternity as "the whole, simultaneous and perfect possession of boundless life,"[60] but the concept is already implicit in Augustine. If the various moments have no unity among themselves, all that remains for them is to crumble into an immense nothingness. Only their total and simultaneous unity has existence, but this unity is eternity itself, and nothing more. Time, in itself, has no substantiality at all. It is only a mirage, a "moving image of eternity." If Augustine

---

[60] Boethius, *The Consolation of Philosophy.*—Eds.

can intellectually dominate his past, it is because he exposes it to the gaze of omniscience. If he can have the intuition of the continuity of his existence, it is because he sees it as a temporal reflection of eternity. The articulation of moral self-awareness is the same articulation of the three times on the axis of eternity.

The idea of the individual as a complex and dramatic unity that forms and assumes itself at the crossroads of the three times has become so incorporated into Western tradition that it inspired all modern personality psychology. Sixteen centuries after Augustine, Maurice Pradines, in his *Traité de Psychologie Générale* (1948), would define consciousness as "the memory of the past prepared for the tasks of the future." Even in Freud, to whom much of the blame (or credit) for the dissolution of the unity of the self is erroneously attributed, personality is the result of an arbitration progressively imposed by consciousness on the antagonistic impulses of the Id and the Super-ego. Nothing could celebrate the final victory of unity more clearly than the famous prophecy of the father of psychoanalysis: "Where Id was, there ego shall be."

A completely different perspective emerges in *Company*. Here, an old invalid man, on stage, listens to episodes of his life—the life of Samuel Beckett himself—narrated and commented on, in a monologue, by a faceless voice. Is it the "voice of consciousness"? Yes and no. It speaks of him either in the second person or the third. The one who, in the present, recalls the past, no longer knows if this past is his own, a third party's, or an invented character's. And the voice challenges the elderly man's sense of identity with a formidable question: if you don't remember your own birth, how can you be sure that the life you are recalling is the same as the one whose birth you think is yours?

Like Augustine, Beckett's character—indistinguishable from the author—sketches his memories on the contrasting surface provided by an invisible interlocutor who transcends the narrator and has the authority of a formative instance. The result, therefore, differs depending on the identity of this interlocutor. The eternity and omniscience of God give Augustine's biographical self-image the unity of a story assumed as a personally responsible creation. But Beckett's interlocutor is not omniscient: he is only more astute than the character. He is the critical reason, a corrosive potion that dissolves the temporal unity of the self through epistemological demands that he cannot meet. The bedridden elderly man does not even have the power to say "I" consciously, but perhaps he is also not to blame for his sins or credited with his achievements. The fragmented self, unable to tell its own story, is a victim of its own existence and therefore has no responsibility for it. Augustine's narrative rises from the dark depths of the heart to the divine light, which, in response, grants him participation in his own unity and clarity. Beckett's narrative comes from an external darkness that obscures the little light the ego thought it possessed.

In the transition from one extreme to another, Olsey documents some stages of the "crisis of narrative memory" that, like a guiding thread, runs through the entire history of modern Western mentality. He dates the beginning of the "crisis" to Jean-Jacques Rousseau's *Confessions* (1782), but he is wrong. It was already fully established in René Descartes' *Meditations on First Philosophy* (1641), which presents itself as an interior autobiography, the narrative of a cognitive experiment.[61] The horrendous confusion that the philosopher produces there between the concrete existential self and the abstract concept of the self as absolute self-awareness (*cogito ergo sum*), moving from the first to the second without noticing that he jumped from temporal order to deductive order, is one of the most prodigious mutilations ever imposed on the autobiographical consciousness of Western man. The entire problem of Beckett was already there. As Jean Onimus observed: "Set yourself in the Cartesian *cogito* at its point of origin, . . . and you will see Beckett's man in all the extent of his misfortune."[62]

The Cartesian self cannot narrate its history because it is only an isolated abstract form in space, severed from temporal experience. If the philosopher, however, presents it in narrative form, it is because, literally, he does not realize what he is doing. Cartesianism is not the opening chapter of the dissolution of narrative self-awareness—I attributed this dubious honor to the autobiographical fragments of Niccolò Machiavelli[63]—but it is an important episode in the process. Descartes' incongruity will be vastly amplified by Immanuel Kant through the idea of the "transcendental self." This astonishing creature of German philosophy has the authority to demarcate the boundaries of experience accessible to the poor existential self without being limited by them, and without opening even a narrow crack for the existential self to see beyond these boundaries. It is called "transcendental" precisely because it closes the doors to the "transcendent." Installed in the middle heights of the transcendental self, just a little above the existential self, Kant does not allow anyone to rise above him. The perverse satisfaction with which he believes to determine the "limits of human knowledge" shows that he had the awareness of being something like, in initiatory climbs, the "guardian of the portal," a kind of metaphysical Pasionaria shouting to the seekers of eternity: *No pasarán! No pasarán!*

---

[61] See further "Descartes and the Psychology of the Doubt," in Chapter Four.—Eds.

[62] [Free translation—Eds.] Jean Onimus, *Beckett: un Écrivain devant Dieu* (Desclée de Brouwer, 1967).

[63] See further "Machiavelli or the Demonic Confusion," in Chapter Four.—Eds.

I have no doubt that Beckett's interlocutor is Kant's transcendental self. Kant, on the one hand, believed that human knowledge is limited to sensory experience, space, and time; on the other hand, he said that the data from experience are a chaotic crumb, to which consciousness imposes its own unity. But, left to itself, without the background of eternity, consciousness itself crumbles. Even more clearly than in Descartes, the isolated and desperate man of Samuel Beckett is present and manifest in Kant's *Critique of Pure Reason* (1781). By prohibiting consciousness from accessing eternity, the transcendental self makes consciousness itself inaccessible and evanescent. Hence the apparent logic and profound absurdity of the demand that comes from the darkness: the idea that only the self that clearly remembers its own birth would have the authority to assert that its history is its own. This is entirely based on a Kantian prank, and this prank, in turn, has as its premise a colossal ineptitude: it assumes that the only legitimate self-awareness would be that of a being who could consciously observe its own birth. But for that, it would have to exist temporally before entering temporal existence. In real experience, every beginning, every gestation, occurs in darkness: light is a progressive conquest. Narrating one's life without being a witness to one's own birth is not an undue pretension: it is simply the real condition of human experience. The transcendental self, pretending to critique experience, establishes premises that deny the possibility of all experience and, therefore, of critique itself. Beckett is aware of the humorous nature of his speculations. But the Kantian humor is pathetically involuntary.

Olsey's study has the merit of elaborating the fundamental concept of the "crisis," but, in exemplifying it, it is very incomplete. Descartes is only mentioned in passing, and Kant's name does not even appear. Unforgivable is the omission of Proust, who spent his life trying to solve Augustine's problem of time, as well as Arthur Koestler, who, in *Darkness at Noon* (1940), documented the reduction of self-awareness, under the pressure of modern totalitarianism, to a "grammatical fiction."

The author also shows no sign of associating the "crisis of memory" with a parallel and inseparable process: the epidemic of consciously falsified autobiographical and biographical narratives for the sake of political propaganda, a phenomenon observed in France for at least a century before that not-very-conscious-liar Rousseau. It would be impossible, in fact, for the dissolution of self-awareness not to come along with the progressive loss of the sense of intellectual responsibility and the formidable expansion of amorality, manipulative cynicism, and sadistic cruelty.

The destruction of the civilizational foundations of human existence does not begin on battlefields or stock exchanges: it begins in quiet offices where seemingly harmless men—whether philosophers or UN bureaucrats—try to be wiser than God. It makes no sense to dissociate the crisis of self-awareness from the modern rejection of the sense of eternity, and it is not possible to accept the dissolution of self-awareness while trying to preserve, at the same time, high moral standards of conduct. At this end of an era, the historical consequences of intellectual decisions made three, four, five centuries ago take the form of totalitarianism, widespread violence, genocide, and, above all, the universal empire of lies.

Those who seek a remedy for these evils in political action will have to understand, sooner or later, that their root lies in the ethereal regions of abstract thought. And those who, out of personal affection, dedicate themselves to abstract thought must examine, with all the sobriety of consciousness, the devastating effects of seemingly harmless abstractisms created by philosophers of past centuries.

In this sense, philosophy is politics, and politics is philosophy.

The Unity of Subject and Object

A handout from the Philosophy Seminar, July 15, 1999

The modern philosophical cycle begins with the shift in focus that Descartes introduces to thought, diverting it from the "naive" certainty of the external world to the supposedly solid ground of the cogito. From then on, the subject, considered as a solitary soul engaging in dialogue within an environment devoid of beings and things, will be taken as the Archimedean point of all philosophical meditation. The solitary subject is directly linked to the universality of God, and, guaranteed by this link, can deduce the entire science of God, the cosmos, and himself from within, through deduction, disregarding the experience of the external world. Spinoza takes this to the extreme, pushing solitary deductivism and disdain for the experience of the external world to their ultimate consequences.

While the empiricist school emerges in England in reaction to this solipsistic extremism, it, from Locke to Hume, accepts only sensations as a foundation. These sensations, considered atomistically and summed inductively (the only accepted method), cannot provide the certainty of universal truths or even the unity of the thinking self.

Apparently, this school rejects the primacy of the self and seems to take us out of the Cartesian domain. However, this is a false impression. In reality, empiricism only regards objects in the external world as occasions for sensations, and since sensations occur in the subject, these objects are never viewed directly but always through the subject's perspective.

Subjectivism is the hallmark of all so-called modern philosophy, with little difference between the two rival schools, rationalist and empiricist.

This becomes evident in the final confluence of these two schools in Kant's critical philosophy, where the subject, through a priori forms, becomes the mold and reason for the unity of the world itself. The object, in this context, recedes to the unattainable distance of the "thing-in-itself," defined as what the object is, independently of what the subject knows of it, ultimately defined by its (albeit negative) dependence on the subject.

The priority of the subject over the object is thus the unwavering constant of the modern philosophical cycle. To go a step further, there are only two paths left. The first is to deny the subject itself, breaking down even the purely subjective unity bequeathed by Kant. This is the path taken by psychoanalysis, analytical philosophy, and deconstruction. The second path is to restore the ontological status of the object. Husserl attempted this path but, still captive to Cartesianism, reverted to taking the solipsistic consciousness as the starting point and could never free himself from the inevitably idealistic consequences of this approach.

In my view, the path to the restoration of the object must take a radically different direction.

This path involves denying the epistemological priority of the subject outright by simply acknowledging that it could not be a subject if it were not also an object. To continue along these lines, it is necessary to define what is meant by subject and object. The proposed definitions are as simple as can be imagined: the subject (of knowledge) is what receives information, and the object is what emits information, at least in the understanding of the subject. With these terms defined, we immediately understand that the subject, considered strictly as a subject distinct and separate from any object, could know nothing because it would not have itself as the object of its knowledge. The Cartesian *ego cogitans* cannot be a pure subject, as it knows something about itself and, therefore, has itself as an object.

More generally, no pure subject is conceivable, as it would only receive information without ever emitting it, and thus, it could know nothing about anything, not even about itself. In the very act of defining itself as a pure knowing subject, it would be asserting *ipso facto* that it knows nothing and cannot, therefore, be a knowing subject.

On the other hand, a purely objective entity that only emitted information without receiving any is inconceivable. This would be equivalent to pure action without any feedback, contradicting the very notion of the continuity of action over time and could only be fulfilled in the intrinsically absurd hypothesis of an action without duration.

Therefore, if the knowing subject cannot be what it is without also being an object, and if, on the other hand, the object cannot be a radical non-subject, the inevitable conclusion is that the condition of subject and the condition of object mutually demand each other and can only be separated in words. At best, subject and object are names of functions that, however, to be exercised, require each other not only in the subject but also in the object. Each of them possesses both functions and can only be subject and object to each other because each is, in itself, both things.

Up to now, all attempts to bring subject and object together—such as in scholastic realism or phenomenology—have tried to do so in the relationship between a given subject and a given object. But it is evident that this union could not take place on the level of mere relation if it were not already given in the constitution of each of them—that is, in the respective constitutions of two entities that are, each on its own, inseparably subjects and objects. Every skeptical doubt regarding human knowledge arises precisely from the hypothesis of a gap between subject and object, an hypothesis that cannot be proven and cannot be contested from the moment we take the pure knowing subject (solipsistic) as the starting point in the study of this relationship, and we take the terms of the relationship as if they were, one, the pure knowing subject, and the other, the pure known object. There is no way to bridge the gap between representation, which will always and inevitably be in the subject, and the represented object, which will always and by hypothesis be outside it.

But if we understand that the union of subject and object should not be sought in the relationship but, rather, before it, in the constitution of each of them—that is, in the respective constitutions of two entities that are, each on its own, inseparably subjects and objects—then we also understand that a union that is in the very constitution of an entity cannot be undone by the simple relationship it enters into with another entity. On the contrary, this relationship can only manifest, through the reciprocity of emitted and received information, the indissoluble union of subject and object, now considered not in each of these entities taken separately, but in the interrelation of the subjective-objective of one with the subjective-objective of another. This relationship is what we call knowledge, and it is essentially the union of subject and object, with the skeptical disjunction applying only *in verbis*. At a glance, all skeptical doubt is reduced to a mere word game. At the same time, the walls of the subjectivist prison are forever demolished, along with the columns of the Kantian palace.

May those who have eyes to see perceive the tremendous philosophical consequences of these observations and understand that the true principle of all science lies therein.

The Height of Human Progress

Diário do Comércio, February 4, 2008
A inversão revolucionária em ação (2015)

Sigmund Freud used to say that the history of Western thought had been marked by three humiliating defeats successively imposed on the presumptions of the human ego: first, Copernicus demonstrated that the planet we inhabit is not the center of the universe; then, Darwin taught that man is not a superior being, but merely an animal among others; finally, Freud himself provided proof that individual consciousness is not even the master of itself but the plaything of unconscious forces.[64]

The idea of the progress of knowledge as an exchange of grand illusions for increasingly depressing truths permeated so deeply into the worldview of the educated classes that other episodes in the history of ideas were interpreted according to it, almost automatically. Between Copernicus and Darwin, Newton and Galileo had taught that our impressions of the sensible world are subjective and deceptive, with only measurable quantities capable of being objects of certain knowledge. Kant demonstrated the impossibility of knowing anything positive about God and the immortality of the soul. Between Darwin and Freud, Marx revealed that the history of ideas itself is only the apparent externalization of hidden economic interests. Comte officially prohibited inquiries into what we cannot know through the methods of Newtonian science, and, finally, a contemporary of Freud, Max Weber, drew from this the most lethal of

---

[64] Sigmund Freud, *A General Introduction to Psychoanalysis,* trans. G. Stanley Hall (New York: Horace Livelight, 1920).—Eds.

consequences: not only are good and evil arbitrary choices, but scientific knowledge itself is not possible without some initial arbitrary choice.

In the following decades, the downgrading of the human species continued relentlessly. Behaviorism replaced the very notion of the "psyche" with a set of conditioned reflexes not much different from those determining the behavior of a rat or, ultimately, an amoeba. Structuralism and deconstruction abolished the Marxist notion of the meaning of History as a residue of humanistic illusions. Genetics, neurophysiology, brain-computer models, and pharmacologically-based psychiatry reduced to nothing the claims of Freudian psychology. Ecology portrayed humans as badly behaved and destructive beasts, harmful to nature. Finally, the philosopher Peter Singer elevated chickens and pigs to the status of human rights bearers, equal even to a sublime creature like himself.

Thus, one by one, the "narcissistic illusions"—as Freud called them—of a species that dared to proclaim itself the image and likeness of God came falling down. The history of scientific ideas, seen from this perspective, is a history of intellectual humility.

However, there are three problems here.

The first is that not all theories included in this narrative are equally true. Galileo made the Sun the center of the universe, not just the solar system. Marx swore that capitalism would restrict the market, instead of expanding it. Evolutionism remains a debatable hypothesis. And psychoanalysis has been so demoralized that Lacan, in an attempt to save it, had to discover an unconscious part in it and claim that this, and not what Freud knew, was genuine psychoanalysis. It makes no sense to equate scientific truths, dreadful errors, and idiotic fantasies as rising steps of cognitive ascent.

The second problem: each of the steps in this alleged ascent was climbed at the cost of some monstrous falsification of historical data. The same scheme was always used: to forcibly embed, in some past doctrine, meanings totally foreign to the time it was enunciated and to the mentality of its author.

Copernicus never imagined that heliocentrism would remove "man" from the top of the created universe. This interpretation was invented a century later by Giordano Bruno. And, to those who intended to draw some materialistic conclusion from it, Bruno himself warned: do that, and you will become so stupid as to doubt your own existence (this literally happened when deconstructionism proclaimed the "non-existence of the subject").

Darwin's doctrine, by placing the human being at the summit of animal evolution, could not simultaneously lower him to the level of any other beast. The very word "evolution" expresses an upward level, not a descent. This should be obvious at first glance, even without the help of the final paragraphs of *The Origin of Species*, which celebrate evolutionary ascent as a divine work of *intelligent design* (oh, horror!).

Freudian doctrine, yes, seems to lower the human being, insofar as it reduces consciousness to a product of unconscious factors. But, if the transition to the self-conscious level resulted from the destruction of narcissistic illusions of childhood, how could the destruction of yet another illusion be a lowering and not an ascent? Freud himself never gave up the bet that the Ego would eventually absorb and overcome the Id, which, incidentally, constituted the central promise of psychoanalysis. When speaking of the lowering of human pretensions, Freud used a figure of speech that unilaterally emphasized only one aspect of his own work, omitting the dialectical compensation of which he was perfectly aware. And he did the same with the teachings of Copernicus and Darwin to forcefully transform the two into precursors of himself.

From then on, making history of ideas through extemporaneous analogies became a universal trend, lowering the public understanding of the past to a succession of vulgar gossip against human dignity. The encyclopedic summary of these gossips constitutes the prevailing historical view, like a dogma of faith, in the minds of virtually all our contemporaries. It resurfaces daily in newspaper editorials, parliamentary speeches, and school essays, with global unanimity, and serves as an argument to justify political, economic, and strategic decisions, as well as to arbitrate domestic discussions and give the appearance of importance to nonsensical university theses.

The third problem is that none of those allegedly humiliating discoveries made the intelligentsia humbler. On the contrary: each one of them was celebrated as a victory of reason and enlightenment against the darkness of the past, resulting in increasingly delusional effusions of pride and increasingly unlimited claims to power.

Copernicus and Newton provided arguments for the revolutionaries of 1789 to concentrate more power in their hands than any tyrant of antiquity and kill more people in one year than the Inquisition had killed in three centuries.

Positivism and scientism gave birth to countless enlightened dictatorships, some of which understood the killing of priests, nuns, and Indians (especially Christianized Indians) as a superior expression of human rationality.

Marxism, I don't even need to say. Who doesn't know the *Black Book of Communism*?[65] Are the barbaric deeds it describes monuments to intellectual humility?

Behaviorism and subsequent psychological schools developed in their practitioners the ambition to shape others' behavior as if it were an industrial product. Ecology reinforced this ambition, creating global control projects that determine even what you can or cannot eat and force you to fill out a stack of forms to pick a bunch of bananas.

Eric Voegelin called "historiogenesis" the symbolic view of history as an ascending process that, culminating in the narrator's person, made his era the supreme holder of human knowledge. Initially, he thought that this scheme was an invention of modernity, but then he discovered that it already existed in ancient Egypt and Mesopotamia. Historiogenesis is a deforming mental tic that reappears in every era, thanks to the incoercible tendency of human beings to make themselves the navel of the universe.

Modernity only added the especially ridiculous detail of describing the glorious ascent leading to itself as a process of rational self-limitation and increasing intellectual humility. With this, the umbilical centric conception of history became a caricature of itself, consisting of the supreme intellectual glory of modern times.

Christopher Lasch: the New Elite and the Old Masses

O Imbecil Coletivo (1996, 2021)

The last warning left by Christopher Lasch: there is a new dominant elite in the world, distinct from the bourgeoisie. Its members do not rule through ownership of the means of production, but through information dominance. More ambitious than their predecessors, they are not satisfied with power over material wealth and people's labor force alone; they want to shape minds, values, lives, and the very essence of existence. They don't merely want to possess the world; they aim to reinvent it in their own image, regardless of the consequences (they call this "social engineering"—and it stings!). Like the bourgeoisie, they are steeped in false consciousness, using discourse to legitimize their interests in the name of

---

[65] Harvard University Press, 1999.—Eds.

everyone's well-being. However, unlike the bourgeoisie, they don't need intellectual intermediaries to create their narrative, and intellectuals, with the typical unfaithfulness of intermediaries, often change sides. This new class invents its own discourse and is immune to the vacillations of hired intellectuals because it comprises intellectuals themselves. We are in the midst of the tyranny of the *intelligentsia*.

This warning constitutes the central message of *The Revolt of the Elites*,[66] the last book prepared by the sociologist behind *The Culture of Narcissism* shortly before his death. The words of the dying carry weight that others lack. Christopher Lasch's words risk being dismissed lightly because—as with all his writings, which resonate primarily with university-educated readers—they address the same audience for whom they allocate a significant share of responsibility for the state of affairs in the world.

Their thesis, at first glance, isn't vastly different from James Burnham's in *The Managerial Revolution* (1941). Burnham heralded the rise to power of a new class of executives and technocrats, whose mastery of modern administration granted them greater influence than nominal capital owners.

However, during Burnham's time, the managerial class was quite distinct from the university *intelligentsia*. They were the technicians, the men of action who made decisions for pragmatic reasons, disregarding with sovereign disdain the subtleties of intellectuals, whom they contemptuously called "eggheads." The intellectuals, at that time, were thoroughly contaminated with Marxism, viewing the managers as a disguised—and therefore doubly odious—expression of the old capitalist class. They did everything to undermine Burnham's thesis. Who would have thought back then that they themselves would eventually become, through a twist of history, the protagonists of the managers' revolution? The new class referred to by Lasch occupies the same position in the system as Burnham's managers, but their minds are composed—yolk, white, and shell—of pure university material: intellectuals have become the managers.

The causes that led to this turn of events are well known. Administration became even more complex, requiring experts in sociology, psychology, communications, and related fields—who had to recruit them from the ranks of the *intelligentsia*. Simultaneously, business leaders became aware of their role as virtual shapers of a new culture: managers became intellectuals. Added to this was the fact that disillusionment among intellectuals with Marxism led them to

---

[66] Christopher Lasch, *The Revolt of the Elites and the Betrayal of Democracy* (New York: W. W. Norton & Company, Inc., 1996).—Eds.

abandon their role as auxiliary forces for a hypothetical revolutionary proletariat and decide to act on their own: egghead-managers became social engineers, inventors of new ethical and political criteria, imposed upon populations reduced to the role of dazzled and astonished spectators by the alliance of a modernizing state with the omnipresent market. The revolution, forgotten by the masses, became the occupation of the elites.

Lasch's book does not detail how this new class came to power but, in compensation, it extensively describes and discusses its ideas and value criteria. These criteria, transmitted to the masses through the educational system and the communications industry, quickly take on the function of unquestionable dogmas in their minds, inspired by the inconceivable mixture of cultural relativism and moral absolutism that today constitutes the formula for "political correctness." The formula is extravagant: members of the new elite see no contradiction between demanding unrestricted sexual freedom and calling for severe legal punishment for a lustful gaze occasionally cast by a male at a pair of female legs; nor between unrestricted freedom of speech and repressive policing of vocabulary to remove any expressions capable of offending political, racial, sexual sensitivities, etc. But the peculiarity of their *forma mentis* has an explanation. According to Karl Marx, bourgeois thinkers tended to think in empty abstract categories because they lived far removed from direct engagement with matter. Lasch extends this diagnosis to the new elite: "They [thinking classes] live in a world of abstractions and images, a simulated world that consists of computerized models of reality—'hyperreality,' as it has been called—as distinguished from the palpable, immediate, physical reality inhabited by ordinary men and women."[67] Their main function is to create, interpret, and market symbols, which is why one of the scholars cited by Lasch, Robert Reich, collectively called them "symbolic analysts." Hence their tendency to imagine reality as pliable and soft material, docile to any engineering: "Their belief in the 'social construction of reality'— the central dogma of postmodernist thought—reflects the experience of living in an artificial environment from which everything that resists human control (unavoidably, everything familiar and reassuring as well) has been rigorously excluded."[68] Symbolic analysts have such difficulty adapting to the limits of physical reality that they spend a good part of their lives in athletic and dietary efforts to prolong their youth indefinitely, but they continue to die at the same age as ordinary people who resign themselves to the inevitability of aging and death.

---

[67] Lasch (1996), 20.—Eds.
[68] Ibid.—Eds.

The new class does not live apart only from the physical world, but also from the other classes, much more than the old bourgeoisie. Observing an unprecedented elitization of American society, Lasch writes: "There has always been a privileged class even in America, but it has never been so dangerously isolated from its surroundings." Removed, first of all, geographically: ensconced in glass towers and gated communities; secondly, culturally: the new class comes entirely from a few hundred elite institutions where education is infinitely better than in the public school system; and thirdly, linguistically: they master codes and information incomprehensible to the mass of the population, and further increase the distance through the abusive use of specialized jargon.

Isolated from the present world, hypnotized by incalculable power that leads them to believe they are at the pinnacle of civilization, symbolic analysts end up isolating themselves from the past and their cultural heritage. At the height of their intellectual prestige, they revert to a kind of barbarism that characterized, in José Ortega y Gasset's classic analysis, *the revolt of the masses*.[69] The mass-man, according to Ortega, was the presumptuous, resentful, and arrogant heir who squandered the painfully accumulated heritage of ancestors; he was the spoiled child, the *señorito satisfecho* incapable of recognizing any moral or cultural superiority. In the name of inconsequential fashions and abstract utopianism, this type threw away all values and knowledge that he could no longer comprehend, attempting to improve the world but only succeeding in plunging it from crisis to crisis. Hence the importance of the elites: "From Ortega's point of view, one that was widely shared at the time, the value of cultural elites lay in their willingness to assume responsibility for the exacting standards without which civilization is impossible."[70] But now the situation has changed. Instead of the masses, Lasch says:

> Today it is the elites, however . . . who have lost faith in the values, or what remains of them, of the West. For many people the very term 'Western civilization' now calls to mind an organized system of domination designed to enforce conformity to bourgeois values . . . All these habits of mind, I submit, are now more characteristic of the upper levels of society than of the lower or middle levels.[71]

---

[69] *The Revolt of the Masses* (New York: W. W. Norton & Company, Inc, 1932); *La rebelión de las masas* (Madrid: Revista de Occidente, 1930)—Eds.
[70] Ibid., 26.—Eds.
[71] Ibid., 25–27.—Eds.

In short, Ortega heard the rooster crow but did not predict where it would crow the next day.

What to make of all this? The importance and value of these analyses are evident. Their timeliness remains to be assessed. To many, they may seem bold and intriguing in their novelty, especially to those still bound to a Marxist view of classes and ideologies (though one doesn't need to be Marxist in all other respects, of course). But, just as Lasch's diagnosis seemed identical to Burnham's while being different, it also seems different from Ortega's while being identical. Because Lasch—like almost all intellectuals outside of Spain, except for a few scholars of Hispanic affairs like Ernst-Robert Curtius—read Ortega very poorly. He understood him solely through *La rebelión de las masas*—a collection of incomplete articles, as the author himself repeatedly (and unsuccessfully) warned. He didn't even glance at the rest of the philosopher's works, where the antecedents and continuation of his argument are found. There, he could discover, for example, that Ortega's distinction between elite and masses has no socioeconomic sense but is only psychological and ethical, inspired, as it is, by the Hindu doctrine of castes and *dharma*, which Western sociology terms do not translate: there are "men of the elite" among proletarians and "mass-men" in the dominant class. He could discover, worse still, that by "masses," Ortega specifically meant—as is explicitly stated in *España invertebrada* (1921)—"the masses in those groups which have the greatest potentiality of power—the middle and the upper class,"[72] especially the masses of students who filled the universities, that is, the future egghead-managers in Lasch's analysis. In *Misión de la Universidad*[73] (1944), a text almost contemporary with *Rebelión*, Ortega made it clear that the new barbarian he called mass-man was "above all the professional man, more learned than ever before, but at the same time more uncultured—the engineer, the physician, the lawyer, the scientist." Ortega's analysis is from 1928. It remained unknown to the world, buried under the false connotation almost universally attributed to his term "masses," to the point that there have been two images of Ortega since then: one of a center-left Ortega in Spain, which read him; one of an extreme-right Ortega in the rest of the world, which read his interpreters. Lasch's analyses may seem unprecedented to the non-Hispanic world.

However, we, in Brazil, cannot appeal to the tattered excuse that we are not Spanish. Here, the revolt of the elites was diagnosed five decades ago by the Austro-Brazilian historian and literary critic Otto Maria Carpeaux (who read Ortega very well). In a memorable—and unjustly forgotten—essay published in

---

[72] Ortega y Gasset, *Invertebrate Spain* (New York: Howard Fertig, 1974).—Eds.
[73] *Mission of the University* (London and New York: Routledge, 1991), 45.—Eds.

the volume *The ashes of purgatory*[74] under the title "The idea of university and the ideas of the middle classes," he attributed the phenomenon of revolutionary barbarism mainly to the "intellectual proletariat" that universities annually dumped into the market to form the new rising middle class: "This new middle class is a child; but a dangerous child, full of the resentments of the declassed, furious against books it no longer knows how to read and whose lessons no longer guarantee social ascent."[75] It is an almost literal description of the hordes of daddy's little boys who now demand the removal of Shakespeare and Homer from American university curricula and their replacement with "non-colonialist," "non-*machista*," etc., literature.

But let us not disregard Christopher Lasch's last warning, however belated it may be. For the intellectual decline in America went much deeper than he imagined. It even contaminated its most lucid critic. Were it not so, he would not dedicate so many pages to the meticulous examination of second-rate ideologues, of merely local importance, while simultaneously omitting a closer look at the philosopher from whom his book draws inspiration as an overt postmodern counterpart to *La rebelión de las masas*. Nor would he sacrifice the idols he unmasks by methodically adding the cautious qualifier "and women" to the word "men" when used in the sense of *humanity*. Nor would he suggest, as a remedy for the diagnosed malady, a return to the tradition of Deweyan pragmatism—a tradition that, by depreciating the notion of "objective truth" in favor of mere useful consensus, has done much to weaken the American mind and generate the current state of affairs. For these weaknesses, and above all for the inescapable tendency to provincially attribute universal significance to everything that happens in the United States, Lasch's work is itself, to some extent, a symptom of the situation it describes.

However, this situation is so intellectually depressing that in the midst of it, it became a notable achievement for someone finally to grasp the social reality that Ortega diagnosed in 1928 and our Carpeaux in 1942. And if there is an indisputable benefit of Christopher Lasch's book, it is that, both by what the author reveals of others' fragility and what he unintentionally exposes of his own, it can help eradicate any rustic fascination with intellectual life in the so-called First World.

---

[74] Otto Maria Carpeaux, *A cinza do purgatório,* "A idéia de universidade e as idéias das classes médias" (Rio de Janeiro: CEB, 1942).—Eds.
[75] [Free translation] Ibid.—Eds.

The East Versus the West

Unpublished manuscript, 2017

The total destruction of the West would not even be conceivable if only criticism, no matter how corrosive, were opposed to the real and supposed evils of the targeted civilization. It was necessary to raise on the horizon the image of an alternative, an anti-model invested with all the virtues lacking in the criticized civilization. Only then would the criticism lose the air of mere theoretical objection and transform into practical guidance towards a real goal. This goal, in turn, could not be reduced to the embellished image of a future socialism, which, precisely because it was only a hypothetical ideal, would lose half of its attacking power.

This is how, almost automatically, the cursed West found itself opposed to the most obvious and easiest alternative model, whose simple location in space seemed predestined for this role: the East.

The invasion of Eastern ideas began in the nineteenth century with Madame Blavatsky's Theosophical Society, university Orientalism, and the trend of Oriental themes in the visual arts and music. It soon underwent a considerable upgrade by the hands of Carl Jung, the highly erudite Romanian historian Mircea Eliade, and numerous first-rate scholars such as Heinrich Zimmer, Karlfried Graf Dürckheim, and Ananda K. Coomaraswamy.

But until then, it was nothing more than the rescue of spiritual, intellectual, and aesthetic values of genuine worth, which could do no harm to the civilization of the West. On the contrary, the fact that it opened itself to these values only demonstrated the authenticity of its universalistic pretensions and its ability to absorb, without prejudice, all sorts of knowledge.

The cult of the East only took on the features of a bellicose confrontation through the works and influence of a figure considered one of the greatest incarnations of reactionary traditionalism in the twentieth century, whose decisive contributions to the "Spirit of '68" are still the most poorly kept open secret in the world.

I am referring to the French doctrinaire René Guénon (1886–1951), who ended his days in Egypt as a devout Muslim. His book *Orient et Occident* (*East and West*), published in 1924 under the guise of a mere comparative study, is a true declaration of war, culminating in the outline of a plan for the cultural and even military occupation of the West by Eastern forces, especially Islamic ones.[76]

Whether out of genuine ignorance or cunning, Guénon reduces the civilization of the West to a mixture of capitalism, scientific materialism, and pseudo-popular religions. The last remnants of spirituality he sees in it are the decadent Masonry and Catholicism reduced to an "exoteric"[77] perspective, already without contact with the "sources of the primordial Tradition." Sources located, of course, in the East, more specifically in the regions of Central Siberia, Malaysia, and Tibet, traversed by Ferdinand Ossendowski in 1920 according to the narrative of *Bêtes, Hommes et Dieux*[78] (1922), where the famous explorer claims to have penetrated the underground sanctuary of the "King of the World." Coincidence or not, these regions are the same where the majority of the "Seven Towers of the Devil" are concentrated, centers of diabolical influence on the entire planet, according to Guénon himself.[79]

Of all the signs of Catholic spiritual vigor at the time—the apparitions of Fatima, the miracles of St. Padre Pio, the flourishing of Catholic intellectual life in the first half of the twentieth century—Guénon wanted to know nothing. For him, everything that did not have a direct channel with the unknown temples of Agartha and Shamballa was at most *exoteric* if not pure and simple anti-tradition.

From this one-sided image of a spiritually devastated West, Guénon saw only three possible outcomes: the definitive fall into barbarism, the restoration of the

---

[76] Carvalho suggests the reading of his essay "In the Claws of the Sphinx: René Guénon and the Islamization of the West" (2016), which is partially reproduced in this *Reader* (see Chapter 8) and published in full in the author's posthumous work *O saber e o enigma* [Knowledge and the enigma], (2022).—Eds.

[77] He gives universal application to the distinction between "esoterism" and "exoterism," which, strictly speaking, only formally applies to the Islamic case. ["Religion is considered a purely exoteric, more of a popular element, which has divine authority only in social and external aspects. As for internal aspects, to access them, you would need an esoterism that would allow you to understand what Frithjof Schuon called the 'transcendent unity of religions' . . . In the explicit, legal and official sense, the distinction between exoterism and esoterism only exists in a single tradition: Islam. It corresponds to the distinction between *shari'ah* and *tariqa*. On the one hand, religious law is mandatory for everyone; on the other, the spiritual "way," of free choice, only for selected and gifted people. Excerpt from Carvalho's book *O saber e o enigma*.—Eds. Although "exotericism" and "esotericism" are more common than "exoterism" and "esoterism," this *Reader* adopted the latter, as used by the translators of Rene Guenon's works, when Carvalho is addressing the project of power of the French thinker.—Eds.]

[78] Ferdinand Ossendowski, *Beasts, Men and Gods* (New York: E. P. Dutton & Company, 1923).—Eds.

[79] *René Guénon et les Sept Tours du Diable* (Paris: Maisnie Trédaniel, 1990).

Catholic Church under the secret guidance of Islamic spiritual masters, and the occupation of the West by Islam, either through cultural invasion or *manu militari*.

In contrast to the caricatural reductionism of his view of the West, the image he had of Eastern civilizations was so charmingly idealized that he even proclaimed that Bolshevism would never penetrate China, so solid were the "spiritual defenses" (sic) of Chinese tradition. Not only did it penetrate, but it established a lasting genocidal tyranny whose violence far surpassed that of the Soviet Union and its satellite countries. A powerful magnet in the vicinity must have momentarily disoriented the needle of the "infallible compass" that Michel Valsan believed to see in René Guénon.

The following generation of Guénonians did not change their rhetoric. Seyyed Hossein Nasr, in *Knowledge and the Sacred* (1981), describes the entire intellectual history of the West as mere preparation for the advent of the Savior, René Guénon. In *Ideals and Realities of Islam* (1966), he only contrasts the beautiful ideals of Islamic civilization with the sad realities of the West, without realizing that this comparison of the virtues of one with the flaws of the other could well be inverted.

For decades, Orientalist devotion was a private cult within groups of intellectuals and wealthy enthusiasts, inspiring countless pilgrimages in search of "wisdom"[80] and the establishment of meditation and spiritual retreat centers such as Monte Verità in Ascona,[81] Switzerland, Hermann Keyserling's "School of Wisdom" in Darmstadt, Germany, and Georges Gurdjieff's famous castle at Prieuré des Basses Loges in Avon, France.

From the 1950s onwards, however, largely promoted by the show business industry and celebrities in literature and the arts, the trend of Eastern doctrines and practices expanded to vast segments of the population in Europe and especially in the USA. This constituted a phenomenon that can only be accurately described as *mass deculturation*—certainly the roughest blow suffered by Western civilization before the Islamic invasion that would come in the 1990s.

The contribution of the *beat generation* poets to the popularization of the Eastern trend was not insignificant:

Not only did the Beats adapt the wisdom teachings of the East to a new, peculiarly American terrain, they also articulated this teaching in the

[80] Harry Oldmeadow, *Journeys East: 20th Century Western Encounters With Eastern Religious Traditions* (Bloomington: World Wisdom Books, 2004).
[81] Martin Green, *Mountain of Truth: The Counterculture Begins: Ascona, 1900–1920* (University Press of New England, 1986).

vernacular, jazzy rhythms of the street, opening up what had been the domain of stuffy academics and stiff translators . . . the voices of American poets recounted the teachings of the Buddha to the general public for the first time.[82]

In 1962, with the founding of the Esalen Institute in Big Sur, California, the "spiritual" revolt against modern Western culture had already reached the dimensions of a unified and self-conscious movement. The Institute quickly became the focal point of what would later be designated as the *New Age*.

To further aggravate the situation, both in America and Europe, the Orientalist wave came together with a new style of cultural criticism that spread rapidly in the media and universities, represented by the Frankfurt School and figures like C. Wright Mills, Margaret Mead, and Saul Alinsky, among others. From their writings, modern Western civilization emerged, in the mildest of hypotheses, exactly as René Guénon had described it: an *anomaly*, a deviation from the universal human pattern, a disease that had to be eliminated at all costs. Although operating in apparently distinct fields, culturally, New Age and New Left were working towards the same end. In fact, without the concurrent contribution of the New Age, the New Left would have been confined to the superficial field of politics *stricto sensu*, without support in the tremendous revolution of customs, feelings, and lifestyles that marked the 1960s and 1970s.[83]

Here, the strict adherent of Guénon or Frithjof Schuon may argue that their masters, as well as all "authentically traditional" esoteric organizations, abhor the New Age and therefore cannot have anything to do with the vulgar Orientalism of Esalen and the Beats or any other form of "pseudo-initiation" or "counter-initiation." But this argument is ineffective, as noted by one of the most eminent disciples and interpreters of René Guénon,

> hostile in principle to a world governed by that metaphysical 'Newtonian' law called 'cyclical degeneration,' initiatic organizations and secret societies cannot play anything but a double role, apparently contradictory but, *in re*, complementary: to restore, to each 'qualified' individual, the level of original consciousness, designated as the primordial or Adamic state, and, in a less confessable manner, to

---

[82] Carole Tonkinson (ed.), *Big Sky Mind. Buddhism and the Beat Generation* (New York: Riverhead, 1995).
[83] Andrew Jamison and Ron Eyerman, *Seeds of the Sixties* (Berkeley: University of California Press, 1994).

accelerate in a 'subversive' mode the process of collective decay that alone will allow the advent of a new cycle.[84]

You couldn't ask for a more explicit confession of the discreet partnership of "initiation" with "pseudo-initiation" and "counter-initiation."

The Intellectuals and Time

O Globo, June 22, 2003
A felicidade geral da nação (2023)

Since the eighteenth century, the main driving force in Western societies has been the "progressive" intellectual class—reformist or revolutionary. Their ideas, initiatives, and influence precede and guide the actions of other classes, so much so that in any modern nation, no law, institution, or commonly used argument cannot be traced back to its obscure origins in the discussions of small groups of intellectuals. The expansion of beliefs in concentric circles is now a well-known process, formalized as a technique in the discipline of "social engineering." International organizations like the UN and UNESCO, headquarters of activist intellectuals, have specialized courses for trainers of "social movements:" in every "spontaneous" protest by the poor, hungry, marginalized, and abandoned, indigenous people, beggars, prostitutes, and street children, there is always the hand of some technician in the service of planetary administration. That a greater power uses the small and helpless as weapons to destroy intermediate powers and concentrate all means of action in its hands is undoubtedly one of the cyclical constants in world history. The novelty is that today the process is conscious, organized, scientific—and, from planning to the last details of execution, the work of intellectuals.

If, despite this evidence, the intellectual class has no awareness of being the ruling class, if its members do not feel the weight of the responsibilities of supreme leaders of the historical process, it is partly because it does not suit them, partly because it is in the nature of intellectual power to act in the long term, so that its holders rarely live long enough to see the results of their ideas, let alone to answer for them.

---

[84] [Free translation—Ed] Jean Robin, *Les Sociétés Secrètes au Rendez-Vous de l'Apocalypse* (Paris: Guy Trédaniel, 1985), 13.

There's nothing more dangerous than an activist intellectual when joining others in the effort to forget what everyone did yesterday. Each new project for a "better world" was born this way—and there's no need to say how they end.

A certain lack of commitment to practical effects is also necessary for inner freedom, without which there is no intellectual life. Ernest Renan confessed that he could not think without ensuring that the ideas he thought would not have any consequences. But do not think that this is the height of irresponsibility. Renan, in order to be able to write delightfully, demanded only the right not to be always taken seriously. That's not even the height of it: it is the ease with which so many intellectuals enjoy this freedom while making plans for the future of society and, all the while, growing impatient with the world that does not obey them. Ninety percent of the stylish opinions in circulation could not have been produced without this delirium of omnipotence: the total absence of moral scruples combined with complete mastery of the means to change the world.

* * *

The reduction of the historical process to economic causes is generally considered a doctrine of "vulgar Marxism" in contrast to "authentic Marxism," supposedly much more differentiated and subtle.

One of the claims that support this certainty is that "Marx himself" recognized the existence of other relevant historical forces, affirming that economic causes only predominate "in the end."

It is also claimed that Marx, at one point, expressed surprise at the fact that the plays of Sophocles or Shakespeare retained their dramatic force long after the socio-economic conflicts of the context wherein they were produced had dissolved.

However, regarding the first assertion, the fact is that in Marx's own work, explanations using economic causes prevail overwhelmingly, with not a single example of a historical event attributed to "other forces." The acknowledgment of their existence remains an abstract, generic hypothesis with no function in the explanatory machinery of Marxism.

As for his surprise at the permanence of the classics, what does it reveal other than the underlying expectation that, if things were not like that, all creations of the spirit would dissipate along with the economic conditions that supposedly motivated them?

There is no "intellectually noble Marxism" in contrast to "vulgar Marxism." All Marxism is vulgar.

Dreaming of the Theory of Everything

Diário do Comércio, December 2, 2012
Os histéricos no poder (2018)

Perfect logical proof is independent of human passions and whims. It disregards witnesses and even the existence of human beings. It imposes itself with the impersonality of earthquakes and planetary cycles. However, these are, on the scale of the universe, limited events. Infinitely above them, the perfect logical proof imposes itself with the absolute authority of divine will.

One who possesses a perfect logical proof can accept disagreement as a fact, not as a right. Ultimately, he will explain every divergence as a result of ignorance or perversion and, sooner or later, will wish to suppress it through indoctrination or force.

Fortunately, perfect logical proofs only exist in the ideal realm; they do not concern the realities of the world. Even the most exact science admits that it exists in a realm, not of definitive truths, but of probabilities and uncertainties. This does not prevent many scientists from continuing to dream of the "theory of everything": the unified and complete explanation of nature and everything that exists within it—including human beings with all their thoughts, desires, emotions, beliefs, and values.

Devotees of this ideal, when they speak of it, hasten to acknowledge that "we are still far" from achieving it. The apparent modesty of this confession conceals the faith that it will be achieved. It also includes the forgetfulness that, in the past, there were those who believed they had already achieved it, at least possessing in broad outlines the founding principles of the entire nature and being capable, therefore, of applying them to all domains of knowledge and action, shaping society, laws, culture, education, and the human mind.

In none of these cases did the foundation reach the level of a perfect logical proof. It always included some unproven, sometimes incongruent or incomprehensible assumptions. But, in any case, compared to the rest of the opinions in circulation, the "general theory" seemed to be the closest to a perfect logical proof, making it difficult for its spokespersons to resist the temptation to arrogate the unlimited authority of a divine commandment, stifling all opposition as irrational and unscientific.

This happened at least three times in history. The first was when Sir Isaac Newton, having successfully deduced some natural phenomena from mechanical principles, expressed the hope that soon all other phenomena could be explained by the same principles. The subsequent development of the sciences showed that the dream was impossible.

However, in the eighteenth century, as Sir Isaac's prestige spread throughout Europe, this dream was taken as reality and consecrated as a doctrine under the name of "mechanicism." Soon, mechanicism transformed into a social reform project and began to cut off heads—including those of some "mechanicists" dissatisfied with the political consequences of the doctrine.

The second time was when Charles Darwin's evolutionary doctrine, barely published, and although it was not a theory of everything but a comprehensive explanation of the variety of living beings, was already applauded as the general key to human history and the scientific foundation of both race war and class struggle. Adopted with slight modifications by the two totalitarian regimes vying for power in the early twentieth century, it served as the ideological foundation for the organized killing of around 200 million human beings.

The third was the proclamation of Marxism as the supreme scientific explanation of historical evolution and, in the words of Jean-Paul Sartre, "the unsurpassed philosophy of our time." Look how that turned out.

In all three cases, the pious attempt to dig an impassable gap between the "purely scientific" core of these theories and their malevolent historical-social effects is futile, attributing the latter exclusively to subsequent ideological distortion and contamination of "pseudoscience." Scientific theories do not descend readymade from the heaven of pure ideas. All carry at their core some ideological element, however discreet and unwanted, which sooner or later rises to the surface of history.

Newton did not conceive his theory of gravity just to explain certain facts of nature but as part of a comprehensive project to destroy Trinitarian Christianity and replace it with a religion of "absolute unity" inspired by esotericism.[85] One must be very naive not to notice the reach of the underlying totalitarian ambition.

Darwin and Marx were much more explicit about the foreseeable consequences of their theories: the former accepted genocide as a normal fact of nature, the latter as an indispensable instrument for the establishment of the socialist paradise.

The utopian delight with which so many scientists dream of the "theory of everything" and strive to refine logical instruments to substantiate it does not seem to be a harbinger of better days for the human species.

---

[85] On this topic see John Maynar Keynes lecture "Newton, the Man" (1942) and Michael White "The Last Sorcerer" (New York: Basic Books, 1997).—Eds.

Fashionable Prejudice

Bravo! magazine, August 2000

The comparison of value between cultures is inevitable.

As an unconditional admirer of the playwright Ariano Suassuna, I write this article to suggest that the Suassuna theoretician of culture resign and go home to write new plays, something he hasn't done for quite some time.

I began to consider this suggestion on the day he, in a magazine article,[86] accused Gilberto Freyre of being racist for writing, in *The Masters and the Slaves,*[87] that in the confrontation between the Portuguese and the indigenous, the more advanced culture had the upper hand over the backward one. I responded, in the same magazine, that attributing the victory of one people over another to cultural factors instead of to racial superiority was, by definition, the opposite of racism. It was also a well-known fact that Freyre became famous in the 1930s precisely for opposing the racial theories then in vogue with the cultural explanations he learned from Franz Boas at Columbia.

Unhappy to find himself caught in the act of nonsense, Suassuna came back swinging in the next issue of the magazine, alleging three reasons:

1. There are indications that Freyre, in his youth, before studying with Boas, had racist ideas.

2. By admitting the superiority of one culture over another, Freyre simply transferred prejudice from the racial to the cultural realm. In reality, all cultures are equal: there are no better or worse ones.

3. Believing in cultural superiority is the sin of Eurocentrists who "do not love our land."

Calling them "reasons" is a euphemism. The first is a fool's trick, the second is fashionable prejudice, the third is an involuntary joke.

1. The Gilberto that Suassuna accused of racism was the anthropologist from Columbia, author of *The Masters and the Slaves.* Suddenly he is no longer: he is a provincial teenage Gilberto, imbued with foolish ideas that he would later abandon during his learning at Columbia and openly contest in *The Masters and the Slaves.* First, Suassuna plucks a sentence from the book and points to it as proof that Gilberto is racist. Once it is proven that there is no

---

[86] "Biologia e Cultura," *Bravo!* Magazine, issue 33, 2000.—Eds.
[87] *The Masters and the Slaves: A Study in the Development of Brazilian Civilization* (California: University of California Press, 1987); *Casa-Grande e Senzala* (Rio de Janeiro: Maia & Schmidt, 1933)—Eds.

racism in the sentence, the accuser, to avoid admitting that he was wrong, alleges that the defendant was racist before writing it. The name for this, in legal practice, is chicanery.

2. Then, to restore the impugned accusation in the field of textual confrontations through tortuous insinuations, Suassuna seeks to give a racist connotation to the idea that there are superior and inferior cultures. He knows perfectly well that this insinuation is false, firstly because if culture is not conditioned by race, if men of any race can participate in any culture and become expressions of it—like the black Pushkin is a high expression of Russian culture or the Pole Conrad is of English culture—then obviously, the judgment made about a culture does not imply any assertion about races.

Even discounting the dishonesty of the insinuation it conveys, it remains to discuss, in itself, the belief in the absolute equivalence of cultures, in favor of which Suassuna dispenses with providing any argument, limiting himself to affirming it with the naive and dogmatic faith of someone who has never thought about the matter.

Now, cultures are composed of human works and acts—a domain that, not being determined by natural fate (including that of race), is entirely subject to decisions, choices, preferences, and exclusions, implying therefore, at every turn, the idea of "better." The pursuit of the better guides everything from the decisions of legislators to the choices of a theme by an artist, of a material and form by a builder, of a location in the forest by a hunter, of a stretch of river by a fisherman, of a wife by a man, and of a husband by a woman. Everything, absolutely everything that happens in the domain of culture is always something that could have been done differently, but human beings chose to do as they did because it seemed the best to them. To say better and worse is to say superior and inferior. Without this pair of concepts, nothing in the cultural world makes sense.

The assertion that there are no superior and inferior cultures implies that within each of them, there is also no better or worse: that a clumsy and foolish warrior chief is as good as a victorious hero, that false and ineffective science is as good as efficient and true, that a failed and crude work of art is as good as a realized and perfect one, that an inhibiting and paralyzing religion is as good as one that opens to the human spirit the knowledge of the deepest mysteries of souls and worlds.

If within each culture there are better and worse manifestations, why should then the comparison of value between manifestations of the same genre in different cultures be prohibited? Either each culture is a closed, incommunicable whole, metaphysically sealed, or this comparison is possible, legitimate, and necessary.

Furthermore, for cultures to be absolutely autonomous and non-comparable in the field of values, it would be necessary to reduce human beings to what their culture has made of them, stripping them of all the general characteristics of the biological species that unite them to all other humans, and in the name by which they may have rights and values that their culture does not recognize, but that exist for the rest of humanity. For example, the unwanted baby in certain indigenous tribes, before the advent of the Brazilian National Indigenous People Foundation, only had one right: to be buried alive. In this case, if we respect cultural relativism, we deny these babies the right to life, which we unconditionally defend for white, black, Arab, and Chinese babies, granting indigenous society a right that we deny to our own: the right to rid itself of socially inconvenient individuals. Cultural relativism, ultimately, results in absolutizing the autonomy of cultures, denying the unity of the human species, which, however, is implied in the very notion of "culture" as a specifically human phenomenon that distinguishes our societies from animal societies. Besides being morally monstrous, it is logically absurd.

More than just fair and legitimate, the comparison of value between cultures is indeed inevitable for anyone who, starting from their native culture, tries to understand any other. If the traveler does not realize that in France university education is "better" than in Brazil, that in Brazil racial relations are "better" than in the United States, that in the United States education is "better" than in Zambia, that the English political regime is "better" than that of Cuba, then they are simply blind and foolish. *Mutatis mutandis*, if the literate person does not realize that English poetry as a whole is "better" than French poetry, that German classical music is "better" than English music, that Dostoevsky's novels are "better" than those of Joaquim Manoel Macedo, then they are a lost cause.

The peremptory assertion that there are no differences in culture, that "everything is equal, nothing is better," is a foolish conclusion that contemporary pseudo-education draws from reading anthropology works that teach, right from page one, the precept of methodological relativism.

This relativism is, obviously, relative. If anthropological science, when studying cultures, refrains from comparative judgments of value, this is a basic methodological precaution aimed at avoiding prejudiced judgments. But it is also obvious that a science that excludes differences of value from its field of study has no minimal ability to tell us, then, whether these differences exist or not. All anthropology can assert is that this, strictly speaking, is not an anthropological question—which does not mean that it is not an ethical, pedagogical, aesthetic, etc., question. Anthropological relativism is a methodological prejudice, not an objective conclusion about the existence or nonexistence of what this precept precisely places outside the field of study of anthropology. To say otherwise is to assert that science is all the more qualified to make pronouncements on the existence of an object the less it is part of its field of study. In this sense, algebra should provide us with the proof of the existence of microbes, and microbiology the resolution of second-degree equations.

To deduce from methodological relativism objective relativism, and from refraining from examining differences of value their positive nonexistence, is a puerile error that only the most complete lack of critical sense, combined with perfect ignorance of the subject, would allow to be enshrined in a self-evident and unquestionable dogma.

Furthermore, this error leads to perfectly hallucinatory cognitive consequences. Methodological relativism in the view of cultures and societies is an achievement of Western science, and not a recent one. It dates back to the beginning of the [twentieth] century. Other times and peoples completely ignored it, and therefore the naive assertion of one's own superiority is a constant trait of practically all known cultures, starting with the so-called "primitive" ones. Now, if all cultures are equal, those that know relativism are as good as those that ignore it, and therefore it is equally acceptable, from a relativistic point of view, to declare that they all are the same or that some are infinitely better than others. Any relativism that pretends to be more than a mere methodological precaution ends in a short circuit.

3. Finally, Ariano Suassuna's declaration of relativistic faith contrasts singularly with his assertion of enthusiastic and intolerant nativism, ready to condemn Eurocentrists who "do not love our land." For, if all cultures are equally valuable, why should we love "ours" more than others? Is there a reciprocal implication between the value of culture and the place of birth registration? A man must be really confused not to notice that his proclamation of absolute cultural relativism is, in the same act, the complete repudiation of any nationalism that claims to be taken seriously. Suassuna is both a relativist and a nationalist at the same time, and he does not even remotely realize that, in the name of the universal equivalence of cultures,

nothing can be alleged against Eurocentrism that does not equally turn against Third Worldism, Brazilianism, Africanism, etc.

For you to get an idea of how deeply this sinks us into the quagmire of absurdity, note the following. Excluding all rational reasons for choice based on religious, ethical values, etc., adherence to this or that "culture" can only be one of two things: either it is the arbitrary choice of a dilettante—and, as *de gustibus non est disputandum,* there is no sense in moral indignation against those who make a different choice—or it is an inescapable natural fate. In this latter hypothesis, it would only remain to explain whether the fate is of a geographical order, our ideas and feelings being linked to a territorial root as Thomas Buckle pretended, or if it is of a racial order, each man receiving in his DNA his ancestral culture and not being able to escape it even by changing countries. We would therefore be reduced to choosing between Buckle's national-geographic ideology and Houston Stewart Chamberlain's explicit racism.

The most extraordinary thing in all this, however, is not the mere logical contradiction of nationalism and relativism: it is the fact that the latter is entirely "made in the USA." The proclamation of the equivalence of cultures, with the consequent imputation of criminal racist intentions to anyone who denies it, is the guiding dogma of the American academic inquisition (to the unmasking of which Saul Bellow dedicated his last novel, *Ravelstein*). Money from the Big Brother from the North now freely flows into the pockets of any Brazilian activist intellectual who agrees to give academic support to ideas that demoralize Brazilian civilization and promote among us the American model of racial democracy: ethnic groups, with strong racial and cultural identity, under the arbitration of a smiling supracultural paternalistic State committed to divide and conquer.

The nationalism that Suassuna defends nowadays, and which has nothing to do with the authentic nationalism of which he was a spokesman in his early plays, consists of local elements unified and coerced by the imperialist doctrine of multiculturalism. It is a dissolvent and suicidal nationalism, calculated to generate a postcard-like "Brazilian-ness" on a globalist and anti-national doctrinal background.

When a talented man, at the height of success, starts mindlessly repeating a discourse invented by smart alecks to induce him to collaborate in the destruction of what he loves most, it's time for him to shut up and go home to think.

The Rise and Fall of Human Consciousness

Excerpt of a lecture on the "1995 UNESCO's Report of the World Commission
on Culture and Development," delivered at the Casa de América Latina in
Bucharest, Romania, July, 1997.
O futuro do pensamento brasileiro (1997, 2016)

How is it possible for human intelligence to reach a state of crudity,
simultaneously naive and brutal, attempting to arbitrate age-old moral and cultural
differences based on simplistic political frameworks?

Why is it that as the opinion of the educated class becomes globalized through
computerization and the telecommunications network, it concurrently loses
critical thinking and intellectual acuity to the extent of confusing concrete political
norms with universal ethical principles? In short, what has transpired in history
and human development for us to descend so far?

Introduction

Without the slightest claim to provide these questions with a conclusive answer,
I can, however, associate the described facts with two historical cycles, one distant
and the other recent.

The first of these cycles is the one in which human consciousness gradually
emerges from the obscure womb of collective discourse to assert itself as a bearer
of autonomous light flowing directly from universal truths. The second goes
precisely in the opposite direction: it marks the return of collective discourse to
the status of supreme authority, endowed with the right to subjugate and crush
individual consciousness.

The Cycle of the Emergence of Autonomous Individual Consciousness

The cycle of the emergence of autonomous individual consciousness manifests
itself between the peak of the Egyptian and Babylonian Empires (2000 BC) and
the advent of Christianity. The cycle of its retraction begins more or less during
the reign of Henry VIII in England (1509–1547) and, faster than the first, is close
to reaching a peak in the era in which we live.

In the great empires of antiquity, we do not see the emergence of any kind of
thought, science, religious knowledge, or even mystical vision that is not
organically intertwined with the fabric of collective beliefs that form, so to speak,
the "official" ideology of society or the state. At that time, social organization is,

as Eric Voegelin[88] demonstrated, the very embodiment of known truth. Not that individual thought was repressed; it simply did not exist as a recognizable unity.

The first sign of a break with this state of affairs comes from a people of shepherds, who until then had lived in the background: the Hebrews. Among the Hebrews, Truth does not immediately emerge as the living constitution of a State, but as a special type of knowledge passed directly from God to certain individuals, the prophets. The prophet, far from being immediately the embodiment of collective belief, as was the Egyptian pharaoh, king-priest, and incarnation of divinity, was often a man among others, without special authority; he was often a marginalized and vilified individual who had to struggle against the community and prove his truth through a victorious confrontation with collective belief. It was not a dialectical proof but a wager on the truth of the prophecy: the accomplished fact proved the accuracy of the prophetic message, the error of collective obstinacy. But many prophets were killed by the community before they could prove the truth of what they said.[89]

This is the original message that the Hebrews bring to the world: truth—the word of the universal God—can be known by an individual without the participation of the community. The proof of truth is not in the unanimity of collective belief embodied in a king-god, but in the reliability (*emunah*) of the message that, no matter how improbable it may seem to collective consensus, ends up proving true through the unfolding of historical facts.

A second decisive step toward the autonomy of individual consciousness is taken by Greek philosophy, in the golden period from Socrates to Aristotle. I will highlight here only the figure of Socrates. He no longer brings, like the Hebrew prophets, a message whose content is rejected by the community. He openly contests common beliefs, in the name of the demand for a consistent and universally valid discourse. Truth is a function of an *apodictic* (= incontrovertible) proof that cannot be imposed on everyone because only he who consents, freely, to follow the steps of dialectical demonstration has access to it. The free individual, who thinks and investigates honestly, has access to self-evident universal truths, possession of which is denied to those who merely echo collective discourse.

---

[88] Order and History, 5 vols. (Baton Rouge: Louisiana State University Press, 1956–1987).

[89] The Hebrew prophet, often being a scapegoat for social guilt without (or before) having risen to the status of chief or king, anticipates the Christian mystery that makes the innocent victim the bearer of truth. See René Girard, *The Scapegoat* (Johns Hopkins University Press, 1989), original *Le Bouc émissaire* (Paris: Grasset, 1982); and *La Route antique des hommes pervers* (id: ibid., 1985).

As the Hebrew prophets were stoned and killed, Socrates was also sentenced to death. The main differences between them were: 1) the prophets were virtual rulers or leaders of their people, who sometimes accepted their guidance, sometimes rejected it with violence, whereas Socrates claims no kind of power or authority and willingly admits to being the defenseless witness of truths that will only become evident and obligatory in another world, after death, and that in this life will remain as a secret accessible only to philosophers; 2) the prophets appealed to the proof of facts, which, even after their death, ended up imposing itself on the entire community, whereas Socrates only resorts to dialectical proof, much more subtle and elusive, whose reliability is revealed only to those few who participate in the investigation for the truth. The authority of truth, in Socrates, is outside the realm of history and the senses.

The decisive step in the conquest of the autonomy of individual consciousness as the bearer of universal truth occurs with the advent of Our Lord Jesus Christ. Like the prophets and like Socrates, He is also the bearer of a solitary truth rejected by the community, and like them, He is condemned to death. However, unlike the prophets, He announces no historical fact destined to confer public authority on this truth after the death of its bearer; even the resurrection is witnessed only by those who had accepted the message before the Master's death. And, unlike Socrates, He appeals to no technique of rational proof. On the contrary, He ostentatiously declares that His message is nonsense in the light of all appearances, whether sensible or rational, that it is a mystery, and that each man has access to it through faith, that is, an inner wager, a free decision, an act of courage and trust to which nothing obliges him, neither in the sphere of facts nor in the sphere of arguments. St. Paul the Apostle will emphasize these differences most forcefully, condemning simultaneously the two forms of misunderstanding, the Jewish and the Greek: the Jews, he says, demand *miracles* (sensible proofs), the Greeks demand *arguments* (rational proofs), but the truth is a mystery that transcends perceptions and reasons.[90] It is evident that by this Paul does not deny all legitimacy to the demand for facts and reasons, which is valid in its own plane, but he emphasizes that in both cases the subject of knowledge imposes conditions on the truth to admit it as consensually valid truth, and that in the case of essential Truth, this requirement is unwarranted because it is not a question of fitting truth into the cognitive criteria of the community, but of healing the soul, through faith and baptism, so that it becomes capable of *personal* access to the truth. On the other hand, Christ does not present Himself only as the bearer of truth but as the *living incarnation* of truth, and He promises men not only

---

[90] 1 Cor. 1:22–23.

knowledge but real and complete integration into the life of truth, that is, a true eternal life.[91]

From the Hebrew prophets to Jesus, passing through Greek philosophy, the external authority, the social approval of truth becomes increasingly tenuous, the means of proof less and less consensual and more internal, increasingly distant from the centers of worldly power and closer to the center of the human heart, to the solitary consciousness of man who, as St. Teresa of Avila would say, is "*solo con el Solo,*" solitary with the solitary truth. Christ on the cross is the solitary truth, the perfect identity between the individual soul and universal truth, both rejected by social consensus.

The foundation of all Christian civilization will consist of millions and millions of solitary acts of adherence to an invisible and externally unproven truth. As long as men are capable of this kind of inner decision, Christianity will expand over the world.[92]

It is not surprising that, as the Christian dogma itself consolidated into a rational theological system (at the end of the Middle Ages) and the Church fully acquired the authority of the dominant social consensus (in the Renaissance), thus satisfying the two opposing mentalities, those of the "Greeks" and the "Jews," and relinquishing its specific ground, which is that of inner freedom, in the same measure, Christianity will weaken and move towards oblivion.

The Cycle of Dissolution of Individual Consciousness into Supposed "Collective Consciousness"

It is precisely here that the second cycle I mentioned begins.

One of the early signs appears in the field of sciences, with the distinction established by Lord Bacon between the primary and secondary qualities of sensible objects. The primary qualities are weight and extension. The secondary ones are taste, color, etc. The difference is that the primary qualities can be

---

[91] Not by coincidence, the three stages of this cycle correspond to the three senses that the word "truth" respectively holds in Hebrew, Greek, and Latin. The Hebrew "emunah" carries the sense of "trust" in a promise. In Greek, *aletheia*, truth is "evidence," a patency, something seen. The Latin "veritas" conveys the meaning of a reliable narrative, an exact recapitulation of facts. See Julián Marías, *Introducción a la Filosofía* (Madrid: Revista de Occidente, 1958), 86; *Reason and Life: The Introduction to Philosophy*, trans. Kenneth S. Reid and Edward Sarmiento (New Haven: Yale University Press, 1956). Indeed, in the Hebrew tradition, truth is projected into the future, in anticipation of the fulfillment of the promise. In Greek philosophy, truth is an intellectual vision. In Christianity, it is the accomplished fact: the incarnation of Our Lord Jesus Christ.

[92] *O Jardim das Aflições*, § 24 [The Garden of Afflictions] (1995, 2015).

precisely measured and, therefore, confirmed by collective consensus, while the secondary ones are "subjective" and vary from individual to individual. At first, this division has only a practical sense: it aims to circumscribe aspects of reality that are more accessible to scientific study. However, gradually, it acquires the significance of a metaphysical law that divides reality into a "more real" and another "less real" realm. The difficulty of measuring secondary qualities turns into a decree that expels them from the objective world, now constituted solely of weight and extension. For Descartes, extension is the quintessential quality of physical substances. It was in vain that Leibniz protested, arguing that substance could not be defined solely by extension, and that something more needed to be added to determine its individuality, preventing substances from being confused with the mere schema of their kind.

The scientific prestige of the "extended substance," based on the ease it offers for consensual confirmation, eventually made it the only reality. The mathematization of nature turned it into a set of conventions accepted by the scientific community and considered "more real" than the world of "subjective sensations," i.e., the world of mountains and trees, birds and animals, men and houses where we all live.

Scientific consensus is valued here, akin to the old communal consensus. More or less at the same time, modern nation-states are formed, and in an attempt to theologically legitimize the power of nations, a highly successful theory, developed by Sir John Fortescue, asserts that each nation is a "mystical body," with subjects being mystical parts of the king's body just as the faithful were parts of the mystical body of Christ. This mere figure of speech assumes the role of a dogmatic truth, disregarding the fact that the faithful integrated into the body of Christ through an intimate participation based on free choice, while the condition of being a subject of this or that king was merely an external demographic circumstance. Through a linguistic trick, the territorial community embodied in the king thus assumed the figure of a living character, endowed not only with self-awareness but also with the authority emanating from divine inspiration.

In the following centuries, the clash of "progressive" and "conservative" tendencies occurs, but both currents are allied at one point: both contribute to strengthening the myth of the substantiality of collective consciousness. Enlightenment and French Revolution philosophers create two notions that will play a decisive role in this regard: "public opinion" and the "general will."

As I pointed out in *O Imbecil Coletivo* (The Collective Imbecile) in 1995, modern consensual thought among intellectuals was born in the clubs, assemblies, and literary salons where the French Revolution was generated—in the 'Republic of Letters.' It was there that, for the first time, modern intellectualism felt the force of its union and was crowned queen under the title of "public opinion." In fact, this term did not designate the opinion of the masses but the common sentiment of the educated elites. The characteristic of these clubs, which differentiated them, on the one hand, from scientific societies as we know them today and, on the other hand, from medieval university debating centers, was the complete absence of rational criteria for validating arguments: it was the empire of 'opinion'—in the Greek sense of *doxa*, or pure belief. Theoretical questions of epistemology, metaphysics, economics, and even natural sciences were decided there by shouting, according to the preferences of the majority. The true doctrine was not the one that coincided with reality, but the one that best expressed the aspirations of the collective, in the language most flattering to the passions of the moment.

Already in the properly revolutionary phase, "public opinion," which until then had been a mere criterion for consensual assessment of "truth," acquires the force of an authority, becoming one of the sources of law, now named the *Volonté Générale*. The "general will" is the fundamental principle of laws and government acts, and its authority is absolute and irrevocable.

The conservative ideological reaction, coming from German historians and philologists, takes the form of an apology for traditions, which ends up asserting, against the autonomy of individual consciousness, the substantive reality of "national spirits."

But at the same time that aristocrats' heads were rolling in Paris, in placid Königsberg, Immanuel Kant quietly promotes a revolution with even more devastating consequences. On one hand, he assembles seemingly unbeatable arguments against the human claim to objectively know things as they are. All our knowledge, he says, merely projects onto the objects provided to it the innate schemes of our own cognitive apparatus: the *a priori* forms of perception (space and time) and rational knowledge (categories). If Kant had stopped there, he would have been just another skeptic. However, more devastating than his destruction of classical metaphysics was his reconstruction of the foundations of certainty. The *a priori* forms are certainly subjective, he affirms, but they are universal and necessary. Thus, the guarantee of the truth of knowledge does not lie in the objective connection between knowledge and things but in the universality of the subjective. I can be sure that I am in the truth when I know, *a priori*, that my thought aligns with the universality of subjective schemes, i.e., with a kind of super-consciousness that transcends all individual consciousness. As this super-consciousness, in turn, cannot be divine (for, according to Kant, we can know nothing of God except through faith), it can only be the consciousness of the human community, substantialized, personalized, and made more conscious than individuals.[93] In one fell swoop, Kant separated consciousness from bodily individuality and attributed it to an abstract universal. With this, Kant definitively opened the doors of history to all the attacks of totalitarianism on the freedom of individual consciousness, a freedom that, notwithstanding, Immanuel Kant himself, with remarkable inconsistency, proclaimed to respect above all.

The Rise of the Priesthood of Darkness

From then on, all ideologies, all factions, without notable exception, would seek pretexts for new and repeated expropriations of consciousness, consistently transferring the burden of knowing the truth from the individual to the collectivity, diverging only on which collectivity should be designated for such investiture.

- For Hegelianism, the bearer of reason is no longer the flesh-and-blood man but the State that humanizes him, and outside of which he is nothing more than a fierce and mute beast.

- Positivism attributes absolute authority to the scientific community, which, free from subjective illusions, adheres to Bacon's correct measurement of primary qualities.

- Marxism disqualifies individual thought as a mere reflection of class ideology and transfers the seat of consciousness to social classes, especially the proletariat.

- Pragmatism reduces all knowledge to the expression of practical projects and, as collective projects must inevitably prevail over individual ones, reduces the cognitive activity of the individual to an obedient collaboration in the social construction of useful knowledge.

- Psychoanalysis demotes individual consciousness to a distorted mirror of unconscious passions and childhood complexes and ultimately recognizes no other authority capable of knowing objective truth than . . . the international psychoanalytic community.

---

[93] Hence the affinity that Lucien Goldmann discovers between Kantism and Marxism. See Lucien Goldmann, *Introduction à la Philosophie de Kant* (Paris: Gallimard, 1967); Lucien Goldmann, *Immanuel Kant* trans. Robert Black (London & New York: Verso, 2011).

But it's not only in the field of theory that individual consciousness undergoes the most violent attacks. Everywhere, established power and opposing factions vying for power use every subterfuge and encourage the creation of new methods to subjugate it:

• Soviet and Chinese communism, building on the discoveries of neurophysiologist Ivan Pavlov, developed the technique of "brainwashing" to block the free exercise of consciousness and compel individual minds to mold themselves by collective discourse.

• Nazi fascism elevates massive propaganda to the level of a great art— the State is the grand spectacle that keeps the masses hypnotized under its spell.

• In democracies, a residue of political freedom coexists with the enslavement of consciousness by political and commercial propaganda, armed with the most refined techniques to obscure individual judgment and shape the behavior of the masses: subliminal messages, hypnosis, information bombardment, neurolinguistic programming, psychological administration, behavioral engineering—all means to elude the vigilance of the conscious self are mobilized to reduce individuals to a statistically predictable and programmable mass.

Scientists and academic philosophers, in general, remain insensitive to the paradox that so many powerful practical means are created to subjugate an entity that, according to their theories, should be inherently defenseless and docile by nature. Instead of studying the alarming phenomenon of the grand lie that contradicts itself, they limit themselves to signing manifestos in defense of freedom of consciousness while striving to create new theoretical arguments to prove that this freedom does not exist, that individual consciousness is only an epiphenomenon or a complete illusion:

• For analytical philosophy, professed by intellectuals who, in politics, continue to be advocates of individual liberties, everything in the individual that constitutes his most essentially personal sphere—values, religious beliefs, traditions, perceptions, feelings—has no meaning whatsoever, and only mathematical language, a standardized code of communication for the academic class, can bear objective truths.

• For Whorf's general semantics, the possibilities of thought are already performed in the structure of each language, leaving men only to think according to the prejudices embedded in the language they speak.

- Sartrean existentialism, which begins by defending complete individual freedom, ends by concluding that the only possible use of this freedom is submission to a collectivist ideology.

- For deconstructionism, human consciousness has no substantiality whatsoever; it is just a crystallization of signs, casual, provisional, and multisensory like any other that forms in the immeasurable network of language.

But not all intellectuals limit themselves to elaborating theoretical discourses against consciousness. Some draw practical consequences from the depreciation of consciousness that threaten to lead to results even more formidable than those obtained by Soviet communism and Nazi fascism:

- The Italian ideologue Antonio Gramsci, whose thought posthumously exerted great influence in Europe from the 1960s to the 1980s and remains significant in Brazil,[94] takes a step beyond Marx. If Marx said that an individual's thought is only an echo of the ideology of his class, Gramsci extends this generalization to all human mental activity, concluding that science, art, and philosophy have no purpose other than to express the political forces of each era. Therefore, man has not been endowed with intelligence except to integrate into ideological combat. Consciousness here becomes *ancilla propagandae*.

- In the same vein, albeit for various reasons, is the pragmatism of Richard Rorty, for whom, since no rational arbitration of issues dividing men is possible, all that remains is for each faction to try to "subtly instill" its way of speaking into public opinion, which will obligate it to think collectively like each faction itself.

The list of assaults on consciousness that I have just presented is far from exhaustive. These are just samples. A minimally satisfactory list should also include, at least, Klagesian dualism that tragically and irreversibly opposes "spirit" and "soul," Jacques Monod's biological philosophy, Skinner's psychology, sociobiology, pseudo-Eastern doctrines of the New Age, and even Heideggerianism, which views human consciousness as a casual aggregate without any organizing center or hierarchical principle.

But there's no need to continue the enumeration. The examples I cited suffice to show that the hatred of individual consciousness, the desire to deny it in theory and destroy it in practice (as if the very existence of such practical will were not the contradiction of this theory), are common traits of almost all major

---

[94] And, evidently, in the U.S. and elsewhere.—Eds.

philosophical, scientific, and ideological currents of the last two centuries. The number and virulence of their manifestations are increasing, in geometric scale, throughout the nineteenth century and our own [twentieth century].

The ascending line of this increasingly clear trend actually marks a descent: over these two centuries, we are descending from the peak where the evolution that goes from the Hebrew prophets, through Greek philosophy, to the advent of Our Lord Jesus Christ had led us. We are losing the prerogatives of autonomous individual consciousness and submitting, in theory and practice, to the demands of a self-deified society that, under modern, scientific, and progressive pretexts, ultimately promises to return us to a state of mental subjection where the indistinct mass can conceive nothing beyond what is dictated by the discourse of an all-powerful ruler.

Let no one be deceived, thinking that the rise of this new—or very old—kind of tyranny can be stopped by fragile expedients such as the struggle for "human rights" or the defense of private economy (the two icons of neo-democratic left and neoliberal right, whose futile worship is performed by the well-intentioned men of both parties, unwittingly becoming servants of the true enemy who laughs behind the curtain at both). I have already demonstrated in my book *O Jardim das Aflições* (*The Garden of Afflictions*) (1995) that the extension of legal rights brings with it the expansion of the State's police power and that the privatization of the economy is perfectly compatible with the increase of state power to the point where it becomes the absolute master of citizens' private lives, shaping values, reactions, and feelings with an effectiveness that not even Hitler or Stalin dared to dream.

The power that is currently expanding in the world and seeking to become unlimited is not solely of a political, economic, or military nature; it is a sociological, cultural, psychological, and ultimately spiritual—or more precisely, anti-spiritual—power. If we understand that it cannot attack the Spirit directly, it seeks to destroy its abode in this world, which is the human heart, the intimacy of each person with themselves, that inner region where, as Antonio Machado said, *quien habla solo espera hablar a Dios un día* ["he who speaks alone hopes to speak to God one day"].

It is an inhuman and anti-human power, whose movements are invisible on the small scale to which are accustomed social scientists, activists, and all those who boast of being realists and practical people. To see it, one must rise to the height of the spiritual history of the world—a path that is closed to most intellectuals today, who, out of pride, pettiness, prejudice, or weakness, have ended up becoming the main allies of this power in its effort to destroy consciousness.

It is within the framework of this gigantic movement that one must seek to understand the singular document whose abbreviated description occupied the first part of our lecture. It illustrates the eager and almost reckless willingness with which leading intellectuals are ready to collaborate, in the name of the most beautiful pretexts, with a cause that can be described as nothing less than monstrous. It shows to what extent so-called intellectual activity can become, in our time, a threat to the integrity of intelligence, which, fundamentally, is nothing other than the integrity of consciousness. At the very least, it demonstrates how dangerous it is for an intellectual to abandon the sphere that is proper to him, which is the deepening of his own consciousness, to heed the flattering invitation to become the forger of a new world.

Today, more than ever, the beautiful ideals of the future, in the name of which activist intellectuals mobilize millions of souls around the world, echo the old promise heard by Adam and Eve in Paradise: *You will be like gods*. But today, the most deceptive of promises dares to transform itself into a sacred commandment, bearing the name of collective solidarity, condemning as enemies of humanity all those who refuse to heed its call.

When this call is formalized on a global scale, when the false moral commandment solidifies into a legal obligation, disobedience to which is punished with all the rigor of the law, then the times will be ripe for the final unmasking of the great parody of spirit, freedom, truth, and goodness. For now, all we can do is watch with anguish and sorrow the rise of the priesthood of darkness, ascending the steps of the temple, holding in its hands its breviary of ignorance.

Chapter 4

Cognitive Parallax in Modern Philosophy

Work and Life in Philosophy

O Globo, September 13, 2003
A felicidade geral da nação (2023)

When we speak of the "work" of a poet, a novelist, what is meant by that is not everything he wrote but only the formally literary part, published or publishable. What remains—drafts, letters, oral statements—is biographical material that does not affect the judgment of the "work," although it may contribute indirectly to its understanding. Even from the published part, sometimes only a small fraction is aesthetically relevant. This is because art is inherently a search for form—identifiable, material, stable form. The "meanings" that generations of readers believe they find there may vary, but, precisely for that reason, they presuppose the permanence of form (nothing proves this better than the obsession for documenting—fixing—those supposedly revolutionary artistic manifestations that are proclaimed fluid and transient in principle).

Philosophy, on the contrary—all philosophy—essentially consists of "meaning," which the philosopher seeks to convey by all means at his disposal, including literary means. The value of this meaning is not conditioned by the greater or lesser success of its verbal expression. All we have left of Aristotle are drafts, fragments, and lecture notes. His "books" are not books: they are posthumous arrangements. The published part, which Cicero praised as "a river of gold" in eloquence, has been irretrievably lost. If this happened to a poet, a writer of fiction, we would, at best, have a great failed writer: subjective intention that does not translate into form, or that loses it, is the very definition of artistic failure. What would Shakespeare be without his plays, his sonnets, reduced to dreams and sketches of intentions? But Aristotle's philosophy subsists entirely in the ruins of his written expression. And Plato's oral teaching, reconstructed from a thousand and one clues, is considered more important today than his entire published work, of which it constitutes the keystone.

Do you understand the difference?

This is because philosophy, as a search for meaning, is a permanent reinterpretation and rectification of itself, rarely admitting to closing itself in a finished and unalterable expression. Hence, a draft, an excerpt from a letter, a loose sentence can sometimes illuminate the whole to such an extent that they end up assuming a very high position in the hierarchy of the philosopher's thoughts. The best ideas of a philosopher do not necessarily coincide with his cleanest and finished writings. This is when, as in the case of Leibniz or Husserl, almost the entire work consists more of notes than works ready for publication. Not by chance, the father of philosophers, Socrates, left no written work. He is the oral thinker par excellence.

Therefore, the relationship between "work" and "life" cannot be the same in literature and philosophy. The idolatry of the "text," in which the University of São Paulo has addicted entire generations of students, only served to erase the distinction between philosophy and philology. Not that the analysis of the text is unimportant. But it is not enough: sometimes, the best of a philosophy lies in what the philosopher only thought, without reaching the point of writing—an observation that, applied to literature, would be pure nonsense.

Of course, not everything in a philosopher's life is equally significant in terms of understanding his philosophy. There is, in it, as in any life, an extensive strip that consists only of the chaos of raw, fragmentary, semi-conscious, and even impersonal experience, from which the philosopher strives to grasp the internal nexus that, once conscious, will integrate into his philosophical thought, whether it is written or remains in intention. It is this transition from experience to explicit consciousness that marks the difference between the pure existential matter of a philosophy and its personalized intellectual form, with the philosopher being responsible for the latter, not the former.

On the other hand, there are acts, choices, and maturely thought-out decisions that must, without hesitation, be understood as interpretations, applications, or extensions that the philosopher gave to his own guiding principles.

It is in this, and not in that aspect of the work-life relationship, that the signs of the *cognitive parallax* should be sought. It would be childish to demand from a philosopher that "coherence between words and actions," literal, material, and stereotyped, that moralists demand from public figures. What can and should be demanded is that the part of life that clearly and consciously integrates into the thought universe of a thinker should not be, by its meaningful content, a formal contradiction of the principles of his philosophy. And even in this case, it will still be necessary to distinguish between a momentary lapse, a structural incongruence, self-deception, or premeditated cunning. The case of Machiavelli is clear: the publication of a conspiracy recipe implicitly asserts that this conspiracy will not be carried out, at least as it is in the book. But Machiavelli was too clever not to realize this. "The Prince," therefore, is not a scientific description of political society: it is a "myth." Interpreters today are almost unanimous on this point.

The choice of Max Horkheimer and Theodor Adorno for a "high standard of living" in the midst of the general misery they blamed, precisely, on the high standard of living classes, cannot be considered either a moral inconsistency or a sign of involuntary blindness but rather the conscious expression of a gnostic cynicism that hated evil without loving good. Like all gnosticism, the philosophy of the Frankfurt School is hatred, not of evil, but of Being.

Mutatis mutandis, Karl Marx's proud disdain for the bastard son he had with the maid is not an "inconsistency" either. It is proof of something that Marx himself recognized but that his admirers today refuse to see: that his adherence to the cause of the poor had no minimum ethical sense—it was only the logical, cold, and amoral consequence of a certain interpretation of History.

Cognitive Parallax

Excerpt of "O futuro da pústula," *Diário do Comércio,* August 14, 2006
O mundo como jamais funcionou (2014)
and *Introdução à filosofia de Louis Lavelle* (2021)

For years, I have been investigating a phenomenon in the history of ideas in Western modernity, which I named "cognitive parallax" and define as the shift between the axis of a philosopher's real experience and the axis of his theoretical construction. From the beginning of the study, the results of which I began to present in my courses in 2001, and in newspaper articles in 2002, I made it clear that I considered this phenomenon an abnormality, a deviation of human intelligence, which revealed itself to be inferior to the standard set by ancient philosophers. Between the two axes, a scotoma, a blind spot, appeared, revealing a serious lapse in consciousness that should not be expected even in ordinary people, let alone in thinkers of great prestige. The result was that there emerged, in theory, arbitrary discontinuities, epistemological abysses between aspects of reality, that in the personal experience of the respective thinker were perfectly continuous. The most grotesque symptom was the philosopher enunciating general theories about the human species that miraculously did not apply to his own person or, worse yet, were incompatible with the fact that he was writing what he wrote.

When Kant, for example, asserted that we only know phenomenal appearances but not things in themselves, this assertion was incompatible with his naive expectation that, starting from a mere sensible sign—the printed letters—the reader would come to grasp the core of his thought. If we could not jump from sensible phenomena to their own substances, much less could we, through them, grasp the substance of a subjective intention signified by them—a leap even greater than that required to apprehend, in an appearance of an elephant, the reality of an elephant. If Kant's words meant anything, the theory enunciated by them meant nothing, and vice versa. Kant's philosophy, in short, was incompatible with the fact that we could read it in the author's books.

Plato, Aristotle, or Augustine never paid a similar price. Perhaps because they had a clear understanding that philosophy was not just a school discipline but a rule of life, they never reasoned against the data of their own consciousness. When they focused on an object, they did so not only with reasoning ability but with the total functioning of their concrete individual consciousness. In other words, they spoke perfectly seriously. When Plato placed human beings between angels and beasts, he knew that he himself was there. When Aristotle defined man as a rational animal, he made it clear that he himself was a rational animal. When Augustine spoke of man's natural inclination to sin, he offered his own sins as examples. The reality these philosophers spoke of was the same in which they lived. Their philosophy was a reflection on experience, not the hypothetical construction of an invented world that, by definition, could not contain the real person of its inventor. Not that they invented nothing. But when they did invent, they did not sell their invention as reality. What surprised me was to discover the increasing frequency with which modern philosophers allowed themselves to fail in this obligation, teaching from their professorial chairs theories with which, in their real lives, they could not possibly agree, but pretending that their listeners should accept them as pure reality.

The parallax thus defined is a specific phenomenon, perfectly distinct, historically identifiable.

* * *

The lack of attention to personal experience and the philosopher's self-limitation to logical discourse can lead to disastrous errors that will persist over time. For example, Hume's denial of causality had significant consequences. Denying the existence of causality renders all metaphysics unfeasible—but the problem is that Hume's critique of the notion of causality is not valid; it's nothing more than a logical trick.

Hume asserts that when we witness any process unfolding, we observe only separate episodes but mentally link them according to the idea of cause. However, if I pay attention to my real experience, I see exactly the opposite: I witness unified processes, and only in a second moment am I able to analyze them and break them down into parts. The separation was made by me; it did not occur on its own in reality, where, on the contrary, phenomena arise in a single chain of events. Reasoning in Hume's manner, I would have to conclude the following: when I see a billiard ball in motion and then see another billiard ball move after the first collides with it, I connect the two movements according to the idea of cause. But where does the movement of the first ball end, and where does the movement of the second ball begin? I don't see that; I'm unable to determine the point at which the union of completely distinct episodes would occur.

Hume makes a very simple observational error. He should have noticed that what we call a cause is nothing more than the beginning of a process, and what we call a consequence is the end of that process. If the cause is completely separated from its consequence, there will be, in reality, no consequence at all. Therefore, the unity of the phenomenon will define the causal process. Unfortunately, this went unnoticed, and critiques like Hume's of the notion of cause—and, on another level, also of the notion of subject—were decisive for the intellectual fate of a philosopher like Kant. These are extreme cases of *cognitive parallax*, denying, in the realm of theory, everything the individual believed in practice. A chasm opens between the domain of philosophical speculation and the domain of the philosopher's actual life.

The Philosophies and Their Structure

Diário do Comércio, October 9, 2014
A cólera dos imbecis (2019); *Maquiavel ou A confusão demoníaca* (2020)

The structure of a philosophy is both the most evident and simultaneously the most hidden aspect of it. Evident because it is present in all its parts, even the smallest and humblest, which are nothing outside of it. Hidden because it is only present in the background, as the key to the locking of the whole, and never as a part or an explicit theme in any of its components.

A philosopher who takes the structure of his own philosophy as a theme to expound upon is already, at that very moment, incorporating it as a part of a larger structure.

One consequence of this is that the structure cannot be revealed by any "textual analysis," no matter how meticulous and careful it may be, as such analysis only leads to the structure of the exposition or the written work, whose relationship with the structure of philosophy itself is varied and ambiguous. The method to apprehend the structure of a philosophy must adhere to the following principles:

(1) Every philosophy, however abstract and disinterested it may seem, is an intervention in the course of human affairs. It always aims to modify or reinforce the state of things in society, culture, science, religion, customs, or even in the human condition as a whole.

(2) For this purpose, it conducts an in-depth examination of the obstacles, cognitive or of any other kind, that hinder or complicate its achievement, attempting to create the intellectual and practical means to remove them.

(3) Its structure, therefore, is defined as an articulation of ends and means. What is the proposed historical-cultural goal, and what is the strategy, both cognitive and persuasive, used to legitimize and enable it?

In other words, the structure of a philosophy only reveals itself when the discourse in which it is expressed is examined not as a pure system of ideas and doctrines, but as a human action, the intervention of an intellectually privileged individual in the lives of his supposedly less endowed peers willing to listen to him.

Now, the examination of discourse as a form of human action is the specialized field of rhetorical studies, the art of persuasion. To grasp the structure of a philosophy, the articulation of its ends and its means, it is necessary to examine it from a rhetorical standpoint, considering it as an effort of persuasion aimed at producing, through modifications in the cognitive sphere, specific effects on historical-social life or even on human life in general.

What often leads to the forgetting of this obviousness is that the exposition of philosophical ideas is generally done through a logical-dialectical discourse that disregards the appeal to rhetorical persuasion and aims to position itself in the field of strict demonstration, intellectual certainties immune to the allure of oratory.

However, this discourse, as such, is not "the" philosophy but merely the set or system of intellectual means by which it seeks to achieve its ends. If we examine it "in itself," without subordinating it to the ends it must serve, we lose ourselves in an infinity of "philosophical problems" or detours without ever grasping the structure of the philosophy in question, a structure that precisely consists of the articulation of its ends along with its means.

In the effort to discern this structure, it is necessary to understand the logical-dialectical discourse as part and instrument of an effort of persuasion, which is, an undertaking that, viewed as a whole, can only be rhetorical in nature.

Therefore, the method to discover the structure of a philosophy lies in the rhetorical analysis of its discourse, discerning in it the four elements that classical treatises define as constituting every rhetorical discourse: the "discourse situation," that is, the historical, social, cultural, and psychological framework in which it emerges and in which it intends to intervene; the "audience," that is, the specific public it addresses and upon which it intends to exert influence; the "objective" or goal, that is, the specific modification it aims to introduce into the framework; and finally, the discourse itself, that is, the set of means of argumentation, proof, and persuasion put into action to achieve this end.

Fortunately, the objective or goal—the "for what," ultimately, the philosopher is doing what he does—is explicitly stated in most philosophies. It is enough to look for it.

The difficulty lies in that it is not always found in the parts considered most important or noble in the philosophical work—sometimes it only appears in personal letters or minor works—so that the scholar, especially when trained in a teaching tradition that privileges the analysis of texts as such and focuses on the most prestigious ones, can get lost in a tangle of difficulties and never ask himself where, after all, the philosopher is leading him. This is how the most refined sophistication of analytical methods can become a precise technique for not understanding anything.

Although I am not aware of any case where the objective has remained completely hidden, the philosopher may have a good reason to keep it discreet when he considers it too dangerous or revolutionary to be displayed in public in the most noble and conspicuous parts of his written work. In this case, it is necessary to seek it in minor and occasional writings, whose strategic importance in the whole escapes the attention of the average analyst, dazzled by the prestige of the "great works." This is precisely the case with Immanuel Kant, Descartes, and Machiavelli.

Philosophical Ambition

Diário do Comércio, October 14, 2014
A cólera dos imbecis (2019)

There is no modest philosophy. Every philosophy is a long-term, large-scale intervention in the world of human events. While the decrees of rulers pass and crumble into oblivion, philosophies remain active and influential, affecting or shaping the course of scientific, moral, political, and religious discussions even centuries or millennia after the death of their creators. They reveal an almost miraculously self-renewing force.

Thousands of biographies of Napoleon and Julius Caesar would not bring back their empires, but sometimes a scholarly debate or an essay of reinterpretation is enough for a philosophy that seemed forgotten to rise from the ashes. Whether adorned with the prefix "neo" or not, it interferes in contemporary life as if it were published yesterday.

Don't think that this phenomenon is solely due to the zeal of late admirers and disciples who, against the will and without the slightest participation of their dead masters and inspirers, prevent the flame from extinguishing. On the contrary, it was these very masters and inspirers who, conceiving long-term goals and deploying the most complex and powerful cognitive strategies in their service, consciously left open or fostered the possibility of successive rebirths.

In some philosophies, the ambitious goal is so evident that it doesn't even need to be declared. No one can doubt that St. Augustine, Aquinas, or Pascal dreamed only of expanding the hegemonic dominion of the Catholic Church and converting, if possible, all of humanity. This is evident in every line they wrote. The three only differ in the intellectual strategies with which they plan to achieve this goal, which are beyond the scope of this article.

In other cases—Marx, for example, or Nietzsche—the goal is so emphatically reiterated that merely mentioning these names immediately brings to mind the image of socialist utopia or the Superman who emerges sovereignly free in the desert of nothingness after the destruction of all values.

However, more interesting is the case of those philosophers who whisper their goals so discreetly, almost in secret, that they can go unnoticed or be neglected for decades or centuries by scholars who see nothing more in their works than the powerful architecture of means, taking it as the end.

The slightest hesitation of the philosopher to prominently display the statement of ends on the portico or at the top of his philosophy can lead to this result. Because the ends, in themselves, are, so to speak, prior to philosophy and, determining its overall form, are not affected by it except in regard to its means of realization.

The ends of a philosophy are not exclusive to it; they can be shared by a multitude of non-philosophers who may not even have the intellectual vigor to understand it. The most didactic example in this regard is the aforementioned case of Augustine, Aquinas, and Pascal. Did they want to expand Christianity? Yes. Is this the goal that guides their entire philosophical effort? Yes. But how many men wanted the same without being philosophers?

What characterizes and distinguishes philosophy amid so many other human endeavors is the peculiar sophistication, richness, and precision of the intellectual means it puts at the service of its project. While others preach the ends and try to achieve them in practice or die for them on the battlefield, the philosopher strives to remove the most arduous cognitive obstacles that stand between present humanity and the achievement of these ends, erecting new intellectual frameworks that make it viable.

These obstacles can consist of common-sense beliefs, errors of perception or reasoning, religious, scientific, or even philosophical doctrines that are misguided, inadequate or misinterpreted symbols that block the imagination, weaknesses of the human psyche, and so on.

Josiah Royce rightly distinguished between the "spirit" of a philosophy and its "technical realization"—the inspiring ideal and the finished form of its crystallization into a philosophical work. The sphere of problems involved in "technical realization" is so extensive, the task of solving them so arduous, the intellectual equipment that must be used (and sometimes created) in their construction so complex, and the absorption by the reader so often difficult, that, if not warned about the underlying ends and ideals, one can prolong the examination of the machinery indefinitely to the point of taking it as if it were the end in itself. Not to mention, of course, the vain pleasure that erudite pedantry can derive from the endless dissection of technical minutiae, where fundamental questions are postponed indefinitely in the name of an appearance of "rigor."

To make matters worse, many elements of "technical realization" even have autonomous value, allowing them to be integrated into other philosophical projects alien or hostile to the original ends they served. You don't have to be a Thomist or a Marxist to take advantage of entire portions of Thomism or Marxism.

In the end, the deviation of focus is less easily committed with philosophers who openly declared their ends, or with those where these are self-evident, than with the ambiguous and slippery types who, out of fear of scandal or aversion to controversy, preferred to be more discreet or obscure.

Fewer mistakes are made by avoiding the essential in the interpretation of Marx, St. Thomas Aquinas, or Pascal than in that of Machiavelli, Kant, or Descartes.

More Parallax

O Globo, December 28, 2002
Maquiavel ou A confusão demoníaca (2020);
A morte do pato (2023)

Some readers have asked me for further explanations about the so-called "conceptual parallax" I mentioned the other day. I'll try.

Every philosophical statement about reality in general, humanity in general, or knowledge in general necessarily includes, among the objects to which it applies, the real person of the speaker and the discursive situation in which the statement is made.

Whatever a man says about these subjects, he also says about himself. No one has the right to set himself up, without further ado, as an exception to a theory that claims to deal with the genus or species to which he himself belongs.

This elementary methodological precaution was neglected by practically all the most important philosophers of the so-called "modern" cycle, as well as by many schools of thought that dominate the contemporary intellectual universe.

As a result, we have an imposing gallery of doctrines that tell us nothing about the world in which they were produced, much less about the real people who created them, but everything about an invented world that does not include them and which they merely observe from outside, from an imaginary vantage point. This vantage point corresponds, structurally and functionally, to that of the "omniscient narrator" in works of fiction, who is not affected by the course of the narrated events. Constructed with fictional technique, but totally unaware of the expedient they employ, these philosophies are works of fiction that do not dare to present themselves as such.

Some examples:

1) Descartes says he will seriously examine his own thoughts and begins to do so in the form of autobiographical introspection. In the middle of the way, he loses the thread of his personal and concrete self, of his biographical self, and begins to speak of a generic and abstract self, the "philosophical self." He is not aware of the leap and believes he continues to do autobiography when he is only doing logical construction. He ends up believing that he is really this philosophical self, under whose shadow the real self disappears completely. The result: his self-observation falls into the grossest errors, such as forgetting that the temporal continuity of the self is an assumption of the *cogito* and not a conclusion obtained from it.

2) David Hume says that our general ideas have no cognitive value because they are only fortuitous clusters of bodily sensations. At no moment does he realize that David Hume's philosophy, being composed of general ideas formed in this way, also cannot be worth much. The philosopher's state of alienation in creating his philosophy could not be more complete.

3) Machiavelli teaches that the Prince must seize absolute power and then get rid of those who helped him rise. Now, who could have helped the Prince more than the philosopher who taught him the formula for the conquest of absolute power? If the Prince took him seriously, he himself, Niccolò Machiavelli, would be the first to be thrown into the trash along with his book, evidence of the crime. Contrary to the general praise that consecrates Machiavelli as the first "realistic" observer of politics, the Prince is an idealized model that can only be described in literature precisely to the extent that no contemporary can embody it in reality. Alienation reaches its peak when Machiavelli says that all the evils of the State come from contemplative intellectuals who, unable to act in politics, theorize about it—precisely what he is doing. Moreover, Otto Maria Carpeaux had already pointed out that Machiavelli's view of politics is not political: it's aesthetic.

4) Karl Marx assures us that only the proletariat, being the last and extreme victim of alienation, can realistically grasp the entire course of the alienating process and, therefore, free themselves from it. Only the proletariat, in short, has adequate historical consciousness. But isn't it extraordinary that the first, the very first, to personify this proletarian consciousness is a bourgeois? I'm not saying that this is impossible, but, in light of Marxist theory, it is a remarkably unlikely exception. Karl Marx passes over it with the greatest innocence, without even noticing a focus deviation, a parallax between the character he represents and the content of his speeches. In Karl Marx's world, there is no Karl Marx.

And so it goes. I have dedicated my courses to the meticulous examination of these and many other similar cases for some years now. The most interesting aspect is the fictional critique of fictional philosophy. In fact, the best critical observers of philosophical alienation were fiction writers, mainly Dostoevsky, Kafka, Pirandello, Ionesco, and Camus. *Demons*, *The Trial*, *Henry IV*, *Rhinoceros*, and *The Stranger* are pieces of an immense literary indictment of the claims of modern philosophy. Saul Bellow's contrast between the "intellectual" and the "writer" is valid here: on one side, the builder of elegant alienations; on the other, the spokesperson for "authentic impressions," sometimes simple truths that burst the intellectual balloon. You've seen it before, haven't you? When I grow up, I want to be a "writer."

Machiavelli or the Demonic Confusion

Maquiavel ou A confusão demoníaca (2020)

The purpose that moved me in this study was not to investigate what the succession of historical versions did to Machiavelli, but, on the contrary, to deconstruct this edifice and ask to what extent Machiavelli himself was aware of the historical results he wanted to produce. Without this, we would risk consecrating as the supreme method of historical interpretation the mere summation of the projections, often self-serving, that other men and times cast on the original intentions of the author.

My question, therefore, was: how did Niccolò Machiavelli understand himself, and to what extent can we, with relative certainty, map the horizon of his consciousness? A horizon of consciousness is defined not only by what it encompasses but above all by what escapes it. The very plurality of contradictory interpretations of Machiavelli's thought emerges, at least in part, from the blind spots that appear in decisive articulations of this thought, causing certain developments given to him by interpreters and successors to be nothing more than a flowering of cancer cells born of the prodigious mental confusion from which they germinated.

Few thinkers throughout history have been revealed to have as many blind spots in their vision of the world and themselves as those that this present study reveals in Machiavelli. Often astonishingly, he not only fails to understand the events he explores but also does not understand himself, sowing his writings with unprocessed and generally unnoticed contradictions. It is not surprising that such a nebulous and confusing thought, made even more complex by a whole network of self-denials and disguises, could generate such disparate and contradictory historical consequences.

The Liar

"I never say what I believe, nor do I believe in what I say"—these words make of Machiavelli a living embodiment of the "liar's paradox" and immediately places his reader at the heart of the problem I named "existential self-reference": does

128

the confessing liar speak the truth at the moment of confession or does he lie about all previous moments? Did he lead a life of lies, or does he lie about the history of his life? Under these conditions, interpreters quickly realized that understanding Machiavelli was impossible without elucidating the exact relationship between the expressed meaning of his text and the unexpressed truth of his existence. The results they reached were most divergent, but four personal details about Machiavelli's life and work should not be forgotten.

First: The man who deemed himself capable of teaching a citizen of humble origin to rise to the highest echelons of power never showed the slightest sign of having learned his own lessons. All he achieved in life was to hold a subordinate position for fourteen years, lose it due to political imprudence, regain it partially by the favor of new rulers, exercise it for another two years, and then die.

Second: He displayed the greatest contempt for intellectuals who, incapable of political action, tried to influence the course of public affairs through written work, yet he was never anything but one of them.

Third: While his work portrays him as a cold, pessimistic, and malicious observer, in political practice, he repeatedly showed signs of naive and almost pathetic credulity. This professor of opportunism never knew how to seize opportunities. "He was always on the wrong side and had luck only once: when he, the republican, died before the death of the Republic of Florence."[95] In his youth, he bet that Cesare Borgia only committed violence on behalf of the papacy because he intended to dethrone the Pope and reign in his place as a lay ruler. However fitting this may have been with Machiavelli's own goals, it was neither in the plans nor within the capacity of the general. After this first incarnation of the "prince" was aborted, new prediction errors awaited the prophet. After the Florentine republic fell, he allowed himself to be deceived by the hope that the new rulers he had helped to fight would keep him in office . . . due to his loyalty to the fallen government! Weeks later, he was fired and imprisoned. Finally, in exile, for years he deluded himself about the possibility of returning to public administration by flattering the powerful in the most degrading way. They reciprocated with total disdain, until, at the end of his life, sick and exhausted, he partially regained his duties thanks to the pity he inspired in his former foes, losing them again due to imprudence and regaining them—again out of charity—shortly before his death.

---

[95] Otto Maria Carpeaux, *História da literatura ocidental* (Rio de Janeiro: Edições O Cruzeiro, 1959), 485.

Fourth: He taught the prince to rise to power with the help of allies and then kill them, but obviously, he himself, as the author of the plan and therefore one of the prince's greatest allies, would have been one of the first to die if the plan were put into action. He despised the inventors of never-realized ideal governments, but over the years, he gave no sign of having realized that he owed his survival precisely to the fact that his ideal government plan had never been realized.

To say that this man is a realist, in the most demanding sense of the term, is unsustainable. We will see in what partial sense he admits this qualification. But whatever that sense may be, it must be compatible with the observation that Machiavelli was also a utopian idealist, not only in his political thought but in the almost complete absence of a conscious connection between this thought and his more direct and visible personal experience. The apparent realism with which he accepts the limitations of human action and describes the miseries of politics conceals not only the prophetic utopianism of the Third Rome but the absolute incapacity of the inventor himself to examine his invention from the point of view of his own real position in existence. Hence the need to embody an imaginary character—the new Moses—and describe the world from the perspective of this fiction, concealing the depressing reality that contrasted with it. I call this displacement between the axis of theoretical construction and the axis of lived experience "cognitive parallax," another permanent characteristic of modern thought.

One of the most obvious manifestations of parallax occurs when the fact that an individual says or writes something proves the falsehood of what he says or writes: there is no clearer example of this than a coup plan that includes, as one of its basic conditions, the liquidation of the author of the plan. Later on, I will explain this concept more clearly, but the general notion I convey here is sufficient for the reader to note that parallax is by no means synonymous with conscious lying, hypocrisy, or dissimulation. Behind these veils, the "Machiavellian" liar, hypocrite, or dissimulator truly believes in something. It is in this subjective or imaginary truth, and not in the disguises that conceal it, that the parallax lies—the gap between basic beliefs and the reality of one's life. Beneath all the feints, detours, disguises, and cunning of the "Machiavellian" liar, there lies the residue of irremovable naivety of one who is incapable of becoming aware of his own situation and, furthermore, of making a comparison between it and the content of his general convictions translated into text for publication. Dante Germino asks: why does Machiavelli remain for us, in Croce's words, "an enigma that can never be solved"? And he answers: "Because he was confused. Why was he confused?

Because he lived in what Voegelin himself called 'The Age of Confusion,' in which the foundations of Western civilization were crumbling around him."[96]

However, it would be even more naive to explain Machiavelli through his "unconscious." Just as in the liar's paradox, the victim of cognitive parallax is not completely unaware of himself but lives in a half-light between truth and lies, unable to establish himself in the first place because it would immediately dispel the lie, but also unable to lie completely because the lie adopted as the guiding thread of action would become the truth of his existence: the true existence of a liar.

Descartes and The Psychology of Doubt

Three excerpts from *Visões de Descartes* (2013)

Descartes assures us that the sequence of *Meditations* leading from questioning the external world to the discovery of the *cogito* is not merely a logical scheme, a hypothetical articulation of thinkable thoughts, but a lived experience, a reliable account of thoughts thought. However, several clues in the text suggest that this assertion should not be taken too literally. I noticed them from the first reading but had to revisit them many times, unable to avoid the question: To what extent did that narrative adequately correspond to the facts, and from which point did it become an invented model, designed to bring order and meaning to experiences that would have actually unfolded much more imprecisely and hazily, if not entirely differently?

To complicate matters, that sequence of thoughts presented itself as a model, a paradigm that should repeat itself in an identical or similar manner, with similar or identical results, in every person willing to reexamine the foundation of their beliefs. Edmund Husserl, in his *Cartesian Meditations*, titled precisely for this reason, asserts that things are indeed this way. At least once in life, he says, every aspiring philosopher must sweep away their structure of beliefs and, like Descartes, rebuild everything from ground zero, the self-awareness of the thinking Self.

To learn how to do this, I had to deeply immerse myself in Descartes's lesson before being able to grasp Husserl's, which extended and radicalized it. A simple

---

[96] Dante Germino, "Was Machiavelli a 'Spiritual Realist'?," panel at Eric Voegelin Society meeting (Washington: Eric Voegelin Society, 2000).

analytical rereading of the author's main texts was unnecessary and insufficient for this task. Unnecessary because in this type of investigation, the essential had already been done by Martial Guéroult, whom I have no intention of surpassing. Insufficient because, if the philosopher had kept any secrets, I could not find a sign of them in the texts if I had not first glimpsed them imaginatively. And the fact was that at that moment, I glimpsed nothing.

I decided, then, to start at the beginning: to reenact in my own mind the succession of *Meditations* that goes from methodical doubt to the discovery of *cogito ergo sum* as the absolute foundation of all certainty. But it wasn't just about repeating, in order, a series of "thoughts." Thoughts presuppose perceptions, memories, feelings, fantasies. What I wanted was not only to repeat a sequence of reasonings but to mentally reconstruct the inner experiences that Descartes condensed into this reasoning. As one extravagance begets another, I resorted to a method that no philosophy teacher would find very respectable, but seemed most suitable in that situation: the "affective memory" method with which the great Russian actor Constantin Stanislavski—whose works I had been studying under the guidance of Eugène Kusnet—constructed his characters by evoking situations from his own life, analogous to those he would have to portray on stage.

This method seemed even more appropriate because Descartes himself, as I just said, claimed that his *Meditations* were not an intellectual construction but the account of lived experiences. Much later, studying Paul Friedländer's *Plato: An Introduction* and the works of Eric Voegelin, I confirmed that my decision was not as crazy as it seemed: with these two illustrious authors, I learned that understanding philosophical ideas cannot be achieved by analyzing texts alone or by reconstructing the cultural atmosphere from which the texts emerged. It requires the meditative tracking of the real experiences from which ideas were born.

I began to reread the *Meditations* as if they were a play, in which I should play the role of René Descartes in the imaginative reconstruction of his cognitive experiences using the Stanislavski method.

What a surprise it was to discover that this was much more difficult than I could have ever imagined! Descartes condenses everything into a few pages, giving the impression that the sequence of meditations flowed through his mind with the naturalness of running water. But the effort to pull from my affective memory some analogue of methodical doubt, the "Evil Genius," and the absolute certainty that the Thinking Self has of itself encountered so many obstacles and contradictions that I couldn't help but conclude that, as an account of lived experiences, the *Meditations* were not very reliable. Descartes *simply could not have* lived those experiences exactly as he narrates them.

That it is possible to doubt our sensations, our imaginations, and our thoughts is something any of us can testify to. It is also possible to put the whole sphere of our representations in parentheses, reducing the "world" to an evanescent hypothesis.

However, after performing these operations, Descartes assured us that he had found, at the core, the certainty of doubt: doubt is a thought, and in the moment that I think it, I cannot doubt that I am thinking it. The self-confidence of the thinking ego in its own metaphysical solidity emerged as a powerful psychological compensation for the loss of belief in the reality of the "world."

However, meticulous in describing the thoughts that lead him to a state of total doubt, he is strangely evasive about this state itself. In fact, he doesn't even describe it; he merely states that it happened and, jumping immediately from the description to deduction, proceeds to draw the logical consequences that the acknowledgment of this state imposes on him.

To give some plausible consistency to my performance in the role of Descartes that I intended to portray in my inner theater, I needed to do what he did not: examine and describe not only the mere content of some particular doubts but the act of doubting itself, *the state of doubt.*

And the first realization that imposed itself on me as undeniable was the following: doubt was not properly a "state"—a static position in which I could remain, as one remains sad or absorbed, motionless or lying down. It was an alternation between a yes and a no, an impossibility of stopping at one of the terms of the alternative without the other coming to dispute its primacy. For the yes or the no, as soon as accepted as definitive, would immediately eliminate doubt, which is made of their antagonistic coexistence and nothing more.

But this antagonism, as I soon perceived, is not static: it is mobile. The mind in doubt incessantly passes from one term to the other, without finding a point of support where it can rest and "be" at. However, as each of the terms is the negation of the other, the mind could not stop at it without, for a moment, denying the other: *and, precisely in that instant, it is not in doubt*—it is affirming or denying, affirming one thing and denying another, even if it cannot persevere in the affirmation or denial without a thousand reasons to abandon it. In the moment it denies or affirms, doubt suppresses itself as doubt, turning to argue in favor of one hypothesis and against the other, struggling to stabilize itself in affirmation or denial; but it fails, and it is in this failure that doubt consists precisely. The fatal conclusion followed: *a doubt that does not question itself, a doubt that,*

suspending the alternation, imposes itself as a "state" and remains, is impossible.
By taking doubt as a "state," omitting that it was an alternation between two
antagonistic moments, Descartes objectified it and made it a certainty. The famous
assertion "I cannot doubt that I doubt at the moment I doubt," which Descartes
takes as an expression of the most obvious truth, actually expressed a pure
psychological impossibility. More accurate would be to say that, when doubting,
I put everything in doubt, including doubt itself. Doubt is not a state; it is a
succession and coexistence of antagonistic states; it is an inability to be at.[97]

What was happening here was that Descartes confused doubt with negation,
more precisely with hypothetical negation. I can indeed produce a hypothetical
negation and repeat it indefinitely. I can even expand it—hypothetically, of
course—until it encompasses the entirety of what I believe to know. But I cannot
"doubt" what I believe without at the same time affirming it repeatedly, as only
then can I intersperse with its successive affirmations their respective negations,
and with these their affirmations, and so on, whose vicious circle constitutes
doubt.

Now, hypothetical negation is not the same as doubt, but it is its logical
counterpart, its reduced, conceptualized, and fleshless version, separated from the
living experience of antagonism that constitutes the psychological substance of
the experience of doubt. Hypothetical negation is the "doubt" as it appears in the
thinking self, not in consciousness, not in the soul. Descartes always uses the term
"doubt," but in fact, he is only talking about hypothetical negation, therefore only
about the thinking self, not about consciousness or the soul. When, in the *Second
Meditation*, he recounts the emotions he felt at finding himself unable to contest
the negations he had made the day before, he talks about the soul, indeed, but not
as the active center of doubt, but as the passive victim of the effects provoked in
it by the thinking self. In other words, by giving hypothetical negation the
dimensions of "doubt," Descartes substitutes the soul for the thinking self and,
speaking of the latter, believes he is speaking of the former. But if the thinking
self has such primacy over the soul, how would it not also have it over everything
the soul knows? The priority of the *ego cogitans*, which will later be affirmed as
the conclusion of the sequence of thoughts, is already given from the beginning

---

[97] When I say "succession and coexistence," I may seem to be uttering a monumental
contradiction. But the yes and the no that compose doubt are coexistent in one aspect,
successive in another. Logically coexistent as terms of contradiction, they are
psychologically successive, that is, they enter the stage of consciousness cyclically,
rotationally: one enters, the other exits, like day and night, which coexist in the sky and
succeed each other at a point on earth.

in the mere formulation of "doubt." The reasoning of the *Meditations* is entirely circular, offering as an answer only what was already contained in the question.

Put in these terms, the Cartesian *cogito* merely repeated Socrates's argument against the skeptic, that one cannot deny without affirming the negation, without affirming something, therefore. But, seen in this way, the Cartesian discovery amounted to very little: far from having established a new foundation, critical or negative, for the world of knowledge, it had only demonstrated again, through the tortuous paths of a rather imprecise psychological self-description, the logical primacy of affirmation over negation. However, the acknowledgment of this primacy was, at the same time, the denial of doubt as a founding act.

But if doubt, as such, could not serve as a critical foundation, it remained to ask what grounds make it possible. And this was the decisive point because if there was something "behind" doubt, it would be that something, not doubt, that Descartes sought as a firm foundation and believed to have found in the acknowledgment of doubt.

Descartes claims that doubt is a certainty in the moment it is thought. But this is false: what is certain is the subsequent reflection that affirms the reality of the experience of doubt. In the very moment of doubt, as we have seen, there is an alternation between affirmation and negation, and therefore the impossibility of affirming any state if, by state, we understand, as we should, the coincidence between a judgment of fact and the feeling that values it negatively or positively, as occurs in sadness, anger, haste, hope, etc. Doubt is not a state, for the simple reason that in it, the feeling, which can be anxiety, hope, curiosity, etc., does not coincide with a specific judgment but arises precisely from the impossibility of affirming or negating a judgment. It is rather a moment of suspension between states, a restless void that contains in germ various possible states—at least two— and does not resolve into any of them without suppressing itself. The mind, therefore, is never "in" doubt; it only passes through it, precisely as a transition between states. It is only when doubt ceases to be a present experience to become an object of reflection that this retrospective and narrative certainty arises: "*I have not been able, so far, to stabilize myself in negation or affirmation.*" There is, therefore, not only a logical distinction but also a factual separation between doubt as a present experience and doubt as an object of recollection and reflection—and it is the latter that is certain and indubitable,[98] not the former, even though Descartes confuses one with the other and presents to us, as direct intuitive evidence, what the result of subsequent reflection is. It is only this reflection that,

---

[98] "Certain and doubtless" or "uncertain and doubtful" are predicates that do not apply to the fact itself, but to the judgments we make about it.

by giving a name to the alternation just experienced, artificially confers the unity of a "state" on what is, in fact, a succession of states that mutually suppress each other or a coexistence of purely potential states, each of which can only be actualized at the cost of excluding the others. By conferring positive consistency to the void of alternation as a state, Descartes, in the same instant, transforms doubt into mere hypothetical negation, taking as an effective psychological state that which is only the logical concept of a possible state.

* * *

Based on the symbol of old cameras, in which the viewfinder's focus did not coincide with that of the lens, I coined the term "cognitive parallax" to denote the structural displacement between the axis of a thinker's real-life experience and the axis of his theoretical construction. If we compare Saint Augustine's *Confessions* with Descartes's *Meditations*, we will see that the difference between these two spiritual autobiographies lies in the fact that, in the former, philosophical speculations remain very close to the inner voice of the sinner confessing his sins, whereas, in the latter, the constructive impulse of the mind takes flight on its own and, ends up far from the immediate consciousness, the heartfelt "hombre de carne y hueso," as Unamuno would say. The difference is structurally determined by the ideal audience to which the two discourses are addressed: Augustine writes to a God whom he knows he cannot deceive. Descartes writes to a scientific audience whom he fervently wishes to persuade of the absolute novelty of his discoveries. There can be no greater contrast than that which emerges from the comparison of these two voices: the voice of the sinner confessing with heart in hand and the voice of the aspirant to the title of head of the school. The distance of each of these voices from the "cardiac" center of consciousness is quite different.

* * *

Another extraordinary thing is the fact that the fundamental argument of the *Meditations on First Philosophy* was entirely copied from *Amphitryon*, a play by Plautus, in which we find exactly the same sequence of thoughts based on the hypothesis of the evil genius. What is the evil genius? The evil genius is a hidden force that has sown in the human mind a set of false impressions—the image of this world—in order to lead the mind into error. The character in *Amphitryon* escapes from this terrifying hypothesis precisely by the discovery of the certainty of *cogito ergo sum*. Benjamín García-Hernández[99] shows that the argument is

---

[99] Benjamín García-Hernández, *Descartes y Plauto. La Concepción Dramática Del Sistema Cartesiano* (Madrid: Tecnos, 1997).

exactly the same and that this comedy by Plautus was among Descartes's bedside books, so he could not legitimately claim ignorance of the debt to the illustrious predecessor he does not mention. The fact that he manifestly concealed the source of his main argument shows that the desire to impose himself as a revolutionary innovator predominated in his soul over the sincere intention of seeking truth. If a thinker can conceal under a reasoning construction even a raw material fact like the existence of a historical source, how much more easily will he not cover up, under this construction, the voice of the inner conscience that shows him in symbols the truth of his life? *Cognitive parallax*, which will be shown in much more striking ways in later cases, already appears here under subtle camouflage, but with all the force of its distorting potential. This distortion, evidently, not only affects Descartes's work but also the entire vision that, based on it, Modernity constructed regarding its own origins. Descartes came to be celebrated as the "discoverer of subjectivity," when in fact, what he did was replace the profound and genuine subjectivity of the confessing self with the pseudo-subjectivity, peripheral and artificial, of the constructive mind. Subsequent thinkers, such as David Hume, Immanuel Kant, and Karl Marx, will show an even more advanced state of alienation, but the gap between the truth of the soul and mental construction is already fully evident in René Descartes.

It is also characteristic that, in *The World*, where Descartes first exposes his scientific conceptions about the constitution of the universe, he does not try to explain how the world was created and constructed by God, but how God would build, at the very moment Descartes writes, another world if He simply found the materials to do so. The entire world described in *The World* is an artificial and hypothetical world, constructed entirely in Descartes's mind—and it is built exactly like a machine, where everything operates driven by mechanical impulses. There is a passage from Alain, I do not remember in which book, where he says that Descartes looked out the window, saw people walking on the street, and had the impression that they were mechanical dolls, not human beings endowed with a soul. This means that the mechanical conception he creates of the world is entirely invented in his mind, and he does not affirm that this is the real world— nor does he affirm, nor deny. He simply says that if God were to create the world now, He would do it this way and that. That is, he is offering God a universe project. He is not only redoing philosophy, redoing theology, redoing all knowledge, but he is remaking the world itself from his mind. Needless to say, this entire conception was demoralized over time—I think there is no longer any pure mechanist in the world, especially after quantum physics. But at the time, that impressed a lot, it was a great success, and for about two centuries, it can be said that mechanism, reinforced by the contributions of Newton and Galileo, became the dominant philosophy in the Western world. Even demoralized as an explicit doctrine, mechanism survived, unnamed, through the deep marks it left on European culture. The most characteristic was undoubtedly the belief that human conduct can—and should—be controlled in a purely mechanical way through the interplay of impressions and stimuli. This idea was put into circulation by Abbot Dubos in 1740, in his *Réflexions Critiques*.[100] No one remembers the book or the author anymore, but who can deny that the same idea inspires the behavioral engineering that has now replaced pedagogy as the matrix of virtually all early childhood education programs in the Western world?[101]

Kant and the Primacy of the Critical Problem

A handout from the Philosophy Seminar, February 1996

If the primacy of methodical doubt is nothing more than the primacy of a verbal equivocation, then Kant's primacy of the critical problem also falls under suspicion. If human knowledge must pay preliminary reverence to the awareness of its limits, why should it not also submit to the demand for a preliminary justification for the claim to know these limits?

Kant's immediate motivation to investigate the limits of human knowledge was the profound irritation caused by Emmanuel Swedenborg's accounts of visions of heaven and hell. The only passages in Kant's work where we sense that the author's usual analytical coldness gives way to a tone of sarcasm and passionate controversy are those in which Kant seeks to reduce the testimonies of the Swedish mystic to hallucinations of a diseased mind. The essay *Dreams of a Spirit-Seer* precisely marks the transition from the pre-critical phase to the maturity of Kantian thought. It is evident that critical philosophy aims less to *provide* a foundation for scientific knowledge than simply to elucidate the foundations taken as presupposed, while denying any scientific basis for mystical and metaphysical knowledge, thus reducing religion to a set of moral commandments without any cognitive support.

---

[100] Jean de Viguerie, *Itinéraire d'un historien. Études sur une crise de l'intelligence, XVIIe.–XXe. Siècle* (Paris: Dominique Martin Morin, 2000).
[101] Pascal Bernardin, *Machiavel pédagogue ou Le Ministère de la réforme psychologique* (Paris: Notre-Dame des Grâces, 1995).

But what's curious is that the critical philosopher, so careful not to be deceived by dogmatic presuppositions, presupposes not only the validity of physical science but also the ability of reason to know its own limits. Beyond the realm of *a priori* judgments and sensory experience, according to him, lies only the domain of the unknowable: *thinkable*, Kant admits, but unknowable. However, how could one determine the limits of the knowable without knowing something about the supposed unknowable whose outer edge coincides precisely with these limits? If reason knows the limits of the sensible and, at the same time, establishes its own limits, how could it also determine the limits of the third field, specifically different, which is that of *rationalized experience*, or science, if, as Kant himself says, it is only the imagination that connects the rational and the sensible? To be consistent, Kant should have said that there are no limits to science except those of the imagination. For, to the extent that it operates guided by reason and sensory experience, imagination, in the Kantian perspective, will not only give us thought, but knowledge, rightly so. And if that's the case, why dogmatically reject the possibility of, starting from the sensible, imaginatively scaling the degrees of the supra-sensible? Nothing in Kantism proves that this is impossible or even difficult.

The limits of a particular capacity can only be of two kinds: intrinsic and extrinsic. Intrinsic limits are those that can be known *a priori* and analytically, by deduction from their concept. However, according to Kant, no *a priori* deduction can migrate, simply put, to the domain of facts, since knowledge of this domain is only valid when it is inductive and based on experience. Therefore, the intrinsic limits of human knowledge, if known, would be purely formal and would not apply to the knowledge of any real and determinate object. They would be, so to speak, empty, hypothetical limits that, in practice, would limit nothing.

As for extrinsic limits, they can only be determined inductively, from varied effective knowledge concerning various species of objects; and, being extrinsic, they could never be necessary and unconditional, but only accidental and contingent.

Seeking to determine, *a priori*, the real limits of human knowledge, which is impossible according to Kantism itself, or to prove by induction from contingent facts that these limits are necessary and unconditional, the proposal of critical philosophy is, to say the least, a fallacy through and through.

The first and most basic of the limits pointed out by Kant is that the field of experience is circumscribed by the two *a priori* forms of sensibility, space and time. But what is in a determined place is also, *a fortiori*, in the infinite supra-spatial; and what happens in a determined moment also happens, *a fortiori*, within eternity—two *a priori* necessities of the most obvious kind that, on their own, would undermine the famous limits that critical philosophy sought to establish.[102]

Even more fallacious is Kant's refutation of St. Anselm's argument. St. Anselm asserts that the existence of God is self-evident by mere analysis, since the infinite and necessary Being cannot be deprived of existence, as every privation is a limitation, contradictory to infinity. Moreover, the very possibility of a limitation is a contingency, contradictory to necessity. Kant objects that analytical judgments have purely rational validity and do not apply to beings in the real domain, which can only be known through experience: to exist is to exist "outside" thought, and therefore existence can never be deduced from mere concept.

In this objection, Kant presupposes that our mind can create, as a mere hypothesis, the concept of an absolutely necessary being, meaning that this concept can be mere "content" of thought. That is to say, the concept of the necessary being would be only *hypothetically necessary*. However, for this concept to be solely and exclusively a creation of our mind, without any objective reality, it would have to be *necessarily hypothetical*, meaning it would have to completely exclude the possibility of being more than a mere hypothesis. Now, this exclusion is self-contradictory. No logic in the world can determine that a hypothetical necessity is *necessarily* hypothetical because this would be the same as denying, in advance, all necessary character, affirmed at the same time by the mere concept. We can, of course, imagine a false necessity, but when we say it is false, we are saying that it is not necessary in any way. A hypothetical necessity is either an unproven necessity, which, if proven, will be shown to be necessary, or it is a false necessity. What is logically impossible is to conceive that a hypothetical necessity is *necessarily* hypothetical, that it cannot be true in any way, for this would deny its status as a hypothesis and replace it with the categorical judgment that affirms its falsehood. The infinite and necessary Being cannot, therefore, be conceived as a *mere* "content of our mind." In fact, to conceive it in this way, giving positive logical content to a self-contradictory

---

[102] Additionally, sensory experience is not only delimited by space and time, but also by quantity. However, as Benedetto Croce demonstrated [*Aesthetic as Science of Expression and General Linguistic*, 1909] *Estetica come Scienza dell'Espressione e Linguistica Generale* (Bari: Laterza, 11ª ed., 1965), we can perceive space independently of time, time independently of space, and quantity independently of both. Furthermore, as Croce insightfully observed, we could not perceive quantity without also having the perception of singular individuality, in its non-spatial and timeless nature. Thus, there is no reason why necessary being cannot be perceived with the senses, as by definition, it is impossible for necessary being to be necessarily excluded from any possibility of phenomenal manifestation.

concept, is much more difficult than knowing something positive about the Absolute. It is easier to know God than it is to know the "necessary necessarily hypothetical."

On the other hand, if the *real* existence of the necessary being cannot be deduced analytically from the concept of its necessity, if necessity excludes contingency (and thus the possibility of non-existence), and if the phenomenal reality is necessarily subject to logical categories, then, in Kantian terminology, the ontological argument is a synthetic *a priori* judgment, not a purely analytical judgment: the real existence of the necessary being is not *contained* in its mere definition, but *a priori*, we know that it demands it, as a property, exactly as in the geometric judgments mentioned by Kant.

More than logically certain, the ontological argument is self-evident. *I call self-evident the judgment that cannot have a univocal opposite, i.e., one whose opposite cannot even be formulated without the fatal flaw of ambiguity.* As far as I know, this characteristic of self-evident judgments had not been emphasized until now. In this case, what is the opposite of the judgment "The necessary being necessarily exists"? Is it "The necessary being necessarily does not exist" or "The existence of the necessary being is not necessary"? It is impossible to decide. The opposite of St. Anselm's argument is *unformulable.* Therefore, to reject this argument is to abdicate the very sense of the unity of discourse, to fall into the double language that will eventually lead us where Kant arrived.

However, the root of all these absurdities lies precisely in the dogmatic faith that Kant, imitating Descartes, places in the human power to doubt. For how can we, in fact, doubt our ability to know the absolute? If we know nothing, radically nothing about the absolute, we cannot even formulate our doubt about the possibility of knowing it. Hence the need to have a point of support in the absolute to formulate doubt; but since, at the same time, Kant has already taken this doubt as an infallible starting point and cannot renounce it in any way, the only option left is to seek this point of support in the very limits of knowledge, elevated to absolute and unconditional, by a most singular logical twist. Thus, we can know nothing about the absolute, except that it is "beyond" the limits of our knowledge, which, not being determined by the absolute (of which we know nothing) and not being contingent and revocable realities (since they are proven by mere analysis, being valid *a priori*), become the absolute itself! Because if thought cannot deduce anything about what is outside it, how can it then know its "limits" unless these are necessary *a priori*? Being necessary *a priori*, they are unconditional; but they are also total, encompassing human knowledge as a whole and not just in some parts and aspects: and the unconditional whole is evidently absolute. Therefore, the proof that we cannot know the absolute is based on the knowledge we have of the absolute, with the name changed to the "limits of knowledge." If this were not an iconoclastic attack on an idol of Modernity, I would say that the only comment worthy of this thesis of Kantian philosophy is that it is puerile.

From a theological standpoint, the enthronement of the limits of knowledge as the new absolute in place of the old God has a consequence that is most clear: the absolute comes to be defined as the non-human, the human as the non-absolute. This abyss, in turn, is absolute: God is everything outside the limits of the human, and the human is everything outside and below the divine realm. In other words, *the exclusion of the human from the divine realm becomes an absolute in itself.* The fact that Kant later attempts to rescue, by the force of practical reason and pietistic faith, the connection between man and God, after having demonstrated that it is absolutely impossible, only shows that he was not very aware of what he was doing. For if the exclusion of man from the divine realm is an absolute necessity, not even the grace of an omnipotent God could revoke it.

In reality, there cannot be *necessary* limits to human knowledge, as the human condition is precisely defined by contingency and freedom. All limits to human knowledge must be contingent, and this is precisely what allows, on the one hand, differences in cognitive capacity among individuals and, on the other hand, the progress of knowledge. The attempt to establish the limits of human knowledge, *a priori*, is self-contradictory and absurd at its core, reducing critical philosophy to a senseless pretension, to the "dream of a spirit-seer" who imagines being able to pull himself out of the water by his own hair, like Baron Munchausen, and contemplate from within his own external limits, like those Escher stairs whose top merges with the first step.

Therefore, more naive than the dogmatic confidence of classical rationalism in the cognitive power of reason, and more visionary than the claim of mystics to an experimental knowledge of God, is the trust in the human power to doubt those principles that underpin the very possibility of doubt. More naive than any dogmatism is the very principle of critical philosophy, which claims to deduce contingent limits and inductively establish necessary limits. More naive than our ancestors who believed in revelation and reason are we, who believe in Descartes and Kant, assuming that the negativity of their starting point is evidence of methodological modesty when, in reality, it conceals the most superhuman of pretensions: the claim to establish absolute limits to human knowledge. A pretension superior to that of God himself, who did not enclose the forbidden fruit with bars but left it within reach of Eve's curiosity.

* * *

Certain philosophies ignore their most obvious practical implications and, as a result, trigger historical effects contrary to those intended by their authors, who, if they saw them, could only try to shift the blame for the legitimate consequences onto the misunderstanding of devoted disciples.

Kant seeks to subjugate philosophy to Christian *faith*, resulting in de-Christianizing philosophy and sapping philosophical vigor from Christianity. Like Descartes, he is a religious zealot who strengthens atheism while imagining to defend religion.

He twists the philosophical gaze, diverting it from the given object to the cognitive structures of the subject. These structures become not only the only safe ground, but also the only object worthy of interest.

Simultaneously, all universality ceases to be objective universality, becoming mere uniformity of cognitive structures of the human species, that is, collective subjectivity or, as it has come to be called, *intersubjectivity*.

Categories are no longer modes of being, but modes of our cognition, any discourse we engage in only concerns ourselves, and the object remains eternally separate from us in the glass case of the unknowable "thing-in-itself." There is no way out of the mental prison except through the categorical imperative that orders us to believe in God. Still, as we have to believe in Him without ever being able to *know* if He exists, any attempt to rationally justify faith will forever be a game of words. One would have to explain finally why this God, in whom we must believe and whom we must judge to be good by categorical imperative, categorically imposes a specific faith and the use of reason, while prohibiting us from using reason to prove the truth of faith. Kant's philosophy is a schizophrenic division: it juxtaposes, side by side, an obedient fideism and a pre-positivist scientism without possible internal communication. Now, between an irrational and authoritarian religion and the denial of all supra-sensory knowledge, any sensible person would opt for the latter, and that is precisely what happened: Kant generated positivism, which gave rise to widespread materialism. Only a naive person would not foresee this consequence, and it was precisely because of foreseeing it that scholastic philosophers insisted on reconciling reason and faith instead of mechanically juxtaposing them without internal connection as Kant does. Kant represents a regression of Christian consciousness, which, through him, falls into splitting contradictions already overcome by scholasticism—a scholasticism that Kant almost completely ignored, as his only source on the subject was the manuals of Christian Wolff.

To make matters worse, the *a priori* forms of subjectivity described by the *Critique* are universal and necessary, that is, they encompass every possible cognizant subject. There is no way to exclude God from this, assuming that God thinks and knows humanly, which the Church says is precisely the business of the Second Person of the Trinity. And there we have the supreme extravagance of Kantism: knowing nothing about God, we are ignorant if He thinks, but at the same time, we already know everything about how He thinks—a conclusion that Kant does not affirm because he does not even perceive it, but that is logically implicated, inescapably, in everything he asserts. Truly I tell you: it seems like a joke.

A die-hard Kantian may object that knowing the human thought of Jesus is not to know absolutely anything about His divine thought—a disastrous objection that would result in digging the abyss between man and God, within Christ Himself, which Kant has already dug in the soul of all of us, an abyss over which Christ is precisely the bridge. Something tells me that when Jesus warned, "Whoever is not with me is against me," the pious, clumsy sage of Königsberg perhaps was not entirely absent from His considerations.

Chapter 5

On the Revolutionary Mind

The Revolutionary Mentality

Diário do Comércio, August 16 2007
A fórmula para enlouquecer o mundo (2014)

Since it got around that I am writing a book called "The Revolutionary Mind," I have received many requests for a preliminary explanation regarding the phenomenon designated by this title.

The revolutionary mind is a perfectly identifiable and continuous historical phenomenon, whose developments over five centuries can be traced in a multitude of documents. This is the subject of the research that has occupied me for some years. "Book" is perhaps not the right expression because I have presented some results of this study in classes, lectures, and articles, and I don't even know if I will ever have the strength to reduce this enormous material to an identifiable printed format.[103] "The revolutionary mind" is the name of the subject and not necessarily of one book, or two, or three. I have never been very concerned with the editorial formatting of what I have to say. I investigate the subjects that interest me, and when I reach some conclusions that seem reasonable to me, I convey them orally or in writing as opportunities arise. Transforming this into "books" is a hassle that, if I could, I would leave to an assistant. Since I have no assistant, I keep postponing this work as long as I can.

The revolutionary mind is not essentially a political phenomenon but a spiritual and psychological one, although its most visible field of expression and its fundamental instrument is political action.

To facilitate matters, I use the expressions "revolutionary mind" and "revolutionary mentality" to distinguish between the concrete historical phenomenon, with all the variety of its manifestations, and the essential and permanent characteristic that permits grasping its unity over time.

"Revolutionary mentality" is the state of mind, permanent or transitory, in which an individual, or group, believes himself authorized to reshape the whole of society—if not human nature in general—through political action. He believes that, as an agent or bearer of a better future, he is above all judgment by present or past humanity, only having to answer to the "court of History." But the court of History is, by definition, the future society that this individual or group claims to represent in the present. Since this society can only witness or judge through this same representative, he becomes not only the sole sovereign judge of his own

---

[103] Some of Carvalho's findings on the *Revolutionary Mind*, along with other original philosophical contributions, still remain sparsely published in articles and recorded lectures, and have not yet been compiled for publication.—Eds.

acts but the judge of all humanity, past, present, or future. Authorized to accuse and condemn all laws, institutions, beliefs, values, customs, actions, and works of all times without being judged by any of them, he is so above historical humanity that it is not inaccurate to call him Superman.

Self-glorification of Superman, the revolutionary mentality is totalitarian and genocidal in itself, regardless of the ideological contents with which it may fill itself in different circumstances and occasions.

Refusing to answer to anything but a hypothetical future of his own invention and firmly determined to destroy, by cunning or force, any obstacle that opposes the re-molding of the world in his own image and likeness, the revolutionary is the greatest enemy of the human species, next to whom the tyrants and conquerors of antiquity seem modest in their pretensions and remarkably circumspect in the use of means.

The advent of the revolutionary to the forefront of the historical stage—a phenomenon that begins to take shape around the fifteenth century and manifests itself with full clarity at the end of the eighteenth century—ushers in the era of totalitarianism, world wars, and permanent genocide. Over two centuries, revolutionary movements, the wars undertaken by them, and the massacre of civilian populations necessary for the consolidation of their power have killed far more people than all the wars, epidemics, earthquakes, and natural disasters of any kind since the beginning of the world's history.

The revolutionary movement is the greatest scourge that has ever befallen the human species since its advent on Earth.

The expansion of genocidal violence and the imposition of increasingly stifling restrictions on human freedom accompany the spread of the revolutionary mentality, *pari passu*, among ever broader segments of the population. Whole masses imbue themselves with the role of avenging judges appointed by the tribunal of the future, granting themselves the right to commit crimes immeasurably greater than all those the revolutionary promise claims to eradicate.

Even if we do not consider deliberate massacres and only examine the revolutionary performance from an economic perspective, no other social or natural cause has ever created as much misery and caused as many deaths from malnutrition as the revolutionary regimes of Russia, China, and various African countries.

Whatever the future of the human species may be and whatever our personal conceptions, the revolutionary mentality must be radically eradicated from the repertoire of admissible social and cultural possibilities. Otherwise, by forcing the birth of a supposedly better world, it may turn it into a gigantic abortion and the millennia-long journey of the human species on Earth into a senseless history crowned by a bloody end.

Although distinct revolutionary ideologies are all, to a greater or lesser extent, threatening and harmful, their evil does not lie so much in their specific content, or the strategies they use to achieve it, as in the fact of being revolutionary in the sense defined here.

Socialism and Nazism are revolutionary not because they respectively propose the dominance of a class or a race, but because they make these banners the principles of a radical re-molding not only of the political order but of all human life. The evils they foreshadow become universally threatening because they do not present themselves as local responses to momentary situations, but as universal commandments imbued with the authority to reshape the world according to the mold of a hypothetical future perfection. The Ku Klux Klan is as racist as Nazism, but it is not revolutionary because it has no project of global reach. For this reason, it would be ridiculous to compare it, in terms of danger, to the Nazi movement. It is a pure and simple police problem.

Therefore, it is necessary to emphasize that the sense attributed to the term "revolution" here is both broader and more precise than the word generally has in historiography and present social sciences. Many socio-political processes, usually denominated "revolutions," are not truly "revolutionary" because they do not partake in the revolutionary mentality. They do not aim at the complete re-molding of society, culture, and the human species, but are solely intended to modify local and momentary situations, ideally for the better. For example, a political rebellion aimed only at breaking the ties between one country and another is not necessarily revolutionary. Nor is the simple overthrow of a tyrannical regime with the goal of aligning a nation with the freedoms already enjoyed by neighboring peoples. Even if these endeavors employ large-scale military resources and cause spectacular changes, they are not revolutions because they aspire only to correct immediate evils or even to return to a lost previous situation.

What unmistakably characterizes the revolutionary movement is that it superimposes the authority of a hypothetical future on the judgment of all humankind, present or past. Revolution is, by its very nature, totalitarian and universally expansive: there is no aspect of human life that it does not intend to subject to its power, and there is no region of the globe to which it does not seek to extend the tentacles of its influence.

If, in this sense, various political-military movements of vast proportions must be excluded from the concept of "revolution," on the other hand, several seemingly peaceful movements of purely intellectual and cultural nature, whose evolution over time leads them to become political powers with claims to universally impose new standards of thought and conduct through bureaucratic, judicial, and police means, must be included in it. The Hungarian rebellion of 1956 or the overthrow of Brazilian President João Goulart [in 1964], in this sense, were by no means revolutions. Neither was the struggle for American independence, a special case that I will have to explain in another article.[104] But undoubtedly, revolutionary movements include Darwinism and the set of pseudo-religious phenomena known as the New Age. All these distinctions will have to be explained separately later and are mentioned here only as a sample.

* * *

Among other confusions that this study dispels is one that reigns over the concepts of "left" and "right." This confusion arises from the fact that this pair of words is used, in turn, to designate two completely distinct orders of phenomena. On the one hand, the left is the revolution in general, and the right is the counter-revolution. There seemed to be no doubt about this when the terms were used to designate the two wings of the Estates-General. However, the evolution of events caused the revolutionary movement itself to appropriate the two terms, using them to designate its internal subdivisions. The Girondins, who were to the left of the king, became the "right" of the revolution, to the extent that, with the king beheaded, the followers of the old regime were excluded from public life and no longer had the right to their own political denomination. This retraction of admissible "rightism," by attributing the label "right" to one of the wings of the left itself, later became a routine mechanism of the revolutionary process. At the same time, genuine counter-revolutionary remnants were often forced to ally with the revolutionary "right" and merge with it to retain some means of action within the framework created by the revolution's victory. To further complicate matters, once counter-revolution was excluded from the repertoire of politically admissible ideas, counter-revolutionary resentment continued to exist as a psychosocial phenomenon and was often used by the revolutionary left as a pretext and rhetorical appeal to win over segments of the deeply conservative and traditionalist population, which had revolted against the revolutionary "right" prevailing at the moment. The appeal of the [Brazilian] Landless Movement ("MST") to agrarian nostalgia, or the pseudo-traditionalist rhetoric adopted

---

[104] See further in Chapter 5, "The Globalist Revolution."—Eds.

occasionally by fascism, makes us forget the strictly revolutionary nature of these movements. Mao Zedong himself was taken, for some time, as a traditionalist agrarian reformer. It's also needless to say that, in the internal disputes of the revolutionary movement, the factions often accuse each other of being "rightist" (or "reactionary"). The Nazi rhetoric that professed to destroy both "reaction" and "communism" corresponded, on the communist side, to the double and successive discourse that first treated the Nazis as primitive and anarchic revolutionaries and then as adherents of "reaction," committed to "saving capitalism" against proletarian revolution.

The terms "left" and "right" only have an objective meaning when used in their original sense of revolution and counter-revolution, respectively. All other combinations and meanings are occasional arrangements that do not have descriptive scope but only opportunistic utility as symbols of the unity of a political movement and demonizing symbols of its objects of hatred.

In the United States, the term "right" is used simultaneously to designate conservatives in the strict sense, counter-revolutionaries to the core, and Republican globalists, the "right" of the worldwide revolution. But the confusion in Brazil is much worse, where the counter-revolutionary right has no political existence, and the name that designates it is used, by the ruling party, to name any opposition that comes from within, even from left-wing parties, while the left-wing opposition uses it to label the ruling party itself.

For me, it is clear that these terms can only be given some objective descriptive value by taking the revolutionary movement, as a whole, as the demarcation line and opposing it to the counter-revolutionary right, even where it has no political expression and is only a cultural phenomenon.

The essence of the counter-revolutionary or conservative mentality is the aversion to any comprehensive transformation project, the stubborn refusal to intervene in society as a whole, the almost religious respect for regional, spontaneous, and long-term social processes, the denial of all authority to the spokespersons of the hypothetical future.

In this sense, the author of these lines is strictly conservative. Among other reasons, because he believes that only the conservative point of view can provide a realistic view of the historical process, as it is based on the experience of the past and not on conjectures of the future. All revolutionary historiography is fraudulent at its core because it interprets and distorts the past according to the mold of a hypothetical and otherwise indefinable future. It is no coincidence that the greatest historians of all time have always been conservatives.

If, considered in itself and in the values it defends, the counter-revolutionary mentality should properly be called "conservative," it is evident that, from the point of view of its relations with the enemy, it is strictly "reactionary." To be reactionary is to react in the most uncompromising and hostile manner to the diabolical ambition to rule the world.

Psychosis of the Enlightenment

Jornal do Brasil, April 24, 2008

One of the constitutive traits of the revolutionary mentality is the irresistible compulsion to take a hypothetical—supposedly desirable—future as a categorical premise for explaining the present and the past. From this perspective, human history is seen as a linear trajectory—although interrupted by abominable resistances—toward the advent of a state of affairs in which the total course of events will find its consummation and its reason for being.

That there is a psychotic inversion of the order of causes in this is something that does not even remotely shine on the horizon of the revolutionary (un)consciousness, so enchanted in the ecstatic contemplation of its own beauties that even the maximum clarity of the obvious becomes a dense and impenetrable darkness in its eyes.

Even more comical, or tragicomic, is this inversion when, in the manner of the Enlightenment, the expected future is described as the triumph of scientific rationality over the obscurantism of barbaric beliefs. For the future-centric conception of history, turning the hierarchy of the necessary and the contingency upside down, already carries within it the complete destruction of logic, the scientific method, and any possibility of a rational understanding of reality. It was not in vain that Paul Ilie, in his masterful study *The Age of Minerva,*[105] characterized the mental style of the Enlightenment as "counter-rational reason."

It is not surprising that, more than two hundred years after unleashing the greatest and most enduring epidemic of revolutions, tyrannies, and genocides ever recorded since the beginning of time, the vanity of the Enlightenment still continues to parade itself as the champion of freedom and human rights, as if it were permissible for a philosophy to recognize itself solely by the ideals declared

---

[105] University of Pennsylvania Press, 1995, 2 vols.

in its propaganda and not by the inevitable and predictably unfolding realization of its premises.

The ideal of a society governed by "scientific reason" is the very core of the Enlightenment proposal, and it gave rise to the two bloodiest tyrannies the world has ever known, one founded on evolutionary biology, the other on the Marxist science of history and economics. The most recent and meticulous comparative study of these two regimes, by Richard Overy,[106] highlights the "cult of science" as the first and essential similarity between them. Auschwitz and the Gulag are the materialized utopia of the Enlightenment.

And don't come to me with the nonsense that the Enlightenment not only generated totalitarian dictatorships but also American democracy. On the one hand, the British Enlightenment that influenced American independence had nothing of the Voltairean and encyclopedic rebellion against religion and traditions.[107] On the other, even this softened version of the Enlightenment discourse was not entirely subscribed to by the Founding Fathers, who modified and Christianized it to such an extent that there is practically not a single statement or legal provision in the Declaration of Independence, the U.S. Constitution, or state constitutions, whose biblical inspiration is not abundantly documented. No rational argument has ever been presented against the mass of evidence assembled by Benjamin F. Morris in the thousand-plus pages of *The Christian Life and Character of the Civil Institutions of the United States* in 1864. All that the "Enlightenment Party" could do to try to impose a caricatured, "French," version of secular militant atheist statehood as pure American constitutionalism, was to make that book disappear, and then panic when it was reissued in 2007 by American Vision.

---

[106] *The Dictators: Hitler's Germany, Stalin's Russia* (New York: W. W. Norton, 2004), 637*ff.*
[107] See Gertrude Himmelfarb, *The Roads to Modernity: The British, French and American Enlightenments* (New York: Vintage Books, 2004).

To Understand Kant

Diário do Comércio, October 16, 2014
A cólera dos imbecis (2019)

In 1762, Kant wrote: "I would find myself more useless than the common laborer if I did not believe that this attitude of mine [philosophy] can give worth to all others in establishing the rights of humanity."[108]

A slow-maturing man, at the age of thirty-eight, he discovered what would become the constant goal of the rest of his life: "establishing the rights of humanity," demolishing the authority of tradition and habit, creating a rational society governed by a rational State educating rational human beings ready to act according to the dictates of universal rules, instead of following their instincts like animals or priests, like a medieval peasant.

Everything he did from the moment of that statement of principles was to serve this goal, to which even the most remarkable philosophical achievements he accomplished along the way are subordinated as means to an end.

He believed that this end was not only desirable but inscribed in the historical evolution of humanity itself, as a final goal to which everything tended in a tortuous and problematic, but constant and irreversible way. When Kant recognizes that humans may fail to achieve this goal, he makes it clear that no other exists: thus, between the Kantian rational society and barbarism, *tertium non datur*.

Kant's philosophical work, as a whole and in its parts, invariably aims at achieving goals that will affect the entire society, culture, politics, morality, religion, law, education, family relationships, human life, in short, in its entirety.

Kant was by no means an isolated, otherworldly, disinterested thinker, engaged in abstractions that only attract an insignificant number of specialized scholars. Like Plato, Luther, or Karl Marx, he was a reformer of humanity, a reformer of the world. That was what he wanted to be, and that was what he became. Nothing he wrote and taught can be understood outside of this grandiose—or, if you will, megalomaniac—project.

What can obscure this reality to the point of making it elusive are three factors:

1. In most of his works, Kant uses such an unusual vocabulary and such abstruse language that it seems more intent on limiting the circle of his

---

[108] AK 20:44 quoted in *Immanuel Kant, Practical Philosophy*, trans. and ed. Mary J. Gregor and Introduction by Allen W. Wood (Cambridge University Press, 1996)—Eds.

readers to the dimensions of an esoteric sect than on influencing the broader public.

2. Some specific parts of his philosophy are so complex, difficult, and brilliantly executed that they tend to appear as isolated monuments, relegating the broader objectives they serve to a discreet background.

3. For this reason, many scholars of Kantism, including some of the most competent, tend to describe the structure of Kant's thought by taking these monuments as the articulating centers of the whole, reducing everything else to the status of peripheral opinions or even to episodes of purely historical-biographical value.

Against these three factors, there remains the undeniable fact that Kant himself repeatedly proclaimed, until extreme old age, the same general, constant, and final goals that inspired him. No clever interpretation of a philosophy should obscure the way the philosopher himself understood it.

It is true that these goals only appear in smaller writings and not in the "masterpieces" like the *Critique of Pure Reason*, the *Critique of Practical Reason*, and the *Critique of Judgment*. Still, the fact that Kant continued to reiterate them long after the publication of these works shows that he never lost sight of the goals he wanted to achieve, and much less was he dazzled by his partial successes to the point of allowing them, by themselves, to take the place of the greater ambition.

On the contrary, if he gave long and concentrated attention to certain specific problems, it was not because he had deviated from this ambition but because he understood that it could not be realized in the historical-social world without these problems being solved first.

When, in an effort to subject human destiny to the rule of reason, he dedicates himself to the critical examination of reason and its limitations instead of uncritically extolling the virtues of rational power, Kant shows only that he is a serious warrior who does not enter into battle without meticulously assessing the possibilities and limits of the weaponry he carries. And when he restricts the reach of reason instead of extending it to infinity, he does nothing but concentrate the forces of his army rather than dispersing them.

This is precisely what his contemporary Napoleon Bonaparte would learn to do on the battlefield.

Of all the world reformers, Kant was perhaps the most subtle and ingenious. Avoiding addressing the popular masses, restricting his audience to highbrow intellectuals, he saved himself from gross attacks that Luther and Marx never lacked and imposed himself on the world with an aura of unassailable respectability, like a mysterious and distant deity.

Above all, the fact that he treated his ideals not as dogmatic truths but as sources of endless problems, contradictions, and difficulties allowed his influence to reach far beyond explicit adherent groups and to spread anonymously everywhere, until it acquired what Antonio Gramsci dreamed of obtaining for the Communist Party: *the omnipresent and invisible power of a categorical imperative.*

The Pseudo-Realism of Machiavelli

Maquiavel ou A confusão demoníaca (2011, 2020)

As I explained above, I do not intend to solve the [Machiavelli] enigma here; my goal is merely to articulate its data in order to emphasize the importance of this enigma as one of the constant elements that have traversed the intellectual history of the West since the sixteenth century.

To do this, one can start with Antonio Gramsci's undeniable observation that, while *The Prince* is composed of elements drawn from the usual conduct of Italian politicians of the time, its complete design is not a reality but a project. To bring this project into reality, Machiavelli himself had no political power but only the intellectual's weapon: the written word. Interestingly, he disdained this weapon and its users. Leo Strauss notes that, in this aspect, Machiavelli aligns with Socrates's realism against the unlimited trust that the sophists placed in the power of discourse as an instrument of social transformation.[109]

He claims that nothing replaces military power. However, this refers to the immediate practical context and the person of the prince acting within it, not to his prophet, Machiavelli himself. What Machiavelli casts into the waters of the future is merely the discourse's fishing hook, to bring forth the new era lying at the bottom of the sea of possibilities.

Realizing this possibility depends on knowledge of the laws of historical necessity. Machiavelli boasts of being the first to possess this knowledge (we will see what it consists of), thus enabling him to open unprecedented perspectives for humanity. This pertains not only to the theoretical understanding of society but also to the creation of a new world.

---

[109] Leo Strauss, *Thoughts on Machiavelli* (University of Chicago Press, 1958), 223–225.

In this sense, he anticipates the operation that Hegel will describe as follows:[110]

> Every single man is but a blind link in the chain of absolute necessity by which the world builds itself forth (*sich fortbildet*). The single man can elevate himself to dominance (*Herrschaft*) over an appreciable length of this chain only if he knows the direction in which the great necessity wants to move and if he learns from this knowledge to pronounce the magic words (*die Zauberworte*) that will evoke its shape (*Gestalt*).[111]

Analyzing this passage, Eric Voegelin sees in Hegel not a philosopher committed to describing the structure of reality but a sorcerer-conjurer, determined to shape it according to the image of a hypothetical future:

> Hegel betrays in so many words that being a man is not enough for him; and as he cannot be the divine Lord of history himself, he is going to achieve *Herrschaft* as the sorcerer who will conjure up an image of history—a shape, a ghost—that is meant to eclipse the history of God's making. The imaginative project of history falls in its place in the pattern of modern existence as the conjurer's instrument of power.[112]

Voegelin strangely does not make the same judgment regarding Machiavelli, to whom the analysis equally applies. Instead, he designates him (in a deliberately unpublished work) as "a healthy and honest figure, most certainly preferable as a man to the contractualists who try to cover the reality of power underneath an established order by the moral, or should we say immoral, swingle of consent."[113] Voegelin even gives him the status of a "spiritual realist," placing him shoulder to shoulder with Plato, Aristotle, Saint Thomas, Leibniz, and Schelling. The spiritual realist, according to the great philosopher from Louisiana, is a thinker who, with a proper awareness of humanity's position in the structure of reality,

---

[110] "Hegel was of course obsessed with the political weakness of Germany; living in the Napoleonic period of collapse, of negation, he hoped, following the dialectic, for the reaction, for the reaffirmation of German might. He aspired, Dr. Sabine believes, to be the Machiavelli of a new Germany"—John Bowle, *Politics and Opinion in the Nineteenth Century: An Historical Introduction* (New York: Oxford University Press, 1954), 43.

[111] Friedrich Hegel, *Phänomenologie des Geistes*, D 324 quoted in Eric Voegelin, *Hegel: A Study in Sorcery, The Collected Works of Eric Voegelin: Published Essays 1966–1985* (Baton Rouge/London: Louisiana University Press, 1990), vol. 12, 221.

[112] Eric Voegelin, *Hegel: A Study in Sorcery, The Collected Works of Eric Voegelin: Published Essays 1966–1985* (Baton Rouge/London: Louisiana University Press, 1990), vol. 12, 213–255.

[113] Eric Voegelin, *History of Political Ideas. Renaissance and Reformation* (Missouri: University of Missouri Press, 1998), vol. 4, 37.

does not confuse immanence with transcendence and, therefore, harbors no illusions about the perfectibility of this world. Although Voegelin later abandoned the use of this concept and, according to his disciple Dante Germino, revised his judgment of Machiavelli,[114] the truth is that, from the strict point of view of the comparison with the idealistic falsification of reality, this judgment is not at all inappropriate. If there's one thing Machiavelli cannot be accused of, it's disguising power relations under an enchanting veil or betting on a future society liberated from repression and fear. On the contrary, his Third Rome is entirely founded on the fear of authority. Later, Voegelin himself admitted that this alone was not enough to make Machiavelli a "spiritual realist." He even conceded a strong "demonic" element in the Florentine thinker, which, while not contradicting the judgment on that particular point, significantly modifies the overall assessment of Machiavelli. Voegelin died before being able to explain this modification better, and I intend no conjecture about it here. What seems evident to me is that realistic pessimism about the perfectibility of the world is entirely compatible with Machiavelli's intention to summon a new world through the commanding words launched to the princes of the future by a revived Moses. And if I see no way to escape the conclusion that, in this, he was a predecessor to Hegel's sorcery, it is precisely because he is by no means a new Moses but, as we will see, an anti-Moses, the secularist parody of the Hebrew prophet.

The Parody of Prophecy

It's worth examining this more carefully.

Machiavelli never denies the existence of God, the prophetic power infused in Moses by Divine Providence, or the presence of divine influence in the later expansion of Christianity. Rather, all of this is condensed by him into the concept of "Fortune" (*Fortuna*), the set of determining factors of destiny beyond human control. Virtue (*Virtù*), defined not in a moral or religious sense but as a simple willpower, the ability to decide and act, becomes the opposition to Fortune. This especially applies to leaders, the princes.

According to him, ancient Rome was born from the *Virtù* of its founders but became corrupted and weakened by the dissolving influence of Judeo-Christianity, the child of God, that is, of "Fortune." The Second Rome, the Rome of the Popes, whose formidable power rested on the disintegration of nations through the deleterious influence of a doctrine of resignation and compassion, emerged from Judeo-Christianity. Machiavelli attributes all the evils of European

---

[114] Dante Germino, "Was Machiavelli a 'Spiritual Realist'?" (Eric Voegelin Society Meeting, 2000).

peoples, especially Italy, to this influence. Both the liberation of Italy in the short term and the establishment of the Third Rome in an indeterminate future must, therefore, be the work of *Virtù* that rebels against *Fortuna* and revokes the decrees of Providence by an act of will.

Machiavelli believes in free will and urges men to use it willingly against God. It is, therefore, impossible that he was not fully aware that, by donning the mantle of Moses, he did so as an upside-down Moses. The parodic inversion could not be more evident.

This simultaneously discards the sanitized images of Machiavelli-the-Scientist or Machiavelli-the-Artist, as well as naive criticisms that saw the Florentine bureaucrat as a vulgar immoralist.

Giving "Machiavellian" advice to princes is obviously a sin against morality. However, assuming the prophetic authority to fight against Providence and attempt to reverse the divine course of history is not an "immorality." It's not even political perversion. It's metaphysical rebellion, a sin against the Holy Spirit.

The parodic nature of the undertaking becomes even clearer when viewed from a chronological perspective. Until 1513, Machiavelli (born in 1469) had only written relatively unimportant administrative documents. *The Prince*, produced in that year, precedes the *Discourses on the First Decade of Titus Livius* by four years, the *Life of Castruccio Castracani* by six, the *Art of War* by eight, and the *Florentine Histories* by twelve. Clearly, Machiavelli's conception of government, with the prophecy of the advent of the reformer prince, was ready and completed the moment its author created, retroactively, a global interpretation of history to justify it. His interpretation of the past is pre-molded by his foresight of the future. This curious inversion of the structure of time is repeated almost invariably in all thinkers who marked the modern cycle: Hobbes, Locke, Kant, Hegel, Auguste Comte, Karl Marx, and even Nietzsche. With the utmost nonchalance, each of them believes to have glimpsed the future and takes it as a premise to explain the past. This phenomenon is what I call *pseudoprophetism*, one of the structural characteristics of modern thought and especially of the revolutionary mentality, in the explicit sense I give to this term.

Even more curious is the relationship between the content of the two essential books, *The Prince* and the *Discourses*, and the function that Machiavelli gave them in the implementation of his own political career. The first is dedicated to Lorenzo de Medici, the ruling prince, and deals mainly with principalities. The second has republics as its central subject and is dedicated to two private citizens with some prospect of becoming rulers. Obviously, the prophet seeks to guard against any potential missteps in the realization of his prophecy. The foresight of the future could serve as a premise for a drastic reinterpretation of the whole of history, but not to unequivocally guide Machiavelli's own career. The Third Rome is an absolute certainty, even more firmly established than the past, as the latter is its function, but it is still uncertain whether it will come in the form of a principality or a republic. It's advisable to be prepared for both eventualities, flattering both possible types of rulers in advance.

Making prophecies for the rest of humanity is one thing; for oneself, it is another. Imagine if Moses, while showing the people the way through the waters of the Red Sea, simultaneously took precautions by renting a little boat. By showing awareness of this distinction, our new Moses, like Don Quixote, proves that he is "*loco si, pero no tonto.*"

The Globalist Revolution

Digesto Econômico magazine, September–October 2009
A filosofia e seu inverso & Outros estudos (2012)

For anyone wishing to navigate today's politics or simply understand something of the history of past centuries, nothing is more urgent than obtaining some clarity about the concept of "revolution." Both in public opinion and in the academic sphere, there is great confusion about this, simply because the general idea of revolution is often formed based on fortuitous analogies and blind empiricism, rather than seeking the deep and permanent structural factors that define the revolutionary movement as a continuous and overwhelming reality for at least three centuries.

Just to give an illustrious example, the historian Crane Brinton, in his classic *The Anatomy of Revolution*, seeks to extract a general concept of revolution from the comparison between four major historical events nominally considered revolutionary: the English, American, French, and Russian revolutions. What is common among these four processes is that they were moments of great ideological ferment, resulting in substantive changes to the political regime. Would that alone be enough to classify them uniformly as "revolutions"? Only in the popular and impressionistic sense of the word. Although, in the dimensions of this writing, I cannot justify all the conceptual and methodological precautions that led me to this conclusion. What I have to observe is that the structural differences between the first two and the last two phenomena studied by Brinton are so profound that, despite their equally spectacular and bloody appearances, they cannot be classified under the same label.

One can legitimately speak of a "revolution" only when a proposal for a comprehensive change in society is accompanied by the demand for the concentration of power in the hands of a ruling group as a means of achieving this change. In this sense, there have never been revolutions in the Anglo-Saxon world, except for Cromwell's, which failed, and the Anglican Reformation, a very particular case that is not discussed here. In England, both the revolt of the nobles against the king in 1215 and the Glorious Revolution of 1688 sought to limit central power rather than concentrate it. The same happened in America in 1776. And in none of these three cases did the revolutionary group attempt to change the structure of society or established customs; instead, they forced the government to conform to popular traditions and customary law. What can be common between these more restorative and corrective processes and the cases of France and Russia, where a group of enlightened individuals, imbued with the project of a completely new society in radical opposition to the previous one, takes power firmly resolved to transform not only the system of government but also the morals, culture, customs, the mentality of the population, and even human nature in general?

No, there were no revolutions in the Anglo-Saxon world, and that fact alone would suffice to explain the global preponderance of England and the United States in recent centuries. If, in addition to the structural factors that define them— the project of a radical change in society and the concentration of power as a means of realizing it—there is anything common to all revolutions, it is that they weaken and destroy the nations where they occur, leaving behind nothing but a trail of blood and the psychotic nostalgia for impossible ambitions. France, before 1789, was the richest country and the dominant power in Europe. The revolution inaugurates its long decline, which today, with the Islamic invasion, reaches pathetic dimensions. Russia, after a semblance of artificial imperial growth made possible by American aid, dismantled itself into a no-man's-land dominated by bandits and the unrestrained corruption of society. China, after the miracle of starving thirty million people in a single decade, only saved itself by renouncing the revolutionary principles that guided its economy and willingly surrendering to the abominable delights of the free market. As for Cuba, Angola, Vietnam, and North Korea, I won't say anything: they are theaters of Grand Guignol, where chronic state violence is not enough to hide indescribable misery.

All misunderstandings surrounding the idea of "revolution" come from the prestige associated with this word as a synonym for renewal and progress.

However, this prestige comes precisely from the success of the English and American "revolutions," which, in the strict and technical sense in which I use this word, were not revolutions at all. This same semantic illusion prevents the naive observer—and I include therein much of the specialized academic class—from seeing the revolution where it happens under the camouflage of slow and apparently peaceful transmutations, such as the implementation of world government that is unfolding today before the astonished eyes of the masses.

The sufficiently distinctive criterion to eliminate all hesitations and misunderstandings is always the same: with or without sudden and spectacular transmutations, with or without insurrectional or governmental violence, with or without hysterical accusation speeches and the general killing of opponents, a revolution is present whenever a project for a profound transformation of society, if not the entirety of humanity, is on the rise or in the process of implementation, through the concentration of power.

It's because they do not understand this that liberal and conservative currents, opposing the most conspicuous and repugnant aspects of some revolutionary process, often end up unconsciously fostering it under some other aspect, whose danger escapes them at the moment. In today's Brazil, the exclusive concentration on the evils of the Workers Party (PT), the "Landless worker's movement" (MST), and such can lead liberals and conservatives to court certain "social movements," under the illusion of being able to exploit them electorally. What escapes the vision of these smart asses is that such movements, at least in the long term, play an even more decisive role in the implementation of the new socialist world order than that of the nominally radical left.

Another dangerous illusion is to believe that the advent of planetary administration is an inevitable historical fate. The ease with which small Honduras broke the legs of the globalist giant shows that, at least for now, the power of this monstrosity consists only of a monumental publicity bluff. It is in the nature of every bluff to extract its vital substance from the fictitious belief it manages to inoculate in its victims. I frequently see liberals and conservatives repeating the most foolish slogans of globalism, such as the idea that certain problems—drug-trafficking, pedophilia, etc.—cannot be addressed on a local scale, requiring the intervention of a global authority. The absurdity of this statement is so obvious that only a general state of hypnotic stupor can explain why it enjoys any credibility. Aristotle, Descartes, and Leibniz taught that when you have a big problem, the best way to solve it is to break it down into smaller units. Globalist rhetoric can do nothing against this methodological rule. Enlarging the scale of a problem can never be a good way to tackle it. The experience of certain American cities, which have virtually eliminated crime from their territories using only their local resources, is the best proof that, instead of enlarging, it is necessary to diminish the scale, subdivide power, and confront evils on the scale of direct and local contact, instead of being intoxicated by the grandeur of global ambitions.

That globalism is a revolutionary process cannot be denied. And it is the most vast and ambitious of all processes. It encompasses the radical mutation not only of power structures but also of society, education, morality, and even the most intimate reactions of the human soul. It is a complete civilizational project, and its demand for power is the highest and most voracious ever seen. There are so many aspects that compose it, such a multiplicity of movements that it encompasses, that its own unity escapes the horizon of vision of many liberals and conservatives, leading them to make disastrous and suicidal decisions just as they strive to halt the advance of the "left." The idea of free trade, for example, which is so dear to traditional conservatism (and even to myself), has been used as a tool to destroy national sovereignties and build on their ruins a universal Leviathan. A correct principle can always be used in the wrong way. If we cling to the letter of the principle without noticing the strategic and geopolitical ambiguities involved in its application, we contribute to turning an idea created to be an instrument of freedom into a tool for the construction of tyranny.

Science and Democracy

Diário do Comércio, March 12, 2007
A fórmula para enlouquecer o mundo (2014)

If you believe that "science" can both enjoy public authority and adhere to Karl Popper's principle of falsifiability, you are wishing for the impossible. No public authority can have the right to change his mind at the first *exemplum in contrarium* that appears and announce that he might change his mind again the next day if a second example challenges the first. The freedom of scientific research essentially depends on the certainty that nothing scientists say will have serious consequences that they cannot change with the same freedom with which they move from one hypothesis to another. As soon as a scientific hypothesis is endorsed by the state and becomes obligatory by law, or is accepted by society and becomes a general belief, it evades the principle of falsifiability and can no longer be altered except by the action of pressure groups and mass propaganda. Science, at least in its ideal self-definition, is the opposite of democracy: it is the power to impose the opinion of one against the authority of all, as long as the former better meets the demands of the method. It is the symmetrical opposite of majority rule.

However, the claim of Popperianism coexists so well with the assertion of public authority that one would say that certain proponents of scientific knowledge are completely unaware of the implications of what they say.

Moreover, the principle of falsifiability is a bottomless pit: one cannot claim a fact against a generalization if that fact does not contain within itself the germ of a new generalization, at least implicitly. And every new generalization is, like its predecessors, only a provisional hypothesis. A provisional hypothesis can last a minute, two minutes, three days, a century, and be suddenly overturned. But if, before being overturned, it already has public authority and becomes the basis of laws and institutions, the scientific community does not have the magical power to retroactively nullify the social and historical consequences of the changes it has legitimized based on the now-rejected hypothesis. The public authority of science is a fraud, in the most essential and inescapable sense of the term. The exercise of science, to the extent that it assumes the permanent right to change its mind, requires the renunciation of all public authority due to the absolute impossibility of bearing the lasting consequences of faith in transitory hypotheses. There can be no public authority without public responsibility, but, being impossible to punish the entire scientific community for dereliction of duty, as one might punish a ruler, this community is forced to renounce its public authority to preserve its own freedom of scientific inquiry.

The peaceful coexistence of "science" and "democracy," if not the forced fusion of the two into the "ideal of reason" as a guide for the people, is just one of the many delusions of Enlightenment that have impregnated the popular imagination to the point of naively taking as homogeneous and identical that which is actually diverse and incongruent.

Revolutionary Inversion in Action

Diário do Comércio, July 21, 2008
A Inversão Revolucionária em Ação (2015)

Both in newspaper articles and in lectures, I have presented some conclusions from an extensive study undertaken on the revolutionary mentality. The main conclusions are as follows:

The revolutionary mentality, as documented in the writings and actions of all revolutionary leaders since the fifteenth century, without any notable exception, does not consist of adherence to this or that specific socio-political proposal but in a certain structure of apprehending reality, characterized by the inversion of temporal and causal order and the subject-object relationship, leading to a variety of secondary inversions.

These inversions do not constitute merely a "spiritual disease," in the sense that F. W. von Schelling and Eric Voegelin give to the term, but a mental illness in a strict clinical sense. The revolutionary mentality is a specific variant of "delusional interpretation," a syndrome described pioneeringly by psychiatrist Paul Sérieux [and Joseph Capgras] in the classic book *Les Folies Raisonnantes. Le Délire d'Interprétation.*

Observations from Dr. Sérieux:

> While, in general, systematized demented psychoses rest on predominant and almost permanent sensory disturbances, all the cases that we have gathered here are, almost exclusively, based on delusional interpretations; hallucinations, always episodic when they exist, play almost no role in them . . . The 'delusional interpretation' is a false reasoning that has as its starting point a real sensation, an exact fact, which, due to associations of ideas linked to tendencies, to affection, assumes, with the help of wrong inductions and deductions, a personal meaning for the patient . . . Delusional interpretation is distinguished from hallucination and illusion, which are sensory disturbances. It also differs from the delusional idea, an imaginary conception, invented point by point, not deduced from an observed fact.[115]

It also differs, according to the author, from mere false interpretation, that is, ordinary error, for two reasons: (1) "Error is, for the most part, correctable; delusional interpretation, uncorrectable." (2) "Error remains isolated, circumscribed; delusional

---

[115] [Free translation] Paul Sérieux and Joseph Capgras, *Les Folies raisonnantes. Le Délire d'interprétation* (Paris: Alcan, 1909).—Eds.

interpretation tends toward diffusion, toward radiation; it associates with similar ideas and organizes into a system."

On a future occasion, I will explain the specific difference between the revolutionary mentality and other varieties of delusional interpretation. Here, I only intend to illustrate something I have said and repeated dozens of times: the inversion of reality is such a constant and omnipresent factor in revolutionary thought of all times that we can practically find samples of it in whatever the spokespersons of revolutionary ideologies say about matters of their political interest. The number of available examples is so immense that the only difficulty for the researcher is the *embarras de choix*, the choice of the most obvious and illustrative cases.

I randomly select an article by Mr. Leonardo Boff, "What future awaits us?"[116]

Quoting Arnold Toynbee, the author says that a constant in the decline of civilizations is the rupture of the balance between the quantity of challenges and the response capacity of each civilization: "When the challenges are such that they exceed the response capacity, civilization begins its decline, enters a crisis, and disappears."

Applying this concept to the description of the current situation, Mr. Boff says:

> Our civilizational paradigm, developed in the West and spread throughout the globe, is springing leaks on all sides. Global challenges, especially those of an ecological, energy, food, and population nature, are of such gravity that we have lost the ability to give it a collective and inclusive response. This type of civilization is going to dissolve.[117]

After outlining, with the help of Eric Hobsbawm and Jacques Attali, some possibilities of catastrophic development of the situation, Mr. Boff states the only hope that remains, in his view: "Humanity, if it does not want to destroy itself, must elaborate a global social contract with the creation of instances of global governance with the collective management of nature's scarce resources." In short: socialist world government.

All the facts mentioned in the article are real but systematically placed in the wrong contexts.

---

[116] "¿Qué futuro nos espera?" [Spanish]; "Que futuro nos espera?" [Portuguese], July 11, 2008.—Eds.

[117] [Free translation].—Eds.

1. The challenges mentioned by Mr. Boff to illustrate Toynbee's thesis do not illustrate it but deviate far from it. What Toynbee has in mind are not material difficulties like those mentioned but, above all, the simultaneous pressure of an "internal proletariat" and an "external proletariat," both committed to destroying the targeted civilization. The first can be exemplified by illegal immigrants who receive all sorts of benefits from the U.S. government (denied even to legal residents) and, with this, strengthen themselves to antagonize local culture and advocate for the disintegration of the U.S. The "external proletariat" is represented by the multitude of organizations engaged in a violent and incessant anti-American campaign, in which Mr. Boff himself is a prominent voice at least on the Brazilian scale. The action of these two proletariats is intensely fostered and subsidized by proponents of world government, who then present the resulting weakening of the U.S. as an impersonal and involuntary phenomenon, disguising the self-fulfilling prophecy through an appeal to "historical constants."

2. Of the four challenges mentioned by Mr. Boff—ecological, food, population, and energy crises—the first three affect the West much less than communist and Islamic countries and their respective areas of influence. There has never been an ecological disaster comparable to the effects of the explosion in Chernobyl or the general pollution in China, nor is there a population drama comparable to that of China, nor a food shortage as alarming as observed in African countries under Islamic and communist rule (Sudan, Zimbabwe). If a paradigm was ever threatened by the three problems that Mr. Boff points out, it is the anti-Western paradigm of China, Russia, and Islamic countries. In the West, instead of overpopulation, there is depopulation today; instead of food scarcity, there is endemic obesity; and nowhere in the world are ecological risks, real or imagined, under as strict control as in developed capitalist countries. How could a civilization be threatened with imminent extinction by challenges that are absent or under control within it? And how could it be replaced with advantage by a "new paradigm" inspired precisely by nations that succumb defenselessly to these same challenges? The inversion of reality here is so symmetrical, so evident, so literal, so naive even, that one could not wish for a clearer and more didactic example of delusional interpretation.

As for the energy crisis, it does not exist in the U.S. but is a possible risk that becomes imminent thanks to the action . . . of whom? Of the same proponents of world government, such as Pelosis and Obamas, who block the opening of new oil wells by all means, causing the nation with the largest oil reserves in the world to become dependent on foreign suppliers. These, in turn, with the money they collect from their biggest customer, finance not only propaganda campaigns against it but even terrorist movements, while they arm themselves to the teeth for the "war of all the people," (a phrase from General Giap adopted by Hugo Chávez) against the "imperialist dominator" that feeds them. As a result of the "breakdown of the imperial order—in Mr. Boff's words—we enter a collective process of chaos . . . Globalization continues, but balkanization prevails with regional domains that can generate conflicts of great devastation . . . This extreme situation calls for an equally extreme solution." The extreme solution is, obviously, the one pointed out above, planetary socialism.

In other words, of the four "challenges" that, according to Mr. Boff, make Western civilization unviable and call for the advent of world government, three exist only among the enemies of the West, and the fourth is inoculated in the West by those enemies, by spreading diseases to sell remedies.

Mr. Boff, being himself one of the agents of the operation—albeit one of the more modest—knows all of this. His perception of the facts is accurate. It is his interpretation of the scenario that is entirely inverted, detail by detail, compulsively, to create a system of errors in which revolutionary treachery can appear as the highest expression of good and virtue.

Thesis on the Worldwide Revolutionary Movement

Lecture delivered at the West Point Military Academy on April 14, 2007
O Foro de São Paulo: a ascensão do comunismo latino-americano (2022)

For the information of the readers, below are some notes I took for the address I will deliver today to officers of the General Staff, both American and Brazilian, at the United States Military Academy at West Point. These are just an outline for oral development, but in future articles, I will provide more details.

1. The revolutionary movement is a unique and continuous phenomenon over time, at least since the fifteenth century. Each generation of revolutionaries is aware of being the heir and perpetuator of those that came before. This is abundantly documented in their writings. It is a fact, not an interpretation of mine.

2. The movement is continuous, but not linear or unidirectional. It progresses through mutations and internal revolutions and feeds on its own failures,

which provide the next generation with powerful motivation for a critical deepening of goals and strategy. As its declared goals change from generation to generation, the general movement has sufficient flexibility to absorb or repel partial movements, according to the strategic and rhetorical needs of each situation. The same partial movement can be considered revolutionary at one moment and counter-revolutionary the next.

3. The conscious continuity of the revolutionary movement does not imply in any way that subsequent generations assume responsibility for the errors and crimes of previous generations. The awareness of historical continuity that is affirmed on the factual level is denied on the moral judgment level. Since, from the perspective of the revolutionary movement, guilt belongs to the past, the innocence of each new generation of revolutionaries is a presupposition of the very existence of the movement. Therefore, the old revolutionaries, if they possess any guilt, do so as figures of the past and not as revolutionaries. Their guilt is attributable to "their time," not to their revolutionary activity itself. The enemy of the movement, on the contrary, bears not only his own guilt but also that of his real or figurative ancestors, when he is not also accused of the crimes of the revolution: after killing a handful of reactionaries, the revolutionary hates them even more because these villains forced him to kill them, staining his pure hands with blood.

4. The revolutionary movement does not identify itself with any of its particular goals, but it also cannot define once and for all the permanent "essence" behind all of them. This essence, in fact, cannot be defined substantively, only negatively: (1) the movement is effectively a movement, a permanent agitation in search of (2) a moving goal that cannot be defined in the present because only the future that finally realizes it will have it before its eyes as an object of knowledge. The revolutionary movement is therefore both a permanent movement and a futuristic movement. The future, by definition, remains in the future. The day of reckoning for the revolutionary with his own conscience is automatically postponed. The thing closest to an examination of conscience in the mind of a revolutionary is the criticism of predecessors.

5. The revolutionary movement is, from its origins, an effort to take the place of the Christ announced in the Apocalypse and replace Him with a terrestrial agent in the role of savior of humanity. The concrete ends of the movement thus take advantage of the dignity of a mystery that can be vaguely announced but cannot be revealed before the end of times. Hence, the lack of

commitment of the revolutionary movement to its own concrete goals, which it changes or abandons at will.

6. It is useless to use the rhetoric that opposes ideals to deeds against the revolutionary movement, in any of its eras or versions. The revolutionary movement swaps ideals with the same ease with which it absolves itself of responsibility for its own deeds. It lives on the tension between mutable ideals and its own unacknowledged deeds. Two other tensions articulate this (see diagram): between the cult of the saints of the revolutionary pantheon and the devastating criticism of revolutions; and between perpetual movement and the hope for an "end of history," a static paradise of universal justice and peace.

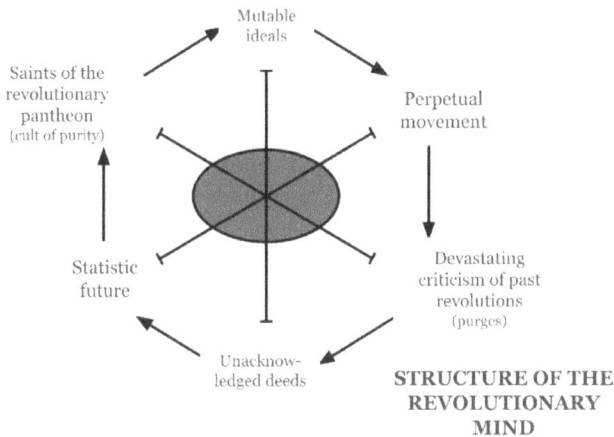

Fig. 1. The structure of the revolutionary mind.

To Understand the Worldwide Revolution

Diário do Comércio, May 14, 2007
A fórmula para enlouquecer o mundo (2014); *O Foro de São Paulo* (2022)

I promised to explain the "theses on the world revolutionary movement" in more detail. As these explanations are long, I will subdivide them into several articles, returning to the subject whenever there is an opportunity. I start with the first paragraph: "The revolutionary movement is a unique and continuous phenomenon over time, at least since the fifteenth century. Each generation of revolutionaries is aware of being the heir and perpetuator of the previous generations. This is abundantly documented in their writings. It is a fact, not an interpretation of mine."

Whatever the state of affairs, there is no conscious political attitude without knowledge of the historical antecedents that produced it; and not only of the immediate factual antecedents but also and mainly of the enduring, long-term elements that do not exert a direct causal influence on the current situation, but shape and determine the general framework in which everything happens, from afar.

When the discourse of a political agent repeats that of characters from two, three, or four centuries ago, whom he does not know and could not purposefully quote, sometimes this fact can be explained by the simple residual persistence of old turns of language, impregnated in the general culture and passively assimilated by the speaker. But when this verbal coincidence is added to the identity of the values and objectives expressed through the discourse, then it is likely that the action of this agent continues a sequence started long before him, to which he serves, with greater or lesser awareness of his participation, in an effort spanning many centuries. If, furthermore, by tracing the origins of his language, we can reconstruct an uninterrupted transmission chain that, from generation to generation, has come from the pioneers of the idea to its last passive repeater, then it is clear that we are facing an identifiable, continuous, and self-conscious "historical movement."

A historical movement can encompass and contain many political, cultural, and religious movements, which constitute its partial, local, and temporary versions, and can be quite different and even contrasting with each other without ceasing to contribute, therefore, to the unity of the whole that drags them inexorably toward the achievement of a general meaning already formulated, essentially, from the beginning.

A historical movement does not act on its own; it is not a magical force nor, as Hegel would say, a "cunning of reason" that operates and achieves its goals through invisible logic, bypassing the conscious intentions of individuals and generations. It is, on the contrary, the temporal continuity of a set of symbols, values, and objectives that are consciously internalized and subscribed to by individuals who place themselves at its service. Only, in each of these individuals, the knowledge of the values they serve does not imply a comprehensive awareness of the totality of the encompassing movement. In some of them, yes. In each generation, there is at least a nucleus of "intellectuals" who know where the movement they serve comes from and where it is going. But most of those involved may only be aware of the immediate partial undercurrents. This is more than enough to ensure the perfect integration of their actions into the overall meaning of the historical movement.

To the lay observer, the unity of the movement may escape him entirely, mainly because he does not know how to distinguish it from three other types of unity that may appear behind the multiplicity of human actions:

(1) The spontaneous unity of historical development. The growth of capitalist economy, for example, does not result from any plan and is not a process directed by anyone. It results, as Ludwig von Mises said, from the sum of an innumerable quantity of individual acts, each of them rational in itself but unconnected in the whole, practiced by economic agents for their personal and group goals.

(2) The concrete and deliberate unity of an explicit political, social, religious, or cultural movement, endowed with an identifiable command and a mass of militants, faithful, or conscious adherents of that unity. Catholicism or communism are characteristic examples. To distinguish them from the general historical movement, I will call them "special movements."

(3) The invisible unity of the "secret power" or "conspiracy." In this case, unity exists only for the leaders, the drivers of the process, and their immediate collaborators. The mass of anonymous helpers, gathered in smaller units without contact with each other, has no clear idea—and sometimes no idea at all—of the larger articulation or the overall purpose they serve.

Although the unity of a historical movement may have elements taken from these three models, none of them explains it. A historical movement is not a pure spontaneous development but a conscious and prolonged effort to take things in a certain direction. But it also differs from special movements in that it does not need to have a hierarchical command structure, at least not permanently. It also differs from the conspiratorial unity because this hierarchical structure, when it exists, does not necessarily have to remain secret.

The unity of a historical movement rests entirely on the appeal of certain symbols that condense and give substance to lasting desires, ideals, and objectives. Once adopted as a banner of struggle by some special movement, these symbols spread and take root so deeply in the culture that their cohesive strength can be renewed at any time by some other special movement that is directly or indirectly inspired by the previous one. A succession of special movements inspired by the same core of symbols and values, spanning epochs without organizational connection to each other, forms a historical movement on its own, even if the consciousness of continuity becomes quite tenuous or is shared only by an intellectual elite without direct command over the whole. If it continues in the same direction, it cannot be said to have stopped or been extinguished. A historical movement can alternately crystallize as a special movement around a known hierarchical command of all participants or, conversely, split into so many independent cells that it seems to have dissolved, not only in adverse times but even in times when the winds are most favorable, and it can count on vegetative growth supported by the pure spontaneous development of social facts. Sometimes, a brilliant leadership capable of maintaining conscious control of the movement for some time appears, sometimes it is necessary to wait until the spontaneity of events creates the conditions for this, but in both of these times, the revolutionary movement continues, unshakeable.

No one will ever understand the world revolutionary movement while continuing to view it only through the prism of the special movements that integrate it. How to explain, for example, the sudden rise of leftism in the world after the fall of the USSR, which, according to general expectations, should have heralded its end? The surprise at the phenomenon is so great that many prefer even to deny it, taking refuge in a psychotic illusion. But its explanation is simple if you understand that the communist movement, organized from the command centers in Moscow and Beijing, was only a partial and temporary embodiment of the revolutionary movement, which continued to develop in other contexts in other latent and discreet forms, ready to come to the forefront as soon as the Soviet-Chinese version failed, as it did indeed. It is depressing, for example, to note how the United States, in the 1950s, while openly combating communist expansionism and Soviet espionage, welcomed with open arms the philosophers of the Frankfurt School, who already brought with them the germ of the *New Left* destined to flourish in the following decade with a force, virulence, and breadth never dreamed of by communist parties. Fighting a special movement without considering its connections with the overall revolutionary movement is risking strengthening the latter at the very moment one imagines defeating it. In fact, the Soviet elite itself had much more flexibility and an incomparably broader strategic horizon than the intelligence professionals and strategic analysts in the United States could imagine then. These individuals, besides focusing on the communist movement in isolation, outside the revolutionary tradition, still considered this movement only a pseudopod of Soviet power when, in fact, Soviet power was only a local and temporary embodiment of a historical current that came long before it and that survived the dissolution of the USSR perfectly well.

The unity of the historical movement must be sought, above all else, in language. It's the recurrence of guiding motifs (in the sense that this expression has in literature and music) that marks the continuity of the movement. And at the moment when this continuity is not only that of a vague "cultural influence," but of revolutionary organizations that generate their successors and reincarnate in them after their apparent disappearance, then the characterization of the historical movement is clear and indisputable, and there is no excuse for not seeing its unity beneath the apparent variation, however bewildering it may be.

For those who know the history of the revolutionary movement as a whole, this unity, which the layman finds so difficult to see, shines through even in seemingly insignificant details. When, for example, Mr. Lula declares himself a Catholic and then, with the most callow expression, claims that he is qualified to receive communion without confessing because he is a man "without sins," anyone who attributes this to the personal foolishness of the president is infinitely more foolish than he. The phrase echoes a *leitmotif* of the revolutionary movement, circulating at least since the fifteenth century: the essential impeccability of the revolutionary, clean and holy *a priori,* and unconditionally. Ah, it's just a verbal coincidence!, say the wisest observers. It is not. The entire mentality of Mr. Lula was shaped by the direct and persistent teaching of Mr. Frei Betto,[118] who is the very incarnation of revolutionary heresy, no different from that of the Cathars and Albigensians. Mr. Lula, in this case, may not be aware that he is a ventriloquist's dummy sitting on the lap of a tradition of five centuries. But Mr. Frei Betto, who thinks with the necessary historical perspective, knows perfectly well for what purposes he trained his disciple.

---

[118] A Brazilian Dominican friar proponent of Liberation Theology, closely associated to the communist movement and to Cuban dictator Fidel Castro.—Eds.

Chapter 6

Marxism, Intellectuals, and Cultural Revolution

An Enemy of the People

O Globo, December 22, 2001
A Nova Era e a Revolução Cultural: Fritjof Capra & Antonio Gramsci (2014);
O irracional superior (2023)

In Dostoevsky's *Demons*, published in 1872, one revolutionary says to another:

> Do you know that even now we are dreadfully strong? . . . Listen, I've
> counted them all: the teacher who laughs along with the children at their
> God and at their cradle is already ours. The lawyer who defends an
> educated murderer on the grounds that he is more highly developed than
> his victims and that in order to get some money, he couldn't help but kill,
> he is already ours. The schoolboys who kill a peasant for the thrill of it
> are ours. Jurors who acquit all criminals without discrimination are ours.
> The prosecutor in the courtroom who trembles in fear that he is not
> sufficiently liberal, is ours, ours. . . . Do you know, do you know how
> much we can take just with ready-made little ideas?[119]

Almost half a century before the storming of the Winter Palace, a century
before the global spread of Antonio Gramsci's works, the novelist had already
grasped the macabre strategy of "cultural revolution," to which the founder of the
Italian Communist Party gave only a theoretical embellishment but which, in
essence, was already in action since the eighteenth century, in salons where
aristocrats delighted in the ideas of Diderot and Rousseau without realizing that
their only purpose was to legitimize their beheading.

Men who boast of being practical—businessmen, politicians, military
commanders—are the slowest to perceive the practical significance of certain
cultural fashions without overly apparent political content, in which they see
nothing but academic curiosities or even legitimate moral demands, but whose
effect, temporarily obscured by the variety and confusion of the words that convey
them, sooner or later, manifests itself in the most brutal way. Invariably, this effect
is one: mass political murder, genocide.

In general, only two types of observers are aware of this connection: activist
intellectuals who wish to produce it and independent scholars. The former have
every interest in keeping it hidden under a veil of diversionary pretexts, moral,
aesthetic, pedagogical, economic, etc., under whose profusion the victims do not
grasp the unity of the underlying revolutionary process. The latter, when trying to

---

[119] Fyodor Dostoevsky, *Demons*, ch. 8, trans. Robert A. Maguire (Penguin Classics,
2010).—Eds.

alert society to what is happening, are almost invariably rejected as alarmists and paranoid by that same part of the social fabric that the revolution will extirpate in the most cruel and bloody manner.

Just the observation of this fact is enough to undermine the Gramscian theory of the "organic intellectual," according to which classes create intellectuals tailored to the defense of their interests: with sinister regularity, from Voltaire to Antonio Negri, it is always the enemy of the ruling class that is courted by it, while the intellectual who would like to preserve the system, disbelieving in the goodness and usefulness of revolutions, is stigmatized, at the very least, as eccentric and marginal.

Dostoevsky, who defended monarchy and religion, always remained an "outsider," while revolutionary writers were received in elegant circles, where they enjoyed all the esteem and consideration—when not blind trust—of their future victims. Nikolai Berdyaev, an aristocrat by birth, a revolutionary by conviction, recounts in his memoirs how, in his youth, he liked to scandalize princesses and countesses with fiery speeches against morality and hierarchy. Only later, learning that they had all died in the Revolution, did he realize that he had contributed recklessly to the achievement of a heinous crime. The case shows that not even the most active collaborators of the "cultural revolution" need to have a full awareness of the purpose to which their seemingly innocuous or piously idealistic acts contribute when added to millions of other similar acts, practiced at the same time by a scattered legion of militants, collaborators, and sympathizers who are unaware of each other. At the top, only a very limited elite has the intellectual vision of the whole, which does not need to be "directed" like an organized conspiracy but only subtly guided, from time to time, by timely interventions. Automatism, the spirit of imitation, and the irresistible attraction of fashions do the rest.

Even when it does not directly result in the seizure of political power, cultural revolution leaves deep and indelible marks on the body of society. Two recent studies by Roger Kimball, publisher of *The New Criterion*—*Tenured Radicals: How Politics Has Corrupted Our Higher Education*[120] and *The Long March: How The Cultural Revolution of the 1960s Changed America*[121]—show how the tireless psychological warfare waged by activist intellectuals against religion, morality, logic, and common sense has produced, in American life, practically irreversible catastrophic results: the collective loss of the most elementary standards of judgment, the premature intellectual decrepitude of students, the endemic spread

---

[120] Ivan R. Dee, (1990) 1998.—Eds.
[121] Encounter Books, 2000.—Eds.

of drugs, rampant crime. Not coincidentally, the same intellectuals who consciously strove to create this state of affairs (many of them in the service of the KGB or Chinese espionage, as is now known thanks to the opening of the Moscow Archives) are the first to reap double political benefits from their own acts, attributing the results of them to the "system," to the "intrinsic corruption of capitalism," etc.

One must be very blind not to perceive that the identical thing is happening in Brazil, with the aggravating—truly despairing—factor that studies like those of Kimball (and similar others) are neither translated nor are there equivalents produced by the local intelligentsia, divided between the majority of furious activists and the minority of intimidated, silent, or accommodating and complicit observers. As a result, the mere attempt to diagnose the situation is rejected— even by the "establishment"—as impudent audacity and intolerable abuse, if not as an extreme right-wing conspiracy.

The cultural revolution [in Brazil] has already achieved its greatest triumph, which is to make its own discussion prohibitive. I will spare readers the account of the constraints, threats, and boycotts I have suffered in response to my simple initiative to analyze and show in broad daylight the progress of a revolution that would like to continue flourishing in the protective shadow of the implicit, the nebulous, and the undeclared. But when an independent writer, isolated, without political connections or protectors of any kind, is fought not by arguments but by backstage maneuvers and collective mobilizations of hatred, as if he were a ruler or a powerful mass leader, then intellectual activity is already entirely subjected to the canons of the "cultural revolution," and anyone who dares to oppose them, even in pure theory, even on a personal basis and without any intention of reacting politically to the course of events, is already considered a dangerous element and an enemy of the people.

The Nature of Marxism

Jornal da Tarde, December 18, 2003
A felicidade geral da nação (2023)

Having investigated the nature of Marxism for decades, I have concluded that it is not just a theory, an "ideology," or a political movement. It is a "culture," in the anthropological sense, an entire universe of beliefs, symbols, values, institutions, formal and informal powers, rules of conduct, discourse patterns, conscious and unconscious habits, etc. Therefore, it is self-founding and self-referential, capable of understanding nothing except on its own terms, not admitting a reality beyond its own horizon or a criterion of truth above its self-proclaimed ends. Like any culture, it places a value on its own subsistence that must be defended at all costs, far above the demands of truth or morality, as it constitutes the totality of which truth and morality are partial elements. Hence, the claim to hold it accountable on behalf of them sounds to its ears like an intolerable and absurd revolt of the parts against the whole, a senseless violation of ontological hierarchy.

The constitution of its identity includes self-defense mechanisms that impose severe limits on rational criticism, resorting, when really or imaginarily threatened, to mythological apologies, collective self-deception, outright lies, mechanisms of exclusion and liquidation of inconveniences, and the sacrificial rite of the scapegoat.

Those who believe it possible to "challenge" Marxism through a well-founded attack on its "principles" are deluded. The unity and preservation of its culture are, for the Marxist, above all considerations of intellectual and cognitive order, and thus the expressed "principles" of the theory are not properly "the" foundation of Marxist culture: they are only the verbal, imperfect, and provisional translation of a much deeper foundation that is not cognitive but existential, identified with the very sacredness of the culture that must remain untouched. This foundation can be "felt" and "experienced" by members of the culture through participation in the collective atmosphere, common endeavors, memory of past glories, and hope for future victory, but it cannot be reduced to any particular verbal formulation, no matter how elaborate and prestigious. Hence it is possible to be a Marxist without accepting any of the previous formulations of Marxism, including Marx's own. Hence it is possible to participate in the Marxist movement without knowing anything about its theory, just as it is possible to reject the theory critically while continuing to collaborate with the movement in practice. The critical assault on theoretical formulations leaves the existential foundation intact, which, when attacked, retreats to the impregnable shelter of silent certainties or simply produces new substitute formulations that, if inconsistent with the first, prove to the Marxist only the infinite richness of the ineffable foundation, capable of preserving its identity and strength under a variety of contradictory formulations that it infinitely transcends. Marxism has no "principles," only ineffable impressions in constant metamorphosis. As the reality of human life can only be experienced as a knot of tensions that change over time without ever being resolved, the contradictions between the various formulations of Marxism will make it a perfect microcosmic imitation of real existence, within which the Marxist can spend a lifetime immune to external tensions, with the additional advantage that those within are somehow "under control," attenuated by the internal solidarity of the movement and shared hopes. If Marxism is a "Second Reality," in the sense of Robert Musil and Eric Voegelin, it is so not only in the cognitive sense of false ideal representations, but in the existential sense of active, practical falsification of the experience of life. Hence any people subjected to the dominant influence of Marxism come to live in a closed mental space, oblivious to the reality of the external world.

I will elaborate further on these explanations in the next article, a summary of those I offered in my recent debate with a professor from the School of Law at University of São Paulo, to which my interlocutor responded that I thought this way because I had "serious emotional problems"—without realizing that, in doing so, he provided the best exemplification of my theory.

Specific Differences

Jornal da Tarde, January 8, 2004
O camarada Enrolevich (2024)

Characterizing Marxism as culture, it is necessary to provide more precision to the diagnosis by highlighting some specific differences.

Marxism is not an autonomous cultural process, but a transmutation that occurred within the worldwide revolutionary movement which by then already had a century-old tradition and a defined identity, to the point of being commonly referred to simply as "the movement" or "the cause," despite the coexistence of a multitude of currents and subcurrents in dispute.

The *Communist Manifesto* of 1848 presents itself as the overcoming and absorption of this disorderly movement into a higher totality. From then on, the relationship between Marxism and other revolutionary currents was that of the boss with his employees, whom he can summon, dismiss, expel, or call back at whim.

This allowed Marxism to condemn existential protests of sexual order as petty-bourgeois revolt or to challenge nationalism as the worst enemy of proletarian revolution, only to call upon both to serve under its ranks shortly afterward. Its capacity for absorption and expulsion is limitless, since it is only accountable to its singular priority, which is its own subsistence and expansion.

Any consideration of truth or morality is pragmatically demoted to the condition of *ancilla revolutionis*. Taken to its ultimate conclusion, its opportunism and complete lack of commitment to the truth can be measured by the consistency with which the communist movement announces its imminent victory against capitalist nations while simultaneously swearing that it does not even exist materially, denouncing any attempt to identify its network of organizations and methods of action as paranoia and "conspiracy theory." Here too, the comparison with dogmatic religions is inappropriate. No religious fanaticism has produced this kind of mass sociopathy.

The fundamental difference between Marxism and other cultures is that for the latter, the decisive test is adaptation to the natural environment, the organization of the economy. Any culture that fails in this regard is doomed to disappear. Marxism, on the contrary, whose complete economic failure in all the nations it dominated is notorious (it is worth noting that no economic organization has ever managed to starve tens of millions people at once, as in the "Great Leap Forward" of Chinese agriculture), seems to derive the most extraordinary advantages from this result, gaining prestige and political strength as it becomes more fragile and dependent on the help of capitalist countries.

Its inability to effectively exploit a territory, compared to its brutal efficiency in expanding within alien territory, shows that Marxism does not exist as a culture in the full sense, capable of asserting its value against the resistance of the material environment, but only as a parasitic subculture embedded in a society it did not create and with which it cannot compete.

As a parasitic subculture of modern Western culture, Marxism is not capable of replacing it but is capable of weakening it and leading it to death. The parasite, however, cannot survive outside the body it exploits, and the weakening of the host organism gives room to the rise of another competing culture, the Islamic one—this one indeed a culture in the full sense—to whose anti-Western struggle Marxism ends up serving as an auxiliary force, while seeking to use it for its own ends. The Islamic adherence of important Marxist thinkers like Roger Garaudy and the "anti-imperialist alliance" of communists and Muslims are symbols of a much more complex process of absorption of Marxism, which some Islamic theorists describe as follows: the struggle for socialism is the initial and lower stage of a broader revolutionary process that will add "spiritual liberation" to the "material liberation" of peoples, through worldwide conversion to Islam. At the same time, Marxists believe they are directing the process and using Islamic rebellion as they once used various nationalist movements, suffocating them afterward.

Whether Marxists are the shock troops of the Islamic revolution or Muslims are the vanguard of the communist movement is the more interesting question for those who want to know where the world will go in the coming decades.

On Cultural Marxism

O Globo, June 8, 2002
A morte do pato (2023)

According to classical Marxism, the proletarians were natural enemies of capitalism. Lenin added to this the idea that imperialism was the result of the capitalist struggle for the conquest of new markets. The inevitable conclusion: the proletariat was also an enemy of imperialism and would refuse to serve it in a generalized imperialist conflict. Being more attached to their class interests than to those of their imperialist bosses, they would avoid recruitment or use their weapons to overthrow capitalism instead of fighting against their proletarian comrades from neighboring nations.

In 1914, this syllogism seemed liquid and certain to all Marxist intellectuals. What a surprise it was, then, when the proletariat embraced patriotic preaching, enlisting massively and fighting bravely on the battlefields for "imperialist interests"!

The general astonishment found brief relief in the Bolshevik success of 1917, but it soon worsened into panic and depression when, instead of spreading to developed capitalist countries, as the manuals predicted, the revolution was stifled by the general hostility of the proletariat.

Faced with facts of such magnitude, a normal brain would think of correcting the theory. Perhaps the interests of the proletariat were not as antagonistic to those of the capitalists as Marx and Lenin claimed.

But a Marxist brain is never normal. The Hungarian philosopher György Lukács, for example, found it the most natural thing to share his wife with someone interested. Thinking with this mindset, he concluded that it wasn't the theory that was wrong: it was the proletarians. These idiots couldn't see their "real interests" and willingly served their enemies. They were crazy. Normal was György Lukács. It was up to him, therefore, to discover who had produced proletarian insanity. A skilled detective, he quickly found the culprit: it was Western culture. The mixture of Judeo-Christian prophecy, Roman law, and

Greek philosophy was a hellish potion concocted by the bourgeoisie to deceive the proletarians. Driven to despair by such a distressing discovery, the philosopher exclaimed, "Who will save us from Western culture?"

The answer didn't take long to appear. Felix Weil, another notable mind, found it very logical to use the money his father had accumulated in the grain trade as an instrument to destroy, along with his own domestic fortune, that of all other bourgeois. With this money, he founded what came to be called the "Frankfurt School:" a Marxist think tank that, abandoning the illusions of a universal uprising of the proletarians, dedicated itself to the only viable undertaking left, destroying Western culture. In Italy, the founder of the Communist Party, Antonio Gramsci, had come to a similar conclusion when he saw the working class betray revolutionary internationalism, joining en masse the ultranationalist variant of socialism invented by the renegade Benito Mussolini. In fact, the Soviets themselves no longer believed in the proletariat: Stalin recommended that Western communist parties recruit, above all, millionaires, intellectuals, and celebrities from show business. Contradicted by the facts, Marxism would get back at it through self-inversion: instead of transforming social conditions to change mentalities, it would change mentalities to transform social conditions. It was the world's first theory that professed to demonstrate its truth by proving the opposite of what it said.

The instruments for this emerged soon after. Gramsci discovered the "cultural revolution," which would reform the "common sense" of humanity, leading it to see the martyrdom of Catholic saints as a sordid capitalist publicity maneuver, and making intellectuals, rather than proletarians, the elected revolutionary class. The men from Frankfurt, especially Horkheimer, Adorno, and Marcuse, had the idea of mixing Freud and Marx, concluding that Western culture was a disease, that everyone educated in it suffered from an "authoritarian personality," that the Western population should be reduced to the condition of a mental patient and subjected to "collective psychotherapy."

Thus, after classical Marxism, Soviet Marxism, and the revisionist Marxism of Eduard Bernstein, the first social democrat, the fourth modality of Marxism was inaugurated: cultural Marxism. As it did not speak of proletarian revolution or openly preach any violence, the new school was well received in the circles responsible for defending the Western culture it professed to destroy.

Expelled from Germany due to unfair competition from Nazism, the Frankfurtians found in the USA the ideal atmosphere of freedom for the destruction of the society that had welcomed them. They then endeavored to demonstrate that the democracy to which they fled was just like the fascism that drove them away. They called their philosophy "critical theory" because it abstained from proposing any remedy for the world's ills and sought only to destroy: destroy culture, destroy trust between people and groups, destroy religious faith, destroy language, destroy logical capacity, and spread an atmosphere of suspicion, confusion, and hatred everywhere. Once this goal was achieved, they claimed that suspicion, confusion, and hatred were proof of the evil of capitalism.

From France, the school received invaluable help from the "deconstructionist" method, an academic charlatanism that allows challenging all products of human intelligence as malicious tricks with which white males oppress women, blacks, gays, and everyone else, including pets and plants.

The American local contribution was the invention of the linguistic dictatorship of "political correctness."

Within a few decades, cultural Marxism became the predominant influence in Western universities, the media, show business, and publishing. Its macabre dogmas, coming without the label of "Marxism," are imbecilically accepted as supra-ideological cultural values by the business and ecclesiastical classes whose destruction is its only and unavoidable goal. It's hard to find a novel, a film, a play, or a textbook today where the beliefs of cultural Marxism, often not recognized as such, are not present with all the virulence of its slanderous and perverse content.

Such was the widespread propagation of this influence that everywhere the old idea of tolerance has turned into Marcuse's "liberating tolerance:" "All tolerance for the left, none for the right." Here, those who veto and boycott the spread of ideas that displease them do not feel they are practicing censorship, they consider themselves paragons of democratic tolerance.

Through cultural Marxism, the entire culture has become a war machine against itself, leaving no room for anything else.

We Are Nowhere

O Globo, January 12, 2002
A morte do pato (2023)

The conventional political spectrum places Soviet and Chinese communism on the left, Nazi fascism on the right, and moderate socialism, called "Fabian" in Europe and the U.S. due to the Fabian Society, in the center, equivalent to what is known as social democratic. All established vocabulary, academic and parliamentary discussions, and barroom debates assume that this is the distribution of ideas and parties on the ideological map of the universe. If there is a fully established consensus, a peaceful point, a neutral zone where everyone agrees, it is this.

However, a brief examination demonstrates that this scheme is false, self-contradictory, and unfeasible. From an economic standpoint, the two ends of the scale are indistinguishable from the middle. Communism is based on state control of the economy, as is Nazi fascism, and democratic socialism likewise. If socialism, as defined by Karl Marx, is state control of the means of production, then all three regimes claiming to encompass the universe of possible ideologies are socialist. What utility can a differentiating scale have, for an objective view of the facts, which begins by rendering all the facts it encompasses indistinct from a standpoint as vital as the economy?

In this scale, there is no room, for example, for anarchism or the classical liberalism of Adam Smith and the American Constitution. There is no place for any system that does not maintain strict control over the economy. There is no place for anything other than socialism. This scheme is not a distinctive criterion or a scientific tool for describing facts. It is a prosthesis, a straitjacket, a bridle that prevents the human mind from thinking and forces it, willingly or not, knowingly or not, in the direction of socialism. It excludes from the realm of what is thinkable ideas that escape the socialist framework and makes the march toward socialism always appear as the universally explanatory key behind every historical succession.

It is evidently a fraud, and it is not surprising that it has spread thanks mainly to Soviet propaganda. The one who started this was precisely Stalin. Who else could it be? Almost all leftist rhetorical clichés, including the more modern-looking ones, trace back to Stalin and the KGB. The KGB was the greatest leftist think tank that ever existed. It had more intellectuals on its payroll than any cultural institution in the world. Although it arrested and killed tens of millions of people, its main occupation was not to arrest or kill, but to establish language standards and shape the discourse of leftist propaganda. But propaganda was understood broadly: it covered all spheres of human communication. Cultural and artistic trends, styles of thinking, literary, theatrical, and cinematographic prestige and discredit, canons of truth and scientific falsehood—everything was manufactured there, spreading at lightning speed thanks to a network of millions of docile agents, militants, bought collaborators, and sympathizers who, spread across all corners of the Earth, injected into the markets of their respective countries these unlabeled products that the public easily swallowed as spontaneous creations of local inventiveness and fortunate coincidence.

The cultural history of the twentieth century would be unthinkable without the KGB. Almost half of what was thought, argued, published, and staged in Europe and the U.S., from the 1930s to the 1980s, originated there. A comprehensive history of this overwhelming influence has not yet been written. Still, monographic studies are so abundant and conclusive that anyone wishing to express an opinion on the culture of this period has no right to ignore the central role of the largest organization that produced, disseminated, and controlled ideas that ever existed in this world. It would be like writing the history of medieval Europe without taking into account the Papacy.

Only the conjunction of cunning lies with sly ignorance can explain the absence of this brutal and overwhelming reality in the conception of the mental history of modern times made by the chattering classes. But when a scholar becomes aware of this reality, he can no longer help but perceive, in so many leftist discourses that imagine themselves new and original, the passive echo of instructions issued by the KGB five or six decades ago. Anyone who undertakes this study will be surprised to see the decisive role that unconsciousness, automatism, and copycatting play in the mental life of the classes that believe themselves intellectually active.

Until the 1940s, it was common for intellectuals of greater prestige to place Nazi fascism alongside communism among subversive and revolutionary movements dedicated to the destruction of everything conservatives loved. These two movements—one emerging from the other—could poke each other occasionally, but nothing compared to the joint attack they mounted against old liberal democracy. So much so that when, after years of secret collaboration, Hitler and Stalin publicly acknowledged their complicity, no one was very surprised, except for the communist circles deluded by Stalin's façade of anti-fascism.

It was the Nazi aggression against the USSR that changed everything. An aggression so unexpected that Stalin, when faced with the perpetrated fact, refused to believe what he saw, and took a long time to give up the hope of restoring an alliance with Hitler. The USSR's entry into the war suddenly made Western countries, out of pure opportunism, retroactively endorse the Stalinist doctrine, which placed Nazism and fascism on the "right" and made them an antithesis to, rather than the Siamese brother of, communism. The complete falsehood of the scheme, swept under the rug for a while, came to the surface again with the rapid dissolution of the partnership between Western powers and the USSR after 1945 and the onset of the "Cold War."

However, for Soviet propaganda, the scheme gained a new utility: to qualify its former allies in the fight against Nazi-fascism as Nazi-fascists. And so it was decreed by Stalin. The canine loyalty of some and the simian mimicry of others did the rest. Half a century later, the imbecilic stereotype still exerts its relentless dominion over the mind of the "intelligentsia." Wherever it starts talking, the nonsense comes back: communism on the left, Nazism and fascism on the right, Fabians and social democrats in the middle.

And we, the people, nowhere.

Invisible Ruler

Jornal da Tarde, April 24, 2003
A felicidade geral da nação (2023)

The Marxist doctrine of "ideology" has so permeated culture that even individuals entirely disengaged from any leftist activism find it natural to expect every idea or theory to be ultimately explained as an instrument of the ambitions of a class or group, and therefore as a self-interested distortion, a self-justifying myth, or propaganda.

From this perspective, there is no longer objective knowledge. The only way for a person to escape ideological imprisonment is to accept it as an unavoidable fate and incorporate it into his habitual worldview, like a horse eating its own reins, hoping to become a jockey by doing so. The new objectivity of the "organic intellectual" no longer consists of seeing the world as it is, but of transforming it into something else in order to be able to say later that it is, in fact, exactly that.

Currents of thought entirely unrelated to Marxism accidentally gave this insane doctrine some accidental legitimization.

Nietzsche abhorred socialism. Still, by rejecting any claim to truth as a self-flattering illusion of sickly contemplatives and consecrating the "thirst for power" as the ultimate foundation of reality and human action, he ended up providing both Bolshevik and fascist socialisms with an admirable pretext to discard the scruples of rational argumentation and willingly adhere to the brutality of "direct action" advocated by Georges Sorel.

Freud, politically a conservative, gave impetus to the destruction of faith in knowledge by denouncing all manifestations of human intelligence, whether in art, science, philosophy, or religion, as camouflages of sexual repression. Inadvertently, he thus placed the power of sexual fantasy at the service of socialist propaganda, as soon as the Frankfurt School believed it had discovered, in repressed desire, the genetic equivalent of the proletarian workforce "despoiled" by the capitalist superego. From then on, all the world's sexually frustrated individuals became potential leftist militants.

Many other intellectual trends and schools, sometimes staunchly anti-Marxist, contributed to the goals of socialism: eroding the popular credibility of Western philosophical and religious traditions, but having no political expression of their own, they ended up being absorbed as ideological warfare tools by the only current of thought that, besides being a doctrine, was a political strategy and an organized militancy. Thus, as it was intellectually demoralized, Marxism renewed itself almost inexhaustibly, calling to its aid newer and newer pretexts adapted from pragmatism, analytic philosophy, or even the psychedelic and anarchic messianism of the New Age. The latest acquisition was the anti-Western rhetoric of radical Islamism. And now even the "traditionalism" of Guénon and Evola can serve to help it a little . . .

No doctrine withstands so many incorporations without losing its identity. But sometimes, this is useful. As its organism became accustomed to so many foreign foods, Marxism, now in the Gramscian version, flexibilized its organizational structure, dissolving the old monolithic parties into a complex network of associations and channels with infinitely varied labeling—from political groups to charitable entities, "meeting groups," and abortion clinics, as well as drug trafficking gangs and kidnappers—, which the advent of computers and the internet allows to keep united and ready at any moment for sudden actions of global reach, as seen in the "peace" marches that almost managed to save, *in extremis*, the most tyrannical and genocidal regime on the planet.

Unrecognizable as an individualized doctrine, Marxism continues politically as the only globally organized force. In the cultural sphere, it has become the dominant influence that, without a name, almost invisibly moves currents of opinion worldwide.

Every time you ask, in the face of an idea, whom it serves before asking whether it is true or false, you are the one serving this invisible master. The Marxist doctrine of ideology, a lie in the service of the "thirst for power," sees everything as lies in the service of power, and like any self-fulfilling prophecy, it has the gift of making those who follow it, even without knowing they follow it, become exactly what it says they are.

The Farce of the Farce

O Globo, January 26, 2002
A morte do pato (2023)

In the famous *Fashionable Nonsense: Postmodern Intellectuals' Abuse of Science*, Alan Sokal [and Jean Bricmont] tested the scientific erudition of contemporary left-wing masters—Althusser, Foucault, Derrida, Lacan, and the like—and demonstrated that they were all charlatans of the lowest kind.

The Australian historian Keith Windschuttle, in *The Killing of History*, proves that in terms of historical knowledge, they fare no better. Add to this the merciless logical examinations undertaken by Roger Scruton in *Thinkers of the New Left* and the apocalyptic description that Roger Kimball presented in *Tenured Radicals* of the mental devastation of American universities under the influence of these gurus and, at the bottom of it all, there is only one question: how was it possible that, for half a century, the leftist intelligentsia, the most pretentious literate caste that has ever existed, the one that most candidly assumed the mission of guiding the world, allowed itself to be guided by the most stupid, perverse, dishonest, and incapable?

The answer is that we are facing a collective phenomenon of neurotic rationalization, with all the lethal consequences that the effort to escape from reality can have on human intelligence. "Neurosis is a forgotten lie in which you still believe," said my late friend Juan Müller, a genius in clinical psychology. When the storm of facts threatens to remove the lie from the unconscious rubble, the soul clings to increasingly desperate, inconsequential, and foolish subterfuges to avoid the shock of light, the liberating revelation of long-denied guilt.

The guilt, in this case, could not be more inescapable. Everywhere it gained power, socialism proved the evil and genocidal essence of the supposedly beautiful ideals that inspired it.

Explaining a hundred million deaths, the Gulag and the Laogai, as accidental and epidermal effects of the application of ideas that remain sublime and generous in themselves is more than human discourse can bear.

Morally, socialism and Nazism are indistinguishable. Want an example? Read Maxim Gorky, the extremely compassionate Gorky of *Mother*, which still brings tears to both puerile and senile militancy. He advised his fellow fighters: "class hatred should be cultivated by an organic revulsion as far as the enemy is concerned . . . The enemy is our inferior, and is a degenerate not only on the physical plane but also in the moral sense."[122] Dr. Goebbels could not have said it more brilliantly. How can one not conclude with Sartre that Robespierre, the weakling, did not kill enough people?

Investing all the force of their talents in defending such monstrosities has made entire generations of left-wing intellectuals accomplices in crimes against humanity, exactly in the sense in which these crimes are defined in the Criminal Code of the very homeland of Sartre and Bourdieu: "Deportation, enslavement or the massive and systematic practice of summary executions, abduction of persons followed by their disappearance, of torture or inhuman acts, inspired by political, philosophical, racial or religious motives, and organized in pursuit of a concerted plan against a section of a civil population."[123]

The persistent embellishment of genocide is guilt enough to feed the soul of the leftist intelligentsia with terror at the mere possibility of a Nuremberg Trial for the crimes of communism. Since 1956, with the release of Khrushchev's Secret Speech, this terror has been growing, reaching a height at the fall of the USSR and the opening of the Moscow archives. As it grew, the neurotic defenses stiffened, the subterfuges proliferated, and rhetorical counterattacks and diversionary maneuvers became more inventive.

Everything the leftist literate caste has written and said since the 1950s is nothing more than a succession of desperate performances to escape consciousness of their guilt. Everything: moral blackmail, intimidation of witnesses, histrionic affectations of horror at liberalism, logical acrobatics designed to separate a platonic ideal Marxism from its historical consequences. *In*

---

[122] Vaksberg, *Le mystere Gorki*, 286–287, quoted in Stéphane Courtois et al, *The Black Book of Communism: Crimes, Terror, Repression* (Harvard University Press, 1999).—Eds.
[123] French Penal Code, Book II, Title I: Crimes Against Humanity and Human Persons, Chapter II, Article 212–1.—Eds.

extremis, the demolition of logic, language, and culture was called for. When reality can no longer be denied, the sense of reality itself must be destroyed. Unable to extinguish the light, they gouge out the eyes of the audience. If all of humanity adheres to semiotics, deconstructionism, ethno-history, relativism, absolute historicism, etc., no one can reasonably associate ideas with acts, or acts with consequences: everything becomes uncertain, and no one has to bear the dreadful consciousness of having done what they did. The leftist elite will have saved face at the cost of plunging humanity into darkness.

The reflections of this self-induced hallucination of the most cowardly and mendacious intellects that have ever occupied the public stage of the West have gone very far—and the farther, the more grotesque. Not even a perfect charlatan can compete, in ridiculousness and misery, with mimics of charlatans: such is the difference between the leftist intelligentsia of Europe and that of the Third World. The farce of the center reverberates on the periphery as an imitation of a farce. Farce of the farce. If in an Althusser, or a Foucault, the existential lie retained at least the authenticity of the inner tragedy it concealed, not even those shreds of dignity remain for their Brazilian imitators. The social effects of their double pretense are prodigious: all the cultural and political history of Brazil in the last fifteen years can be described as progressive loss, by the chattering classes, of the most elementary moral discernment, diluted in the mixture of pseudo-intellectual chatter in universities and pseudo-ethical vociferation at the podiums.

At the height of the pantomime, those who taught criminals the technique of kidnappings and the principles of paramilitary organization; who for forty years flattered the criminal soul until instilling in it self-beatifying pride and ambition for unlimited power; who proclaimed from the lecterns and pulpits disdain for all morality, all law, all authority; who thus placed the entire society in the dock before a jury of murderers and kidnappers—these same people, when the monster they created escapes their control and turns against some of them, suddenly appear in public disguised as champions of order. They weep for their dead comrades, something they never did for thousands of victims of their own thoughts, turned into bloody actions by the fertile coexistence on [the penitentiary of] Ilha Grande.[124] In their faces, no sign of remorse. No doubt, no moral unease. It is because to have problems of conscience, one would have to have a conscience. Free from this evil, they go to Mardi Gras during the long bloody carnival wearing

---

[124] Ilha Grande: a prison in Rio de Janeiro where, in the late 1960s and early 1970s, communist political prisoners taught common criminals guerilla warfare tactics, bank robbery, and kidnapping, laying the foundation for criminal organizations, such as "Comando Vermelho" ("Red Command"), which remains active.—Eds.

their new costume with the naturalness of those who were born to it. Not even the slipperiest Parisian charlatans would be capable of this. The Brazilian lie has depths that its own models do not know.

The Collective Imbecile

O Imbecil Coletivo (1996, 2021)

The success of Richard Rorty in Brazil seems strange since the local intellectual milieu is predominantly Marxist and would have every reason to reject pragmatism as a capitalist ideology. However, the ground for Rorty's entry had been prepared by three decades of Gramscian hegemony. Gramsci, the most influential Marxist theorist in Brazil, was not a pure Marxist, but a mix of a pragmatist, through the lineage of his master Antonio Labriola. Labriola not only agrees with pragmatism in general but, by a significant coincidence, his "philosophy of history" is identical to that of Richard Rorty in particular, to a point where both blatantly disagree with Karl Marx: in denying that history has a "meaning." This denial is obviously incompatible with the ideology of "progress," inherent to Marxism. The sudden interest of progressive intellectuals in philosophies that deny the meaning of history is evidently a consequence of the depressive sentiment following the failure of international communism. Unable to adhere to the optimistic view of communism, they sought refuge in a nearby ideology, capable of accounting for the seemingly absurd course of historical evolution, without requiring them to break with the atheistic and materialistic background of Marxism. Some endeavored, for this purpose, to search for and rescue old materialisms that Marxism believed it had absorbed and overcome. Others sought a rapprochement with "bourgeois" materialist currents, such as the analytical philosophy of Russell and Wittgenstein (widely read in Brazil in the 1980s) and, naturally, pragmatism. First, there was the fad of Charles Sanders Peirce, a fifth-rate philosopher who was erected as a totem in certain Brazilian academic circles. But the best came with Rorty, whose points of similarity with Gramsci give him irresistible appeal in the eyes of the local intelligentsia.

One of these similarities, the most significant, is the denial of objective knowledge and the consequent reduction of intellectual activity to propaganda and manipulation of consciousness. Both Gramsci and Rorty deny that human knowledge can describe reality and declare that the only purpose of our cultural and scientific efforts is to express collective desires. For both, there are no universal concepts or valid universal judgments, but universals can be "created" through propaganda, making all people share the same beliefs, or rather, the same illusions. The function of the intellectual is therefore to generate these illusions, and, as Rorty says, "gradually instill them" in the minds of the people. They differ only on the identity of the intellectual: for Rorty, it consists of the academic community; for Gramsci, it is the Party or "collective intellectual."

These two phantasmagorical entities—tasked with directing the consciousness of beings devoid of consciousness—and themselves formed of individuals who have no consciousness whatsoever, share the greatest contempt for arguments and evidence and a pronounced taste for psychological action that shapes the feelings of the masses without allowing for discussions or providing explanations for the demand for "truth." In both, the cunning of manipulating reality replaces the intelligence of knowing it. Manipulating reality? No. Manipulating its image in the public's mind.

Much like Peirce and Rorty's academic community, Gramsci's "collective intellectual" does not have the real unity of an organism, but the functional, and more or less conventional, unity of a club or an army. For this very reason, it cannot be intelligent; it cannot have intuitive perceptions. What is it to be "intelligent"? It is to grasp, at a glance, the objective unity of a set of data, arranging them in a framework immediately available to all psychic faculties, will, feeling, imagination, etc. This simultaneity of information allows the individual to react as a whole to situations, without the mediation of a long and complex decision-making process. It is "presence of mind," alert consciousness that enables full and effective adaptation to changes without loss of biographical continuity, or the sense of life. How could a collective entity rise to this level of consciousness? To understand and decide as quickly as an individual, it has to place an individual at the top and follow his decisions without discussion. But to preserve internal democracy, it has to submit decisions for the approval of all members and await the final outcome of discussions, during which thousands of deviating factors interfere, such as the intrusion of other issues, competition between vanities in assemblies, etc.—and in the end, the final decision will be a mechanical arrangement of pressures and compromises, not the immediate response of consciousness to a perception of reality. The "collective intellectual" has to choose between the unity of a tyranny and the multiplication of languages; between explicit or implicit submission to any individual consciousness and dissolution into a collective unconsciousness that, sooner or later, will be manipulated discreetly by some clever individual; ultimately: between declared tyranny and concealed tyranny.

While the principle of the "collective intellectual" prevailed only within the Communist Party, its cult of unconsciousness affected only those directly engaged in left-wing movements, preventing them from seeing the most obvious and glaring facts, such as the Moscow Trials, the economic failure of the USSR, the Gulag, etc.

With the fall of the communist hierarchy, however, the spirit of the "collective intellectual" leaked from the dying body of communism to intellectuals in general. Nowadays, particularly in Brazil, intellectual life as a whole imitates, through the uniformity of themes and values, the internal discussion in the old Communist Party, the collective processing of ideas by a mass of militants to obtain, through the sum of votes, the infallible definition of the "party line."[125] With this, individual intelligences lose all ability to operate independently, understand nothing by themselves and, confirming a widespread rumor about the uselessness of autonomous consciousness, only show themselves capable of acting in an atmosphere of unanimous agreement, of "participation" in the collective sentiment. Since everyone is immersed in this collective, no one sees it from the outside, just as fish do not see the water. Intellectual life is thus reduced to the mutual confirmation of beliefs, prejudices, feelings, and habits of the literate group. It becomes tribalized.

Anyone who sees this involvement as a passing phenomenon that only scratches the surface of history would err due to excessive optimism. It has an anthropological dimension; it affects the destiny of the human species in the cosmos: it only takes a generation of "collective intellectuals" to dominate the world and lose the individualization of consciousness, the prize of a millennial evolutionary effort.

The idea of the "collective intellectual" has a compromising origin. It was born in clubs, assemblies, and literary salons where the French Revolution was generated—the "Republic of Letters." It was there that the class of modern intellectuals first felt the strength of its union and was crowned queen under the title of "public opinion." In fact, this term did not designate the opinion of the

---

[125] And what the hell is the difference between "party line" and "politically correct" anyway? What good did it do to destroy the machine of communist mental censorship if now it's the entire intellectual establishment that comes down on us like a pack of commissars to monitor, patrol, pressure, blackmail, threaten, and denigrate? Worse still, sheltered under the general conviction that "communism is dead," the new commissars are free to act just like the old ones without anyone being able to accuse them of being communist. It's the ultimate trick of the most histrionic of ideologies: pretending to be dead to mug the gravedigger.

masses but the common sentiment of the educated elites.[126] The characteristic of these clubs, which differentiated them, on the one hand, from scientific societies as we know them today and, on the other hand, from the centers of debate in the medieval university, was the complete absence of rational criteria for validating arguments: it was the empire of "opinion"—in the Greek sense of *doxa* or pure belief. The true doctrine was not the one that coincided with reality, but the one that best expressed the aspirations of the collective, in the language most flattering to the passions of the moment. After the storm of the Revolution passed, the scientific and university institutions of the victorious bourgeoisie naturally refrained from organizing themselves according to the example of revolutionary societies, but according to the established models of the medieval university and the scientific circles of the Renaissance. Everyone knew that the "Republic of Letters" had served to agitate the masses but could not serve to produce knowledge. It is not surprising, therefore, that the model of the revolutionary debating society was later adopted by those excluded from the new order: the socialist intelligentsia. But it would not remain confined there forever. If, over the course of the twentieth century, an atmosphere of a Jacobin club quietly takes hold of the entire cultural life, this is largely due to the proletarianization of universities, which, from generators of a scientific and governing elite, have turned into centers for the professional training of the masses (transferring, of course, the burden of forming the elite to more discreet, if not secret, institutions).[127]

The democratization of education opened access to intellectual and scientific professions to millions of people. What was once an elite, a handful of geniuses exchanging ideas through private correspondence and a few academic publications, has become an innumerable crowd. The quantitative swelling, accompanied by reduced demands, resulted in a formidable decline in standards: the intellectual proletariat, spread across thousands of institutions and occupied with daily professional tasks, no longer even attempts to keep abreast of the march of ideas in the world. Each professional has resigned to being unable to follow the

---

[126] It was there—and not in the American universities of the 1980s—that the "revolt of the elites" began, as described by Christopher Lasch in his book *The Revolt of the Elites and the Betrayal of Democracy*. All the characteristics Lasch attributes to modern intellectual elites—abstract utopianism, the view of reality as a pliable substance subject to any reformism, thinking based on models rather than facts, etc.—were already present in the revolutionary *intelligentsia* of 1789. [See "Christopher Lasch: The New Elite and the Old Masses," in Chapter 3.—Eds.]

[127] It's significant that the century of democracy, of government by the masses, is also the century of secret power—the CIA, the KGB, Mossad, etc. These entities have influenced contemporary history much more than all parliaments and elections combined.

succession of discoveries, not even in their own specialty; each moves through a tunnel, unaware of where the others are going. To compensate for the imbalance caused by specialization, a prosthesis called "general culture" is then grafted onto the specialist, and soon universities have to unleash a wave of "specialists in general culture" onto the market. Mainly composed of those who failed to specialize in anything else, the new profession is occupied either with adorning the cake of professional knowledge with a cherry of culture as a leisure activity and completely disconnected from any reference to practical life, or with outlining a synthesis between culture and practice in the form of ideological indoctrination. Thus, the very nature of university-level professions has been perverted: the university graduate professional no longer has to be an intellectual capable of forming a reasonable personal opinion; they are a worker, an employee, following the collective script, as the middle-class officials and manual laborers did in the past. Therefore, as scientific information accumulates, the capacity, necessity, and simple desire to absorb it decrease on the other side.

With the advent of tertiary capitalism, where the predominant industry is that of "cultural goods," the intellectual proletariat has expanded to encompass most of the population in rich countries and almost the entire middle class in poor countries. As a result, higher cultural production had to meet a prodigious demand for cheap emotions, now dignified with "intellectual" prestige. The gossip of the old show business magazines, for example, invaded historical research, taking on the appearance of respectable academic activity. Driven by the need to flatter the most vulgar passions, higher culture ended up being shaped by the criteria of pure marketing, with the *collective imbecile* circularly confirming that there is no truth above the taste of the majority.

In this atmosphere, rational discussion becomes impossible: consensus forms in waves of feelings that vaguely stir in the air and produce brief chills on the skin. Beliefs mold and dissolve in an impressionistic atmosphere, like moving ink blots on wet paper. It is the time of rhetoric, psychological persuasion, and vaguely camouflaged blackmail that takes the place of argumentation. And finally, the state of affairs claims its elevation to the status of norm and law: the Boehms, the Feyerabends, the Kuhns, the Rortys emerge, advocating the legitimacy of rhetorical argument, emotional appeal, and even subliminal influence as means of scientific proof.[128] The notion of "truth"—which the first generation of

---

[128] Recognizing the reality of rhetorical interference in the course of scientific investigation is one thing; accepting rhetorical argumentation as a criterion of scientific truth is another. The attacks of the "holist" movement on positivist scientism have resulted mainly in the

intellectual proletarians had already reduced to a conventional formalism, emptying it of its ontological substance—fades away completely and is finally ostentatiously denied. Ideas gain followers through emotional contagion; and once dominant, they no longer need to even claim the pretense of truth. They have a better argument: the force of numbers, which spreads fear of isolation in the souls of recalcitrants, vaguely identified with misery and madness. Beneath the festive adherence to new intellectual fashions, the persuasive machinery of psychological terror grinds ominously.

In summary, these are the dominant trends in scientific and philosophical debate in the world today. In older countries that retain values inherited from the Middle Ages and the Renaissance, these trends can sometimes be offset by some critical and organizing reaction. But the new countries, which entered history after the French Revolution and absorbed little from the legacy of previous centuries, have no defense against the spirit of the "collective intellectual," which tends to be identified, in an unconscious dogmatism, as the only possible incarnation of the idea of higher culture. Becoming an "intellectual" there is not about acquiring certain knowledge and demonstrating capability in certain genres of investigation or creation, but about being accepted in certain circles, speaking in a certain tone, and acquiring certain mannerisms that recognize caste identity. Hence, a great philosopher living in isolation may end up being excluded from the cultural history of the country, as happened with Mário Ferreira dos Santos,[129] while the socialite, popular in certain groups, will become a famous intellectual even if he leaves no work worth reading and discovers nothing worth knowing.

Brazil is the promised land of the "collective intellectual."

---

establishment of an inverted scientism. Positivism arrogated to existing science the merits and authority of the pure ideal of apodictic knowledge. Holism, noting that scientific practice falls far short of this ideal, simply assumes existing practice (including rhetoric) as the norm and disregards the ideal. However, it does not relinquish the authority of the scientific caste; instead, it adds to it the prestige of non-scientific forms—literary, religious—of knowledge. The modern academic only acknowledges the poverty of their specialized scientific knowledge in order to better pose as a Renaissance *uomo universale* and offer opinions on all subjects.

[129] Mário Ferreira dos Santos (1907–1968) was a Brazilian philosopher who authored the *Enciclopédia das ciências filosóficas* [Encyclopedia of Philosophical Sciences] in 48 volumes, among which his magnum opus *Filosofia Concreta* [Concrete Philosophy]. Carvalho considered him the greatest Brazilian philosopher and published an introduction and study guide to his work, which had until then been neglected by the Brazilian academic establishment.—Eds.

The New World Order Guru

Diário do Comércio, April 3, 2006
O mundo como jamais funcionou (2014); *O Foro de São Paulo* (2022)

Some readers find it strange that in the midst of the communist rise in Latin America I diverge from the explosive present to engage, here and in other publications, in an apparently untimely combat against Immanuel Kant and the Enlightenment.

Some may even imagine that I developed a grudge against the hunchbacked little man from Königsberg due to his physical resemblance to that of Turin (Antonio Gramsci). However, I have nothing against little people, except when they harbor enormous monsters within. In another article, I briefly described the latter. His German predecessor seems much less dangerous. Often, he appears in the media with the smiling features of a lover of peace and freedom. No one can deny that he really was that, but in philosophy, words are not valued for their dictionary-standard meaning, but for the specific and fully developed concept they name. When we examine what Kant understood by peace and freedom, knowing that this is also how the current candidates for world rulers understand them, we cannot help but perceive that the philosopher's resemblance to the founder of the Italian Communist Party is not only anatomical but also moral—especially in the ability both had to beautify the ugliest historical realities they were planting in the soil of the future with idealistic language.

In general, the increasing and more organized influence of intellectuals in the centers of world power and the widespread adoption of "cultural warfare" as a primary instrument of domination make politics incomprehensible to those who cannot closely follow the march of ideas. It is a deadly illusion to imagine that a "practical" sphere still exists separately from cultural, religious, and philosophical debate. *Soi-disant* "pragmatic" politicians or business leaders, who boasted of looking with contempt at seemingly Byzantine discussions among academics, are today a dying breed. To destroy them, activist intellectuals need only conceive strategies that remain far removed from the horizon of their practical immediacy. The victory of Gramscism in Brazil is explained, in large part, by the intellectual indolence of political and business leaders outside the left. In the U.S., nothing is debated in Congress, decided in the judiciary, or undertaken in the executive without first passing through the scrutiny of think tanks, where intellectuals of considerable caliber create the categories of thought that then guide all subsequent discussion. If you try to follow the unfolding of events without knowing the most remote intellectual presuppositions behind power conflicts, you end up understanding nothing. One of these presuppositions is Kant's philosophy.

Presented in an abstruse style that repels even philosophy students, it is the last thing a "practical man" would be interested in. Precisely for this reason, it is becoming a reality right before their eyes, without them having the slightest idea of where it threatens to lead them.

A few observations are enough to highlight the seriousness of the matter.

Firstly, the Kantian notion of "eternal peace," so appealing to sentimental individuals due to its vague biblical resonance, means nothing other than "world government." In an important study,[130] Fr. Michel Schooyans, a Belgian philosopher who has also taught in Brazil, demonstrates that the new uniform legislations imposed on the world by the UN, such as the mandatory acceptance of abortion I referred to in one of the previous articles,[131] are directly inspired by Kant. The rapidly evolving global government that the UN is constructing is the exact legal translation of what Kant understood as the "human community." According to the philosopher, this community spontaneously emerged from the fact that humans are all endowed with the same faculty of "reason." But reason, for Kant, is not the same as it was for ancient and medieval thinkers. They understood it as the simple gift of speech and coherent thinking, a distant reflection of the divine Reason that created and sustains the world. Thanks to this gift, humans could grasp something of the divine and cosmic order of the world, ordering their own soul's life accordingly within the limits of their capabilities. For Kant, on the contrary, reason is the supreme and unsurpassable legislative authority, which owes no satisfaction either to a pre-existing divine order or to any facts of the real world that do not fit into its sovereign self-regulation. Students of the history of philosophy are aware that the Enlightenment, in general, was characterized by the advocacy of abstract universality, with complete disregard for the variety of singular facts. In the French Revolution, thousands of individual heads were severed to bring those remaining into the beautiful universality of reason. Kant loved it. The rigidity of his abstract moralism knew no bounds. Now, imagine what can result from transforming this into the guiding principle of world order. Eliminating nations that do not fit perfectly into the new global order will be as easy as guillotining dissenters. If Colombian culture, for example, is resistant to abortion due to its desire to remain faithful to its Christian origins, the international credit of Colombia is cut off, just as the head of the poet André Chénier or the physicist Lavoisier was once severed. This is actually

---

[130] *La face cachée de l'ONU* (Paris: Ed. Sarment Fayard, 2000); *The Hidden Face of the United Nations*, trans. Rev. John H. Miller (St. Louis: Central Bureau, CCVA, 2001).
[131] "O estupro das soberanias nacionais" ["The rape of national sovereignties"], published in 2006.—Eds.

happening, and it is a tempting solution, especially because the Colombian government is waging a successful war against drug trafficking, which the emerging global order would prefer to liberalize as a legitimate trade (a widespread campaign in this regard is subsidized by Mr. George Soros, who simultaneously invests heavily in building the new order and buying land . . . in Colombia). For those who want to fit the planet into a uniform legal model, crushing opponents and recalcitrant individuals with the good conscience of an apostle of eternal peace, nothing is more inspiring than Kant's abstractions.

However, long before instilling these malignant ideas into the heads of Genevan bureaucrats, Kant had already done irreparable harm to human intelligence. By consecrating the empire of uniform "reason" over the multiplicity of facts, he created the scientistic dogmatism that allows entire continents of reality to be abolished under the pretext that they are resistant to scientific study, and then gives this same science, which admits its inability to study them, the authority to declare that they do not exist. This idolatry of the method produced tragicomic results. The epidemic of anthropological charlatanism in the twentieth century was among them. Based on the Kantian premise that from a factual judgment one cannot deduce a value judgment, nor from value a fact, obtuse social scientists professed to abstain ascetically from making value judgments about the cultural realities they studied and ended up drawing from this vow of chastity the conclusion that, in this field, differences in value did not exist at all. The equality of cultures before Kant's supreme Reason is now a dogma imposed on all nations by the politically correct pedagogues of the UN. The bibliography aimed at persuading the world that, for example, the Aztec rituals of human sacrifice were as decent a custom as Franciscan charity is immeasurable.

When Prof. Peter Singer firmly asserts the human rights of chickens, extending to differences between animal species the same precept that has been so successful regarding differences among cultures, he is being rigorously Kantian.

From the same inspiration comes the sublime rule that, as genetic science cannot perceive any difference between a human being and a chimpanzee at three months of gestation, human beings are not really different from chimpanzees. Strengthened by Kant's authority, each individual science believes itself authorized to proclaim that everything beyond the reach of its methods is perfectly nonexistent. Any janitor knows that a human embryo, once grown, can become Plato or Michelangelo, and that no chimpanzee embryo can expect an equally promising future. But, as embryology does not study anything that happens to embryos after they cease to be embryos, this difference is Kantianly abolished in favor of the sovereignty of the method. And long ago, the suppression of this difference ceased to be a mere academic speculation; it has become law, and the heads cut off along the way are neither those of chimpanzees nor chickens.

Another incalculable misfortune that Kantism brought to humanity is the rigid and stereotyped separation between "science" and "religion." According to Kant, the former concerns what we can "know," while the latter concerns what we can only "hope for," that is, desire and imagine. In short, there prevails the difference between "knowledge" and "belief." A scientific theory can be proven or contested. In a religious doctrine, you only believe or disbelieve, with no possibility of rational arbitration. This distinction has so deeply permeated the Western soul that it has ended up determining the daily use of these respective words in the media, schools, public, and private discussions. This is perhaps the most successful terminological dogma of all time. Even in the automatism of the unconscious, religion has become synonymous with "faith," end of story. But this is a puerile and unsustainable concept, complete nonsense. No religion in the world begins with "belief." It always starts with a succession of events that mark the sudden and humanly inexplicable collective penetration into a sphere of higher reality, where all existence appears transfigured by a new meaning. I say "events" because that's what it's about. The crossing of the Red Sea may have turned into a matter of "belief" for subsequent generations, but for those who lived through the event, it was nothing of the sort. Jesus Christ could say to the cured blind and paralyzed: "Your faith has saved you." But it's pure metonymy: healing, if it were purely a matter of faith and not a fact of the physical order, would be fraud and nothing more. With the passage of time, as the living memory of the testimonies fades, access to these facts may require some "faith," but it makes no sense to confuse the nature of a fact with the way of knowing it centuries later. Either these miracles happened, or they did not. Shifting the problem to a distant past is just avoiding the problem. Seventy-six percent of American doctors today believe in miraculous cures because they see them happening daily and know that they are even more frequent than cures by usual therapeutic means. Jesus Christ himself, when asked [by his disciples] if He was truly the sent one of God or if they should wait for another, did not respond with a "doctrine" to be believed or disbelieved, but with facts to be confirmed or contested (see Matthew 11:1–6). Religions only become a matter of "belief" for an audience that is far removed, in space or time, from their original sources. Direct knowledge and scientifically responsible study of miraculous events are the only intellectually valid avenues to religion. The rest is an empty discussion among ignorant chatterers sitting on the periphery of reality. Nowadays, however, any fact deemed miraculous is automatically excluded from official discussion unless it is a fraud or an illusion, that is, precisely because it is not miraculous in any way and can be explained by some facile psychologism or sociologism. Once inconvenient data is expelled, Kantian "reason" reigns absolute in its mole hole. Kantism, a consecration of intellectual cowardice that shies away from everything it does not know, blocks the possibility of coming to know it. No dogmatic authoritarianism in history has been as petty and as harmful as this. In other articles, I give examples of its disastrous effects on culture, history, and moral life. [132]

For now, I only ask that you not come to me with that soft talk that Kant had the best intentions, that it was all the fault of the exaggerated zeal of misunderstanding disciples. The perverse consequences of Kantism, like those of Hegelianism and Marxism, did not come centuries or millennia later; they were almost immediately subsequent. A thinker who believes he can turn the entire universe of human knowledge inside out has no excuse for ignoring the most obviously foreseeable effects of the spread of his ideas. It is indecent to move from supreme intellectual arrogance to feigned innocence. One cannot grant this right to Kant, just as one cannot grant it to Hegel, Karl Marx, or even Nietzsche, despite the mitigating factor of madness. Anyone who claims to have understood the integral meaning of human history has a strict obligation to accurately foresee the next episode, at least regarding their own limited field of personal action. If he cannot even do that, it is because he has not reached the fullness of the philosophical self-awareness of a Plato, an Aristotle, a Thomas Aquinas, or a Leibniz. And in that case, we only continue to consider him a great philosopher, and not merely an interesting thinker, out of idolatrous devotion.

---

[132] For instance, see "Kant and the Primacy of the Critical Problem" in Chapter 4 and "To Understand Kant" in Chapter 5.—Eds.

Chapter 7

Revolutionary Minds in Action

There Is Only One Enemy

Diário do Comércio, January 8, 2007
A fórmula para enlouquecer o mundo (2014)

Marxism did not begin with Marx and did not arise from any scientific study of economics. Everything Karl Marx would come to think and say—except for the materialist-dialectical pretext and the statistics he falsified from the famous Blue Books of the British Parliament—was already in the doctrines of messianic heresiarchs since the fourteenth century. Everything: class struggle, revolution, socialization of the means of production, dictatorship of the proletariat, the mission of the revolutionary vanguard. Even the ideas of Lenin and Gramsci are already clearly anticipated there.

John Knox, Jan Hus, Thomas Münzer, and other "prophets" of the origins of modernity are not only precursors of the world revolutionary movement: they are its creators. The ambiguous and reticent tributes paid to them from time to time by some leftist intellectual only serve to inflate the contributions of the more recent left, diminishing that of those founding fathers by artfully placing them back in a supposedly ascending historical series whose top is always, of course, the author of the tribute.

The central idea of the messianic revolution can be summarized in four points: (I) sinful humanity will not be saved by Our Lord Jesus Christ but by itself; (II) the method to achieve redemption is to kill or at least subjugate all the wicked, that is, the rich; (III) the poor are innocent and pure but do not understand their place in the salvation project and therefore must place themselves under the orders of a ruling elite, the "saints;" (IV) the redemptive slaughter will generate not only the best distribution of wealth but the elimination of evil and sin, the advent of a new humanity.

A heresy is not "another religion:" it is, by definition, an internal opposition, born from within Christianity itself, generally through some exotic graft that completely distorts the original message and gives it the most absurd meanings imaginable.[133] It's not surprising, therefore, that the subsequent evolution of the

---

[133] The passionate love that many intellectuals today have for these aberrations reveals not only their hatred for Christianity and their desire to exterminate it by any means possible, but also a lack of intelligence bordering on the monstrous. Bart D. Ehrman, the acclaimed author of *The Lost Gospel of Judas Iscariot. A New Look at Betrayer and Betrayed* (Oxford University Press, 2006), for example, is nothing but a fanatic Gnostic disguised as a university scholar, capable of conducting philological research in various ancient languages but incapable of discerning the most puerile contradictions in his own text. For

revolutionary movement was marked by a permanent tension between heretical faith and the denial of all faith, between pseudo-Christianity and anti-Christianity, between the ambition to destroy Christianity and the desire to preserve something of it to be able to parasitize its authority. This dialectical game confuses the lay observer, who, deluded by apparent differences, loses sight of the profound unity of the revolutionary movement and often ends up serving one of its subcurrents, believing fervently that he is serving a counter-revolutionary, conservative, or even Christian or Jewish purpose in the strict sense of the terms.

With the extinction of the messianic revolutions, the second wave of the revolutionary movement takes the form of explicit anti-Christianity and anti-Judaism. The Enlightenment thinkers of the eighteenth century not only openly preached the elimination of these two traditional faiths, but did not hesitate to invent the most aberrant lies against them, finding it beautiful and having a lot of fun. Today's anti-Christian polemics seem like masterpieces of politeness when compared to the virulence of 18th-century fantasies.[134] It increasingly seems to confirm the thesis of Abbot Antonin Barruel, exposed in his *Histoire du Jacobinisme* (1798), of a plan devised among Voltaire, d'Alembert, Diderot, and Emperor Frederick II of Prussia to roll out a vast defamation campaign aimed at covering the Church with infamy by all unscrupulous means available.

Diderot's case is particularly illustrative. In *The Nun*, he tells the story of a poor girl kept in a convent against her will. The abominable image of imprisoned nuns, circulated by him and other Enlightenment thinkers long before the posthumous publication of the book in 1796, became a condensed symbol of all the crimes attributed to the Church by the fervor of anti-Christian propaganda. In the turmoil of the Revolution of 1789, the symbol transformed into a literal belief. Many revolutionaries who invaded convents, killing monks and nuns *en masse*, solemnly swore to be doing so to liberate the incarcerated virgins who, they imagined, must overcrowd the basements of the cloisters. When eighty abbeys, monasteries, and religious houses in Paris had already been invaded and much blood spilled, the Constituent Assembly, perplexed, received the news that everywhere the nuns and novices had unanimously proclaimed their fidelity to

---

this type of scholar, committed to challenging the original Gospels based on Gnostic texts written two centuries later, university chairs, NBC, the *History Channel*, *National Geographic*, and the entire chic media are always open, for the simple reason that these institutions are funded and controlled by the same core of billionaires committed to manufacturing a bionic religion to replace Christianity in the third millennium.
[134] See, on this matter, Paul Hazard, *La Pensée Européenne au XVIIIe. Siècle* (Paris: Boivin, 1946), a classic in the history of ideas.

their state, even as they ascended the steps of the guillotine. Such was the spirit of the "prisoners."

Diderot, although dying five years before the Revolution, cannot easily be excused for the criminal effects of a hatred he consciously instigated. He cannot, especially because he was always aware that there were and could be no prisoners in the convents, that all the nuns were there of their own will, including the one who inspired him to write the novel, Sister Delamarre, from the Longchamps convent. It was all a premeditated forgery.

For a long time, the whole world believed in Diderot's version, which claimed to have complete documentation of the Delamarre case. In fact, the dossier was in his hands but disappeared soon after the publication of the novel. Found again in 1954 by the researcher Georges May,[135] reading it shows that Diderot was aware of the following facts:

1) In Paris, there were four tribunals, ecclesiastical and civil, to judge requests for release from the monastic career, and the general rule was to grant all requests.

2) The selection of nuns was extremely rigorous. The Church's commitment was to rid itself of false vocations, not to retain them by force.

3) Exactly the opposite of a convent prisoner, Sister Delamarre was the gatekeeper, had the keys, and could come and go as she pleased.

4) The only lawsuit filed by Miss Delamarre was an estate dispute with a relative. To receive the inheritance, a noble title, the nun had to leave the religious order. But soon after giving up the legacy dispute, she happily returned to the convent.

Diderot knew all this, and the correspondence between him and his friend Jacob Grimm shows that the novelist was "bursting with laughter" (*sic*), with the meticulous forgery he was concocting around the story. He not only enjoyed the fierce joy of slander but also indulged in the refinement of very direct mental cruelty. To the Marquis de Croismarre, a pious Christian who wrote to him worried about the fate of the girl, Diderot responded with disturbing fabrications, emphasizing the sufferings of the unfortunate woman in the cloister, and relishing

---

[135] Georges Claude May (1920–2003) was a French academic and researcher, author of several books, including *Diderot et 'La Religieuse'* (New Haven: Yale Univ. Press; Paris: Presses Universitaires de France, 1954). After receiving degrees from the University of Paris and the University of Montpellier, he served in the French Army during World War II, was affiliated with the U.S. Office of Strategic Services and, after the war, took a job as an instructor at Yale University and earned a Ph.D. from the University of Illinois.—Eds.

to the very end the pleasure of keeping the poor man in distress. It is not surprising that Diderot was the favorite writer of Karl Marx, another sadistic sociopath.

Other documents found by Georges May after Diderot's death show that Sister Delamarre died thirty years after the novelist, still as the gatekeeper of the convent, having bravely faced, alongside her sisters, the Revolution's commissioners. The only oppression she suffered came from the enemies of the Church. [136]

If I were to enumerate and analyze all the lies invented by the thinkers of the Enlightenment against Christians and Jews, an entire year of daily editions of a major newspaper would not be enough to contain them. But the fact is that these lies have crossed centuries, deeply ingrained in the popular imagination, resurfacing in new and varied forms and serving to legitimize the massacre of Christians in Russia and Jews in Germany. Intellectuals and artists of great prestige do not hesitate to collaborate in this heinous crime. Everything about the Delamarre case was already well known to historians when, in 1970, Jean-Luc Godard's film *La Religieuse* renewed the effect of the odious symbol invented by Diderot.

But, returning to the central argument, the advent of the Jacobins to power caused a shift in the pole of dialectical tension: from anti-Christian propaganda, there was an open effort to create a simulacrum of Christianity for the consumption of revolutionary crowds. The rhetoric of Terror closely mimics that of the pseudoprophets of messianism: the idea of earthly apocalypse, the radical condemnation of capitalism, the purification of the universe through the killing of the rich, the privileged mission of the "saints," the return of humanity to an era of original purity—all of these resurface, but now with Rousseau's *Social Contract* as a sacred text instead of the Gospels. The caricatured imitation of the Christian *ethos* increasingly gains autonomy, detaching itself from the apparent meaning of Christ's message and parasitizing deeply rooted moral sentiments in the Christian population to turn them into instruments of legitimization of state terrorism, under the inspiration of—as Thomas Carlyle wrote—"a new Fifth Evangelist Jean-Jacques, calling on men to amend each the whole world's wicked existence" [137]

Luciano Pellicani, in his study on *Revolutionary Apocalypse: Ideological Roots of Terrorism*, observes:

---

[136] On the episode, read Jean Dumont, *La Révolution Française, ou, Les Prodiges du Sacrilège* (Paris: Criterion, 1984).
[137] Thomas Carlyle, *The French Revolution: A History*, vol. 3 (London: Chapman and Hall Ltd, 1891).—Eds.

Thus the revolutionary elite, acting on the basis of the diagnosis-therapy of the evils of the world contained in the 'true philosophy,' comes to take on the typical role of the Paraclete in gnostic tradition: it alone knows what is for the good of the city and how to achieve it.[138]

Founded on this omniscient authority, salvation must take the form of redemptive slaughter. Robespierre makes this clear: "popular government in revolution is virtue and terror . . . Terror is nothing but prompt, severe, inflexible justice; it is therefore an emanation of virtue."[139] Pellicani concludes: "This concept of redemption of humanity requires a society organized as if it were a *militarized convent*." The formula will reappear in the guerrilla priests of liberation theology and in the more recent projects of "archbishop" Hugo Chávez.

However, long before that, the revolution's pendulum swings once again to the other side. With the end of the Jacobin cycle, the advent of the Napoleonic Empire, the Restoration, and bourgeois democracy, the new formulas of revolutionary ideology, with Marx and Bakunin, upgrade anti-Christianity, transfiguring it into militant atheism. Karl Marx professes to "hate all gods," and defines atheism as the denial of God through which the existence of man is affirmed. For Marxism, inspired by Feuerbach at this point, God arises from the self-alienation of human powers projected into a metaphysical heaven—as if man had created heaven and earth and then forgotten it, transferring the honors to a nonexistent entity: a theory idiotic enough to seem seductive to millions of intellectuals.

With the rise of atheism, the killings of priests and believers multiply to a degree never dreamed of by Robespierre himself. Between the Mexican Civil War (1857) and the beginning of World War II (1939), no fewer than twenty million Christians died in religious persecutions intended, according to Lenin, to "sweep Christianity off the face of the earth." And the massacre of the Jews had not even begun yet.

But perhaps atheism is not the most authentic trait of this stage of the revolutionary movement. Both Marx and Bakunin openly participated in satanic rituals.[140] And at least in Italy, the praising of Satan became explicit with the poet Giosuè Carducci, one of the greatest inspirers of the local revolutionary movement:

---

[138] Luciano Pellicani, *Revolutionary Apocalypse: Ideological Roots of Terrorism* (London: Praeger, 2003).
[139] M. Robespierre, *Virtue and Terror* (London: Verso, 2017).—Eds.
[140] Read the never contested work of Richard Wurmbrand, *Marx and Satan, Living Sacrifice* (Book Company, 1986).

Hail, O Satan
O rebellion,
O you avenging force
of human reason![141]

Whatever the case, the impact of the killings eventually bothered the revolutionaries themselves, who, in the 1930s, were already thinking of some way to circumvent it. Antonio Gramsci, in the *Prison Notebooks*, teaches that the Church should not be fought but emptied of its spiritual content and used as a sounding board for communist propaganda. The success later achieved in this endeavor can be measured by two facts:

1) The overwhelming influence that communists managed to exert from within and outside the Second Vatican Council, dividing the Catholic Church and causing the largest exodus of faithful in two millennia of Catholicism.[142]

2) The World Council of Churches, the largest Protestant organization in the world, bringing together hundreds of churches in all countries, nominally for "ecumenical" objectives, is notoriously a pro-communist entity that supports and subsidizes terrorist revolutionary movements.[143] The various National Councils of Churches are independent entities, but at least the one in the USA is even more openly pro-communist than the World Council.[144]

Concurrently and in close informal association with communist efforts, a worldwide movement has been developing since the late nineteenth century to create the greatest possible religious confusion through mass occult propaganda and the forced revival of Gnosticism. Phenomena such as the outbreak of pseudo-mystical orientalism of the New Age, the cult of drugs as a "path to inner enlightenment," the wave of dangerous psychic experiments that started at Esalen (CA) and spread worldwide, the proliferation of sects committed to enslaving their followers through destructive mental practices—all of these can be presented to the public as a spontaneous convergence of trends or as an impersonal historical inevitability dictated by the "spirit of the times," but a little research into the

---

[141] *Hymn To Satan*. Original: "Salute, o Satana, O ribellione, O forza vindice, De la ragione!"

[142] See Ricardo de la Cierva, *Las Puertas del Infierno. La Historia de la Iglesia Jamás Contada*, (Madridejos, Toledo, Fénix, 1995); and *La Hoz y la Cruz. Auge y Caída del Marxismo y la Teología de la Liberación* (ibid., 1996).

[143] See Bernard Smith, *The Fraudulent Gospel. Politics and the World Council of Churches* (London: The Foreign Affairs Publishing Co., 1977).

[144] C. Gregg Singer, *Unholy Alliance. The Definitive History of the National Council of Churches and Its Leftist Policies—From 1908 to the Present* (Arlington House, 1975).

sources reveals that it is a unitary, organized initiative, and billionaire-funded by the same self-appointed forces determined to turn the UN into a world government.[145]

The dialectical and pendular oscillation of the revolutionary movement between anti-religion and pseudo-religion, combined with the hallucinatory multiplicity of the currents that feed it, disorients almost the entire public. The eagerness to take a position, endlessly fueled by the media and the school system, leads many people to support movements and ideas whose connection to the central current may not be immediately evident at first glance. How many conservative Christians, wanting to save the Church, have not adhered to anti-Jewish ideas, imagining that the revolution was essentially the work of Jews? How many Jewish intellectuals have joined revolutionary parties without realizing that they were digging the grave of their people? How many Protestants, confusing Catholicism with its revolutionary counterfeit, think that the best thing to do is to destroy the Catholic Church? How many Catholics, intoxicated with doctrinal purity, see Americanism as an enemy and therefore wage war against the only nation that has created a functional synthesis of Christian culture, prosperous economy, and political democracy? How many advocates of capitalist democracy do not believe they can reconcile it with militant atheism that, by eroding the spiritual and moral foundations of capitalism, invites it to become precisely the "idolatry of the market" that communist propaganda accuses it of being, and thus help transfer the monopoly of moral authority to revolutionaries, as well as radical Islamists? By choosing the enemy according to the most salient features that oppose their subjective preferences, all these people only fuel the flames of the dialectical tension from which the world revolutionary movement feeds and strengthens itself. Indeed, there is only one enemy. It cannot be effectively fought without grasping its unity behind the hallucinatory variety of its versions, incarnations, and appearances. Some decades ago, this unity was difficult to see because there was not enough documentation to prove it. Today, the evidence is so abundant that continuing to ignore it is starting to become a kind of criminal complicity.[146]

---

[145] The author had doubts about the feasibility of the initiative to create a world government, which obviously does not prevent its enthusiasts from attempting to implement it. Carvalho compared the world government project to the communist utopia, which, despite being unattainable, resulted in over 100 million deaths in the attempt to achieve it.—Eds.

[146] The question of the place occupied by Islamism in the process described here requires a separate examination, which will be done on another occasion. [See further in Chapter 8

What Does It Mean to Be Socialist?

Jornal da Tarde, October 28, 1999
O imbecil juvenil (2020)

Socialism has killed over 100 million dissidents and spread terror, misery, and famine over a quarter of the Earth's surface. All the earthquakes, hurricanes, epidemics, tyrannies, and wars of the last four centuries, combined, have not produced such devastating results. This is a simple and straightforward fact, accessible to anyone capable of consulting *The Black Book of Communism*[147] and making a basic calculation.

However, since what determines our beliefs isn't facts but interpretations, the devout socialist always has the recourse of explaining this formidable succession of calamities as the effect of fortuitous accidents unrelated to the essence of socialist doctrine. Thus, the beauty and dignity of a superior ideal are believed to remain immune to all the misery of its implementations.

To what extent is this claim intellectually respectable and morally admissible?

The socialist ideal is essentially the attenuation or elimination of differences in economic power through political power. But no one can effectively arbitrate differences between the most powerful and the least powerful without being more powerful than both: socialism must concentrate power capable not only of imposing itself on the poor, but of victoriously facing the entirety of the rich. Therefore, it cannot level differences in economic power without creating even greater disparities in political power. And as the structure of political power does not sustain itself in the air but costs money, it is not clear how political power could subjugate economic power without absorbing it, taking the wealth of the rich and administering it directly. Hence, in socialism, in exact opposition to what happens in capitalism, there is no difference between political power and dominion over wealth: the higher the position of an individual and a group in the political hierarchy, the more wealth will be entirely, and directly, at their disposal. There will be no class richer than the rulers. Therefore, economic disparities will not only necessarily have increased but, consolidated by the unity of political and economic power, they will have become impossible to eliminate except by the complete destruction of the socialist system. And even this destruction doesn't solve the problem because, with no rich class outside the *nomenklatura*, the latter

---

"The USA and the New World Order" and "In the Claws of the Sphinx: René Guénon and the Islamization of the West."—Eds.]
[147] Harvard University Press, 1999.—Eds.

will retain economic power in its hands, simply changing its legal legitimation, and self-denominating themselves as the bourgeoisie. Socialist experience, when it does not condense into bureaucratic oligarchy, dissolves into wild capitalism. *Tertium non datur*. Socialism consists of the promise to achieve a result by means that necessarily produce the opposite result.

Understanding this immediately reveals that the emergence of a bureaucratic elite with tyrannical political power and extravagant wealth is not a mere accident but the logical and inevitable consequence of the very principle of the socialist idea.

This reasoning is within the reach of anyone with moderate intellectual endowment, but, given a certain inclination of weaker minds to believe in desires rather than reason, one could still forgive these creatures for succumbing to the temptation to "take a chance" on the lottery of reality, betting on chance against logical necessity. Although immensely foolish, it is human. It is humanly foolish to insist on learning from one's own experience when we have been endowed with logical reasoning precisely to reduce the amount of experience necessary for learning.

What is by no means human is to reject both the lesson of logic, which shows us the self-contradiction of a project, and the lesson of an experience that, to rediscover what logic had already taught it, caused the death of 100 million people. No intellectually sound human being has the right to cling so stubbornly to an idea to the point of demanding that humanity sacrifice, on the altar of its promises, not only rational intelligence but the very instinct for survival.

Such incapacity, or refusal to learn, reveals, in the mind of the socialist, the voluntary and perverse lowering of intelligence to an infra-human level, a conscious renunciation of that basic discernment capacity that is the very condition of human nature. To be a socialist is to refuse, out of pride, to assume the responsibilities of human consciousness.

Ignoring the Essential

Diário do Comércio, April 3, 2009
O império mundial da burla (2016)

Here are some fundamental historical facts about the communist movement, ignored by the majority and little known, or well forgotten, by the educated minorities, without which it is literally impossible to understand anything about recent history. If you seek to inform yourself about this and begin to take these facts into account, you will see how much obscure information is automatically clarified without the need for great interpretative effort.

1. Communism has been and is, throughout human history, the only—repeat: the only—politically organized movement on a global scale, with ramifications and agents in the remotest places of the planet, disciplined and capable of immediate, coordinated, and simultaneous action upon the first call from its command centers.

2. Despite having a vast number of mass organizations and parties at its service, communism is essentially an underground movement whose command and action plans must remain invisible to outsiders, even in times of legality when various communist organizations operate publicly without suffering the least persecution. The primacy of the clandestine elite over visible leadership is, at least since Lenin, a cornerstone of communist strategy. It is impossible to understand this strategy and the tactics that implement it by only considering the overt actions of the most visible communist leaders in each country, without access to the internal discussions and international connections of each organization.

3. Communism has been and is, worldwide and at all times, the only political movement that has had, and has, unlimited financial resources at its disposal, superior to the greatest fortunes known in the West and to the budgets of many governments combined. Its possibilities of action must be measured on the scale of its resources.

4. Only a tiny fraction of communist activity consists of directly or indirectly recognizable doctrinal propaganda. The larger and more significant part consists of infiltrating and blending into all kinds of organizations—political parties (including liberal and conservative ones), media, unions, state and private companies, cultural, educational, religious, and charitable institutions, the armed forces, Freemasonry, the list is endless—in order to make them instruments of communist strategy and control the entire society through them, making the Party "an omnipresent and invisible power" (the

expression is from Antonio Gramsci, but the technique existed long before him). It is naive to imagine that, once inserted into these entities, communists dedicate themselves to indoctrination or proselytism, as if they were Protestant pastors spreading the Gospel among unbelievers. The mobilization of all forces to serve communist strategy is a tremendously subtle and complex mechanism, involving massive doses of camouflage and misdirection, with many paradoxical moves along the way.

5. It is foolish to imagine communism as a "doctrine" or "ideal," especially when this implies the open preaching of the abolition of private property. The communist movement never had nor needed any doctrinal unity and has proven a thousand times its ability to adapt tactically to the most disparate ideological formulas, successively or simultaneously, completely disorienting the lay observer (including politicians in general and almost all liberal and conservative intellectuals). The most truculent atheistic campaigns, for example, coexist peacefully within the communist movement with the use of religious discourse as a means of reaching the hearts of the masses. *Mutatis mutandis*, the exploitation of extreme nationalist sentiments goes hand in hand with the effort to dilute national sovereignties into larger, regional, or global units, so that behind the scenes, the communist movement benefits from both patriotic resistances and rising global power. The unity of the communist movement is strategic and organizational, not ideological. Communism is not a set of theses: it is a power scheme, the broadest, most flexible, integrated, and efficient that has ever existed. Even radical Islam, currently expanding rapidly, could do nothing without the support of the global network of communist organizations.

6. Even more foolish is to imagine that the logical-formal opposition between the abstract concepts of capitalism and communism translates, in practice, into a mortal conflict between capitalists and communists. The variety of different local and temporal situations corresponds to an infinity of nuances and transitions, with ample space for the strangest (only in appearance) arrangements and complicity. No one will understand anything about the historical world in which they live today without taking into account the long collaboration between the communist movement and some of the largest fortunes in the West, for example, Morgan, Rockefeller, and Rothschild. Classic books on the subject include those by the English economist Anthony Sutton, but as early as 1956, the Reece Committee of the U.S. House of Representatives produced substantial evidence that some billionaire foundations were using their formidable resources "to destroy or discredit the

free-enterprise system which gave them birth."[148] These foundations are now among the most robust pillars supporting the socialist government of Barack Hussein Obama.

The ignorance or misunderstanding of these facts among liberals and conservatives is at the root of their inability to mount a serious resistance to the triumphant march of communism in Latin America. Many still believe, for example, that forcing the FARC to abandon armed struggle and become a legal party will be a great victory for democracy. They do not understand that creating a recognized political force is ultimately the only goal of armed struggle—in Colombia or anywhere else. Guerrillas do not win wars; all they want is a politically advantageous defeat. Therefore, while exchanging gunfire with government forces in the jungle and cities, they place their agents in key positions in legal leftist parties, from where they decry bloodshed and dramatically appeal for a return to legality. They did this in Brazil and are doing it now in Colombia.

Until liberals and conservatives obtain a clear overview of the immensely complex phenomenon of communism, as long as they insist on opposing only the most immediate and repugnant facets of this movement, if not just the communist doctrines considered abstractly, they are condemned to defeat even when they consider themselves victorious.

The fact that there has never been an Anti-Communist International makes it difficult for many people to obtain this comprehensive view, which communists themselves so easily achieve. But the absence of social support cannot serve as an excuse for intellectual laziness. There are always some individual intelligences capable of reasoning above group perspectives. Nothing justifies these intelligences staying on the sidelines of public discussions, leaving the monopoly of the microphone to the ignorant. In this, as in all other human matters, those who have studied nothing are full of simplistic certainties and proclaim them with an air of tremendous superiority, without realizing the ridiculous role they play. Those who have studied sometimes seem crazy or eccentric, but after all, why does anyone study if not to know something that the majority does not know?

---

[148] John O'Donnell (*New York Daily News*, December 21, 1954), quoted in René A. Wormser, *Foundations: Their Power and Influence* (New York: The Devin Adair Company, 1958).—Eds.

The Origins of *Chic* Communism

Zero Hora, September 10, 2000
O Foro de São Paulo: a ascensão do comunismo latino-americano (2022)

In the 1920s, Stalin, rightly judging that it would be very difficult to control a revolution on the other side of the Atlantic, decided that the Communist Party of the United States should not be organized for the purpose of seizing power, but for the financial support and propaganda of European communism. Therefore, American communism was always less dedicated to the organization of the proletariat than to the enlistment of millionaires, Hollywood artists, and renowned intellectuals. For the embellishment of the communist image, it was important that these "fellow travelers" did not become members of the Party, but retained their status as independent personalities so that their expressions of support, activated at opportune moments, seemed like personal and free initiatives, dictated by innocent and spontaneous coincidence between communist objectives and the lofty ideals of a non-political humanity.

The success of this new style, contrasting with the traditional image of proletarian austerity, led to its adoption in Western Europe as well, marking an entire era. More than an era: the "glamour" of chic communism perpetuated a model by which the wardrobe of worldly intellectuals in New York is still cut, envied and imitated by the lettered crowd of the Third World: go to an exhibition of Sebastião Salgado, and you'll know what I'm talking about.

People who are unaware of these facts have a stubborn resistance to believing that such vast effects could have been planned by a discreet, almost secret elite. They prefer to cling to the foolish belief that everything happens spontaneously—a belief that rests on the hypothesis of a metaphysical fluid instead of the concrete action of attentive and clever men over distracted and foolish men. But spontaneous propagation does play some role. The technicians of the Communist International, counting on the ease with which fashions and quirks spread among worldly intellectuals, calculatedly used this effect and called it "raising rabbits."

The elite itself sometimes just has luck. No one could predict that the style of American communism would survive the loss of prestige of the Soviet regime, perpetuating itself in the form of the "New Left," which in the 1960s could continue working for totalitarianism without its beautiful image of independence being contaminated by what was happening in the USSR. But sometimes luck also runs out. The two main architects of creating chic communism, Karl Radek and Willi Münzenberg, ended up dead by order of Stalin as soon as the success of the operation made them useless. The initial idea had been conceived by Radek, one of the pioneers of the Russian Revolution, and implemented under the direction of Münzenberg, a propaganda genius. To give you an idea of Münzenberg's diabolical efficiency, it's enough to mention that he was the creator of the Sacco and Vanzetti myth. Decades after the trial, with the guilt of one and the complicity of the other in the murder of an unarmed man who begged for mercy demonstrated a thousand times that the publicity scheme was unmasked by confessions from members of Münzenberg's team. Yet, what still remains in the popular imagination is the legend of innocent workers sacrificed by a sordid capitalist plot.

An "expert" in enduring hoaxes, Münzenberg was also the inventor of other typical instruments of communist propaganda that are periodically pulled out of the hat and always work, such as the "intellectual manifesto," the celebrity march, and, last but not least, simulated trials, simulated elections, simulated referendums. So, the National Conference of Bishops of Brazil (CNBB) has their role model. The style is the man.

Münzenberg was also the creator of what he called the "politics of righteousness." It is a fundamental element of chic communism: it consists of not confronting democratic society head-on, but parasitizing the prestige of its moral ideals, making carefully selected "fellow travelers" pose as its most representative spokespeople. Thus, the appeal to these ideals can be modulated and directed according to the interests of a strategy that subtly, and as if by chance, leads society further away from them and closer to communist revolution. Recent Brazilian campaigns for "ethics" and "against poverty" were simply the application of this technique: they neither raised the moral standard of the nation nor reduced poverty, but created the atmosphere in which today, the training of guerrillas is funded by government funds without causing the slightest scandal. The spirit of Willi Münzenberg continues to hover over the Brazilian political scene.

Bears and Bureaucrats

Diário do Comércio, September 23, 2014
A cólera dos imbecis (2019)

My plan, this week, was to interrupt the series of depressing considerations about the heinous national and world politics and offer readers something more fun. Everything was set for just that. At 67, for the first time in my life, I took a leisure trip and am in the heart of the Maine forest with my son Pedro and my friend Silvio Grimaldo, hunting black bear.

It's a region of indescribable beauty; the guides are very kind people, so you feel like family. The accommodation even looks like a set of toy houses, and the food is top-notch. Every day the guides take us down a dirt road from where individual trails branch off into the woods to the stand where we perch to wait for the bear, attracted—hopefully—by the bait planted in an open barrel.

My bear hasn't shown up yet, especially because it rained a lot yesterday, and black bears don't like rain, but I'll keep trying. I carry a Browning .300 Winchester Magnum, enough to bring down three bears in a row, and my aim is not entirely bad.

Fig. 2. From left to right: Olavo de Carvalho, his youngest son, Pedro Carvalho and their friend Silvio Grimaldo (Maine, 2014).

I had a good opportunity, therefore, to entertain readers with some hunting stories, but darn it, even here, the hateful globalist politics has arrived, firmly determined to spoil everything and prove that "another world is possible." Of course, it's possible. What will be impossible is living in it without starting to think about suicide at the age of thirty.

It will be a completely managed world, with no room for human spontaneity, where the last semblance of emotion will consist of consuming drugs provided by the government and engaging in industrialized sex. Traces of this world are already seen everywhere, except in Russia, China, and Islamic countries, which prefer more outdated versions of hell.

The situation around here is as follows. Maine has about thirty thousand black bears. To prevent them from eating all the moose calves, about five thousand need to be killed each year. Laws and regulations have already complicated things to the point where not even half of that can be killed. As a result, moose hunting, once a popular sport, has become the privilege of a handful of wealthy people, and even they have to enter a lottery and wait for their chance.

Moose meat is delicious, and in my modest opinion, it is much more decent to eat a dangerous animal that you have killed personally, at your own risk, than to cynically devour a defenseless cow beaten to death at the end of a dead-end bay.

But now, the so-called Humane Society, a gigantic organization subsidized by George Soros and other lovely creatures, has invented a referendum to ban baiting, hounding, and trapping, leaving only the so-called "still hunting," which involves walking through the woods until you find a bear, which is nearly impossible.

Tom Hamilton, our guide, said that in ten years, he only saw one bear like that from afar. The black bear is not as bold as the grizzly. It's a shy animal that hides like a sneaky thief. If the "Yes" vote wins, the bear overpopulation will put an end to the moose, invade human space, and threaten domestic animals. It will be the perfect ecological paradise.

For millennia, human communities have kept themselves safe from ferocious animals thanks to a vast circle of protection consisting of hunters, game wardens, farmers, etc. This is true even today. The typical urban citizen of our day ignores the existence of this circle and imagines that it is simply natural for animals to remain at peace in their "habitat," as if obedient to an immense cosmic real estate registry, only becoming dangerous when their territory is "invaded" by wicked humans.

This is monstrously stupid. The "natural habitat" of a bear or a wolf is not a fixed place: it is where they find food to their liking. It could be a chicken coop, a cattle farm, or a small town. If they don't go beyond that, it's because someone shot them.

The urban idiot, thousands of miles away, intoxicated with marijuana, ideological babble, and TV programs, believes himself protected by the kindness of the beasts and the miracle of "ecological balance." One must be very, very stupid to believe that, left to itself or maintained as an inviolable sanctuary by the worshipers of animalism, Mother Nature will sort everything out in perfect harmony.

This kind mother has already exterminated more animal species than all of humanity's hunters combined. Of all natural factors, man is the least deadly. He is, in fact, the only one concerned with preserving other species. No tiger holds a protest march when one of its relatives eats four hundred poor, unarmed Indians. No grizzly publishes outraged editorials when one of its kind kills dozens of cubs, females, and weaker bears.

Not coincidentally, the entire movement for the protection of animal species was an invention of hunters, such as Theodore Roosevelt in the USA and Jim Corbett in India. Hunters know what is good for animals, for humans, and for reasonable coexistence among species. Politicians and enlightened intellectuals only think of themselves and invent the most beautiful pretexts to control everything.

Do the math. In Maine, where bear hunting is still a common practice, there are forty—yes, forty—times fewer risky situations between bears and people than in Connecticut, where hunting is entirely prohibited, and there are only 450 bears instead of Maine's thirty thousand. Who better protects the human and animal population? Hunters or the government?

Will To Kill

Jornal da Tarde, January 22, 1998
O imbecil juvenil (2020)

Friends and readers ask me for an opinion on abortion. However, inclined by nature towards the economy of effort, my brain refuses to form an opinion on anything unless it finds a good reason to do so. Faced with any problem, its instinctive reaction is to fiercely cling to the natural right to not think about the case. But, in arguing for this right, we end up having to ask why the damn problem exists in the first place. Thus, what started as an attempt not to think becomes an investigation of foundations, i.e., the most philosophical endeavor there is. Future authors of disparaging biographies will say, rightly, that I became a philosopher simply out of laziness to think. But, as laziness prioritizes subjects on the scale of minimum attention, I ended up developing a keen sense of the difference between problems posed by the fate of things and problems that only exist because certain people want them to exist.

Now, the problem of abortion obviously belongs to the latter kind. The questioning of abortion exists because the practice of abortion exists, and not the other way around. That someone decides in favor of abortion is the assumption of the existence of the abortion debate. But what is assumed in a debate cannot, at the same time, be its logical conclusion. The choice for abortion, being prior to all discussion, is inaccessible to arguments. The abortionist is an abortionist by free decision, which dispenses with reasons. This freedom is asserted directly by the act that realizes it and, multiplied by millions, becomes a freedom generally recognized and consolidated into a "right." Hence, the discourse in favor of abortion avoids the moral issues and clings to legal and political ground: it does not so much want to affirm a value, but establish a right (which can, in theory, coexist with the moral condemnation of the act).

As for the content of the debate, opponents of abortion argue that the fetus is a human being, and killing it is a homicide. Supporters argue that the fetus is just a piece of flesh, a part of the mother's body that she should have the right to remove at will. In the current score of the dispute, neither side has yet persuaded the other. Nor is it reasonable to expect they will, as in the present civilization there is no consensus on what is or is not human nature, and there are no common premises that can underpin a resolution.

But the tie itself ends up transfiguring the whole discussion: faced with it, we move from an ethic-metaphysical dispute, unsolvable under the present conditions of Western culture, to a simple mathematical equation whose resolution should, in principle, be identical and equally convincing for all beings capable of understanding it. This equation is formulated as follows: if there is a 50% chance that the fetus is human and a 50% chance that it is not, betting on the latter hypothesis is literally choosing an act that has a 50% chance of being a homicide.

With this, the whole question becomes clearer than the most refractory of brains could demand. In the absence of absolute certainty about the inhumanity of the fetus, removing it presupposes a moral (or immoral) decision made in the dark. We can preserve the life of this creature and later discover that we have vainly engaged our lofty ethical sentiments in defense of what ultimately was just a mere thing. But we can also decide to remove the thing, running the risk of discovering, too late, that it was a human being. Between caution and reckless gambling, is there a choice? Which of us, armed with a revolver, would consider ourselves morally authorized to pull the trigger if we knew there was a 50% chance of hitting an innocent creature? In other words, betting on the inhumanity of the fetus is like flipping a coin for the survival or death of a possible human being.

At this point in the reasoning, all pro-abortion arguments have become arguments against. For here we leave the realm of the undecided and encounter a firmly established worldwide consensus: no defensible or indefensible advantage, no real or hypothetical benefit to third parties can justify risking the life of a human being in a bet.

But, as we have seen, the pro-abortion option is prior to any discussion, which is why the abortionist resents and denounces any contrary argument as "repressive violence." The pro-abortion decision, being the precondition for the existence of the debate, could only seek in the debate the *ex post facto* legitimization of something that was already decided irreversibly, with or without debate. The abortionist could not yield even in the face of irrefutable evidence of the humanity of the fetus, let alone mere assessments of a moral risk. He simply wants to take the risk, even with a zero percent chance. He wants it because he wants it. For him, the death of unwanted fetuses is a matter of honor: it is about demonstrating, through acts and not through arguments, a self-founding freedom that dispenses with reasons, a Nietzschean pride for which the slightest objection is intolerable.

I believe that I have discovered, here, the reason why my brain obstinately refused to think about the matter. It sensed the ineffectiveness of any argument against the brutal and irrational assertion of the pure will to kill. Of course, in many abortionists, this will remains subconscious, covered by a veil of humanitarian rationalizations that media support strengthens and militant vociferation corroborates. But it is also clear that it is useless to argue with people capable of lying so tenaciously to themselves.

A Hundred Years of Pedophilia

O Globo, April 27, 2002
A morte do pato (2023)

In Greece and the Roman Empire, the use of minors for the sexual satisfaction of adults was a tolerated and even esteemed custom. In China, castrating boys to sell them to wealthy pederasts was a legitimate trade for millennia. In the Islamic world, the strict morality that governs relations between men and women was often offset by tolerance for homosexual pedophilia. In some countries, this lasted until at least the beginning of the twentieth century, making Algeria, for example, a garden of delights for depraved travelers.[149]

Wherever the practice of pedophilia retreated, it was the influence of Christianity—and practically only that—that freed children from this fearsome yoke.

But this had a price. It is as if an underground current of hatred and resentment crossed two thousand years of history, waiting for the moment of revenge. That moment has arrived.

The movement to induce pedophilia begins when Sigmund Freud creates a caricaturally eroticized version of the early years of human life, a version that is easily absorbed by the culture of the century. Since then, family life increasingly appears, in Western imagination, as a pressure cooker of repressed desires. In cinema and literature, children seem to have nothing more to do than spy on the sexual life of their parents through the keyhole or engage in the most astonishing erotic games themselves.

The politically explosive potential of the idea is soon seized by Wilhelm Reich, a communist psychiatrist who organizes a movement for the "sexual liberation of youth" in Germany, later transferred to the United States, where it will perhaps become the main driving idea of student rebellions in the 1960s.

Meanwhile, the Kinsey Report, which we now know to have been a fraud through and through, demolishes the image of the respectability of parents, showing them to new generations as sexually sick hypocrites or closet libertines.

The advent of the pill and the condom, which governments happily begin distributing in schools, sounds like the bell ringing for the general release of child and adolescent eroticism. Since then, the eroticization of childhood and adolescence has expanded from academic and literary circles to the culture of the middle and lower classes, through countless films, TV programs, "meeting groups," family counseling courses, advertisements, and so on. Sex education in schools becomes a direct induction of children and young people into the practice of everything they see in movies and on TV.

But up to that point, the legitimation of pedophilia only appears insinuated, smuggled in the midst of general claims that involve it as an implicit consequence.

In 1980, however, *Time* magazine reports that pro-pedophilia arguments are gaining popularity among sex counselors. Larry Constantine, a family therapist, proclaims that "children have the right to express themselves sexually, even with

---

[149] Read the memoirs of André Gide, *Si le grain ne meurt* (Paris: Galliard, 1928); *If It Die . . . An Autobiography* (New York: Vintage Books, 2001).

members of their own family."[150] One of the authors of the Kinsey Report, Wardell Pomeroy, pontificates that incest "can sometimes be beneficial."[151]

Under the pretext of fighting discrimination, representatives of the gay movement are allowed to teach the benefits of homosexual practice in elementary schools. Anyone opposing them is stigmatized, persecuted, fired. In a book praised by Joycelyn Elders, former U.S. Surgeon General (the same one who issues apocalyptic warnings against cigarettes), journalist Judith Levine claims that pedophiles are harmless and that a boy's sexual relationship with a priest can even be a beneficial thing. According to Levine, the real danger lies in parents who project their fears and their own desire for child bodies onto the mythical child molester.[152]

Feminist organizations contribute to disarming children against pedophiles and arming them against the family, spreading the monstrous theory of an Argentinian psychiatrist that at least one in four girls is raped by her own father.

The highest consecration of pedophilia comes in a 1998 issue of the *Psychological Bulletin*, a publication of the American Psychological Association. The magazine claims that child sexual abuse does not cause intense damage in a pervasive way and even recommends replacing the term child sexual abuse, "biased by the use of negatively loaded terms," with "adult-child sex."[153]

It would be unthinkable that such a vast mental revolution, spreading throughout society, miraculously spared a special segment of the public: priests and seminarians. In their case, an extra stimulus, well calculated to act from within, was added to the external pressure. In a recent book, *Goodbye, Good Men*, American reporter Michael S. Rose[154] shows that for three decades gay organizations in the United States have been placing their people in the psychology departments of seminaries to make it difficult for vocationally gifted applicants to enter and force the massive entry of homosexuals into the clergy. In major seminaries, homosexual propaganda has become overt, and heterosexual students have been forced by their superiors to submit to homosexual conduct.

Cornered and sabotaged, confused and induced, it is inevitable that sooner or later many priests and seminarians will succumb to general child and adolescent

---

[150] "Sexes: Attacking the Last Taboo," *Time*, April 14, 1980.—Eds.
[151] Ibid.—Eds.
[152] *Harmful to Minors: The Perils of Protecting Children from Sex* (University of Minnesota Press, 2002).—Eds.
[153] Bruce Rind, Robert Bauserman, Philip Tromovitch "A Meta-Analytic Examination of Assumed Properties of Child Sex Abuse Using College Samples" (Psychological Bulletin, July 1998, vol. 124, No 1, 22–53).—Eds.
[154] Regnery, 2002.—Eds.

debauchery. And when this happens, all the spokespersons of modern "liberated" culture, the entire "progressive" establishment, all the "advanced" media, all the forces, in short, that over a hundred years have stripped children of the protective aura of Christianity to deliver them to the lust of perverse adults, suddenly rejoice because they have found an innocent subject upon whom to cast their guilt. A hundred years of pedophilic culture are suddenly absolved, cleansed, redeemed before the Almighty: the only culprit for everything is . . . clerical celibacy! Christendom will now pay for all the evil it prevented them from doing.

There is no doubt: the Church is accused and humiliated because it is innocent. Its detractors accuse it because they themselves are the guilty ones. Never has René Girard's theory of scapegoating as a device for the restoration of the illusory unity of a community in crisis found such clear, obvious, universal, and simultaneous confirmation.

Anyone who does not perceive this at the moment is divorced from their own conscience. They have eyes but do not see, they have ears but do not hear.

But the Church itself, if instead of denouncing its attackers, chooses to bow before them in a grotesque act of contrition, sacrificing a few pedophile priests *pro forma* so as not to confront the forces that injected them into it like a virus, will have made its most disastrous choice of the last two millennia.

A Corpse in Power

Diário do Comércio, January 15-29, 2015
A cólera dos imbecis (2019)

Why do some people still follow Liberation Theology? Apparently, no reasonable person should do so. From a theological standpoint, the doctrine spread by the Peruvian Gustavo Gutierrez and the Brazilian Leonardo Boff was already demolished in 1984 by then-Cardinal Joseph Ratzinger,[155] two years after being condemned by Pope John Paul II.[156] In 1994, theologian Edward Lynch stated that it had already been reduced to a mere intellectual curiosity.[157] In 1996, the

---

[155] Joseph Cardinal Ratzinger, "*Instruction on Certain Aspects of The Theology of Liberation*" (Congregation for the Doctrine of the Faith, 1984).—Eds.
[156] Quentin L. Quade, ed., *The Pope and Revolution: John Paul II Confronts Liberation Theology* (Washington, D.C.: Ethics and Public Policy Center, 1982).
[157] Edward Lynch, *The retreat of Liberation Theology* (The Homiletic & Pastoral Review, 1994).

Spanish historian Ricardo de la Cierva, who nobody would say was misinformed, declared it dead and buried.[158]

Fifteen years later, it is practically the official doctrine in twelve Latin American countries. What happened? That is the question posed to me by a group of eminent American Catholics and which certainly also interests Brazilian readers.

To answer it, we need to analyze the issue from three angles:

(1) Is Liberation Theology a Catholic doctrine influenced by Marxist ideas or is it merely a communist ruse disguised in Catholic language?

(2) How do Liberation Theology as a theoretical discourse and Liberation Theology as a militant political organization connect with each other?

(3) Once these two questions are answered, we can then grasp Liberation Theology as a precise phenomenon and describe the special "mentality" of its theorists through the stylistic analysis of their writings.

To the first question, both Professor Lynch and Cardinal Ratzinger, as well as countless other Catholic authors,[159] provide remarkably uniform answers: starting from the premise that Liberation Theology presents itself as Catholic doctrine, they proceed to examine it from that aspect, praising its potential just and humanitarian intentions but concluding that, essentially, it is incompatible with the Church's traditional doctrine, and therefore heretical in a strict sense. They add to this the denunciation of some internal contradictions and criticize its social proposals based on a thoroughly demoralized Marxist economy.

From there, they proceed to declare its death, ensuring, in Professor Lynch's terms, that "While still attractive to many North American and European scholars, it has failed in what the liberationists always said was their main mission, the complete renovation of Latin American Catholicism."[160]

Every revolutionary ideological discourse can be understood on at least three levels of meaning, which must first be distinguished by analysis and then hierarchically rearticulated as one of these levels proves to be the most decisive in the concrete political situation, subordinating the others.

---

[158] Ricardo de la Cierva, *La Hoz y la Cruz. Auge y Caída del Marxismo y la Teología de la Liberación* (Toledo: Fénix, 1996.)

[159] For example, Hubert Lepargneur, *A Teologia da Libertação. Uma Avaliação* (São Paulo: Convívio, 1979), and Sobral Pinto, *Teologia da Libertação. O Materialismo Marxista na Teologia Espiritualista* (Rio de Janeiro: Lidador, 1984).

[160] Edward A. Lynch, "The Retreat of Liberation Theology," February 1994 issue of *The Homiletic & Pastoral Review*, New York.—Eds.

The first is the descriptive level, in which it presents a diagnosis, description, or explanation of reality, or an interpretation of some previous doctrine. At this level, the discourse can be judged for its truthfulness, adequacy, or fidelity, either to the facts, to the state of available knowledge, or to the considered doctrine. When the discourse brings a definite proposal for action, it can be judged by the feasibility or convenience of that action.

The second is the level of ideological self-definition, in which the theorist or indoctrinator expresses the symbols in which the interested group recognizes itself and by which it distinguishes insiders from outsiders, friends from enemies. At this level, it can be judged for its psychological effectiveness or correspondence with the audience's expectations and desires.

The third is the level of strategic disinformation, which provides false clues to disorient the adversary and preemptively deflect any attempt to block the proposed action or neutralize other effects targeted by the discourse.

On the first level, the discourse ideally addresses the neutral observer, whose adherence it seeks to gain through persuasion. On the second, it addresses the current or virtual adherent or militant, to reinforce their adherence to the group and obtain from them maximum possible collaboration. On the third, it addresses the adversary, or target of the operation.

Practically all criticisms by Catholic intellectuals of Liberation Theology have been limited to examining it at the first level. They intellectually discredited it, proved its heretical nature, and pointed out the old vices that make any proposal for socialist remodeling of society unfeasible and destructive.

If the mentors of Liberation Theology were sincerely committed Catholics endeavoring to "renew Latin American Catholicism," even if by means contaminated with Marxist ideology, that would have been enough to completely deactivate it. Since this type of critical analysis moved from mere intellectual discussions to become the official word of the Church, with Cardinal Ratzinger's study in 1984, Liberation Theology could be considered, from this angle, extinct and surpassed.

Now read this testimony from General Ion Mihai Pacepa, the highest-ranking KGB officer ever to defect to the West, and you will begin to understand why intellectual and theological demoralization was not enough to put an end to Liberation Theology. In 1959, as head of Romanian espionage in West Germany, General Pacepa heard from Nikita Khrushchev himself: "We will use Cuba as a springboard to launch a KGB-devised religion into Latin America."

The testimony continues:

Khrushchev called the new KGB-invented religion Liberation Theology. His penchant for 'liberation' was inherited by the KGB, which later created the Palestine Liberation Organization, the National Liberation Army of Columbia (FARC), and the National Liberation Army of Bolivia. Romania was a Latin country, and Khrushchev wanted our "Latin view" about his new religious 'liberation' war. He also wanted us to send a few priests who were cooptees or deepcover officers to Latin America, to see how 'we' could make his new Liberation Theology palatable to that part of the world. Khrushchev got our best effort.

. . . Launching a new religion was a historic event, and the KGB had thoroughly prepared for it. At that very moment, the KGB was building a new international religious organization in Prague called the Christian Peace Conference (CPC), whose task would be to spread Liberation Theology within Latin America.

. . . In 1968, the KGB-created CPC was able to maneuver a group of leftist South American bishops into holding a Conference of Latin American Bishops at Medellin, Colombia. The Conference's official task was to ameliorate poverty. Its undeclared goal was to recognize a new religious movement encouraging the poor to rebel against the 'institutionalized violence of poverty,' and to recommend it to the World Council of Churches for official approval. The Medellin Conference did both. It also swallowed the KGB-born name 'Liberation Theology.'[161]

The idea of Liberation Theology, in its essential form, came ready from Moscow three years before the Peruvian Jesuit Gustavo Gutierrez, with the book *Teología de la Liberación*,[162] who presented himself as its original inventor, certainly with the approval of its true creators, who had no interest in public recognition of paternity. The tutor of the child, Leonardo Boff, would enter the scene even later, not before 1977. To this day, popular sources, such as Wikipedia, like trained parrots, repeat that Father Gutierrez was indeed the generator of the thing and Mr. Boff its second father.

* * *

---

[161] Ion Mihai Pacepa, "The Kremlin's Religious Crusade," *FrontPage Magazine*, June 30, 2009 [Free translation. See also Ion Mihai Pacepa and Ronald J. Rychlak, "Liberation Theology," *Disinformation* (Washington, D.C.: WND, 2013).—Eds.]
[162] Lima, Centro de Estudios y Publicaciones, 1971.

If the thing, and even the name that designates it, came ready from the KGB, that doesn't mean that its adoptive parents, Gutierrez, Boff, and Frei Betto, had no merit in its dissemination throughout the world. On the contrary, they played a crucial role in the victories of Liberation Theology and the mystery of its long survival.

The three, but especially the two Brazilians, always acted simultaneously on two levels. On the one hand, they produced artificial theological arguments for use by the clergy, intellectuals, and the Roman Curia. On the other hand, they spread sermons and popular speeches, dedicating themselves intensely to creating the network of activism that would become known as "base ecclesial communities" and would constitute the seed of the Workers' Party. "Base" is indeed the technical term traditionally used in communist parties to designate activism, distinguishing it from leaders. Its adoption by Liberation Theology was no mere coincidence. When pastors transformed into political commissars, the flock had to become the "base."

In his 1986 book *And the Church Became the People*[163] [in Portuguese] Boff confessed that it was all a "bold plan," conceived along the lines of the strategy of the slow and subtle "occupation of spaces" advocated by the founder of the Italian Communist Party, Antonio Gramsci. It was about gradually filling all the decisive positions in seminaries and lay universities, in religious orders, in Catholic media, and in the ecclesiastical hierarchy, without much fanfare, until the time when the great revolution could be exhibited openly.

Shortly after the conclave that elected him in 1978, Pope John Paul I met with twenty Latin American cardinals and was very impressed by the fact that most of them openly supported Liberation Theology. They informed him at the time that there were already more than one hundred thousand "base ecclesial communities" spreading revolutionary propaganda in Latin America. Until then, John Paul I knew Liberation Theology only as theoretical speculation. He had no idea that it could have transformed into a political force of such dimensions.

In 1984, when Cardinal Ratzinger began dismantling the theoretical arguments of Liberation Theology, it had been four years since the "base ecclesial communities" had transformed into a mass party [in Brazil], the Workers' Party, whose activism largely ignores any theological speculation, but swears that Jesus Christ was a socialist because that's what the party leaders say.

In other words, the supposed theological argumentation had already fulfilled its role of fueling discussions and undermining the authority of the Church and

---

[163] *E a Igreja se fez povo* (Vozes, 1986).—Eds.

had been functionally replaced by the open preaching of socialism, where the apparently erudite effort to reconcile Christianity and Marxism gave way to the handling of cheap clichés and word games in which the activism neither sought nor found rational argumentation, but only the symbols that expressed and reinforced its group unity and fighting spirit.

The success of this second endeavor was proportional to the failure of the trio in the theological sphere. It is possible that in Europe or the US, an opinion leader with pretensions of leadership may not survive their intellectual demoralization, but in Latin America, and especially in Brazil, the activist mass is leagues away from any intellectual concern and will continue to lend credibility to its leader as long as they have sufficient political-party support.

In the case of Boff and Betto, this support was nothing short of formidable. After guerrilla warfare spread across the continent by OLAS, the *Organización Latino-Americana de Solidariedad* ("Latin American Solidarity Organization"), founded by Fidel Castro in 1966, failed, activism overwhelmingly took refuge in non-military leftist organizations, which were implementing Antonio Gramsci's ideas on "occupation of spaces" and "cultural revolution." Gramsci's strategy involved massive infiltration of communist agents into all organs of civil society, especially education and media, to disseminate specific, isolated communist proposals, without the label of communism, gradually achieving an overall effect where no one saw any communist propaganda, but where the Party, or equivalent organization, ended up mentally controlling society with "the invisible and omnipresent power of a divine command, a categorical imperative" (sic).

No instrument served this purpose better than the "base ecclesial communities," where communist proposals could be sold under the label of Christianity. In Brazil, the overwhelming growth of these organizations resulted, in 1980, in the founding of the Workers' Party, which initially presented itself as an innocent trade union movement of Christian leftism and only gradually revealed its deep ties to the government of Cuba and various guerrilla and drug trafficking organizations. The party's top leader, Luís Inácio "Lula" da Silva, always recognized Boff and Betto as the mentors of the organization and himself.

Born out of Latin American communism through the "base ecclesial communities," the Party would not be long in returning the favor, founding, in 1990, an entity under the anodyne Gramscian name *Foro de São Paulo* ("São Paulo Forum"), aimed at unifying various leftist currents and becoming the strategic command center of the communist movement on the continent.

According to Frei Betto himself, the decision to create the *São Paulo Forum* was made at a meeting between him, Lula, and Fidel Castro in Havana. For seventeen years, the Forum grew in secrecy, eventually gathering together two hundred affiliated organizations, mixing legally constituted parties, groups of kidnappers like the Chilean MIR, and drug trafficking gangs like the FARC, who swore they had nothing to do with drug trafficking, but then already regularly exchanged two hundred tons of Colombian cocaine annually for weapons smuggled from Lebanon by the Brazilian trafficker Fernandinho Beira-Mar.

When Lula was elected president of Brazil in 2002, the *São Paulo Forum* had already become the largest and most powerful political organization in action in Latin American territory at any time, but its existence was completely unknown to the population and cynically denied when denounced by any investigator. The blockade reached its most intense point when, in 2005, Mr. Lula, already president of Brazil, confessed the existence and activities of the *São Paulo Forum* in detail. The speech was published on the official page of the Presidency of the Republic, but even so, the mainstream media insisted on pretending not to know anything.

Finally, in 2007, the Workers' Party itself, feeling that the protective cloak of secrecy was no longer necessary, began to trumpet the deeds of the *São Paulo Forum* to the four winds, as if they were mundane and well-known. Only then did the newspapers admit to discussing the matter.

Why could the secret now be revealed? Because in Brazil, all ideological opposition had been eliminated, leaving only under the name of "politics" the disputes over positions and accusations of corruption coming from within the left itself, while on a continental scale, the parties affiliated with the *São Paulo Forum* already dominated twelve countries. The "base ecclesial communities" had taken power. Who, at this point, would be concerned with theological discussions or with ethereal objections made twenty years earlier by a cardinal who took the literal meaning of the texts seriously and barely scratched the political surface of the problem?

In the twelve years it remained in power, the Workers' Party expelled all conservative opposition from the scene, sharing the political space with some more rabid allies and with a mild center-left opposition, and governed through bribery, assassination of nuisances, and the systematic appropriation of funds from state-owned companies to finance the party's growth.

The escalation of kleptocracy culminated in the Petrobras episode, where the embezzlement reached the scale of trillions of reais, constituting, according to the international media, the largest case of corporate corruption of all time. This succession of scandals caused some discomfort within the left itself and constant complaints in the media, leading the leftist intelligentsia to mobilize massively to defend the party. For over a decade, Mr. Betto and Mr. Boff have been busy with this activity, in which theology only enters as an occasional supplier of figures of speech to adorn party propaganda. Liberation Theology had finally assumed its deepest vocation.

Anyone who reads the writings of Gutierrez, Boff, and Betto easily discovers their multiple inconsistencies and contradictions. They reveal that this material did not result from any very serious theoretical effort, but from the mere intention of keeping the theologians of Rome busy with complex theological refutations while the militant network spread throughout Latin America, reaching mainly poor populations devoid of any interest or ability to follow these high-level discussions.

Cattle drivers call this "piranha baiting:" they throw a steer into the river so that while carnivorous fish are busy devouring it a few yards ahead the herd crosses the waters safely.

Intellectually and theologically, Liberation Theology has been dead for three decades. But it was never an intellectual and theological movement. It was, and is, a political movement adorned with artificial theological pretexts and unparalleled levity, thrown into the waters of Rome as "piranha bait." The herd passed, dominated the territory, and there are no land piranhas that can threaten it.

Yes, Liberation Theology is dead, but its corpse, elevated to the highest rank of the command hierarchy, weighs on an entire continent, oppressing it, suffocating it, and hindering all its movements. Latin America is now ruled by a corpse.

The Greatest Criminal Plot of All Time

Digesto Econômico magazine, September–December, 2007
O Foro de São Paulo: a ascensão do comunismo latino-americano (2022)

The indisputable pioneer in investigating the *São Paulo Forum* phenomenon was the São Paulo lawyer José Carlos Graça Wagner, a man of extraordinary intelligence, who honored me greatly with his friendship. He was already speaking about the subject, with acute understanding of its historical and strategic importance, around 1995, when I met him. By 1999, the documentation he had been collecting about the origin and actions of the entity filled an entire room in his house, and a testament to the researcher's intellectual rigor was that only from then on did he feel himself in a position to begin writing a book about it. At the time, he invited me to assist him in the endeavor, but I was about to leave for Romania and, with much sadness, I declined the invitation.

Even greater was the sorrow I experienced years later when, upon reestablishing contact with Mr. Wagner, I learned that the project had been interrupted by a sudden and unstoppable wave of financial setbacks and legal battles, which ultimately ruined the health of my friend and his wife, both already elderly. I cannot shake off the suspicion that the perilous investigation he had embarked upon had something to do with the sudden downfall of a professional career hitherto marked by success and prosperity.

He had business dealings in the USA, and it was also there, in the libraries and archives of Miami and Washington D.C., that he compiled most of the material about the Forum. In recent years, the research had taken a peculiar turn. Dr. Wagner hoped to find evidence of an intimate connection between the *São Paulo Forum* and a prestigious entity of the American chic left, the "Inter-American Dialogue." I do not know if this specific proof exists or not, or if it is really necessary to demonstrate something that half of America already knows from other abundant signs, namely, that the loudest leaders of the Democratic Party are notorious protectors of revolutionary and terrorist movements (so that the Forum, if added to the list, would not greatly alter the biographies of these vampiric characters).

What I do know is that the beginning of my friend's personal ruin dates approximately from an interview he gave to *Diario Las Américas*, an important Spanish-language publication in Miami, in which he spoke about the *São Paulo Forum* and its dangerous relations with the "Dialogue." But this would already be the subject of another investigation, and far be it from me to explain *obscurum per obscurius*. Even without being able to promise a solution to this particularly enigmatic aspect of the problem, one thing I can guarantee: Mr. Wagner's archives, recently made available to researchers, allow us to resume the investigation with the hope that within a year we will have at least the internal history of the *São Paulo Forum* reconstructed practically month by month. Then it will be possible to put the question of the "Dialogue" on more solid ground, but before that, another puzzle must be solved, one much more urgent and much closer to us.

I will formulate this puzzle by contrasting two sets of facts:

First: The São Paulo Forum is the largest political organization ever to exist in Latin America and, undoubtedly, one of the largest in the world. It includes all the leftist leaders on the continent. But it is not just any left-wing organization. It brings together more than a hundred legal parties and several criminal organizations linked to drug trafficking and the kidnapping industry, such as the FARC and the Chilean MIR, all committed to a common strategic articulation and the pursuit of mutual advantages. Never before in the world has such an intimate, persistent, organized, and enduring coexistence between politics and crime been seen on such a gigantic scale.

Second: For sixteen years, all newspapers, TV channels, and radio stations in [Brazil]—all, without exception, including those that prided themselves on investigative journalism and courageous exposés—obstinately refused to report on the existence and activities of this organization, despite my repeated warnings about it, in every possible and imaginable tone. From solicitous warnings to insulting provocations, from humble pleas to the most persuasive logical arguments, everything was in vain. When they didn't respond with disdainful silence, they did so with flippant evasions, with entirely aprioristic skeptical objections that dispensed with any examination of the subject, with the wisest observations about my mental health, or with the most stupid and childish mockery imaginable. Reacting to this persistent denial of facts, I had the almost complete minutes of the *São Paulo Forum*'s assemblies and working groups published by the *Mídia Sem Máscara* online newspaper. The voluminous documentary evidence proved incapable of persuading the deniers. They seemed hypnotized, stupefied, and mentally paralyzed in the face of a hypothesis more fearsome than their brains could bear at the time.

The *São Paulo Forum* brings together more than a hundred legal parties and several criminal organizations linked to drug trafficking and the kidnapping industry, such as the FARC and the Chilean MIR.

The publication of the minutes, however, had two important consequences. On the one hand, the official website of the Forum, www.forosaopaulo.org, was hastily taken down, only to return months later in a heavily sanitized version. On the other hand, among journalists and political analysts, the affectation of contempt for the subject gave way to overt, public denial of the very existence of the *São Paulo Forum*. Two figures were particularly prominent in this dirty little job: the Englishman Kenneth Maxwell and the Brazilian Luiz Felipe de Alencastro. To announce to the world the complete nonexistence of the entity I had denounced, both—ironically, historians by profession—used the podium or megaphone of the CFR, Council on Foreign Relations, the most powerful American think tank, thus giving deliberate ignorance (or gross lies) the endorsement of considerable authority. Anyone who still harbors illusions about the intellectual reliability of the academic profession, even when practiced in the so-called "major centers" (Alencastro is a professor at the University of Paris, and

Maxwell is the CFR's supreme consultant on Brazilian affairs), can cure themselves of this ailment by simply noting these facts.

But then the hypothesis of mere organized ignorance begins to give way to the suspicion of a conscious plot much greater than our paranoia could imagine. Important members of the CFR had close contacts with the criminal organizations participating in the *São Paulo Forum*, whose existence they could not therefore ignore.[164] In short, Brazil seemed to be ensnared in the webs of a criminal conspiracy, which involved, at the same time, the entirety of Latin American left-wing parties, the bulk of the national journalistic class, the main drug trafficking gangs on the continent, and, finally, a not insignificant portion of the American political and financial elite.

The gravity of these facts is measured by the breadth and persistence of their concealment. Growing in secrecy, the *São Paulo Forum* became the main engine of historical transformations on the continent, while the general ignorance about it caused public debates—and therefore the entirety of cultural life—to increasingly move away from reality and become a machinery of alienation, further favoring the growth of a power scheme that delightedly fed on its own invisibility. The vertiginous decline in the level of public consciousness under these conditions was not only predictable but inevitable. Circulating opinions became a grotesque dance of irrelevancies, evasions, and massive errors, while violence and corruption grew before the astonished eyes of the public and opinion-makers, each clinging to the most disjointed, untimely, and impotent explanations. Many decades will pass before the psychological devastation resulting from this scenario can be reversed. The fabulous consortium of crimes that determined it has no parallel in universal history.

One of the most grotesque aspects of the situation is how easily the culprits shake off any attempt at denunciation, labeling it a "conspiracy theory." But who mentioned a conspiracy? What we see is a gigantic movement of resources, powers, organizations, and historical currents that, to remain immune to popular curiosity, do not need to hide in basements, but only rely on the public's incapacity to grasp its unmanageable complexity and to believe in the existence of such organized malice.

The Forum is a *sui generis* entity, without correspondence in any time or country. Long after it is extinct, as I hope it will be one day, it will still be an enigma and a challenge to the discernment of historians. For us, it is more than that. It is the "omnipresent and invisible" enemy dreamed of by Antonio Gramsci.

---

[164] See next "Behind the Subversion."—Eds.

Behind the Subversion

Diário do Comércio, June 5, 2006
O mundo como jamais funcionou (2014); *O Foro de São Paulo* (2022)

In early 2001, the Council on Foreign Relations (CFR), a billionaire think tank from which so many presidents and secretaries of state have emerged that some consider it a kind of meta-government of the United States, created a "task force," overflowing with PhDs, chaired by historian Kenneth Maxwell and tasked with suggesting modifications to Washington's policy toward Brazil. The first list of wise advice, published on February 12, emphasized "a new urgency to work with Brazil in combating the drug scourge and its corrupting influence on governments."[165]

At that moment, with the old cartels destroyed, the Revolutionary Armed Forces of Colombia (FARC), deliberately spared by the Clinton administration's Plan Colombia under the pretext that the fight against drug trafficking should be apolitical, emerged as dominant players in the drug market in Latin America. The FARC, a communist organization, had entered the drug market to finance its terrorist operations and quest for power. Since 1990, they had been part of the São Paulo Forum, where they coordinated their actions with the overall strategy of the Latin American left, securing political support that made them virtually immune to persecution in various countries where they operated. In Brazil, for example, despite the hundreds of tons of cocaine they dumped annually onto the market through their associate Fernandinho Beira-Mar,[166] and despite occasional exchanges of gunfire with the Army in the Amazon forest, the FARC were well treated: their leaders freely roamed the streets under the protection of federal authorities and were received as official guests by the Worker's Party government of the State of Rio Grande do Sul. Never before had the relationship between drug trafficking and politics been closer. It risked becoming even more intense because Luís Inácio Lula da Silva, founder of the Forum and therefore the main orchestrator of the common strategy between legal left-wing parties and criminal organizations, seemed destined to be the next president of Brazil.

The increasing integration of drug trafficking and politics therefore made it urgent to combat "the drugs scourge and its influence on governments." And the only way to do that was, evidently, to dismantle the *São Paulo Forum.* Seen from this perspective, the suggestion put forth by the "task force" seemed indeed

---

[165] "Brazil is the Fulcrum: Independent Task Force Urges President Bush Quickly Recast U.S. Policy Towards Brazil" (2001), available at CFR's website.—Eds.
[166] One of the most dangerous criminals in Brazil, sentenced to 320 years in a maximum security prison.—Eds.

timely. But only those who do not understand the subtleties of the meta-government interpret it that way. The literal sense of the phrase, in fact, expressed the symmetric opposite of what the notables of the CFR intended.

For the *São Paulo Forum* to continue meddling with impunity in the internal politics of several Latin American nations, it immediately needed to maintain its status as a discreet or semi-secret entity, and the head of the task force himself helped with that. In an article published in the *New York Review*, Maxwell stated that the Forum simply did not exist because "even the best-informed experts I talked to in Brazil had never heard of the *São Paulo Forum.*"[167]

For a professional historian to rely on the opinions of others instead of investigating primary sources, which were abundantly available on the Forum's own website at the time, was a scandalous proof of ineptitude. At the time, Mr. Maxwell belonged (and still belongs) to the circle of enlightened individuals who were (and still are) listened to with the utmost respect by the Brazilian media, especially *Folha de S. Paulo*. This seemed to provide indisputable evidence that he was indeed a donkey, having acted so extravagantly in pure obedience to his animal nature. But now I notice that this did not explain everything. Shortly thereafter, another highly respected intellectual in asinine circles, Luiz Felipe de Alencastro, professor of Brazilian history at the Sorbonne and columnist for *Veja*, shone in a CFR debate by lending his formidable authority to the thesis of the non-existence of the São Paulo Forum and even added that I was the creator of the legendary organization . . . Making the continental coordination of the Latin American communist movement disappear seemed to have become an established habit at the CFR.

This could have been just an innocent accumulation of misinterpretations if the entity had not simultaneously cultivated another habit: that of good relations with the FARC. In 1999, the president of the New York Stock Exchange, Richard Grasso, a CFR member, paid a courtesy visit to FARC commander Raul Reyes and came out celebrating the community of interests between the Colombian gang and the "progressive" financial elite of the United States. Shortly thereafter, two other CFR members, James Kimsey, emeritus chairman of America Online, and Joseph Robert, head of the real estate conglomerate J. E. Robert, had a lively meeting with FARC founder Manuel Marulanda himself, and then went to Colombian President Pastrana to successfully persuade him to make peace with the narcoguerrillas.

---

[167] "Brazil: Lula's Prospects," by Kenneth Maxwell (The New York Review of Books, December 5, 2002 issue).—Eds.

The division of labor was clear: the potentates of the CFR negotiated with the main military and financial support force of the São Paulo Forum, while their intellectual office boys took care to deflect attention from the operation by proclaiming that the Forum did not even exist. The CFR boasted of its intention to eliminate the influence of drug trafficking on governments while actively contributing to making that influence broader and more fruitful than ever.

The Council on Foreign Relations also included President Clinton, whose infamous Plan Colombia had the main result of eliminating competitors and handing over a quasi-monopoly of the drug market in Latin America to the FARC. In 2002, the Latin American policy of the globalist grandees underwent an upgrade: to the objective of beautifying the FARC was added the commitment to make the president of the São Paulo Forum the president of Brazil. A few days before the 2002 election, the American ambassador Donna Hrinak, who may belong to the CFR but is a member of the board of an entity closely associated with it, the Inter-American Dialogue, shamelessly promoted the leftist candidate, proclaiming him "a realization of the American dream."[168] Although this was illegal and indecent interference of a foreign authority in a national election—causing no scandal only because even imperialist arrogance becomes charming when it works for the politically correct side—and although the verbal formula chosen to do it was an unparalleled absurdity (for it is not known that many Americans had as their supreme ambition to stop working at twenty-four to make a career in a communist party), the expression was so successful that, shortly thereafter, it was repeated *ipsis litteris*, without citation of source, in an article in the *New York Review of Books* that enthusiastically celebrated Lula's victory. Who signed the article? The indefatigable Kenneth Maxwell.

Faced with these facts, would anyone still hesitate to perceive that the connections between the powder-puff leftism of the CFR and the blood-and-feces leftism of the Marulandas and Reyes are more intimate than would fit in the stereotyped image of an essential and irreducible hostility between reactionary capitalists and revolutionary communists? The meaning of events is too transparent, but the brains of our elites are still capable of projecting their own obscurity onto them to avoid drawing the conclusions they impose.

Of course, I do not endorse the idea that the CFR, as an institution, is a pro-communist conspiratorial center. Many of its members are American patriots who would never consciously endorse a policy harmful to their country. But it cannot

---

[168] "The Battle for the White House," by Matias Spektor (Getulio Vargas Foundation, January 2011 issue, v. 3, n.1).—Eds. As of 2024, Hrinak is not merely a member of the CFR, but sits on its board of directors.

be hidden that, inside it, a group of immensely powerful billionaire world reformers have induced the entity to influence the Washington government, almost always successfully, in the most leftist and anti-American direction imaginable. In the United States, this is common knowledge. No one doubts it. Only the "conspiracy theory" used to explain it is discussed. This theory has among its defenders some first-rate intellectuals like Carroll Quigley, a history professor at Georgetown University and mentor to Bill Clinton, or economist Anthony Sutton, author of the classic *Western Technology and Soviet Economic Development* (4 vols.). The fact that the former was an enthusiastic adherent and the latter a devastating critic of the globalist elite further contributes to the credibility of the thesis. And what makes it even more attractive is the fact that the CFR, acknowledging its existence to the extent of offering an explicit denial on its official website, avoids debating with these heavyweights and dozens of other serious scholars who have written about it, and instead prefers to flaunt an easy and fake victory in a confrontation with the populist and caricatured versions of the conspiracy theory, invented by figures like Lyndon LaRouche and Pat Robertson. The fact that the CFR uses this evasive expedient to escape the accusations is a serious indication that they have at least some truth to them.

To assess how much the Brazilian economic, political, and military elite is alienated and out of touch with the world one only need notice that their main source of information about the CFR, the Inter-American Dialogue, and other globalist organizations has been none other than Mr. Lyndon LaRouche, whose *Executive Intelligence Review* is read by the luminaries of the *Escola Superior de Guerra* (Brazilian Superior War College) as if it were the purest example of inside information (he is so well-informed that he even classified me—of all people— as an apostle of globalism, simply because I wrote for a newspaper called *O Globo,* "The Globe." The other known sources in the country are all leftist, and what they have in common with Mr. LaRouche's bulletin is that they monstrously distort the facts by presenting globalist circles as representatives of good old "American imperialism" in unequal struggle against the national sovereignties of the poor countries. I don't know whether to laugh or cry when I see how many Brazilians, who are not at all leftist, take this version seriously and base their strategic analyses and government proposals on it. It's ridiculous and tragic at the same time. With so many primary sources and high-level diagnoses available, why eat garbage and belch out the La Tour d'Argent menu? From the underdeveloped cultural quagmire only ignorance and self-deception bloom.

For example, the most popular Brazilian leftist website [vermelho.org.br] presents the Inter-American Dialogue as filled with "personalities of the most conservative right," and "representatives of the American Establishment." In the USA, even schoolchildren know that "Establishment" means "chic left," that there are not, nor can there be, any "personalities of the most conservative right" inside it, and that if any national sovereignty is threatened by the Establishment, it is that of the USA first and foremost. The long and fierce controversy waged by conservatives and nationalists against the CFR, the Inter-American Dialogue, and globalist circles in general is completely unknown to the chatterboxes of the Brazilian Superior War College and the "bunch of generals" who believe in leftist sources and Mr. LaRouche. Among this crowd of credulous bumpkins, there are numerous sincere patriots. But the destruction of a country begins when its patriots become idiots, leaving the monopoly of cleverness to traitors, conspirators, and revolutionaries.

The history of manipulating Brazilian patriots by cunning leftists is itself a tragicomedy. For decades, the leftist leadership has subjected these people to Pavlovian treatment, based on a one-shock-one-cheese approach, which has proven so effective that many high-ranking officers, ideologically anti-communist, now find it supremely honorable to transform our soldiers into diggers and tractor drivers in service of the "Landless Workers' Movement" (MST). How does one lead a human brain to plunge into this abyss of stupidity? It's simple: just create a team selected from articulate leftists and divide it into two wings, tasked with opposite tasks—one infiltrated in the media, responsible for spreading scandalous lies, fomenting anti-military hatred; the other, well-placed within military circles and the Superior War College, tasked with stroking the ego of the Armed Forces and inducing them to conciliation and collaboration with the continental communist strategy by virtue of their own patriotism, easily converted into anti-Americanism through a skillfully planned flow of false information (including, of course, that provided by Mr. LaRouche). In the first team, notable figures include Caco Barcelos, Cecília Coimbra, and Luiz Eduardo Greenhalgh. In the second, Márcio Moreira Alves, Mário Augusto Jacobskind, and Cesar Benjamin. The duplicity of this treatment leaves the victim disoriented and ultimately subjugated. Amid slaps and kisses, a good portion of our officer corps easily fell for the deception, showing they indeed have the IQ of laboratory mice. The recent lecture by the Army commander in Porto Alegre shows to what extent an institution slandered, marginalized, and trampled upon feels relief and comfort at the humiliating offer of a seat at the table of its traditional detractors.

Similar stratagems have been applied among businessmen and politicians, with equal effectiveness.

That's why it has become so difficult to explain to Brazilians what, among American conservatives, even the slowest of intellects like Pat Robertson understand perfectly well: the globalist elite is the number one enemy of American national sovereignty and, by extension, but only by extension, of all other sovereignties.

Chapter 8

On Power and The New Global Order

The History of Fifteen Centuries

Jornal da Tarde, June 17, 2004
O Foro de São Paulo (2022); *O camarada Enrolevich* (2024)

After the dismantling of the Roman Empire, the churches scattered throughout the territory became the successors of the shattered administration. In the general confusion, while the forms of a new era were barely discernible amid the mists of the temporary, the priests became clerks, magistrates, and bailiffs. The seeds of the future European aristocracy sprouted on the battlefield, in the struggle against the barbarian invaders. In every village and parish, the community leaders who stood out in the defense effort were rewarded by the people with lands, animals, and money, by the Church with titles of nobility and the legitimizing anointing of their authority. They became great landowners, and counts, and dukes, and princes, and kings.

Agricultural property was never the foundation or origin, but the fruit of their power. Military power. The power of a fierce and haughty caste, enriched by the sword and not by the plow, proud not to mingle with others, not to engage therefore in either the cultivation of intelligence, fit only for priests and women, or in that of the land, a task for serfs and tenants, or in business, the occupation of bourgeoisie and Jews.

For over a millennium, Europe was governed by the force of arms, supported by the tripod of ecclesiastical and cultural legitimization, popular obedience translated into labor and taxes, and financial support obtained or extorted from merchants and bankers in times of crisis and war.

Its rise culminated and its decline began with the founding of absolutist monarchies and the advent of the nation-state. It culminated because these new formations embodied the power of the warrior caste in its purest form, self-sourced by direct delegation from God, without the mediation of the priesthood, reduced to the subordinate condition of forced and recalcitrant accomplice. But it was already the beginning of decline because the absolute monarch, coming from the aristocracy, stood apart from it and had to seek support against it—and against the Church—from the Third Estate, which thereby became an independent political force, capable of intimidating the king, the clergy, and the nobility together.

If the medieval system lasted for ten centuries, absolutism lasted no more than three. For even less time will the reign of liberal bourgeoisie endure. A century of economic and political freedom is enough to make some capitalists so incredibly rich that they no longer want to submit to the whims of the market that enriched them. They want to control it, and the instruments for this are threefold:

domination of the state, to implement the statist policies necessary for the perpetuation of the oligopoly; encouragement of socialist and communist movements that invariably favor the growth of state power; and the recruitment of an army of intellectuals who prepare public opinion to bid farewell to bourgeois freedoms and joyfully enter a world of pervasive and obsessive repression (extending to the minutest details of private life and everyday language), presented as a paradise adorned at once with the abundance of capitalism and the "social justice" of communism. In this new world, the economic freedom essential to the functioning of the system is preserved only to the extent necessary to subsidize the extinction of freedom in the political, social, moral, educational, cultural, and religious domains.

With this, the mega-capitalists change the very basis of their power. They no longer rely on wealth as such, but on control of the socio-political process. This control, by freeing them from the adventurous exposure to market fluctuations, makes them a durable dynastic power, a neo-aristocracy capable of weathering fortune's vicissitudes and the succession of generations, sheltered in the stronghold of the state and international organizations. They are no longer mega-capitalists: they are *metacapitalists*—the class that transcends capitalism and transforms it into the only socialism that has ever existed or will ever exist: the socialism of the magnates and the social engineers at their service.

This new aristocracy does not arise, like the previous one, from military heroism rewarded by the people and blessed by the Church. It arises from Machiavellian premeditation founded on self-interest, and through a counterfeit clergy of subsidized intellectuals, it blesses itself.

It remains to be seen what kind of society this self-invented aristocracy can create—and how long a structure so obviously based on lies can endure.

The USA and the New World Order

Os EUA e a Nova Ordem Mundial:
um debate entre Alexandre Dugin e Olavo de Carvalho (2012, 2019)

[A debate between Olavo de Carvalho and Aleksandr Dugin, 2012. Both participants responded to the question: "*What are the historical, political, ideological, and economic factors and actors that currently define the dynamics and configuration of power in the world, and what is the position of the United States of America in what is known as the New World Order?"*]

Excerpt from Olavo de Carvalho's first response

The question is twofold: who are the actors on the stage and what is the position of the USA in the scenario?

Regarding the first question: discounting Catholic and Protestant Christianity, which I will discuss later, the historical forces currently vying for power in the world are articulated in three projects of global domination, which I will tentatively call "Russian-Chinese," "Western" (sometimes erroneously called "Anglo-American"), and "Islamic."

Each has a well-documented history, showing its remote origins, the transformations it has undergone over time, and the current state of its implementation.

The agents that currently embody them are respectively:

1. The ruling elite of Russia and China, especially the secret services of these two countries.

2. The Western financial elite, as represented especially in the Bilderberg Group, the Council on Foreign Relations (CFR), and the Trilateral Commission.

3. The Islamic Brotherhood, religious leaders from various Islamic countries, and also some governments of Muslim countries.

Of these three agents, only the first can be conceived in strictly geopolitical terms, since its plans and actions correspond to well-defined national and regional interests. The second, which is more advanced in achieving its plans for world government, explicitly places itself above any national interests, including those of the countries where it originated and serves as its operational base. In the third, any conflicts of interest between national governments and the higher goal of the Universal Caliphate are always resolved in favor of the latter, which, although currently existing only as an ideal, has its symbolic authority founded on Quranic commandments that no Islamic government would dare to openly contradict.

The conceptions of global power that these three agents strive to realize are very different from each other because they stem from heterogeneous and sometimes incompatible ideological inspirations.

Therefore, they are not similar forces, species of the same genus. They do not fight for the same objectives, and when they occasionally resort to the same weapons (for example, economic warfare), they do so in different strategic contexts, where the use of these weapons does not necessarily serve the same goals.

Although nominally their relations are competitive and contentious, sometimes even militarily, there are immense areas of fusion and collaboration, albeit mobile and shifting. This phenomenon disorients observers, producing all sorts of displaced and fantastical interpretations, some in the form of "conspiracy theories," others as *soi-disant* "realist" and "scientific" challenges to these theories.

Much of the haziness of the global picture is produced by a more or less constant factor: each of the three agents tends to interpret the plans and actions of the other two in its own terms, partly for propaganda purposes, partly out of genuine misunderstanding.

The strategic analyses on both sides reflect their own ideological biases. While trying to take into account all available factors, the Sino-Russian scheme privileges the geopolitical and military perspective, the Western scheme the economic viewpoint, and the Islamic scheme the religious dispute.

This difference, in turn, reflects the sociological composition of the ruling classes in the respective geographical areas:

1) Originating from the Communist nomenklatura, the Sino-Russian ruling class consists essentially of bureaucrats, intelligence service agents, and military officers.

2) The predominance of international financiers and bankers in the Western establishment is too well known to require further emphasis.

3) In various countries of the Islamic complex, the authority of the ruler substantially depends on the approval of the *ummah*—the multitudinous community of categorized interpreters of traditional religion. Although there are a great variety of internal situations, it is not an exaggeration to describe the structure of dominant power there as theocratic.

Thus, for the first time in world history, the three essential modalities of power—political-military, economic, and religious—are embodied in distinct supranational blocs, each with its plans for global domination and its peculiar modes of action. This does not mean that each of them fails to operate on all fronts, but only that their respective historical and strategic visions are ultimately delimited by the modality of power they represent. It is no exaggeration to say that today's world is the subject of a struggle between soldiers, bankers, and preachers.

Although in current discussions these three blocs are almost invariably designated by the names of nations, states, and governments, describing the relationship among them in terms of a dispute between nations or national interests is a residual habit of old geopolitics that does nothing to help understand the current situation.

Only in the Sino-Russian case does the globalist project symmetrically correspond to national interests, and the main agents are the respective states and governments. This happens for the simple reason that the communist regimes, prevailing there for decades, dissolved or eliminated all other possible agents. The globalist elite of Russia and China are the governments of these two countries.

On the other hand, the Western globalist elite represents no national interest and does not identify with any particular state or government, although it dominates many of them. On the contrary: when its interests clash with those of its home nations (and this necessarily happens), it does not hesitate to turn against the homeland itself, subjugate it, and, if necessary, destroy it.

The Islamic globalists cater, in principle, to the general interests of all Muslim states, united in the grand project of the Universal Caliphate. Divergences produced by clashes of national interests (such as between Iran and Saudi Arabia) have not been sufficient to open unhealable wounds in the long-term Islamic project. The Islamic Brotherhood, the primary conductor of the process, is a transnational organization: it governs some countries, is in opposition in others, but its influence is omnipresent in the Islamic world.

The heterogeneity and asymmetry of the three blocs are reflected in the image they have of each other, as evidenced in their propaganda discourses—a system of errors from which it can be strongly suggested that the destinies of the world are in the hands of delusional madmen:

1. The Sino-Russian perspective (now expanded in the form of Eurasianism, which will be one of the topics of this debate) describes the Western bloc as (a) a worldwide expansion of American national power; (b) the material expression of the liberal ideology of the "open society" as advocated predominantly by Sir Karl Popper; (c) the living embodiment of the materialist, scientific, and rationalist mentality of the Enlightenment and, therefore, the archenemy of all traditional spirituality.

2. Western globalism declares no enemies other than "terrorism," which it does not identify in any way with the Islamic bloc but describes, as a residue of barbaric beliefs on the verge of extinction and "fundamentalism," a notion in which the ideological spokesmen of Islamic terrorism and the "Christian right" are indiscriminately mixed, as if the latter were allies of the former and not one of its main victims (so that the fear of Islamic terrorism is used as a pretext to justify the official boycott of Christianity in Europe and the US!).

Russia and China are never presented as potential aggressors but as allies of the West, with China at worst as a commercial competitor. In short: the ideology of Western globalism speaks as if it already embodied an established universal consensus, only being made hostile by somewhat insane marginal and religious groups.

3. The Islamic bloc describes its Western enemy in terms that only reveal its willingness to hate it *per fas et per nefas*, presenting it either as the heir to the ancient Crusaders or as the embodiment of modern materialism and hedonism. The generous collaboration of Russia and China with terrorist groups is certainly the reason why these two countries are almost nonexistent in Islamic ideological discourse. This skirts around insurmountable theoretical incompatibilities. Some theorists of the Caliphate claim that socialism, once victorious in the world, will need a soul, and Islam will give it one.

To the same extent that it cultivates a false image of its competitors, each of the blocs also projects a false image of itself. Setting aside, for now, the Islamic and Western projection fantasies, let's look at those of the Russo-Chinese bloc.

The Russo-Chinese bloc presents itself as an ally of the US in the "fight against terrorism," while providing weapons and all sorts of aid to practically every terrorist organization in the world and to anti-American regimes like Iran, Venezuela, etc., and spreading, even through high-ranking officials, the myth that the attack on the World Trade Center was the work of the American government.

Russia complains of having been "corrupted" by Boris Yeltsin's liberal reforms, of American inspiration, as if before them it lived in a temple of purity and not in the endless rot of the communist regime. It's worth remembering that the Soviet government essentially lived off theft and extortion for sixty years, without ever having to be held accountable, and corrupted the population through the institutionalized habits of bribery, exchanges of favors, and influence peddling, without which the state machine simply did not function.[169] When their assets were divided up after the official dissolution of the regime, the beneficiaries were the members of the nomenklatura themselves, who became billionaires overnight, without severing the ties that bound them to the old state apparatus, especially the KGB ("there is no such thing as a former KGB officer," as confessed by Vladimir Putin).

---

[169] See Konstantin Simis, *URSS: The Corrupt Society: The Secret World of Soviet Capitalism* (New York: Simon & Schuster, 1982) and Alena V. Ledeneva, *Russia's Economy of Favours* (Cambridge University Press, 1998).

Imagine what would have happened in Germany after World War II if the victors, instead of persecuting and punishing the leaders of the old regime, had rewarded them with access to the assets of the Nazi state. That's exactly what happened in Russia: as soon as the USSR was officially dissolved, its agents of influence in Europe and the US mobilized in a successful operation to block any investigation of Soviet crimes.[170] No one was punished for the murder of at least tens of millions of civilians, and for creating the most efficient state terror machine humanity has ever known. On the contrary, the chaos and corruption that followed the dismantling of the Soviet state were not caused by the new free-market system, but by the fact that the first to benefit from it were the lords of the old regime, a horde of thieves and murderers such as had never been seen in any civilized country.

Furthermore, by whining that it was corrupted by American capitalism, Russia forgets that it corrupted American capitalism. Since the 1930s, the Stalinist government, aware that America's strength lay "in its patriotism, in its ethical conscience, and in its religion" (sic), unleashed a gigantic operation aimed, in the words of its main executor, Willi Münzenberg, at "making the West so corrupt that it stinks." Buying consciences, involvement of high officials in espionage and shady businesses, intense propaganda campaigns to weaken the moral beliefs of the population, and widespread infiltration of the educational system ultimately yielded results, especially from the 1960s onwards, radically altering American society to the point of making it unrecognizable.

It was also Soviet action that gave global dimensions to the drug trade, starting in the 1950s. The story is well documented in *Red Cocaine: The Drugging of America and the West,* by Joseph D. Douglass.[171] When Russia complains that after the fall of communism it was invaded by the drug culture, it is merely reaping what it sowed.

None of this vast corruption is a thing of the past. Nowadays, there are more Russian agents in the US than during the Cold War.

China, well fed by American investments, proves that the apparent liberalization of its economy was just a facade for maintaining the totalitarian regime, which is becoming increasingly solid and seemingly indestructible.

Regarding the position of the USA in the global context, let's first examine how Professor Dugin describes it and then consider its reality. According to

---

[170] See *Vladimir Bukovsky, Judgment in Moscow: Soviet Crimes and Western Complicity* (Ninth of November Press, 2019).
[171] Atlanta: Clarion House, 1990.—Eds.

Eurasianist doctrine, the USA is defined as the quintessential embodiment of liberal globalism.[172] Liberalism, as Professor Dugin perceives it in the face of America, is essentially that of the "open society" advocated by Sir Karl Popper. Here is how Professor Dugin summarizes the liberal idea:

> To understand the philosophical coherence of the National-Bolshevik ideology . . . it is absolutely necessary to read Karl Popper's fundamental book, *The Open Society and Its Enemies*. Popper developed a crucial typology for our subject. According to him, the history of humanity and the history of ideas are divided into two (unequal, by the way) halves. On one side, there are the supporters of the 'open society,' which, in his view, represents the normal form of existence for rational individuals (as he considers all men to be) who base their conduct on calculation and supposedly free personal will. This set of individuals logically forms the 'open society,' which is essentially "non-totalitarian" because it lacks any unifying idea or system of values of a collectivist, supra-individual, or non-individual character. The 'open society' is open precisely because it ignores all 'teleologies,' all 'absolutes,' all established typological differences, and therefore ignores all limits that emanate from the non-individual and non-rational domain (supra-rational, a-rational, or irrational, the latter term being more frequent in Popper).
>
> On the other side is the ideological camp of the 'enemies of the open society,' where Popper includes Heraclitus, Plato, Aristotle, the Scholastics, as well as the German philosophy of Schlegel, Fichte, and especially Hegel and Marx . . . Karl Popper shows the essential unity of their approaches and discerns the structure of their common *Weltanschauung*, whose characteristic features are the denial of the intrinsic value of the individual, hence the disdain for autonomous rationalism, and the tendency to submit the individual and his reason to "non-individual and non-rational" values, which always and inevitably leads, according to Popper, to the apologia of political dictatorship and totalitarianism . . .

---

[172] The two elements that this definition merges into one do not have the same origin, nor were they born in solidarity with each other. The first liberal movements of the nineteenth century, emerging alongside independence movements against colonial powers, were markedly nationalist, while the first global governance projects that appeared at the beginning of the twentieth century were inspired by notably interventionist and statist ideas.

The National-Bolsheviks . . . absolutely and unreservedly accept Popper's dualistic view and fully agree with his classification. However, they consider themselves the convinced enemies of the 'open society.' They absolutely reject the 'open society' and its philosophical foundations, namely the primacy of the individual, the value of rational thought, progressive social liberalism, atomistic egalitarian democracy, free criticism, and the Cartesian-Kantian *Weltanschauung* . . .[173]

Now, globalism:

Today, it is evident that the World State conceived as a World Market is neither a distant nor chimerical prospect, because that liberal doctrine [of Karl Popper] is gradually becoming the governing idea of our civilization. This entails the ultimate destruction of nations as remnants of the past era, as the last obstacle to the irresistible expansion of globalism . . . The globalist doctrine is the perfect and complete expression of the 'open society' model.[174]

Liberal globalism is, therefore, the ongoing project aimed at implementing Popper's "open society" model worldwide, necessarily destroying national sovereignties and any metaphysical or moral principles that claim to be superior to individual rationality along the way. It signifies the end of nations and all traditional spirituality, with the former being replaced by a scientific-technocratic world administration and the latter by the blend of scientism, materialism, and relativistic subjectivism that inspires the globalist elites of the West.

Since the USA is the primary center of this project's dissemination and Russia is the main center of resistance (for reasons we will explore later), the clash is inevitable: The main thesis of the neo-Eurasianism is that the struggle between Russia and the United States is inevitable, since "America holds in its hands the steering wheel of globalization, which threatens to destroy Russia, the fortress of spirituality and traditions."[175]

I made a point of reproducing my opponent's opinion in some detail because, although I do not consider it false regarding the mentality of the globalist elites, who are indeed inspired by Popperian ideals, I can prove with little margin of error that:

---

[173] [Free translation—Eds.] Aleksandr Dugin, "La métaphysique du national-bolchevisme," *Le Prophète de l'Eurasisme* (Paris: Avatar Éditions, 2006), 131–133.
[174] Ibid.
[175] [Free translation.—Eds] Vadim Volovoy, "Will A. Dugin's predictions come true?" originally published at Geopolitika, November 2008.

1) The description does not apply at all to the USA, a nation where Popperianism is a recent graft, with no local roots and completely hostile to American traditions.

2) The USA is not the command center of the globalist project but, on the contrary, its primary victim, marked for destruction.

3) The globalist elite is not an enemy of Russia, China, or the Islamic countries virtually associated with the Eurasianist project but, on the contrary, a collaborator and accomplice in the effort to destroy the sovereignty, political-military power, and economy of the USA.

4) Far from favoring free-enterprise capitalism, the globalist project has strongly supported statist and controlling policies everywhere, differing in no way from the interventionism advocated by the Eurasianists. Globalism is only "liberal" in the local sense the term has in the USA as synonymous with "leftist." The globalist project is a direct heir and continuator of Fabian socialism, a traditional ally of the communists. Popperian ideology itself is not liberal-capitalist in the sense of classical liberalism, but, above all, an experimental approach to social engineering.

5) Eurasianism opposes the Popperian "open society" as an abstract ideological model, but since Eurasianism itself is not merely an abstract ideological model but also a geopolitical strategy, it is clear that it targets the Popperian ideology to hit, behind it, a specific national power, the USA, which has nothing to do with Popperian ideology and can only expect harm from it. Worse: American nationalism is a powerful Christian resistance to the globalist ambitions that have been trying to take over the country to destroy it as an autonomous power and use it as an instrument for their essentially anti-national plans. The destruction of American power will remove the last substantial obstacle to the establishment of a world government. Then, only the division of spoils among the three globalist schemes—Western, Russian-Chinese, and Islamic—will remain.

6) Russia is by no means the "fortress of spirituality and tradition," charged by a celestial mandate to punish, through the USA, the sins of the materialistic and immoral West. Today, as in Stalin's time, it is a den of corruption and wickedness like never before, engaged, as the prophecy of Fatima announced, in spreading its errors throughout the world. It should be noted that this prophecy never specifically referred to communism but to the "errors of Russia" in a general sense and announced that the dissemination of these errors, with all the accompanying misfortunes and sufferings, would only cease if the Pope and all the Catholic bishops in the world performed the rite

of consecration of Russia. Since this rite has never been performed, there is no reason not to see in the Eurasianist project a second wave and an upgrade of the "errors of Russia," heralding a catastrophe of incalculable proportions.

7) If today Russia, through Professor Dugin, presents itself to the world as the bearer of the great salvific spiritual message, it is necessary to remember that it has done so twice before:

(a) In the nineteenth century, all thinkers of the Slavophile line, like Dostoevsky, Solovyov, and Leontiev, saw the West as the source of all evil and announced that in the following century, Russia would teach the world "true Christianity." What was seen was that all this spiritual arrogance was powerless to stop the advance of communist materialism in Russia itself.

(b) Russian communism promised to bring the world an era of peace, prosperity, and freedom beyond the most beautiful dreams of past generations. All it managed to do was create a totalitarian hell that neither Attila nor Genghis Khan could have envisioned in a nightmare.

It would be great if every country learned to cure its own ills before posing as the savior of humanity. Aleksandr Dugin's Russia seems to have drawn the opposite lesson from its crimes and failures.

Cold War or Asymmetric Warfare?

Folha de São Paulo, July 27, 2014

Accepted, even in Brazil, as an unquestionable dogma, the popular view of the Cold War as a surreptitious and relentless struggle between two powers that hated each other can now be thrown into the trash can as misleading stereotypes, a fairy tale invented to give lazy brains the illusion that they understood what was going on.

In recent decades, so many facts have been brought to light by the deciphering of the Venona codes (the coded communications between the Soviet embassy in Washington and the Moscow government) and by the plethora of documents unearthed from Soviet archives that practically nothing remains standing of the chic opinion dominant at the time.

In truth, the main occupation of the Soviet government and media during the period was to lie about the United States, while their American counterparts were, with equal zeal, lying in favor of the USSR. Not only lying: covering up their crimes, protecting their agents, favoring their interests over those of friendly nations and, often, over those of the American nation itself.

Instead of the balance of power, which, whether supported or not by obscene moral equivalence, still appears in the vulgar media and in Wikipedia entries as a faithful historical portrait, what we see today is that the USA-USSR conflict was what would later be called "asymmetric warfare," in which one side fights the other and the other fights itself.

Not that there wasn't, on the American side, a determined and vigorous anti-communism, willing to do anything to stop Soviet advances in Europe, Asia, Africa, and Latin America. So many were the personalities who stood out in this fight—journalists, writers, artists, politicians, military personnel, intelligence agents—and so gigantic were their efforts, that this is from where we derive what may be legitimate in the view of the USA as the archenemy of the communist movement. Just mentioning the names of George S. Patton, Douglas MacArthur, Robert Taft, Whittaker Chambers, Joseph McCarthy, Eugene Lyons, Sidney Hook, Fulton Sheen, Edgar J. Hoover, James Jesus Angleton, Robert Conquest, and Barry Goldwater, is enough to understand why anti-communism was projected as a typical image of America, not only abroad but also before the Americans themselves.

However, when examined case by case, what is found is that in each of them the inspiring force was personal initiative and not a government policy; and that, practically without exception, all those who stood out in this fight were boycotted, restrained by Washington authorities (even when they themselves were part of the government), and ridiculed by the media, the education system, and show business, in life or at least posthumously. Often sabotaged and persecuted by their own Republican and conservative peers, fearful of appearing more anti-communist than the prevailing anti-anti-communism in the chic world allowed.

In short: while American society was teeming with anti-communism, official policy, from Roosevelt onwards, and with the notable exception of Ronald Reagan's administration, was systematically one of collaborationism, if not always well disguised.

What explains this is that the Soviet agents infiltrated in the government and in the major media were not fifty some-odd, as the unfortunate Joe McCarthy thought, and who paid for this very modest calculation by becoming the most hated American senator of all time. They were—it is now known—more than a thousand, many of them placed in high positions in the hierarchy, where sometimes they did much more than "influence:" they even determined the course of American foreign policy, always, of course, in a sense favorable to the USSR.

The most classic example was the deterioration of relations between the USA and Japan, which culminated in the attack on Pearl Harbor—an ingenious plan conceived in Moscow to rid the USSR of the danger of a two-front war, playing the Japanese fury against the Americans through a well-coordinated game between Richard Sorge's "Red Orchestra" in Tokyo and presidential adviser Harry Hopkins, in Washington.

But the chapters of the collaborationist saga accumulated in hallucinatory profusion until the Clinton administration, when government encouragement of massive investments in China turned a bankrupt country into a threatening enemy power.

I don't believe this story—perhaps the most well-documented of the twentieth century—has ever been told in Brazil. Even in the USA, it circulates only among intellectuals and professional historians, while the general public still follows the official legend. It's a story too vast and complex for me to attempt to summarize here.

What I can do is suggest some books that may provide the reader with an overview of the state of research today.

Diana West, *American Betrayal. The Secret Assault on Our Nation's Character* (St. Martin's, 2013).

Herbert Rommerstein and Eric Breindel, *The Venona Secrets. Exposing Soviet Espionage and America's Traitors* (Regnery, 2000).

John Earl Haynes and Harvey Klehr, *Venona. Decoding Soviet Espionage in America* (Yale University Press, 1999).

Allen Weinstein and Alexander Vassiliev, *The Haunted Wood. Soviet Espionage in America. The Stalin Era* (Random House, 1999).

Paul Kengor, *Dupes. How America's Adversaries Have Manipulated Progressives for a Century* (ISI Books, 2010).

Arthur Hermann and Joseph McCarthy, *Reexamining the Life and Legacy of America's Most Hated Senator* (Free Press, 2000).

M. Stanton Evans, *Blacklisted by History. The Untold Story of Senator Joe McCarthy* (Crown Forum, 2007).

Robert K. Willcox, *Target: Patton. The Plot to Assassinate General George S. Patton* (Regnery, 2008).

The Future that Russia Promises Us

Diário do Comércio, May 23, 2011
Breve retrato do Brasil (2017)

Professor Aleksandr Dugin, at the forefront of the Russian intellectual elite shaping the Putin government's foreign policy, says that his nation's grand plan is to restore the hierarchical sense of spiritual values buried by modernity. For people with a religious mindset, shocked by the brutal vulgarity of modern life, the proposal may sound quite appealing. However, the realization of the idea involves two steps. First, it is necessary to destroy the West, the source of all evils, through a world war, inevitably more devastating than the previous two. Then, the Eurasianist World Empire will be established under the leadership of Holy Mother Russia.

Regarding the first point: "salvation through destruction" is one of the most constant slogans of revolutionary discourse. The French Revolution promised to save France by destroying the *ancien régime*: it brought it from downfall to downfall to the condition of a second-class power. The Mexican Revolution promised to save Mexico by destroying the Catholic Church: it turned it into a drug supplier to the world and a source of destitutes for American social assistance. The Russian Revolution promised to save Russia by destroying capitalism: it turned it into a graveyard. The Chinese Revolution promised to save China by destroying bourgeois culture: it turned it into a slaughterhouse. The Cuban Revolution promised to save Cuba by destroying imperialist usurpers: it turned it into a prison for beggars. Brazilian positivists promised to save Brazil by destroying the monarchy: they ended the only democracy on the continent and plunged the country into a succession of coups and dictatorships that only ended in 1988 to give way to a modernized dictatorship with another name.

Now, Professor Dugin promises to save the world by destroying the West. Frankly, I prefer not to know what comes next. The revolutionary mentality, with its self-deferred promises, so ready to transform into their opposites with the most innocent face in the world, is the greatest scourge that has ever befallen humanity. Its victims, from 1789 to today, number no fewer than three hundred million people—more than all epidemics, natural disasters, and wars between nations have killed since the beginning of time. The essence of its discourse, as I believe I have already demonstrated, is the inversion of the sense of time: inventing a future and reinterpreting the present and the past in its light, as if it were a certain and proven premise. Inverting the normal process of knowledge, beginning to understand the known through the unknown, the certain through the doubtful, the categorical through the hypothetical. It is structural, systematic, obsessive, hypnotic falsification. Professor Dugin proposes the Eurasianist Empire and reconstructs the entire history of the world as if it were the long preparation for the advent of this beautiful thing. He is a revolutionary like any other. Just immensely more pretentious.

As for the Eurasianist World Empire, with an Eastern pole sustained by Islamic countries, Japan, and China, and a Western pole in the Paris–Berlin–Moscow axis, it is by no means a new idea. Stalin cherished this project and did everything he could to realize it, only failing because he could not, in time, create a maritime fleet with the required dimensions to accomplish it. He erred in timing: he said that the US would not make it past the 1980s. It was the USSR that did not make it.

As Professor Dugin adorns the project with the appeal to spiritual and religious values, instead of the proletarian internationalism that legitimized Stalin's ambitions, it seems logical to admit that the new version of the Russian imperial project is something like a right-wing Stalinism.

But the most obvious thing in the Russian government is that its occupants are the same as those who dominated the country during communism. Essentially, it's the personnel of the KGB (or FSB, as the periodic name changes never changed the nature of this institution). Worse still, it's the KGB with brutally expanded power: on the one hand, if in the communist regime there was one secret police agent for every 400 citizens, today there is one for every 200, unmistakably characterizing Russia as a police state; on the other hand, the division of state properties among agents and collaborators of the political police, who became "oligarchs" overnight without losing their ties of submission to the KGB, grants this entity the privilege of operating in the West, under layers and layers of disguises, with a freedom of movement that would have been unthinkable in Stalin's or Khrushchev's time.

Ideologically, Eurasianism is different from communism. But ideology, as Karl Marx himself defined it, is merely a "cloak of ideas" covering a power scheme. The power scheme in Russia has changed its cloak but remains the same—with the same people in the same places, exercising the same functions, with the same totalitarian ambitions as always.

The Eurasianist Empire promises us a world war and, as a result, a global dictatorship. Some of its adherents even call it "the Empire of the End," a clearly apocalyptic evocation. They just forget to observe that the last empire before the Final Judgment will be nothing other than the Empire of the Antichrist.

Communism After the End

Jornal da Tarde, June 6, 2002
O Foro de São Paulo (2022); *A morte do pato* (2023)

Imagine that, at the end of World War II, with the Führer dead in the depths of his bunker and democracy restored in Germany, a universal tacit consensus decided that the Nazi war crimes should not be investigated or punished, that the Nazi Party would continue to operate legally under various names, that a good part of the concentration camps should continue to function at least discreetly, that no one in the Gestapo or the SS would be dismissed or interrogated, and that some good officials from these lovely institutions should even be put in charge of the nation.

Under these conditions, would you believe in the "end of Nazism"? Or would you rather perceive therein an immense "upgrade" of this satanic movement, stripped of its most obvious and compromising appearance, subtly refined and disseminated in the air like a virus to infect all of humanity?

Would you believe in the "end of Nazism" if, while the means of subsistence and expansion of this movement were preserved, the international media and the elegant opinion instantly decreed the most drastic moral repression against any explicit anti-Nazism, accusing anyone who dared to speculate, even from afar, about the risks of a return of the Nazi regime, under another name, of being paranoid and antidemocratic?

Would you believe in the "end of Nazism" if, after half a century of its alleged extinction, any attempt to investigate and disclose the extent of its crimes was publicly condemned as an inconvenience, a sin, a malicious vendetta? Would you believe in the "end of Nazism" if, in Germany and beyond, any heavier criticism of those who once advocated for this genocidal regime was banned and persecuted as a crime or at least as a sign of mental illness?

Would you believe in the "end of Nazism" if everywhere those who promoted Nazi propaganda were pampered and honored not only as great figures of intellectual and artistic life, but also as defenders of freedom and human rights?

Would you believe in the "end of Nazism" if notorious pro-Nazi militants were rising to power through electoral means in various Third World nations, while in others guerrilla wars, revolutions, and coups inspired by Nazi preaching were erupting?

Would you believe in the "end of Nazism" if the nations that supposedly defeated it were surrounded by an international hate campaign supported by Nazi parties and organizations?

Would you believe in the "end of Nazism" if all those who labeled themselves as "former" Nazis only made very vague and generic criticisms of Hitler's regime, quickly changing the subject, but at the same time continued to attack anti-Nazism as the worst of evils?

So, for heaven's sake, why do you believe in the "end of communism"? The international communist movement has not been dismantled, weakened, or even accused of anything. In Russia, the Communist Party maintains a good number of seats in parliament, the KGB (with its name changed for the thousandth time since Lenin) continues to operate at full steam with budgets higher than those of all Western secret services combined, the Gulag remains full of prisoners. In China, Vietnam, North Korea, and Cuba, one billion, four hundred million people still live under the communist police state which, with each new promise of liberalization made to seduce foreign investors, tightens the screws of repression and strangles any hint of organized opposition. In Latin America and Africa, new communist or pro-communist regimes emerge and, in the face of international media's complacency, violently dismantle all opposition, demolish guarantees of individual freedom and property rights, and foster guerrillas and revolutions in neighboring countries, with the support of drug trafficking networks set up by the KGB and Chinese espionage since the 1960s, now grown to the point of controlling the economies of entire countries. In supposedly triumphant capitalist nations, slogans, values, and criteria from the Marxist "cultural revolution" of the 1960s are officially imposed in schools and homes as unquestionable dogma, while a tricontinental communist lobby rigidly controls the flow of news in major newspapers and TV channels, and Marxist orthodoxy manages to silence the few dissenting voices through intimidation and coercion at universities.

How, in sound consciousness, can anyone who knows these things claim that communism has ended or that it no longer poses any danger?

The ABC of Disinformation

Diário do Comércio, January 10, 2013
O progresso da ignorância (2019)

For those who are concerned about the survival of their brains in a time of the universal shipwreck of intelligence, nothing is more urgent than understanding what "disinformation" really is. The common use of the word as an infamous label to denigrate any opposing opinion is a sure guarantee that true disinformation operations will go unnoticed, a necessary and almost sufficient condition for their success.

There are only two types of genuine disinformation, and each requires much more planning and careful execution than the mere journalistic vice of spreading ideologically seductive lies.

The first type—and by far the most important—is the one that targets not the general public, the ignorant masses, but rather the men of power, those who make far-reaching decisions. Hardly any of these creatures allow themselves to be guided by what is reported in popular media. To influence them, it is necessary to place in their entourage (or win over through bribery, blackmail, etc.) technical advisors who are completely trusted. And even these advisors must be very cautious in handling the flow of information that will lead their bosses to make the wrong decisions, favorable to the enemy who controls the situation from afar. The importance of these operations is immeasurable, much more than the average citizen can imagine, and no one has been (and still is) more skilled in managing them than the good old KGB (now FSB). Thanks to the plethora of secret documents revealed after the fall of the USSR, it is now known that since the 1940s, Soviet agents have shaped some of the main strategic decisions of the Washington government on the international stage, inducing it to work against the most vital interests of the American nation.

The clearest and most didactic example is in the book *Operation Snow: How a Soviet Mole in FDR's White House Triggered Pearl Harbor* by John Koster.[176] "Mole" is the technical term used in intelligence services to designate an infiltrated agent. The mole, in this case, was Harry Dexter White, a senior Treasury official, a trusted man of Franklin Delano Roosevelt, and, as documents prove, a Soviet agent.

The situation in 1941 was as follows. The militaristic and expansionist government of Japan was divided between two currents: one wanted to resume the old war with Russia. The other wanted to help the Nazis against the Western powers. Russia, under German attack since June, could not offer effective resistance to the Japanese on the other side of their territory. A profound connoisseur of the Japanese language, culture, and politics, and placed, moreover, in a position from which he could easily influence the economic decisions of the Roosevelt government, Harry Dexter White was hired by the Soviets to artificially create a conflict between Japan and the US. The sequence of memoranda and strategic studies with which he worsened the economic relations between the two

---

[176] Regnery, 2012.

countries was a stroke of genius, leading Roosevelt to impose drastic limitations on Japanese oil imports that, from the American point of view, seemed simply reasonable, but which in the Japanese context, and in the Japanese language, sounded like true declarations of war. Japan responded with the attack on Pearl Harbor on December 7, 1941—not coincidentally, a day after Russia, free from the Japanese threat, launched a massive counterattack against the Germans.

Psychologically, Pearl Harbor remains to this day a rallying symbol of American patriotism, but, in substantive terms, it was a tremendous victory for Soviet disinformation.

The other type of disinformation is rather a work of social engineering. It does not target the government to shape its decisions, but, on the contrary, comes from the government and its associated centers of power and descends to the popular masses, after decisions have already been made and it is necessary, to implement them, to gain the support of the electorate, keep them in total ignorance of what the high circles are doing, or adjust their conduct to the standards required by the new policy.

These two types can be called micro and macro-disinformation. The difficulties are considerable in both cases, but of a very different nature. If the first is unworkable without maximum secrecy and fine handling of the flow of information, the second requires complete control of the larger and more prestigious means of dissemination, but can coexist with some lesser—or marginal—contention that, statistically, does not affect the sentiments of the popular masses.

In Brazil, this condition is very easy to achieve, as the mainstream media has always been dependent on government funding and dares not bite the hand that feeds it. This is how the major newspapers and TV channels consented to hide the existence of the *São Paulo Forum* until the moment that, having completely dominated the continental situation, it could already appear in public without major risks.

In the US, the situation had to be preceded by a long and complex process of media concentration in the hands of the globalist groups that today vie with Russia for the affections of the Islamic bloc. When these groups put Barack Hussein Obama in government to undermine the national power of the US and carry out a 180-degree turn in American foreign policy, turning the former ally of Israel into the greatest protector that radical Muslims have ever had in the West, the media was already prepared to conceal not only the highly compromising biography of the president but even some of his most ambitious and damaging executive orders, which went into effect without the population knowing anything about them.

The Masters of Failure

Diário do Comércio, April 24, 2006
O mundo como jamais funcionou (2014)

George F. Kennan and Hans J. Morgenthau were both born in 1904, the former in Milwaukee, Wisconsin, the latter in Coburg, Franconia, Germany, emigrating to America in 1937. Kennan surpassed the century mark, living until 2005; Morgenthau died in 1980. Reaching their intellectual maturity in the 1940s, they were destined to create the two theories that, essentially, would determine American foreign policy throughout the second half of the twentieth century: the doctrine of "containment" and that of "political realism," respectively. The former continually guided U.S. relations with communist countries, only being informally and temporarily abandoned during the Reagan administration. The latter, more comprehensive, provided the general concepts with which the State Department views the world. The George W. Bush administration deviated from it in partial aspects but continued reasoning within the intellectual framework it created.

What would happen if these two doctrines were substantially wrong? Engaged in improper international policy, America, the wealthiest and most powerful nation in the universe, with inexhaustible natural resources and the most patriotic, devoted, and creative people the world has ever seen, would play a much lesser role on the global stage than it seemed destined for by the circumstances of its founding and the absolute success of its economic and political system. Its most obvious merits, instead of asserting themselves to the world with the authority of example, would be denied in favor of the anti-example of inhumane and economically failed tyrannical regimes. Its enemies, unable to defeat it by their own ingenuity, would thrive on exploiting its weaknesses, gaining in the fields of Machiavellianism, and deceit, the advantages denied to them in economic, military, and scientific competition. Even defeated in the political and military arena, they would achieve ideological and propaganda victories. A continuous flow of aid provided to other countries—even hostile ones—the most formidable outpouring of national generosity humanity has ever known, often exercised against the material interests of the American people themselves, would not arouse any sympathy for America. On the contrary: it would foster among the beneficiaries a sense of inferiority that they would seek to compensate for with a grotesquely hypertrophied notion of their own "rights." Everywhere ingratitude would transform into patriotic symbolism, envy into virtue, and anti-American hatred into moral obligation. Entire nations that owed their survival to American aid would prefer to approach aggressive and exploitative neighbors—to whom they would feel equal and united by the community of evil—rather than the benefactor in whose presence they would feel humiliated, not only by the difference in material goods but also by their own moral inferiority.

Well, aren't these precisely the things that are happening? Aren't they the exact description of the position that the U.S. occupies in the world? Isn't it time to subject the ideas of Kennan and Morgenthau to radical critique?

Their main weakness comes from their disciplinary origin. There seems to be nothing abnormal about theorists of International Relations being, of course, scholars of International Relations. But the approach that Kennan and Morgenthau take to the problems of the field reflects the dominant tendency of the European and American academic world at the time of their university education, the early decades of the twentieth century. The fashion then was for each scientific discipline to seek independence, carving out its territory according to the autonomous, pure, and uncontaminated nature of its object of study. It was the era of Edmund Husserl's "pure logic," Hans Kelsen's "pure theory of law," Léon Walras's "pure economics," and Carl Schmitt's "pure politics." This obsession with purity arose from a healthy impulse to respect the limits of the various domains of reality (the "regional ontologies" as Husserl called them), reacting against the 19th-century mania of making the most successful science of the moment the model and standard for all others, a mania labeled "scientific imperialism" by José Ortega y Gasset (himself a proponent of "pure sociology," although not under that explicit name).

The reaction towards differentiation was quite sensible, but it generated a kind of scientific jingoism, an autonomist pride: each science, once constituted, allowed itself to solemnly ignore what the neighboring disciplines had to say about its jealously delimited and guarded field. Kelsen, for example, was particularly fierce in his refusal to allow sociological, psychological, or moral considerations to intervene in "pure law" (later he had to concede). The result was that many areas of intersection came to be ignored because they did not fit into any particular discipline. Taken together, they form entire continents of reality. Whatever happened in this zone was considered irrelevant or nonexistent.

In the production of this phenomenon, there was also the interference of another factor. If readers remember what I wrote about Kant,[177] they will have no difficulty in perceiving how Kant's primacy of method may have contributed to turning away from facts becoming a matter of honor for many scientists.

---

[177] For instance, see "Kant and the Primacy of the Critical Problem," "To Understand Kant," and "The New World Order Guru" in this *Reader*.—Eds.

Kennan and Morgenthau (the latter, not coincidentally, a disciple of Kelsen and Schmitt) were deeply affected by this vice. Formally and by definition—thus from the perspective of disciplinary purity—international relations are relations between States. But who said that in the real plot of world history States are the main agents of the process? States form and dissolve like clouds. Wars and agreements make them appear and disappear from the map. Sometimes they are mere diplomatic fictions created by arrangements among other States. Furthermore, States do not act: those who act on their behalf are governments; and governments change objectives according to forces that are not of a state, often not even national, order. To act, the scholastics said, one must *be*. And being means, among other things, having unity and preserving it over time. Behind the States, there are much more cohesive, enduring, and continuous agents, such as the Catholic Church, Islam, Freemasonry, the Communist Party, or certain noble and wealthy families. These entities have permanent objectives that surpass the duration of States and often the horizon of vision of state agents. Their action overlaps state divisions and frequently determines them. By describing the power game in the world essentially as a plot of relations between States, both Kennan and Morgenthau end up, in a Kantian manner, confusing the definition of a scientific discipline with the objective order of reality. Misguided by them, America made mistake upon mistake, first in the confrontation with communism, and now with international terrorism.

In the famous "long telegram" sent from the American Embassy in Moscow to the State Department on February 22, 1946, George F. Kennan, recognizing the immutably aggressive nature of the Soviet regime, proposed a "long-term patient but firm and vigilant containment of Russian expansive tendencies."[178] *Containment* became the permanent basis of American strategy in the Cold War.

Now, at the end of World War II, the USSR's economy was in a shambles. It depended entirely on American aid, which was given to it more generously than to any other allied country. The U.S., on the other hand, emerged from the combat enriched and in formidable industrial expansion. It had on its side the universal prestige of democracy and still the advantage of the atomic bomb, a nightmare that terrorized Stalin. It was in a position to break the spine of the Soviet regime, to reduce it to complete impotence and docility, even without military pressure, through the simple refusal—or threat of refusal—of economic aid. If there is something well proven in History, it is that the Soviet economy has always been crippled, always dependent on American assistance, and, after the war, became

---

[178] "George Kennan and Containment," Office of the Historian, Foreign Service Institute United States Department of State.—Eds.

even more so. The USSR only became a threat to the Americans because they themselves rebuilt it and armed it against themselves.[179] Besides arranging "the best enemy that money could buy," as Anthony Sutton called it, they also fostered its most paranoid ambitions through the excessive concessions made to Stalin by Franklin Roosevelt at the Yalta agreements, under the direct influence of an adviser, Harry Dexter White, who was later found to be a Soviet agent.

The proposal of "containment," at this point, was of abnormal modesty and benevolence. It served only to encourage the Soviets, who unleashed against it one of their most virulent and deceitful propaganda campaigns. In September, a telegram from Nikolai Novikov, the Soviet ambassador in Washington, commissioned and dictated by Stalin himself to be used in this campaign, "informed" that "reflecting the imperialistic tendency of American monopoly capital, US foreign policy has been characterized in the postwar period by a desire for *world domination*."[180] Now, American "containment" was not a publicity slogan; it was the literal expression of the principle adopted in practice, which recognized the legitimacy of the borders reached so far by brutal Soviet expansion and only aimed to prevent them from going further. The idea reflected not only Kennan's suggestion but also the influential doctrine of "balance of powers" that Hans J. Morgenthau was teaching at the University of Chicago and that would compose his 1948 book, *Politics Among Nations: The Struggle for Power and Peace*. Empowered to achieve hegemony, Americans wanted only "containment" and "balance of powers." The greatest proof of this was that they withdrew their troops from Europe as promised, while the Soviet Union made sure to keep theirs there indefinitely. The modesty of American aspirations and the unlimited ambition of the Soviets appeared rigorously inverted in Novikov's telegram and in all the anti-American propaganda campaigns that followed.

Focused on the effort to halt the territorial expansion of the Soviet state, American security services neglected the communist movement as such, which in the meantime infiltrated hundreds of agents into the US government, almost completely dominated the cultural and artistic establishment, spread agents of influence throughout the Western mainstream media, and prepared the internal rebellion that, in the 1960s, led the US to defeat in Vietnam. General Giap, commander of the North Vietnamese forces, astutely observed that while the Americans treated the war as a strictly military matter, they, the Communists,

[179] See Anthony Sutton, *National Suicide. Military Aid to the Soviet Union* (New Rochelle: Arlington House, 1973)—a classic.
[180] Winson Center, Digital Archive. Telegram from Nikolai Novikov, Soviet Ambassador to the US, to the Soviet Leadership, September 27, 1946.—Eds.

were simultaneously fighting on all fronts: moral, cultural, journalistic, etc. And it was precisely on these fronts that they won the final battle, through the American New Left itself, at a time when the Viet Cong army was practically destroyed after the famous Tet Offensive.

Limited by state obsession, the American government, for a long time, followed the norm of only being concerned with an individual or communist group when it had a direct connection to Soviet espionage. Outside of this, communist militancy was considered a simple expression of individual opinions, without greater danger. In the 1960s and 1970s New Left, the links of militancy with communist governments were too tenuous to attract attention. The explanation for this was not genuine independence of leftism from Soviet and Chinese strategy. It was that the communist movement was already beginning to evolve from rigid hierarchical structure to informal and flexible organization in multinational "networks," which in the following decades would harass the US from many sides simultaneously with a global hostility campaign that the American government was not and still is not prepared to face. It was only during the George W. Bush administration that the belated recognition came that the US was now dealing with a new type of war, impossible to fit into usual doctrines.

All of this could have been avoided if the US had not focused its foreign policy on the effort to contain the expansion of Soviet territorial borders, instead of combating the international communist movement on all fronts. To get an idea of how much the US was left behind, just compare the scope of the effort that the Soviets made to dominate the intellectual and artistic environment of Europe and the US since the 1920s,[181] with the modesty of the American reaction, only coming in the 1950s and practically limited to the Congress for Cultural Freedom held in West Berlin in 1956. It is interesting to note that, thanks to communist cultural hegemony within the American academic environment itself, even this modest response was condemned within the US as a morally repugnant imperialist action.[182]

As for the Morgenthau doctrine, its self-designation of "political realism" seems almost like a stroke of involuntary humor. Defining international relations as a field essentially constituted by competition between national interests and emphasizing nationalism as the predominant ideological force, Morgenthauism

---

[181] See Frederick C. Barghoorn, *The Soviet Cultural Offensive* (Princeton University Press, 1960), and especially Stephen Koch, *Double Lives. Spies and Writers in the Secret Soviet War of Ideas Against the West* (New York: Free Press, 1994).

[182] See for example Frances Stonor Saunders, *The Cultural Cold War. The CIA and the World of Arts and Letters* (New York: The New Press, 1999).

served to obscure the three main factors at work in the historical panorama of the last half century: the strategic unity of international leftism, its reorganization into informal networks for the cultural war effort, and its simultaneous action on an unmanageable multiplicity of fronts—precisely the three factors that have been accumulating strength since the 1950s to today—put the US under permanent multilateral siege. Morgenthau underestimated the unity of the communist strategy to the point of proposing that the US try to make alliances with communist countries against the USSR and China, a plan from which, obviously, the Soviets and Chinese took almost unlimited advantage.

These two paragraphs that he published in the *New York Times Magazine* on April 18, 1965, give an idea of the extent of Morgenthau's unrealism and imprudence:

> However, we are under a psychological compulsion to continue our military presence in South Vietnam as part of the peripheral military containment of China. We have been emboldened in this course of action by the identification of the enemy as "Communist," seeing in every Communist party and regime an extension of hostile Russian or Chinese power. This identification was justified 20 or 15 years ago when Communism still had a monolithic character. Here, as elsewhere, our modes of thought and action have been rendered obsolete by new developments.

> It is ironic that this simple juxtaposition of "Communism" and "free world" was erected by John Foster Dulles's crusading moralism into the guiding principle of American foreign policy at a time when the national Communism of Yugoslavia, the neutralism of the third world, and the incipient split between the Soviet Union and China were rendering that juxtaposition invalid. [183]

Now, we know that: First, the "neutralist" movement of the Third World was entirely articulated by the KGB, with the quite reasonable intention of creating anti-American fronts that could not easily be identified as communist. [184] Second, the supposed independence of Yugoslav communism made it a wonderfully effective instrument that the Soviets used to create this "neutralist" hoax. Third, the so-called Sino-Soviet conflict was never real, it was just staged to camouflage

---

[183] *Vietnam and the National Interest*—Eds.
[184] See Christopher Andrew and Vasili Mitrokhin, *The World Was Going Our Way. The KGB and the Battle for the Third World* (New York: Basic Books, 2005).

the global unity of communist strategy and lead Americans to think exactly what Morgenthau thought.[185]

The inefficiency of Morgenthauism, however, has deeper and darker roots than mere unreality. It stems from an incurable internal contradiction. On the one hand, Morgenthau's entire description of the political world is based on the ideas of the Nation-State, national interest, and nationalism. On the other hand, he believed in the viability of a world government and worked for this idea. It was precisely this that made him so beloved in the globalist circles of the Council on Foreign Relations. These circles were and are dominated by groups of *metacapitalist* billionaires, whose plans, global and more civilizational in scale than political-military, go far beyond the horizon of any Nation-State, not to mention any government. Living and thinking within this atmosphere, Morgenthau had the unequivocal proof right in front of him that Nation-States are not the main agent subject of History, but often the helpless object in the hands of more unitary and coherent agents. Concealing the actions of these agents, of which he himself was a valuable intellectual collaborator, Morgenthauism is an extreme case of "cognitive parallax," in which the very existential conditions in which the theory sprouted and developed bring complete denial of the content of the theory.

Old John Foster Dulles was not wrong to wish that the Americans' struggle was not against particular States, but against the communist movement as such. Only, limited by Kennan's perspective, he still saw this struggle in terms of containment and not global cultural warfare, at a time when the communists had already been engaged in this war for a long time. If he erred, it was out of modesty and not out of excessive pretension of his "moralistic crusade"—today more necessary than ever.

The combined effect of the theories of Kennan and Morgenthau on American foreign policy can be measured by the formidable increase in anti-Americanism after the fall of the USSR and by the present state of moral siege in which the US finds itself, unable to even defend the most elemental rights of its sovereignty without immediately arousing a worldwide wave of revolt against it.

---

[185] On these last two points, see Anatoliy Golitsyn, *New Lies for Old. The Communist Strategy of Deception and Disinformation* (Atlanta: Clarion House, 1990.)

In the Claws of the Sphinx: René Guénon and the Islamization of the West

Verbum magazine, 2016
O saber e o enigma (2022)

The profound historical and spiritual transformations that will determine the future of humanity are so distant from our media, our university life, and, in general, from all public debates in Brazil, that surely what I am going to say in this article will seem outlandish and disconnected from immediate reality.

* * *

After describing in somber tones of a genuine Apocalypse the spiritual degradation of civilization in the West, attributing it to the loss of "true metaphysics" and the connections between the Catholic Church and the Primordial Tradition (connections that, in his view, could only have been maintained through initiatic organizations),[186] René Guénon foresaw three possible developments of the state of affairs in the West:[187]

1. The definitive descent into barbarism.

2. The restoration of the Catholic tradition, under the discreet guidance of Islamic spiritual masters.

3. Total Islamization, either through infiltration and propaganda, or through military occupation.

These three options ultimately boiled down to two: either plunging into barbarism or submitting to Islam, whether discreetly or overtly. The outbreak of World War II seemed to indicate that the West preferred the former option, with an ironic detail being the fact that important Islamic religious authorities gave full support to the *Führer*, especially regarding the extermination of the Jews.[188] Macabre coincidence or self-fulfilling prophecy? I do not know.

After the war, the intimate collaboration between Islamic governments and communist regimes in the joint anti-Western effort became so notorious that there is no need to insist on this point. It is worth noting that today, the global left committed to corrupting the West "until it stinks," is the same one that openly

---

[186] Guénon doesn't even mention Protestant churches, as he considered all of them to be anti-traditional deviations. Schuon, later on, would soften this diagnosis without formally challenging it.

[187] *Orient et Occident* (Paris: Véga, 1924).

[188] Barry Rubin, *Nazis, Islamists, and the Making of the Modern Middle East* (Yale University Press, 2014); and David Motadel, *Islam and Nazi Germany's War* (Belknap Press, 2014).

supports the Muslim occupation of the West through mass immigration, as well as boycotts by all means any serious effort to combat Islamic terrorism, so that there seems to be a Leninist agreement between the two blocs to "foment corruption and denounce it." Once again, the same question from the previous paragraph arises, with the same answer.

For the Catholic aspirant, all that the *tariqa*[189] offered was the choice between becoming a Muslim or being Catholic under Muslim guidance. The same choice that Guénon offered to the entire Western world.

I believe that with this, Guénon's intention becomes clearer when he squeezes all religions, especially Christianity, into the forced mold of an Islamic descriptive concept, the exoterism-esoterism[190] distinction. Indeed, how to dominate an entire civilization without first fitting it into the intellectual coordinates system of the dominating civilization, where it will cease to be an autonomous whole and become part of a comprehensive map? It is also obvious that it was not enough to do this in theory: it was necessary to conquer, for this new view of things, the most valuable, intellectually active elements of the target civilization's elite. Only when it began to understand itself in the terms of the dominator, rather than its own, would it be ripe to accept, without major reactions, a broader operation of cultural occupation. Moreover, the reduction of Christianity to the exoteric-esoteric dichotomy, accompanied by the somber diagnosis of the loss of the esoteric dimension, inexorably culminated in the conclusion that the "restoration of Christianity," of its connections with the Primordial Tradition and therefore of the highest dimensions of its spirituality, could only be achieved under the guidance of a "living esoterism," that is, Sufism. To use Guénon's own terms, it was necessary to subject the West to the "spiritual authority" of Islam before subjecting it to its "temporal power."

Frithjof Schuon's theory, according to which the Christian sacraments retained their initiatic power, seemed to diminish somewhat the force of the Islamizing argument, but in reality, it did not do so at all. Without proper spiritual instruction, which only a "living esoterism" could offer, the bearer of a "virtual initiation" remained unaware of having received it and not only remained paralyzed in the midst of the initiatic ascent, but also risked, as a result, suffering all sorts of spiritual and psychic disturbances. Only Sufi spirituality—embodied, in this case, in the person of F. Schuon—could save Catholics from themselves.

---

[189] *Tariqa* is an esoteric Islamic grouping, see "The East Versus the West," in Chapter 3.— Eds.

[190] See "The East Versus the West," in Chapter 3.—Eds.

The Islamization of the West—whether discreet or overt, peaceful or violent—is the central and indeed, sole objective of all of René Guénon's work. It all converges on this goal, not as a mere logical conclusion, but as a kind of single way out, to which the reader—and ideally, the entire West—is being led, within the walls of a labyrinthine construction, by a sense of inexorable fate. Excluding this objective, it would be nothing more than a set of theoretical speculations without purpose, a structure of beautiful but unrealizable spiritual possibilities, something he always denied it could be.

If an explicit confession were needed to confirm it, it would suffice to recall that, precisely at the moment when F. Schuon returned from Algeria with the title of *sheikh*, boasting his intention to "islamize Europe" (sic), Guénon declared that the foundation of Schuon's *tariqa* in Lausanne, Switzerland, was the first and only fruit produced by his decades-long effort.

* * *

What can make this objective nebulous or even invisible to the public eye are two factors:

First: Guénon repeatedly asserts his total disregard for any political activity, movement, or ideology, ensuring that his interests have nothing to do with the struggle for power and are exclusively focused on the spiritual and eternal sphere. This seems to place him, in the eyes of many, incomparably above the current dispute between Islamic countries and the West.

This viewpoint is not exactly false; it is merely empty. It is obvious that Guénon is not vying for political power. He is vying for something infinitely above that, and of which, as he himself explains, political power is nothing but a secondary, almost negligible reflection: he is vying for spiritual authority. He is contending for it with the Catholic Church, positioning himself far above it and claiming to guide it from the sublime heights of Sufi spirituality (not necessarily in person, of course).

He is very explicit about this point. The Catholic Church, at some point in its history, he says, lost contact with the Primordial Tradition and no longer even has an understanding of the "higher parts" of metaphysics: it stops at pure ontology, or the theory of Being, without delving into the supreme mysteries of Non-Being (Schuon prefers to say "Supra-Being").

I have explained on other occasions what seems to me to be the intrinsic absurdity of the doctrine of Non-Being, and I will not revisit that subject here. What matters at the moment is to emphasize that, according to Guénon,

Catholicism, starting from this initial mutilation, has declined sharply to the point of being reduced to mere sentimental devotion for the masses.

Since only those who still possess the original connection with the Primordial Tradition can lift it from this abyss, it is evident that the salvation of the Church and, through it, of the entire West, can only come from outside. From where, precisely?

It cannot be from Buddhism, since Guénon does not even consider it a fully valid tradition.

Nor can it be from Hinduism, because it cannot be practiced outside of India or by those who are not of Indian nationality. All that Hinduism can provide is a deeper understanding of metaphysical doctrine—and indeed Guénon extensively refers to Hindu texts for this purpose—but mere theoretical understanding, while indispensable, cannot by itself provide authentic "metaphysical realization."

From Judaism, even less so, for it would be inconceivable for the Church, having been born from it, to return to the maternal womb without *ipso facto* annulling itself and ceasing to exist.

From Freemasonry? Impossible, not only because of the above-mentioned and unresolved incompatibilities, but also because, according to Guénon, Masonic initiations are only of "little mysteries," secrets of the cosmos and society that do not even come close to touching the heights of supreme metaphysical realization, the "great mysteries."

From obstacle to obstacle—it is not necessary to examine all the alternatives—the inexorable conclusion is that the labyrinth of impossibilities has only one way out: Catholicism can only be restored to its original integrity if it consents to submit to the guidance of Islamic masters. Either that, or the occupation of the West by Muslims. *Tertium non datur.*

That, *en passant*, Guénon and his followers have made several valuable contributions even to the understanding of Catholicism by Catholic intellectuals themselves, especially regarding symbolism and sacred art, is something that no one in their right mind could deny.

But there's nothing strange about that either. What authority could a Sufi master claim to exert over Catholics if, at least in some select points, he did not prove to understand their religion better than they themselves did?

Guénon's "Catholic" articles published in *Regnabit* magazine between 1925 and 1927 do not prove, nor even suggest, that he had accepted the independence, much less the superiority, of Catholicism over Islam. It only proves that, at that time, he still believed in the possibility of directing the course of things in the

Catholic Church through gentle persuasion and infiltration.[191] His departure for
Egypt in 1930, with the firm decision never to return and to communicate with
his audience only through *Études Traditionnelles* magazine from then on, marks
the moment when he lost that hope and, increasingly integrating into Egyptian
esoteric circles (even marrying the daughter of the prestigious *sheikh* Elish El-
Kebir), he passes the ball back to the Islamic authorities who had long guided his
actions within the European framework. How things evolved from that point to
the adoption of the terrorism and "occupation through immigration" policy
(which, of course, would never happen without the approval of Islamic spiritual
authorities), is a story we are ignorant of and which may only be told, perhaps,
several decades from now. What is absolutely certain is that Guénon, from the
beginning of his public activity, declared not to speak in his own name but to
strictly follow the guidance of "qualified representatives of the Eastern
traditions," among whom, it is known today, mainly the *sheikh* El-Kebir himself.
It is utter nonsense to say that Guénon "converted to Islam" in 1930. He had been
a regular member of a *tariqa* since at least the age of twenty-one, which is enough
to show that he was long prepared for the extremely difficult mission he was to
undertake.

* * *

The second factor that hinders the perception of Guénon's identity as an
Islamic agent is the impact of his work on his disciples. Qualified as "the most
dazzling intellectual miracle of our time,"[192] this work sheds so much unforeseen
light on the religious phenomenon and the spiritual decline of the West, and its
contrast with all modern atheist or Christian thought is so great, that it becomes
almost irresistible to view it truly as a miracle, a divine intervention in the course
of history. Seyyed Hossein Nasr, in *Knowledge and the Sacred*,[193] does not
hesitate to present the entire intellectual history of the West as if it were a long,
groping, and semi-blind preparation for the advent of Guénonian insights. Seen in
this way, Guénon's work appears as a supra-historical message coming from the
dawn of time, from the very Primordial Tradition itself and not from a
contemporary Egyptian *sheikh*.

---

[191] The presence of Rama P. Coomaraswamy (son of Ananda) as a professor at a Catholic
seminary proves that even in the 1980s, F. Schuon believed in this possibility, a belief
abandoned by Guénon half a century earlier. Dr. Coomaraswamy, known as a Catholic
theologian and a brilliant defender of traditional Catholicism (I had the pleasure of seeing
him demolish Fr. Gutierrez, a leading figure in "liberation theology," in a debate in Lima,
Peru), was more than a mere member of the *tariqa*: he was Schuon's right-hand man.
[192] Michel Valsân.
[193] State of University of New York Press, 1989.—Eds.

The desire to erase its contemporary roots and to hover above historical contingencies is evident in various passages of this work, reinforced by several expressions of disdain for the "mere" historical perspective, which Guénon considers an illusory veil of passing appearances concealing the reality of eternal things. He even criticizes the Western mentality's attachment to "facts" as if it were a vice of thought.

Jean Robin, characteristically, proclaims Guenonism a providential intervention and "the West's last chance." It is an inalienable right of the enthusiastic disciple to celebrate the master's work with the most emphatic qualifiers. But a qualifier means nothing when separated from the substance it qualifies. One thing is to speak, in general terms, of the "West's last chance"[194]— and we all know that the West needs one. But another completely different thing is to clarify that it is not just any chance, not an abstract and generic "restoration of spirituality" but rather salvation through Islamization. Jean Robin simply omits this point.

It is also very fair to privilege the eternal and immutable above the temporal and transitory. But any faithful Catholic accustomed to the sacrament of confession understands that the leap into the eternal, without passing through the consciousness of the factual details of earthly life, often humiliating and depressing, is not spirituality; it is angelism. The apostle who declares, "It is no longer I who live, but Christ who lives in me," is the same who confesses to bearing "a thorn in the flesh" (2 Cor 12:7) until the end of his days.

The desire to fly to the world of eternal archetypes by leaping over concrete historical reality appears not only in the hagiographic profiles of the "mission of René Guénon" but also in at least three books by important perennialist authors on Islam.

Ideals and Realities of Islam by Seyyed Hossein Nasr,[195] *Understanding Islam* by Frithjof Schuon,[196] and *Moorish Culture in Spain* by Titus Burckhardt[197] barely conceal their rhetorical strategy of depicting Muslim life only through the eternal archetypes it symbolizes, contrasting them, explicitly or implicitly, with the raw factual miseries of the materialistic West. It even becomes a bit naive. Even a child realizes that it is not fair to compare the virtues of one with the faults of the other, instead of virtues with virtues and faults with faults.

---

[194] René Guénon, *La Dernière Chance de l'Occident, Éditions de la Maisnie* (Paris: Guy Trédaniel, 1983).
[195] Beacon Press, 1972.
[196] World Wisdom, 2003; Éditions du Seuil, 1976.
[197] George Allen & Unwin Ltd., 1972.

All this makes it difficult, for both the newcomer and sometimes even for the spokespersons of perennialism themselves, to admit the obvious: René Guénon's work may have all the providential and saving character one desires, provided that the obvious is clearly admitted: that, in the end, it never offered another path of salvation for the West except Islamization.

It is also true that any intelligent Christian, Catholic or not, can benefit from René Guénon's teachings without adhering to the Guenonian project, but how to refuse adherence without knowing or wanting to know that the project exists? Every useful idiot is useful and idiotic to the extent that he denies the existence of the one who uses him.

Many Christians, Catholics or not, felt so outraged by René Guénon's teachings that they made several attempts to refute him and even to ridicule him. These attempts only proved the intellectual superiority of the adversary and fell into ridicule or oblivion.

In this regard, Guénon's disciples were not entirely wrong in considering him insurmountable ("the infallible compass," said Michel Valsân). But Guénon does not need to be fought or defeated. By adopting the pseudonym "Sphinx" in his early writings, he knew that those who did not decipher his message would be swallowed up and reduced to obedience. Those who thrash about amidst cries of revolt, don't fail to deliver him obedience, reluctantly or even unconsciously.[198] Once deciphered, however, the Sphinx has no choice but to gently release its prey, which will emerge from its claws not only free but strengthened.

Back to The Garden of Afflictions

A conversation with the author
on the twentieth anniversary of its publication.

O Jardim das Aflições, 4th ed. (2015)

Silvio Grimaldo: Professor Olavo, I would like to clarify in this conversation whether, and what, you would change or correct in the book *O Jardim das Aflições* (The Garden of Afflictions), which is celebrating twenty years of its first edition.

---

[198] The most typical example is the anti-Guénonian conservative Christians who, revolted by the "decadence of the West," adhere to the Eurasianist politics of Aleksandr Dugin, the spiritual great-grandson of Guénon. They are perhaps the dumbest people in the universe.

Since that time, you have developed your political theory, adding new concepts and analyses that would certainly enrich the history of the idea of Empire as told in the book. Among these more recent developments, I can mention your discovery of the *revolutionary mentality*[199] and the unity of the revolutionary movement throughout the history of the West over the last three centuries, the theory of the three competing globalist blocs,[200] and, finally, your view of American society,[201] which seems to have changed significantly since your move to the US. In *The Garden*, American society appears as a reincarnation of the Roman Empire, but now in a republican, democratic, and Masonic version. However, your weekly articles for the *Diário do Comércio* present us with another America, more conservative, more Christian, less revolutionary, and less expansionist than that presented in the book. What, then, has changed in your view of American society and the US in recent years?

Olavo de Carvalho: The fundamental thesis of the book is that the history of the entire West is marked by the idea of Empire and successive attempts to create it. The limits of this Empire are undefined, and therefore it could expand indefinitely, eventually becoming ideally a global Empire, where what is understood as global in each period is evidently the extent of the visible world. For example, the Roman Empire came to encompass almost the entire known world. As the geographical boundaries expand, with the great journeys, the perspectives of the Empire also broaden. But this permanence of the idea of Empire seemed natural and inherent to political power, which is expansive by its very nature. As soon as power centralizes, organizes, and structures itself, the tendency is to expand. Expansion is primarily motivated by an instinct of self-defense and aims to eliminate external enemies. As long as an Empire has external enemies, it is not entirely secure and ends up imitating the Roman Empire, which gradually subjugated its potential enemies until there were only internal enemies left.

From the dissolution of the Roman Empire onwards, there is an interval, which is, let's say, the feudal balance, a situation in which there was no central government and in which the power structure was fragmented. When the Empire falls, the senators, landowners, the ruling class flee to their farms outside of Rome and create independent centers of power. Then they need to negotiate with each other, and although there are conflicts, no power could overpower the others. With the restoration of the idea of Empire, with Charlemagne, the situation begins to

---

[199] See "The Revolutionary Mentality," in Chapter 5—Eds.
[200] See "The USA and the New World Order," in Chapter 8—Eds.
[201] See next "The Generosity of the American People."—Eds.

change. Charlemagne's Empire dies with him, as his heirs enter into conflict, make disastrous mistakes, and power dissolves; but the idea of Empire remains.

Later, when the Empire fragments due to the emergence of nation-states, each one, as soon as it's formed, asserts itself as an Empire. They not only set out to conquer neighboring territories but also distant territories. We are talking about the colonial period, when nation-states invade regions of Africa, Asia, and the Americas. During this time, several competing projects of Empire begin to emerge: the Portuguese Empire, the Spanish Empire, the British Empire, etc. The great achievement of the British Empire, which is the colonization of America, ends disastrously, with the American War of Independence fragmenting the Empire. And the nation that emerges from this process already asserts itself at the same time as a new Empire, out of the simple need to expand and occupy territory. The Empire sometimes advanced by violent means, as happened in Texas, with the war against the Spanish, and sometimes by peaceful means, as in Louisiana and Alaska, which were purchased.

It does not seem exaggerated to say that the idea of Empire guides the political life of the West since the fall of the Roman Empire. Naturally, each of these attempts to form the Empire is inspired by the Roman Empire. So what we have is a series of successors to Rome. Even Russia clearly asserts itself as the Third Rome. But the Third Rome that succeeded was the United States. The architecture of Washington clearly has Roman inspiration, and all the Founding Fathers were inspired by Roman examples; they all read *Parallel Lives* by Plutarch, and clearly tried to be what was called "Plutarch's Men"—that is, they had a very clear ideal of a ruler. For this success, there was the coincidence of two factors: on the one hand, a set of material circumstances that impelled expansion, and on the other hand, the residual strength of these Roman symbols that gave their successive imitators the idea of what could be done. So, the history of the West is marked by successive reincarnations of the idea of the Roman Empire, culminating in the American Empire.

However, at the time I wrote this book, I only knew American culture through what was exported by the mainstream media and the American publishing market, that is, only that exportable "official" culture. The idea that reached me was that of the politically correct Empire. An Empire that was created under Masonic inspiration, with the idea of neutralizing differences between religions through the recourse of the secular state, which does not take sides in the conflict between various religions and, precisely for this reason, becomes the arbitrator of these conflicts. To arbitrate, it is necessary for the State to have no content, no religious doctrine of its own. Thus, the notion of a theologically empty State is created: a purely political-juridical structure, not theological. At that moment, political-juridical thought supersedes religion. Religion becomes only a matter of individual preferences and therefore ceases to be a comprehensive interpretation of universal value and becomes only the conviction or belief of certain groups. And what becomes the general belief, the doctrine of society, is the political-juridical structure of the State. In this sense, the American Constitution is above all religions. It judges religions.

This is the first effective incarnation of the secular State, since the French secular State declined from crisis to crisis. The French secular State project was a failure, whereas the American was truly a success.

However, when I moved to the United States, I began to become aware of an entire local culture that is not exported, which, although very vigorous here, has no voice in the world, being practically ignored abroad. I am referring to the entire conservative and Christian culture which, to my great surprise, was much more vigorous here than I could have imagined. When I lived in Brazil, I imagined that the conservative Christians here were a bunch of hillbillies who had no influence on society. In part, I was misled by the tone of superiority with which the left referred to this conservative culture, as, for example, in the movie *Deliverance*,[202] where four executives decide to go canoeing on a river in the state of Georgia and encounter a bunch of rednecks and hillbillies, terribly hostile, evil, and mentally retarded, who pursue them through the mountains and cause a series of misfortunes. This image, that there is an enlightened, progressive America, obedient to the laws, and another barbaric America that inhabits the interior of the country, is an inverted view because in these regions occupied by hillbillies and rednecks, crime is minimal, or even nonexistent. Whereas in regions considered enlightened and civilized—especially large cities and state capitals, such as New York, Chicago, and Washington—crime is rampant and uncontrollable. The violence is there, not in the interior. And Hollywood movies convey an exactly inverted view. Those they portray as backward, violent, and murderous hillbillies are, as I discovered in the interior of Virginia, where I live, the most educated, kind, and civilized people in the world. Whereas in large urban centers, we find all kinds of barbarity and violence unknown elsewhere in the country. Furthermore, this conservative Christian culture is presented only as a popular residue, without greater intellectual elaboration. But when you look closely, you discover that the intellectual vigor of this culture is astounding.

---

[202] *Deliverance* (1972), by John Boorman, starring Jon Voight and Burt Reynolds.

In Brazil, however, this culture is not revealed. The United States produces this conservative culture for itself, while the politically correct culture, from the secular state, represents the force of imperial expansion, transmitting its ideology and thought to the rest of the world, wanting to shape it in its image and likeness. Christian conservatives are only interested in competing within the American framework, without interest in converting the population of other countries to conservatism. This was another element that appeared inverted in Brazil, by which I allowed myself to be deceived, reasoning from the sources I had.

The idea of American expansionism, for example, which was presented to me as a guideline of the conservative right, was actually the defining activity of progressives, who want to impose the American system on the world. In the same line are the neocons, but they are not conservatives.

Neocons are people who came from the left and created a justification for the imposition of American democratic institutions on the rest of the world, as George Bush ended up doing in Iraq, imposing a secular state by force. That is, the neocons adopted a clearly revolutionary doctrine, and despite the influence they exerted in Republican governments, they were a tiny fraction of the right, but they appeared, especially in France and Brazil, as the quintessence of American right-wing itself. But neoconservatism fits perfectly well with the definition of a *revolutionary movement*, which advocates the creation of a new society, a new historical situation, through the concentration of power. It should not be surprising, therefore, that most of them came from the left and received a Marxist education, and that none of them were really religious people. Most neocons were of Jewish origin, but disconnected from religious Judaism. That is, they were Jews who became disillusioned with Judaism, then with Marxism, and decided to make another revolution, using the means of the American state.

When I arrived here in the US [in 2005], I started reading material produced by conservatives and realized that they represented a much more vigorous and superior culture than progressives. In all debates, what you see is conservatives having a big advantage. And I soon realized that there was a competition between intellectual and cultural superiority against administrative and financial superiority, so to speak. David Horowitz's book, *The New Leviathan*,[203] shows that the amount of money collected by the Democratic Party and the left is often much greater than the funds of right-wing organizations. The difference is so enormous that the balance of electoral results, which always shows small differences between winners and losers, becomes almost incomprehensible. So

---

[203] New York: Crown Forum, 2012.

how does this conservative right, with little money, compete with this monster subsidized by Rockefellers, George Soros, and *tutti quanti*? The answer lies in its own incessant intellectual vigor, which is flowing. This culture never stops producing ideas, raising debates, publishing books, etc. Finally, I ended up seeing that this America, which from Brazil seemed like a bunch of hillbillies, is the center of American intellectual life. The rest is just the production of a spent ideology and a discourse that has already been discredited.

Therefore, the idea of the US as a Masonic republic, engaged in the construction of the secular state, exists, obviously, and it is this idea that imposes itself as the image of America in the rest of the world; however, internally, things are not exactly like that. There is a fairly balanced struggle between these two Americas within.

* * *

SG: From what you just said, I had the idea that there are two imperial tendencies within the US. I can clearly see the neocons, as you say, committed to exporting an American model of institutional organization, with formal democracy, elections, parliament, freedom of the press, and free trade, to other countries. But the progressive forces, aligned with the Democrats, seem to be committed to exporting something else, another vision that practically subjugates the US to a foreign force, such as international organizations. It is not exactly the American model, but a global model, using the American state as a means of imposing it. But wouldn't this endanger the survival of the American system itself?

OC: Yes. That is an ambiguity of the system. The idea of expansion, of westernizing the world, is common to both currents, but the interpretation each one makes of westernization is different. In fact, there are three different interpretations. There is that of the leftists, which is to end all public authority of religion, transforming it only into a personal option and leaving it cornered, and to create a state authority that is superior to everything and provides the general worldview. It is this current that brings secularism, feminism, gay activism, animalism, and all that cultural heritage that came to the US through the Frankfurt School and that formed what we can inadequately call cultural Marxism. The second current is that of the neocons, who desire the same thing, to expand institutions, but placing emphasis on the American state, which must become the world's policeman. And there is, thirdly, the conservatives proper, the *paleocons*, who are less interested in expanding American power than in defending American sovereignty against its enemies and keeping society faithful to its original traditions, to the constitution, to the Founding Fathers, etc.

These three lines intersect. The neocons no longer have as much expression as before, leaving only the left and the paleocons. Among the latter, some are so radical as to preach total isolationism, like Ron Paul; others advocate a moderate but firm security policy. On the other hand, on the left, there is also a terrible internal ambiguity, because while they want to expand this cultural revolution globally, they want to have alliances with the Islamic world, which, from a moral and cultural point of view, is extremely reactionary. The American left carries this contradiction, placing, for example, radical feminists and militant gay activists as allies of the most violent sexists in history. However, this ambiguity helps the revolutionary movement, which lives on its self-contradiction because it cannot stabilize with a definitive ideal that can be realized in society, and therefore judged by its results; the revolutionary movement needs to continue indefinitely, and therefore needs contradiction and internal conflict.

So, this is the current situation: there are the paleocons, among whom are libertarians and isolationists, and those who have a more military self-defense view of American territory and interests, but both are basically inspired by the same values, differing only strategically. But overall, this conservative worldview is incompatible with that of the secular and expansionist state, which desires to impose American hegemony, or export these elements of the cultural revolution.

* * *

SG: But during this period, not only did your perception of the cultural foundations of American society change, but your own theory of Empire evolved. In the debate with Aleksandr Dugin, you defend the thesis that today there are at least three global governance projects in dispute. Although not all three are reincarnations of the Roman Empire, they are clearly imperial projects.

OC: Although the interpretation I presented about the history of the idea of Empire in *O Jardim das Aflições* (The Garden of Afflictions) is correct, it is incomplete regarding the US. And it was precisely thinking about this gap that it seemed necessary to me to remap the entire set of analysis because, at that time, I was only interested in the historical evolution of the West as successive rebirths of the Roman Empire. I needed to broaden the framework, and it was then that the theory of the three globalist blocs came to me: the Western Anglo-Saxon, the Russian-Chinese Communist, and the Islamic.

Both the Western globalist bloc and the Communist bloc are inspired by the Roman Empire. The Islamic bloc, on the other hand, does not share this inspiration because it believes that Islam has already surpassed Rome. What is the

Roman Empire compared to the Universal Caliphate? Nothing! Additionally, the Islamic bloc has its own source, the Quran.

And where do American Christian conservatives fit in? They are outside of this game. They are not a voice present in the world. They could be if there were, alongside these three global projects, a Christian globalism, but that does not exist.

* * *

SG: Wouldn't this Christian globalism be the very missionary nature of the Catholic Church?

OC: The Catholic Church could have embraced this project. In Malachi Martin's book, *Windswept House*,[204] you can read the story of the conflict between John Paul II and the globalist elite. This elite intended to transform the Catholic Church into a kind of general management of religions, that is, they would abolish what Catholicism specifically has, and it would be dissolved into universal ecumenism. The Catholic Church would have to accept other religions as equals, doctrinally dissolving itself, losing faith, but consolidating itself as a political power, subsidiary to the Western globalist elite. John Paul II neither said yes nor no, trying to play with these elements, taking advantage of the Church's contact with other religions to absorb them. In a way, his intention was to turn the globalist game upside down. It didn't work because John Paul II died—and the subsequent popes are lost like blind men in a shootout. John Paul II was an astonishing genius. Benedict XVI is also in a way a genius, but a theological genius, not a political and strategic genius like John Paul II. He understood all the political forces at play in the West. Benedict XVI was concerned with defending Catholic doctrine, remaining only on the defensive.

With John Paul II, the prestige of the Church in the world grew extraordinarily. He entered the communist world overthrowing everything, like a bull in a china shop. Communist leaders were terrified of that man, who, wherever he went, gathered millions of people to listen to him. He achieved what he wanted and only did not do more because he died. And now we have Pope Francis, who although he is a very likable man, whom everyone likes (even me), but who in my opinion is a simple-minded man. Now, it is not impossible to impose oneself only through charm, without force, as did John Paul II, who possessed both. He attracted through charm when he wanted and frightened by force when necessary. I do not believe at all that Francis understands what is at stake in the world today and what forces are in conflict.

---

[204] New York: Doubleday, 1996.

* * *

SG: In these fifteen years, from the writing of the book in 1995 to the eve of your debate with Aleksandr Dugin [2011], wouldn't there have been another translation of the idea of Empire in the West? The emergence of this Anglo-Saxon globalist bloc does not represent a new incarnation of the imperial project, since now it is not based on the US but presents itself as supra-national?

OC: Yes. This new modality of empire is no longer the American Empire, but rather the supra-national Empire, as Antonio Negri well observed. In this aspect, his diagnosis, which came out five years after *O Jardim das Aflições* (The Garden of Afflictions), coincides with mine. This globalist elite already presented an extra-national project at that time, which only fails to impose itself as global because it has two other major competitors, which also aim to be global. It is important to note that this dispute between the three projects is neither linear nor simple. Sometimes they are in conflict, sometimes they cooperate with each other, and we still cannot say how this story will end.

For example, the communist bloc had to rebuild itself. China had to rebuild its economic system, introducing elements of the free market, so that the country would not starve. And this reconstruction would have been impossible without the help of the Western capitalist globalists themselves, who believed they could absorb China into their bloc. It would become an element of Western globalism fitted into the East. But that didn't work. The Chinese pretended to give in to Western capitalism, but they kept the power structure of the Communist Party and the army intact. In fact, they manipulated the entire West, showing that they are smarter than the globalist elite.

* * *

SG: More or less like Lenin had done with the NEP . . .

OC: Exactly. They repeated Lenin's New Economic Policy, creating a capitalism that exists only in the economic sphere, without interfering in the legal and political sphere. The power structure remained intact.

Something similar happened in Russia after the fall of the USSR. But instead of advantages, Western capital brought disadvantages to Russia. The entry of Western capital was completely uncontrolled and based on corruption, which led the country to lose money. This fueled a nationalist revolt against the West, a revolt embodied in the persons of Putin and Dugin. This nationalist revolt is given an imperial expansionist tone with the Eurasianist idea, which seeks to gather all the discontented of the world against the West, including Muslims. This may even be done to some extent, but the Islamic bloc will never give up its idea of the

Universal Caliphate just to fit into the Eurasianist Empire. They cannot do that because Islam was born as an imperialist project, whose destiny is to dominate the world. It has been so since day one. Islam may pretend to yield to the Eurasianist idea, but what they really want is to Islamize China, Russia, and the West. Thinking about it, from an ideological and cultural point of view, Islam has more vitality than the Eurasianist project, which is a global camouflage of Russian nationalism. But Islam is truly global. So much so that if we look at the Islamic world, we will see that national interests always take a back seat to its cultural and religious unity. In the Eurasian world, there is a permanent conflict between Russian national interest and the idea of Eurasian brotherhood. Just look at Ukraine to see how this Eurasian brotherhood works in reality . . .

The Eurasianist project, however, is very unique. Its main ideologue, Aleksandr Dugin, thought he could gather everything that exists against the West: communism, Nazism, esoterism, paganism, Orthodox Christianity, Islamism, etc. He made Eurasianism a hodgepodge, which works precisely because of this confusion, as everyone can participate based on the most disjointed pretexts. Everything serves as a justification for supporting Eurasianism. This can work for a while, but in the long run, they will have to yield to the rigidity of Islam, which will not be absorbed into Eurasianism in any way. The USSR already tried to dominate the Islamic world, creating leaders like Yasser Arafat. But the Soviet hand that entered there has already been withdrawn, and these Islamic revolutionary groups have prospered, and continue to prosper, even after the end of the Soviet Union. The Germans also tried to absorb the Islamic world. Nazism has already been buried, and Islam continues to live and thrive. Islam, from this point of view, is incorruptible. It will never abandon its principles, on which its survival depends.

* * *

SG: What is the relationship of the globalist elite to the conservative culture that embodies the values of the American revolution?

OC: The traditional American discourse, of the Founding Fathers, the Constitution, and the Bill of Rights, can be used by groups interested precisely in the opposite, as President Barack Obama himself does. He presents himself as an achiever of the American ideal. But speeches of values and ideals are empty. They only acquire meaning when they are incarnated in history in the form of concrete actions. The same body of values can be used to justify completely opposite actions. For this reason, I am not interested in what universities call political philosophy, which is the study of ideals and values, separated from the concrete action that gives them all the sense they have.

Hegel already said that when an ideal becomes incarnate in history, in concrete action, it necessarily produces its opposite, and from this antagonism, historical movement is born. In other words, an ideal produces its opposite and may, perhaps, absorb it or be absorbed by it. Let's take the example of equality before the law, which is a consecrated element in the American Constitution, and in the speeches of the Founding Fathers, etc., but which can easily be transformed into a terribly anti-American force, favoring the destruction of the State, as in the Cloward-Piven strategy. This pair of sharpies discovered that American social security assistance only reached 5% of the population that theoretically had the right to it, because the other 95% did not need it. They imagined that if they put the remaining 95% who had the right, but did not enjoy it, into the welfare system, they would be able to overthrow banks, topple the system, and seize power. What they intended was to create a demand impossible to be satisfied by government bureaucracy. And to do that, to create a crisis of gigantic proportions, they used all the equal rights language of the Founding Fathers. Political theory only exists in the study of the historical and effective embodiment of political ideas, not in the study of values and theories.

Globalists need the American State. But their idea is to weaken the State externally, so that international organizations and economic groups can dominate it, but to strengthen it internally so that it can control the population.

But this is also practiced in Brazil. Our country is increasingly weak in certain aspects, but the government is increasingly strong over and against the population.

Now, how is it possible to use the same ideals and values to pursue a contrary policy? The trick is invariably the same: it is the quantitative expansion of rights, based on Mao Zedong's qualitative leap. Social engineers know that if certain elements of democracy are expanded quantitatively, democracy will turn into something else. It is called the expansion of rights or democracy. But if democracy is expanded, it is automatically annihilated. Democracy is a rule of coexistence among certain groups, but the unlimited expansion of rights makes this coexistence impossible. As the number of rights holders increases, the central power that controls and guarantees these rights automatically increases. The discourse of expanding rights is precisely made to limit rights. In the end, there are more people enjoying that right created, but there are fewer rights, because more decision-making spheres fall under the discretion of the State. The whole Cloward-Piven strategy is based on this. This is how, in the name of equality, a terrible inequality is created between the ruling bureaucratic elite and the rest of the people. This expansion of rights is fostered by the globalist elite precisely to increase, through the control of the American State, the means in their hands to control the population.

The Generosity of the American People

Os EUA e a Nova Ordem Mundial:
um debate entre Alexandre Dugin e Olavo de Carvalho (2012, 2019)

It's not a coincidence that the country where individual freedom is most cultivated is also where participation in charitable and humanitarian community activities is the highest in the world. This aspect of American life is widely ignored outside the US (and completely hidden by Hollywood's militant anti-Americanism), but I see no reason to believe distorted opinions and hateful fantasies from the international media industry rather than what I see with my own eyes every day and can be confirmed, at any time, with substantial quantitative data. Here are some of them:[205]

1. Americans are the people who donate the most to charity in the world.

2. The US is the only country in the world where popular contributions to charity surpass total government aid.

3. Among the twelve peoples who donate the most in voluntary contributions—US, United Kingdom, Canada, Australia, South Africa, Republic of Ireland, Netherlands, Singapore, New Zealand, Turkey, Germany, and France—American contributions are more than double that of second place (United Kingdom). If someone wants to downplay the importance of this data, claiming "They give more because they are richer," forget it: the contributions are not ranked here in absolute numbers, but as a percentage of GDP. Americans simply dig deeper into their own pockets to help the poor and sick, even in enemy countries. The super supportive Russia and China are not even on the list of contributors.

---

[205] The Center on Philanthropy, Indiana University, Giving USA 2010. *The Annual Report on Philanthropy for the Year 2009* (Giving USA Foundation, 2010); *The Center for Global Prosperity, Hudson Institute, The Index of Global Philanthropy and Remittances* (Hudson Institute, 2010); *Charities Aid Foundation, International Comparisons of Charitable Giving* (2006); Virginia A. Hodgkinson et al., *Giving and Volunteering in the United States. Findings from a National Survey Conducted by The Gallup Organization* (Washington D. C., Independent Sector, 1999); Lori Carangelo, *The Ultimate Search Book: Worldwide Adoption, Genealogy and Other Secrets* (Baltimore, MD: Clearfield, 2011).

4. Americans adopt more orphaned children—including from enemy countries—than *all other peoples in the world combined.*

5. Americans are the only people who, in every war they participate in, rebuild the economy of the defeated country, even at the cost of making it a commercial competitor and a powerful enemy in the diplomatic arena. Compare what the US did in France, Italy, Germany, and Japan with what the Chinese did in Tibet, or Russia in Afghanistan.

6. Americans do not offer the poor and needy only their money. They give them their time, in the form of volunteer work. Volunteer work is one of the oldest and most solid institutions in America. Half of the American population dedicates their time to working for free at hospitals, daycare centers, orphanages, and prisons, etc. What other people in the world have made active compassion an essential element of their style of existence?

7. Furthermore, the value that American society attributes to acts of generosity and compassion is such that no finance or industry mogul can escape from making immense annual contributions to universities, hospitals, etc., because if they refuse to do so, they will immediately be demoted from the status of honored citizen to that of public enemy.

Professor Aleksandr Dugin juxtaposes American individualism to Russian-Chinese "holism." He says that in the former, people only act according to their individual preferences, while in the latter, they integrate into larger objectives proposed by the government. But, with all evidence, the governments of Russia and China have proposed killing their own people rather than helping them: no charitable work in Russia and China has ever had the dimensions, cost, power, and social importance of the Gulag, Laogai, and secret police, tentacular organizations tasked with controlling all sectors of social life through oppression and terror.

Secondly, it's true that Americans don't do good because they are forced to by the government, but because they are encouraged to do so by the Christian values they believe in. Freedom of conscience, instead of descending into pure anarchy and everyone fighting against everyone else, is moderated and channeled by the unity of the Christian culture which, despite all efforts by the globalist elite to marginalize and destroy it, still holds sway in the US. John Adams, the second president of the US, once said that a constitution like America's, guaranteeing civil, economic, and political freedom for all, only served a moral and religious people and no other. The proof that he was right is that as soon as the principles of Christian morality began to be eroded from above, by the actions of the government allied with globalist forces and the international left that Professor

Dugin so cherishes as the moral reserve of humanity, the atmosphere of honesty and Puritan rigidity that prevailed in the American business world gave way to an epidemic of fraud like never seen before in the country's history. The phenomenon is widely documented in Tamar Frankel's book, *Trust and Honesty: America's Business Culture at a Crossroad*.[206]

What I say is not only based on statistics. I have lived in this country for six years,[207] and here I am treated with a kindness and understanding that no Brazilian, Russian, French, German, or Argentine (not to mention Cubans or Chinese) has ever enjoyed in their own land. As soon as I settled in this Virginia wilderness, neighbors from all sides came, bringing sweets and gifts, offering to take the children to school, to introduce us to the church of our preference, to show us interesting places in the area, to help us solve bureaucratic problems, and so on. "Good neighborhood" is not a propaganda slogan. It is a living reality. It is an American institution, does not exist anywhere else in the world, and was not created by the government. It dates back to the days of the Jamestown Colony (1607). Although my family and I are Catholics, the first place we visited here was the Methodist Church, the closest to my home. When we arrived, what were the believers doing? Taking up a collection for street children . . . from Brazil! The collection was accompanied by heart-rending speeches and exhortations. I felt ashamed to tell those people that, according to official studies, most Brazilian "street children" have homes, parents, and are only on the street because they want to be. American compassion ignores the lies and deceit of many of its foreign beneficiaries: it arises from the naive belief that all children of God are, at least deep down, faithful to the Father.

Americans are shy and always feel like they are intruding. Immediately after the initial reception, they prefer to keep their distance, not to meddle in your life. They only come close if you invite them. "I don't want to impose" is an almost obligatory phrase when they visit someone. But if you have a problem, or encounter difficulty, they will come running to help you, with the solicitude of old friends. And this is not just for newcomers. Sometimes even Americans themselves, accustomed to hearing ill of their people, are surprised to discover the inexhaustible reserve of kindness in the hearts of their compatriots. Read this testimony from Bruce Whitsitt, a martial arts champion who occasionally writes for the *American Thinker*:

---

[206] Oxford University Press, 2006.
[207] Carvalho moved to the United States in 2005.—Eds.

Both before and after Dad died, good Samaritans came out of nowhere to offer aid and comfort. I discovered that my parents were surrounded by neighbors who had known them and cared about them for many years . . .

After it was all over, I was struck by the unbelievable kindness of everyone who helped . . .

At the end of the day, this tragedy reopened my eyes to the deep-running goodness of Americans. So many people in this country are decent and good simply because they have grown up in the United States of America, a society that encourages charity and neighborliness. Decency is not an accident; in countries such as the old Soviet Union, indifference was rampant and kindness rare because virtue was crushed at every turn. America, on the other hand, has cultivated freedom and virtuous behavior, which allows goodness to flourish. Even in Los Angeles—that city of fallen angels, the last place on earth where I would have expected it—I experienced compassionate goodness firsthand.

. . . Goodness is not something that a beneficent government can bestow; it flows from the hearts of free citizens reared in a tradition of morality, independence, and resourcefulness.[208]

The American nation was founded on the idea that the unifying principle of society is not the government, the armed state bureaucracy, but society itself, in its culture, its religion, its traditions, and its moral values. Professor Dugin, who does not seem to conceive of any other model of social control than the Russian imperial theocracy, where the police and the Church (later the Party) act hand in hand to shackle the people, can only imagine the US as a wild jungle of conflicting selfishness, proving that he knows nothing of American life.

Perhaps there is no other country in the world where the sense of community solidarity is as strong as in the US. Anyone who has lived here for some time knows this, and at the very least is surprised by the presumption that China or Russia are, in this respect, models that Americans should copy.

---

[208]Bruce Whitsitt, "The Great Goodness of America" (*American Thinker*, January 30, 2011).—Eds.

Chapter 9

Return to Consciousness

What Am I Doing Here?

Diário do Comércio, February 8, 2016
A cólera dos imbecis (2019)

The fundamental characteristic of ideologies is their normative nature, the emphasis on the "ought to be." All other elements of their discourse, no matter how dense or sparse their descriptive, analytical, or explanatory content may seem, contribute to this end and are determined by it, to the extent that the norms and values adopted retroactively decide the profile of the described reality, and not the other way around.

This does not mean that ideologies lack rationality; on the contrary, they are rational constructs, sometimes feats of logical argumentation, but built upon evaluative premises and selective choices that can never be questioned.

Hence, as A. James Gregor, the great scholar of the modern revolutionary phenomenon, says, ideological discourse is "deceptively descriptive": when it seems to be talking about reality, it does nothing more than seek surfaces of contrast and points of support for the "better world" whose realization is its objective and its *raison d'être*.

If an individual opts for socialism, he will describe capitalism as its predecessor and adversary, suppressing everything in capitalist society that cannot be described in those terms. If he chooses the Enlightenment view of democracy as the child and culmination of scientific reason, he will describe fascism as pure irrational brutality, suppressing from history the decades of fascist argumentation—equally rational as any other ideological discourse—that paved the way for Mussolini's rise to power.

With this in mind, it is the most obvious thing in the world that none of my writings and nothing I have taught in class is ideological, and to describe me as a "right-wing ideologue," or an ideologue of anything, is only worthwhile as a defamatory pejorative, an attempt to reduce me to the mental stature of the dwarf who labels me as such.

You can search through my books, articles, and lectures. You will not find any speculation about the "good society," let alone a model of it. At most, I may have subscribed here or there, in passing and without paying much attention, to this or that minor normative precept in economics, education, electoral politics, or any other specialized domain, without any attempt to articulate them, much less to systematize them into a general conception, an "ideology."

This should be clear to anyone who can read, and indeed it would be if the fusion of functional illiteracy, malice, and rustic fear of the unknown did not form that indissoluble and unalterably foul compound that constitutes the *forma mentis* of our "opinion formers" today (of course, I refer to the most popular and flashy ones and their vast audience of repeaters in the blogosphere, not to the equally honorable but obscure exceptions, some of which I find in this same *Diário do Comércio*).

It is obvious that these people are incapable of reasoning in the key of descriptive discourse. They do not say a word that is not to "take a stand," or rather, to display a flattering self-image to the readers, for which they must contrast it with some odious anti-model that, if not found, must be invented with mockery, puerile caricatures, and patches of appearances.

The most important thing in life for these individuals is to embody, in the spotlight, certain values deemed good and desirable, such as "democracy," "human rights," "constitutional order," "defense of minorities," etc., placing anything they dislike diametrically opposed to these excellent things.

Some of these individuals have had their personalities so completely engulfed by these conventional symbols of good that they go as far as to regard any complaint, insult, or criticism directed at their distinguished selves as an attack on democracy, a virtual *coup d'état*.

The desire to personify beautiful things like democracy and constitutional order is so intense that in the confrontation between left and right, both sides accuse each other of being "coup plotters" and "fascists." You couldn't ask for better proof that these are mere ideological discourses.

As for my part, my political writings are divided between the search for scientifically grounded descriptive concepts and the application of these concepts to the diagnosis of concrete situations, sometimes complemented by prognoses that, over more than twenty years, have never failed to materialize.

Of these two parts, the first is documented in my seminar handouts, and the second in my newspaper articles. Readers of the latter do not have direct access to the theoretical foundation, but they find in them sufficient indications that it exists, that it is not a matter of loose opinions floating in the air, but, as Martin Pagnan observed, of political science in the strict sense in which his master and friend, Eric Voegelin, understood it.

Among the most praised "opinion makers" in Brazil—whether journalists or academics—not a single one has the required capacity, I won't say to discuss, but to grasp this material as a whole.

I describe things there as I see them through scientific observation instruments, caring little if I "give the impression" of being a democrat or a fascist, a socialist, a neocon, a Zionist, a traditionalist Catholic, a Gnostic, or a Muslim.

In fact, I have been called all of these things, which in itself demonstrates that the labelers are not interested in diagnoses of reality, but only in inventing, in what they read, the hidden profile of the friend or the enemy, to know if, in the ideological struggle, they should praise or ridicule him.

The very variety of ideologies attributed to me is conclusive evidence that I subscribe to none of them, but speak in a key whose understanding escapes the narrow consciousness horizon of the ideologues who now occupy the entire space of the media and university chairs.

Their hysterical and hateful reactions, their feigned poses of Olympian superiority, their malicious and puerile inventiveness, their theatrical caresses of paternalistic condescension interspersed with insinuations, are vivid symptoms of a monstrous collective ineptitude, as never seen before in any era or nation.

What in this country is called "political debate" is of an indescribable intellectual poverty, which alone provides sufficient explanation for the national failure in all domains—economy, public security, justice, education, health, international relations, etc.

I say this because the speaking intelligentsia demarcates the maximum breadth and altitude of a people's consciousness. Its incapacity and baseness, which I have been documenting since the days of *O Imbecil Coletivo* (The Collective Imbecile) (1996), but which after that time went from alarming to calamitous, and from there to catastrophic and infernal, are reflected in the mental and moral degradation of the entire population.

Of all human assets, intelligence—and intelligence means nothing other than consciousness—distinguishes itself from the others by a peculiar distinctive trait: the more we lose it, the less we notice its absence. There, the most obvious connections of cause and effect become an inaccessible mystery, an unthinkable esoteric secret. Disjointed and absurd behavior then becomes the general norm.

For forty years, Brazilians allowed, without complaint, their country to become the largest consumer of drugs in Latin America; they allowed their schools to become centers of communist propaganda and brothels for children; they allowed, without complaint, their superior culture to be replaced by the empire of semi-literate charlatans; they allowed, without complaint, their traditional religion to prostitute itself in the bed of communism, and hurried to seek fictitious refuge in makeshift pseudo-churches where false miracles were sold at high prices; they allowed, without complaint, their brothers to be murdered in increasing numbers, until the entire nation was afraid to venture into the streets and began to imprison itself behind impotent bars for protection;[209] they allowed, without complaint, the government to take away their weapons,[210] and even hastened to surrender them, leaving their families unprotected, to demonstrate how good and obedient they were. After all this, they discovered that politicians were diverting state funds, and then exploded in a cry of revolt: "No! Nobody touches our rich and holy money!"

The popular rebellion against the "communothieves" does not arise from any legitimate moral indignation but emanates from the same money-oriented mentality that inspires the most cynical corrupt individuals.

Not only is money the highest value there, perhaps the only one, but everything seems to be inspired by the rule: "I want some too, otherwise I'll tell everyone." It is obvious that if this mentality did not prevail in our social environment, corruption would never have reached the stratospheric levels it achieved with scandals like the *Mensalão* and the *Petrolão*, etc.

Hatred of evil is not a sign of goodness and honor: it is part of the dialectic of evil to hate oneself, to wage war against oneself, and to proliferate through fissiparity.

Most significant of all is that such a patent, visible, and scandalous moral teratology phenomenon isn't even deserving of a minor comment in a newspaper, when it should be the subject of a thousand sociological studies.

Do you need greater proof that the luminaries of the media and universities have no interest whatsoever in knowing reality, but only in promoting their damned ideological agendas?

That is why, more than twenty years ago, I came to the conclusion that any political solution to the country's woes was, from the outset, rendered unviable by the futile and perverse nature of public discussions.

There was only one way—difficult and laborious, but realistic—to change for the better the course of things in this country, and that course did not pass through political-electoral action. It was necessary to follow, "without stopping, without rushing, and without retreating," as Paulo Mercadante taught, the following steps:

---

[209] Rampant criminality in Brazilian cities rapidly altered their aspect. Most houses and buildings now are surrounded by iron bars and high perimeter walls topped with electric security fences and cameras.—Eds.

[210] A national disarmament campaign began in 2005 in Brazil during Lula's first term as president.—Eds.

1. Revitalize high culture by training young people to produce work worthy of what Brazil had until the 1950s-60s.

2. In this way, purify the publishing market and cultural media, gradually creating a new environment for consuming high culture and thereby sanitizing public debates.

3. Cleanse the mainstream media through pressure, boycotts, and occupying spaces.

4. Cleanse the religious environment—both Catholic and Protestant.

5. Gradually cleanse educational institutions.

6. Finally, raise the level of political debate, making it address the realities of the country instead of getting lost in immaterial clichés and empty rhetoric. This stage would not be reached in less than twenty or thirty years, but there is no "shortcut," no political solution, no salvific ideological formula. Either all these steps are taken, with patience, determination, and firmness, or it will all be nothing more than a pathetic succession of premature ejaculations.

This is the project to which I have dedicated my life, and the articles I publish in the media are nothing but a partial and fragmentary sample of it. To imagine that I did everything that I did just to create a "right-wing movement" is, in the most generous of hypotheses, unbearable stupidity.

As for item number one, do not be impressed by the overeagers who, having superficially absorbed some of my teachings, already want to go out there, shining and pontificating, in a frenzied eagerness to appear as improved substitutes for Olavo de Carvalho.

These are just the froth, soap bubbles that time will take care of dissolving. I still have a good number of serious students who continue to prepare themselves silently to do good work in due time.

Meditation and Consciousness

Diário do Comércio, September 29, 2014
A cólera dos imbecis (2019)

One of the saddest aspects of Brazilian life, for this commentator, is the scarcity or complete absence of spiritual activity in what is written and published, whether in books, in the media, or even in blogs. By spiritual activity, I mean solitary meditation in which consciousness takes possession of itself as self-creation and freedom struggling to realize itself in the spatiotemporal world and there encounters, at the same time, its obstacles and its instruments.

Only by grasping, in this way, the measure and proportion between what we can be and what we are becoming, do we come to know ourselves as a nature inseparably created and creative, in the sense of Scotus Erigena, indescribable therefore as figure and image and only comprehensible as force and conflict until the moment when death, as Mallarmé's sonnet teaches us, fixes us forever in the unchangeable form of a realized and exhausted destiny.[211]

Only those who dedicate themselves incessantly to this activity can pronounce the word "I" with some knowledge or even with some legitimate right. The others, when they say it, designate nothing more than the wholly fictitious figure they would wish, for practical advantage or relief of complexes, to project onto the screen of others' minds or onto their own.

If the non-meditator only comprehends himself in the succession of disguises that he erroneously calls "I," behind which there is nothing but a vague feeling of guilt and anxiety perpetually engaged in denying itself, it is obvious that one who lives in this condition can neither truly communicate with his fellows, only use them as characters in an inner theater that they are unaware of, nor can he, on the other hand, know God, whether to deny Him or affirm Him, except as a gigantic figure of fiction always available to reinforce, alleviate, or conceal guilt and anxiety.

Through the clear consciousness of our partial and limited creativity, we understand that the existence of billions of other small creative forces around us manifests an infinite creativity, and thus we catch a glimpse of God as Pure Act, without form or figure, the incessant creator of all forms and figures. It was this God who said of Himself: "I am that I am." Only He properly has an "I," because the "I" is a creator without form or figure, whose analogue the human being only becomes, and even then partially, through the act of freedom that accepts and assumes being the image and likeness of God.

Do not confuse meditation, on the other hand, with religious confession or with the examination of conscience. It is the prerequisite that gives spiritual substance to these two activities, without which they are reduced to a mechanical cataloging of shameful acts and thoughts, without the slightest notion of their

---

[211] "Such as into Himself at last eternity changes him." Stéphane Mallarmé, *The Poems in Verse*, trans. Peter Manson (Miami University Press, 2012).—Eds.

inner root as well as their dialectical function in the struggle for the self-realization of consciousness.

Perhaps the greatest of sins, the true crime against the Holy Spirit, lies in allowing thinking faculties to detach from the meditative and creative center, acquire autonomy, and assert themselves even as the supreme distinctive characteristics of the human being.

The more these faculties refine themselves, the stronger the tendency to alienate to them a power and prestige that, by right, belong solely to the "I" proper.

Even worse when, consecrated in more or less uniform and impersonal formal codes, they impose themselves from outside onto the individual, corrupting him to the core and rewarding his alienation with the welcoming applause of some intellectual or academic community.

The more one relies on these codes, believing thereby to prove the strength of their intellect, the more the individual sacrifices his birthright for a plate of lentils, becoming a living personification of "science without conscience."

Nothing exemplifies this more clearly than the reduction of philosophy to the logical analysis of language, which still today, under more diversified or camouflaged forms, fascinates immature students eager for academic approval. These students often show one or several intellectual abilities developed to exceptional levels. They only lack the self-aware ego that binds them together and synthesizes them into the form of a "personality," without which all pretense of intellectual responsibility amounts to nothing more than obedience to an external code, that is, a theatrical sham.

Alongside and in contrast to mere ideological homogenization, which in a certain way is less serious, this pathology currently affects a good portion of philosophy and humanities students in Brazil, especially those of the so-called "right," heralding for the coming decades, when Marxist intoxication fades, its replacement by a form of alienation even more sterilizing and difficult to cure.

Signs of authentic interiority are practically absent in the public debates and academic production of this country, which, in this aspect, as well as in many others, has already experienced better days.

Christmas Prayer

O Globo, December 21, 2002
A morte do pato (2023)

Until a certain period in history, the notion of "truth" did not distinguish itself from the feeling of social cohesion expressed in the mythological symbols of cultural identity. "Being in truth" meant being immersed in this identity, it was "being one of us," it was belonging and alliance. Error and lies were "the other," the strange, the "outsider," the foreign, rebellious to assimilation.

The perception of a kind of truth that transcends social identity only begins to appear in Greek theater. A civic rite destined to cement this identity, it simultaneously hinted at the limits of local culture, the irreducible difference between existing society and humanity in general. It did this by choosing the foreigner as protagonist, so that the people would empathize with the enemy killed in battle, or by setting up a conflict of jurisdictions in which the rejected hero highlighted an invisible and universal divine order above the laws of the polis. In the effort to restore hierarchy between greater and lesser order through rational persuasion, the individual hero appeared as the spokesperson for divine truth, for the ultimate meaning of which the merely "general" truth of the community revealed itself as a provisional signifier.

When theater loses persuasive force, suddenly drama becomes reality. Socrates is not a theatrical character: he is the sage of flesh and blood who, through dialectical art, makes his fellow citizens see the demands of the divine order above common beliefs and established habits. The philosopher's life not only embodies, in the materiality of its tragic outcome, the unresolved tension between universal wisdom and concrete social order, but marks the decisive moment when the primacy of transcendent truth integrates into cultural heritage as the measure of all things. From truth as "pertinence" then follows truth as "knowledge," "reason," "discourse," and "Spirit." This leap, this sudden enlightenment of the framework of life, is recorded not only by the birth of organized philosophical inquiry, but by linguistic mutations that prove the discovery of the independence between the spiritual meanings of certain words and the sensible support that, in poetic compression, previously only obscurely pointed to them.

Rejecting the philosopher's invitation to integrate into the spiritual order, the polis was doomed: less than a generation later it is destroyed and absorbed into a new order, not spiritual, but material: the empire of Alexander and the monarchies into which it disintegrated, inaugurating the "Hellenistic" period. It was a period of chaos, tyranny, and despair, but it expanded the historical field in such a way that the next leap no longer occurred in the limited scope of a local culture, but on an imperial stage capable of making it resonate *urbi et orbi:* the discovery of the Spirit in Athens is followed by its incarnation in Bethlehem. This came through a people who, distant and without contact with the Greeks, in their own trajectory and without equivalents, had already surpassed by themselves the illusion of communal truth and learned to live in the pursuit and obedience of the invisible order. The history of the Jews repeats, in their own way, the drama of Socrates: they are the prophetic people, repelled by "this world." From this people emerges the new leap of consciousness, no longer as "discovery," but as "birth": no longer an event on the internal scale of the soul, but simultaneously in it and in the physical world.

Jesus Christ is no longer just the "spokesperson" of the divine order: He is *the* divine order itself that presents itself, healing and reintegrating human order in its origin and meaning. From then on, no local order, no historically given society will have the right to incarnate truth by itself. All know that "truth" and "community" are not mutually convertible terms. All know that they are mortal, transient reflections of the immortal truth that generates and surpasses them. Kingdoms, principalities, republics yield to the injunctions of the invisible order and, humbly, seek to model themselves after it.

Among these four great moments—Greek theater, philosophy, Mosaic law, and the birth of Christ—there is such a patent convergence, that to deny it would be to refuse the very foundation of our lives: for everything we are and do since then is founded on the recognition of a universal truth that transcends the pretensions of historical communities and is never fully known. Everything: science, morality, law, freedom, dignity, and the value of existence. This truth, which begins to insinuate itself obscurely in the plots of dramatists and ends by illuminating the entire Earth as the presence of the incarnate *Logos*, is everything to us. In it "we live, move, and have our being," as the Apostle will say. Without it, we are only the blind tribe that, from the depths of the cave, proclaims itself the sole Sun.

But nowadays, this arrogant illusion reigns again. Doctors and princes, scribes and Pharisees, rich and poor, cardinals and commissioners of the people, deny any truth superior to their gathered authorities and proclaim the absolute reign of "consensus." Their will is law. With each generation, the call of universal order becomes more inaudible, each new society makes its assembly the top and limit of possible consciousness. Everything beyond the assembly is "the other," error, illusion, odious rebellion. Thus decreed Nazism, fascism, and socialism.

Democracy itself, bewitched by them, forgets the Greek, Jewish, and Christian legacy that originated it and condemns to outer darkness everything that strays from "consensus." Two millennia after the birth of Christ, we return to the tribal experience of truth as the identity of "us" against "them." This is what Carl Schmitt called "politics."

Therefore, this Christmas of 2002, my prayer is: Above all "consensuses," Lord, grant us the gift of seeking, loving, and obeying Your truth.

Published Works of Olavo de Carvalho[212]

Carvalho, Olavo. (1994) 2014. *A Nova Era e a Revolução Cultural: Fritjof Capra & Antonio Gramsci* [The new age and the cultural revolution: Fritjof Capra & Antonio Gramsci]. Rio de Janeiro: IAL & Stella Caymmi; 4th and rev. ed. Campinas, BR: Vide Editorial.

———. (1995) 2019c. *O Jardim das Aflições: de Epicuro à ressurreição de César—ensaio sobre o materialismo e a religião civil* [The Garden of Afflictions: from Epicure to Cesar's resurrection—a study on materialism and civil religion]. 1st ed. Rio de Janeiro: Diadorim; 4th ed. Campinas, BR: Vide Editorial.

———. (1996a) 2019. *O Imbecil Coletivo: atualidades inculturais brasileiras* [The Collective Imbecile: Brazilian incultural news]. 1st ed. Rio de Janeiro, BR: Faculdade da Cidade & Academia Brasileira de Filosofia; 12th rev. ed. Campinas, BR: Vide Editorial.

———. (1996b) 2013d. *Aristóteles em Nova Perspectiva: introdução à Teoria dos Quatro Discursos* [Aristotle in new perspective: introduction to the Theory of the Four Discourses]. 1st ed. Rio de Janeiro, BR: Topbooks; 4th and rev. ed. Campinas, BR: Vide Editorial.

———. (1997) 2016. *O futuro do pensamento brasileiro: estudos sobre o nosso lugar no mundo* [The future of Brazilian thought: studies on our place in the world]. 1st ed. Rio de Janeiro, BR: Faculdade da Cidade & Academia Brasileira de Filosofia; 4th ed. Campinas, BR: Vide Editorial.

———. (1998) 2020. *A longa marcha da vaca para o brejo* [The cow's long march to the swamp]. Initially published as Vol. 2 of O Imbecil Coletivo [The Collective Imbecile] 1st ed. Rio de Janeiro, BR: Topbooks; later published as Vol. 1 of O que restou do Imbecil [What was left out from The Imbecile]. 3rd ed. Campinas, BR: Vide Editorial.

---

[212] Abbreviations: **CTPB:** Cartas de um Terráqueo ao Planeta Brasil, "Letters from an Earthling to planet Brazil," a series in ten volumes. **OQRI**: O que restou do Imbecil, "What was left out from The Imbecile," a series in seven volumes. *Publications that did not appear in this *Reader*.

————. (2006) 2015. *A dialética simbólica: ensaios reunidos* [Symbolic dialectic: collected essays]. 1st ed. São Paulo, BR: É Realizações; 2nd ed. Campinas, BR: Vide Editorial.*

————. (2011) 2020. *Maquiavel ou a confusão demoníaca* [Machiavelli or the demonic confusion]. 2nd ed. Campinas, BR: Vide Editorial.

————. (2012a) 2019. *A filosofia e seu inverso & outros estudos* [Philosophy and the inverse thereof & other studies]. 2nd ed. Campinas, BR: Vide Editorial.

————. (2012b) 2019. *Os EUA e a Nova Ordem Mundial: um debate entre Olavo de Carvalho e Aleksandr Dugin* [The USA and the New World Order: a debate between Olavo de Carvalho and Aleksandr Dugin]. 2nd ed. Campinas, BR: Vide Editorial.

————. 2013a. *Visões de Descartes: entre o Gênio Mau e o Espírito da Verdade* [Visions of Descartes: between the Evil Genius and the Spirit of Truth]. Campinas, BR: Vide Editorial.

————. 2013b. *O mínimo que você precisa saber para não ser um idiota* [The minimum you need to know not to be an idiot]. 41 editions. Rio de Janeiro, BR: Record.

————. 2013c. *Apoteose da vigarice* [The apotheosis of dishonesty]. Vol. 1 of CTPB. Campinas, BR: Vide Editorial. Articles from 2005.*

————. 2014a. *O mundo como jamais funcionou* [The world as it never worked]. Vol. 2 of CTPB. Campinas, BR: Vide Editorial. [Articles from 2006].

————. 2014b. *A fórmula para enlouquecer o mundo* [A formula to drive the world crazy]. Vol. 3 of CTPB. Campinas, BR: Vide Editorial. [Articles from 2007].

————.2015. *A inversão revolucionária em ação* [Revolutionary inversion in action]. Vol. 4 of CTPB. Campinas, BR: Vide Editorial. [Articles from 2008].

————. 2016a. *O império mundial da burla* [The world empire of buffoonery]. Vol. 5 of CTPB. Campinas, BR: Vide Editorial. [Articles from 2009].

————. 2016b. *O dever de insultar* [The duty to insult]. Vol. 6 of CTPB. Campinas, BR: Vide Editorial. [Articles from 2010].*

————. 2017. *Breve retrato do Brasil* [A brief portrait of Brazil]. Vol. 7 of CTPB. Campinas, BR: Vide Editorial. [Articles from 2011].

————. 2018. *Os histéricos no poder* [Hysteria in power]. Vol. 8 of CTPB. Campinas, BR: Vide Editorial. [Articles from 2012].

————. 2019a. *O progresso da ignorância* [The progress of ignorance]. Vol. 9 of CTPB. Campinas, BR: Vide Editorial. [Articles from 2013].

————. 2019b. *A cólera dos imbecis* [The wrath of the imbeciles]. Vol. 10 of CTPB. Campinas, BR: Vide Editorial. [Articles from 2014].

————. 2020a. *Edmund Husserl contra o psicologismo* [Edmund Husserl against psychologism]. Campinas, BR: Vide Editorial. [Lectures from 1993].

————. 2020b. *O imbecil juvenil* [The juvenile imbecile]. Vol. 2 of OQRI. Campinas, BR: Vide Editorial. [Articles from 1997–1999].

————. 2020c. *Mário Ferreira dos Santos: um guia para o estudo de sua obra* [Mário Ferreira dos Santos: a guide to study of his works]. Campinas, BR: Vide Editorial.*

————. 2021a. *Introdução à filosofia de Louis Lavelle* [Introduction to the philosophy of Louis Lavelle]. Campinas, BR: Vide Editorial.

————. 2021b. *A consciência de imortalidade* [The consciousness of immortality]. Campinas, BR: Vide Editorial. [Lectures from 2010].

————. 2021c. *O leão e os ossos* [The lion and the bones]. Vol. 3 of OQRI. Campinas, BR: Vide Editorial. [Articles from 2000].

————. 2021d. *Inteligência e verdade: ensaios de filosofia* [Intelligence and truth: essays on philosophy], Campinas, BR: Vide Editorial. [Essays from 1994–2009].

————. 2021e. *Diário filosófico* [Philosophical diary]. Vol. 1, Campinas, BR: Vide Editorial.*

Posthumous publications

————. 2022a. *O saber e o enigma* [Knowledge and the enigma]. Campinas, BR: Vide Editorial. [Essays from 1997–2018].

————. 2022b. *Diário filosófico* [Philosophical diary]. Vol. 2, Campinas, BR: Vide Editorial.*

————. 2022c. *O Foro de São Paulo: ascensão do comunismo latino-americano* [The São Paulo Forum: The rise of Latin American communism]. Campinas, BR: Vide Editorial. [Articles from 2001–2016].

————. 2023a. *O irracional superior* [The superior irrational]. Vol. 4 of OQRI. Campinas, BR: Vide Editorial. [Articles from 2001].

————. 2023b. *Aforismos* [Aphorisms], Campinas, BR: Vide Editorial.*

———. 2023c. *A morte do pato* [The death of the sitting duck]. Vol. 5 OQRI. Campinas, BR: Vide Editorial. [Articles from 2002].

———. *A felicidade geral da nação* [The general happiness of the nation]. Vol. 6 OQRI. Campinas, BR: Vide Editorial. [Articles from 2003].

———. 2024a. *A vingança de Aristóteles* [Aristotle's revenge]. Campinas, BR: Vide Editorial. [Essays from 1994].

———. 2024b. *O camarada Enrolevich* [The 'Enrolevich' comrade]. Vol. 7 of OQRI. Campinas, BR: Vide Editorial. [Articles from 2004].

———. 2024c. Seminarium: páginas de um diário filosófico. Vol. 1: 1979–1997. [Seminarium: pages of a philosophical diary]. Campinas, BR: Vide Editorial.*

(forthcoming) "A formação da personalidade e a Teoria das 12 Camadas da Personalidade" [Personality formation and the theory of the 12 layers of personality], Campinas, BR: Vide Editorial. [Lectures from 2015].*

Index

www.ingramcontent.com/pod-product-compliance
Lightning Source LLC
Chambersburg PA
CBHW070814300326
41914CB00082B/2039/J